THE DRAMA OF THE MIDDLE AGES

AMS Studies in the Middle Ages: No. 4

ISSN: 0270–6261

No. 1. Josiah C. Russell. *Twelfth Century Studies.* 1978.

No. 2. Joachim Bumke. *The Concept of Knighthood in the Middle Ages.* Translated by W. T. H. and Erika Jackson. 1981.

No. 3. Donald K. Fry. *Norse Sagas Translated into English.* 1980.

The Drama of the Middle Ages

COMPARATIVE AND CRITICAL ESSAYS

Edited by

Clifford Davidson, C. J. Gianakaris,
and John H. Stroupe

With an Introduction by
Clifford Davidson

AMS PRESS, INC.

New York, N.Y.

Library of Congress Cataloging in Publication Data
Main entry under title:

The Drama of the Middle Ages.

(AMS studies in the Middle Ages, ISSN 0270-6261; no. 4)
Includes bibliographical references and index.
1. Drama, Medieval—History and criticism—Addresses,
essays, lectures. I. Davidson, Glifford. II. Gianakaris, C.J.,
1934–   . III. Stroupe, John H. IV. Series.
PN1751.D73   809.2   81-68995
ISBN 0-404-61434-5   AACR2

MANUFACTURED IN THE UNITED STATES
OF AMERICA

Contents

Notes on Contributors

DAVID A. BJORK is an Assistant Professor at the University of Chicago, where he teaches medieval music. He is the author of several published and forthcoming articles on liturgical chant.

JEROME TAYLOR is Professor of English at the University of Wisconsin–Madison. His books include a translation of Hugh of St. Victor's, *Didascalion: A Medieval Guide to the Arts*; *Medieval English Drama: Essays Critical and Contextual,* which he edited with Alan H. Nelson; a two-volume selection of Chaucer criticism, edited with R. J. Schoeck; and a translation (with Lester Little) of selected papers by M.-D. Chenu, *Nature, Man, and Society in the Twelfth Century.*

CLIFFORD DAVIDSON is Professor of English at Western Michigan University and Executive Editor of the Early Drama, Art, and Music project sponsored by the Medieval Institute. His extensive publications include articles in major American and European journals. His most recent book is *York Art: A Subject List of Extant and Lost Art Including Items Relevant to Early Drama,* in which he collaborated with David E. O'Connor. He is the editor of *Studies in Medieval Drama in Honor of William L. Smoldon* (1974).

KATHLEEN FALVEY teaches English and Italian at the University of Hawaii at Manoa, where she is an Assistant Professor. She has published articles on Chaucer and medieval Italian drama. Her major work-in-progress is a collection of fourteenth-century Umbrian confraternity plays.

LYNETTE R. MUIR is Reader in French and Director of the Centre for Medieval Studies in the University of Leeds. In addition to work on various projects in connection with medieval European drama, she is preparing a book on *Literature and Society in Medieval France.* Her *Liturgy and Drama in the Anglo–Norman 'Adam'* was published in 1973.

BARBARA C. BOWEN is Professor of French at the University of Illinois in Urbana. She has written widely on farce, and is the editor of *Four Farces* (1967) as well as of *The French Renaissance Mind: Studies Presented to W. G. Moore* (*L'Esprit Créateur,* vol. 14, 1976).

ROBERT EDWARDS teaches at the State University of New York at Buffalo, where he is an Associate Professor of English. He is the author of *The Monte-cassino Passion and the Poetics of Medieval Drama* (1977), and is completing a study of changes in literary form in the Middle Ages. In addition to studies of medieval drama, he has written on aspects of narrative in Old English, medieval French, and Spanish as well as on allegory.

PATRICK J. COLLINS has written on medieval drama and art in several articles and in his book, *The N-Town Plays and Medieval Picture Cycles* (1977). The recipient of a doctorate from the University of California, Berkeley, he is currently an assistant manager for the San Francisco branch of the Occidental Life Insurance Company.

ROBERT W. HANNING is Professor of English and Comparative Literature at Columbia University. He is the author of *The Individual in Twelfth-Century Romance* (1977), *The Vision of History in Early Britain* (1966), and numerous articles on medieval subjects. One of his current projects is a book on the Wakefield Master and his contemporaries.

THOMAS P. CAMPBELL is Assistant Professor of English at Wabash College. He has published in the fields of medieval drama and Old English, and is currently studying the development of dramatic techniques in the liturgical plays of the eleventh and twelfth centuries.

WILLIAM F. MUNSON, an Associate Professor of English at the University of Alabama in Huntsville, has published on the English mystery plays and has a continuing interest in medieval liturgy and the Latin and English drama.

DAVID STAINES, an Associate Professor of English at the University of Ottawa, has primary interests in medieval drama and the Arthurian legends. His previous publications include numerous studies of both medieval and Victorian Arthuriana. He is currently completing an edition of the romances of Chrétien de Troyes for publication by Indiana University Press.

DANIEL P. POTEET II, Dean of the Faculty at Hampden–Sydney College, has published articles on medieval English drama. With Richard Burnham and Robert Hogan, he is one of the authors of *The Abbey Theatre: The Rise of Realists 1910–1915* (1979).

THERESA COLETTI has published numerous articles on Chaucer and medieval drama, and is currently working on a study of images, spirituality, and artistic patronage in the late Middle Ages for the Early Drama, Art, and Music monograph series. She is an Assistant Professor of English at the University of Maryland.

LYNN SQUIRES, the Legal Writing Associate at the University of Washington School of Law, is at work on two books, the first a handbook for legal writers and the second a study of the influence of law in late medieval English drama and art. The latter is to be published in the Early Drama, Art, and Music monograph series.

MERLE FIFIELD, Professor of English at Ball State University, is the author of three monographs, including *The Castle in the Circle* (1967) and *The Rhetoric of Free Will: The Five Action Structure of the English Morality Play* (1974). She is also the author of a number of articles on medieval literature and drama.

NATALIE CROHN SCHMITT is Associate Professor of Theater at the University of Illinois at Chicago Circle. She is the author of a number of articles, including the influential "Was There a Medieval Theater in the Round? A Re-examination of the Evidence" originally published in *Theatre Notebook* in 1968–69.

JOHN WASSON, Professor of English at Washington State University, has collected the dramatic records of Suffolk and (with David Galloway) of Norfolk for the Malone Society. He is currently collecting the dramatic records of Devon for Records of Early English Drama.

STEPHEN SPECTOR is an Assistant Professor of English at the State University of New York at Stony Brook. He is editing the N-town cycle of mystery plays for the Early English Text Society, and is compiling a catalogue of watermark betaradiographs taken from dated medieval manuscripts. He has also published a number of articles on bibliography and manuscript study.

MICHAEL J. PRESTON is the Director of the Center for Computer Research in the Humanities at the University of Colorado at Boulder. He has collaborated in a series of monographs entitled *Chapbooks and Traditional Drama* and has published a *Concordance to the Middle English Shorter Poem*. He is also the author of numerous articles, and presently is systematically concording all the Middle English dramas.

ELIZABETH A. WARNER, Senior Lecturer in Russian Studies at the University of Hull, is the author of *The Russian Folk Theatre* and of numerous articles on Russian folk literature. Currently she is engaged in research on Russian peasant superstitions and witchcraft as well as on the Russian folksong.

Introduction

The labeling of historical periods leaves much to be desired, especially when such terms as *Middle Ages* or *Renaissance* are involved. And with reference to drama, the identification of examples that are *medieval* will surely be seen as lacking in precision. The examples covered under this rubric normally span the period from the ninth century through the sixteenth and even into the seventeenth, though if certain folk dramas are included the cut-off date must be recognized as much later. Furthermore, we are actually dealing with various traditions of the theater involving quite distinct purposes or intentions. In this regard, the drama of the seminal medieval period—a period including at least seven centuries of Western history—ranges from the deepest religious devotion to the purely recreative, i.e., from the striking iconic visualization of sacred scenes in the stylized liturgical drama (and in related ceremonies) to the bawdiest mimic entertainment.[1] The richness of this drama, of which so much has been lost through the decay and destruction of texts and dramatic records as well as visual data, can now hardly be questioned, even though the inclusion of so many riches within the confines of the term *medieval* may continue to trouble us.

Curiously, we are perhaps also a little troubled because, even as scholars, we tend to be somewhat defensive about our concern with the past, especially with a period connected in the popular mind with centuries of superstition and ignorance. The legacy of earlier critics of the medieval drama is very likely still with some of us to a certain extent, and it remains difficult for many to see the achievements of the Middle Ages as anything more than necessary preparation for the brilliance of the Elizabethan and Jacobean age. When we consider the scope and quality of the various

xi

kinds of medieval drama, however, we should come to quite a
different view of them. Some of the greatest cycles, for example,
certainly rival the vision if not the architectonics of *Paradise
Lost,* while some comic scenes are no less lively than Shakespear-
ian comedy. Theatrically, the plays are often not at all naive, but
are representative of the most sophisticated art. Such certainly is
the case with the music dramas in the famous Fleury Playbook,
which presents a perfectly polished and balanced species of drama that has never been surpassed. In no sense ought the best of
the extant medieval plays to be regarded any differently from the
rich resource of medieval architecture which is so widely admired
in Europe. The cathedrals and large churches of the Middle Ages
are especially valued because they could not really be replaced today; each is unique, representing a different approach to the mastery of the craft of masonry and related arts. These buildings
quite simply could not be reproduced today except as copies, and
then as rather pale reflections of the skill of the brilliant medieval
architects and craftsmen who designed them. The cultural milieu
from which they sprang is now no more, and the varieties of style
which the buildings then achieved can no longer be expanded.
This architecture therefore is a valuable monument of our European past, constantly endangered by weather, pollution, war,
vandalism, and other ravages of time. So too are the plays valuable in their way, for they also come from this same milieu, both
monastic and civic. Like the buildings, the play texts themselves
are generally impossible of imitation in our time, and hence we
need to recognize them as the highly prized dramas of our
ancestors.

Of course, as buildings and the art they contain can be subjected to "restorations" which are really vandalism in disguise,
so too the plays are capable of being produced in ways that are
highly unauthentic. Fortunately, bad productions of the plays are
less permanent in their effects than the restoration to which
stonework and painted glass, for example, have been treated.
The York plays as performed at York in the ruins of St. Mary's
Abbey in modern times do not do permanent damage to the play
manuscripts or texts, while some nineteenth century and even
more recent tampering with the York glass can never be repaired.[2]
Yet, because of the intense hostility of the Reformation, the plays
suffered greater losses in the early modern era than the buildings.
The latter could hardly be replaced without great cost, and
though they might be "cleansed" of their contents, they never-

theless were more often than not still needed for the worship services of the community. The religious plays, and the liturgical books which contained many of them, were destined to be deliberately destroyed in great numbers, while non-religious plays tended frequently to suffer the same fate for reasons of indifference and simple hostility to the past.[3]

The indifference and hostility have extended very nearly up to our own time, and unquestionably colored the beginnings of medieval drama criticism in the nineteenth century. The frontispiece to William Hone's *Ancient Mysteries Described* (London, 1823) contains the following verses:

> When Friars Monks and Priests of former days,
> Apocrypha and Scripture turn'd to Plays,
> The Festivals of Fools and Asses kept,
> Obey'd Boy-Bishops and to crosses crept,
> They made the mumming Church the People's rod,
> And held the grinning Bauble for a God.

In the light of expressed attitudes even by editors of the plays, we can also be hardly surprised that few English vernacular dramas have received editions that could be called adequate—a lack that is only now in the process of being rectified.[4] E. K. Chambers' two-volume study, *The Mediaeval Stage* (1903), illustrates genuine dislike for medieval forms of Christianity and an appreciation directed largely toward dramatic elements of the religious plays which later would be seen as forming the elements of a secular theater in the Renaissance. Of course, he also shows intense interest in the folk drama, and indeed devotes a disproportionate segment of his study to these popular forms. Even earlier twentieth-century productions of medieval plays, including William Poel's pioneer production of *Everyman* in 1901,[5] were highly fanciful, hardly recognizing the intrinsic integrity of the plays themselves. Some of the hostility was backed with the tooth of the law, with one director charged in 1910 with a violation of the Blasphemy Act. In 1930, British censorship of the stage would not allow an uncut production of the Chester plays![6] Such attitudes are also surely background to the wretched modernizing inflicted on the York and Chester plays in modern civic presentations—presentations that are, in the words of one critic, "misguided medievalism."[7]

As late as 1955 Hardin Craig was able to assert that the medieval drama "had no theory and aimed consciously at no dramatic effects, and when it succeeded, its success came from the import of its message or from the moving quality of some particular story it had to tell."[8] In a sense, the dissent to this statement had already been presented in Mary H. Marshall's eloquent paper, "Aesthetic Values of the Liturgical Drama," published in the *English Institute Essays, 1950.*[9] Her pioneer article suggests very succinctly the manner in which "formalized symbolic suggestion" becomes the "method" of such a play as the Fleury *Herod,* and she identifies precisely the "iconic quality" of the Latin music-drama. The vernacular religious drama likewise will not sustain the charge that it is lacking in "theory" and "dramatic effects." An English document entitled *A Tretise of Miraclis Pleyinge,* which was written by an anonymous Wycliffite apparently in the early fifteenth century, provides crucial evidence in drawing a connection between this drama and scenes in religious art—a connection that will apply to the continental religious plays as well. The Wycliffite writer insists:

> sithen it is leueful to han the myraclis of God peyntid, why is not as wel leueful to han the myraclis of God pleyed? sythen men mowen bettere reden the wille of God and his meruelous werkis in the pleyinge of hem than in the peyntynge, and betere thei ben holden in mennus mynde and oftere rehersid by the pleyinge of hem than by the peyntynge, for this [painting] is a deed bok, the tother [playing] a qu[i]ck.[10]

It is hard to believe that these comments refer to a childish or mawkish drama without well thought out theatrical effects, different though these might be from the effects of the modern theater.

Fortunately, in the past quarter century the drama of the Middle Ages has become the focus of scholarship as lively and penetrating as perhaps any in the humanities. The intense interest aroused in this drama, to be sure, depends to a considerable degree on a series of scholarly and critical breakthroughs—i.e., books and articles which spurred new approaches to the plays of the medieval period. Of first importance, therefore, is the first volume of Glynne Wickham's *Early English Stages* (1959). With his emphasis on techniques of staging and on the documents which illuminate the spectacle that was medieval drama, Wickham turned attention to the most practical matters of medieval stagecraft. This was also one of the concerns of Arnold Williams, whose influential *The Drama of Medieval England* was published in 1961. Williams's account is frequently "addressed to the general reader, not to the literary scholar" (p. vi), but its implicit in-

terest in the theatrical helped to stimulate work in this aspect of
the medieval drama through the decade of the 1960s. And it has
been an interest that has endured, despite the coming and going
of a number of critical fashions (e.g., the tendency to over-read
the typology of the plays, decried by Williams in an article in
1968[11]). In 1962, David Bevington's *From Mankind to Marlowe*
further probed acting conditions among early plays leading up to
the Elizabethan period, and opened up a rich mine of information about the acting companies and about early professionalism.
There is still dispute concerning some of the specific tenets of
Bevington's book, but there can be no denying that his application of practical questions of the stage to play design was seminal
in establishing a methodology for further study of the late medieval and early Tudor drama.

Likewise of seminal importance is another book for the non-
specialist, M. D. Anderson's *Drama and Imagery in English Medieval Churches* (1963). While at times naive in method, uncritical in its assumptions, and careless in its application of information, this book nevertheless pointed toward a rich store of documentary material that could be drawn upon for the purpose of arriving at a more complete understanding of the medieval stage.
The visual aspect of the drama, previously so often neglected,
now could be placed within the framework of the extant art contemporary with the plays. Use of this kind of evidence will be
noted in such studies as Fletcher Collins's *The Production of Medieval Church Music-Drama* and Rosemary Woolf's long study,
The English Mystery Plays, both published in 1972, as well as in
many other inquiries into the nature of drama.[12] Recent scholarship has tended to be more systematic, providing careful attention to such matters as dating of the analogous art work and to
such aspects as local iconographic peculiarities.[13]

But in some ways the most stimulating books to be published
in the 1960s were the controversial *Christian Rite and Christian
Drama in the Middle Ages* (1965) by O. B. Hardison, Jr., and
The Play Called Corpus Christi (1960) by V. A. Kolve. Hardison's work contains, to be sure, much that has been successfully
challenged, but his brilliant chapter attacking the application of
evolutionary ideas to the history of drama remains solidly respected as a major tenet of our current thinking about the relationship of earlier and later examples of medieval theater. He
called our attention again to the liturgical drama that had been
presented in seemingly such a definitive way by Karl Young in

The Drama of the Medieval Church (1933). This drama could
now be seen as a separate development (and, in some ways, a
higher development) distinct from the vernacular tradition, and
indeed what David Bevington has called the "discontinuity in
medieval acting traditions"[14] has become accepted as historical
fact. In performance, two of these liturgical plays, the Beauvais
Daniel and the Fleury *Herod,* had by then become popular successes through the pioneering efforts of Noah Greenberg and the
New York Pro Musica. And interestingly it was Greenberg's musicological collaborator for his edition of *Herod,* William L.
Smoldon, who, attacking certain crucial points in Hardison's
book, pointed out most forcefully the significance of the music in
the art of the medieval liturgical drama.[15] Likewise, C. Clifford
Flanigan, in two articles, challenged Hardison's view of Christian
ritual through his careful research in the Western liturgy and in liturgical theory.[16]

Kolve's *The Play Called Corpus Christi* was the first to attempt
a full-scale analysis of the aesthetics of the medieval popular and
middle class theater in England, but indeed many of his comments are broadly applicable also to the medieval vernacular drama of the continent. His work is based on careful consideration
of the Wycliffite *Tretise of Miraclis Pleyinge* and the other documents of medieval literary criticism from England. Only now can
many of us fully appreciate Kolve's insistence upon the close association between *play* and *game*—an association that at first was
often misunderstood or dismissed as merely the application to
drama of the popular theory set forth in Huizinga's *Homo Ludens.* While the application of Brechtian ideas in regard to the
plays has on the whole subsided, the connection between the *play*
and *game* remains fruitful, especially in light of careful attention
to the critical texts of the medieval period and to recent studies in
the field of hermeneutics such as Hans-Georg Gadamer's *Truth
and Method* (1975).

It is, of course, impossible here to provide a review of all the
research published in the 1960s and 1970s,[17] but we need to take
note that much of this research was characterized by the widening
of horizons and the new tendency to think of English drama as a
part of a European phenomenon. Both of these tendencies were
recognized in the last major anthology of modern critical writings
to be published on the medieval drama (*Medieval English Drama,* ed. Jerome Taylor and Alan H. Nelson, 1972). The anthology edited by Taylor and Nelson contains some attention to the

liturgical drama, including a reprinting of Marshall's article on aesthetics and the medieval music-drama, and it also takes note of continental dramatic activity. Attention to the continent has additionally appeared in Richard Axton's *Europeun Drama of the Early Middle Ages* (1974) and in William Tydeman's *The Theatre in the Middle Ages* (1978). It has therefore been judged appropriate in the present collection of papers and essays, all of them first published in *Comparative Drama* during the past decade, to include a healthy selection of items on the medieval theater outside of England.

With regard at least to the English drama, the frequent critical superiority of more recent scholarship may perhaps be easily judged when one compares Stanley Kahrl's *Traditions of Medieval English Drama* (1974) with earlier surveys, even with the still useful *English Drama from Early Times to the Elizabethans* (1950) by A. P. Rossiter. This is not to say that all recent scholarship has done its job equally well, of course, since journals continue to publish articles based on outdated asumptions and even books appear which fail to advance our knowledge in any significant way. Some also take up critical concerns in such a limited way that their value is severely restricted, as in the case of Richard Collier's *Poetry and Drama in the York Corpus Christi Play* (1978) which ignores almost all recent developments in the study of these plays. Others, such as Alan H. Nelson's fruitfully controversial *The Medieval English Stage* (1974), have helped to stimulate further research directly, especially by those who have felt that some of the conclusions require either to be contradicted or qualified. It is clear that in the study of medieval drama there is less certainty than there was thirty years ago, and there is also a great deal more that is known about it. The work of uncovering further facts concerning the early drama continues, of course. Dramatic records from England are being edited under the umbrella of Records of Early English Drama at the University of Toronto, and the relationship between early drama and the other arts is being studied much more closely through scholarship being prepared for the Early Drama, Art, and Music project sponsored by the Medieval Institute at Western Michigan University. At the University of Leeds a group of scholars is engaged in compiling a Catalogue of Medieval Plays which will assemble for the first time a subject index of all known European medieval dramas.

In Germany, Walther Lipphardt is provided remarkable evidence toward understanding the liturgical drama and its origins by editing a massive collection of texts of the Easter play, *Latei-nische Osterfeiern und Osterspiele* (1975–   ). Scholarship on the liturgical drama—and on its music—has indeed reached an exciting stage, as the article by David A. Bjork in this collection will demonstrate. It is therefore unfortunate that W. L. Smoldon's full-length book on the music, prepared for publication by Cynthia Bourgeault after his death in 1974, was delayed for so many years, since the fruits of his research have thus been denied to other scholars at the same time that some of his observations certainly have become outdated even before the publication of his work.

From the work of such men as Lipphardt we discover that medieval drama, in spite of differences in language and custom, formed part of the cultural milieu from such Northern countries as Sweden to the Mediterranean and from the British Isles to Eastern Europe. Individual scholars have analyzed the specific developments in each country and region, to be sure. It has not been possible in this collection to cover all the significant geographical locales, but nevertheless attention has been given to such diverse matters as, for example, the Italian Passion Play and French farce, the latter a genre which appears to have been admired by its English imitators who thus can speak for its dramatic power even across linguistic boundaries.

From the standpoint of methodology, the present book attempts also to illustrate a representative spectrum, with attention to matters that range from aesthetics to questions of iconography, philosophy, and even law. Analysis is presented from several perspectives to show precisely how religious scenes translate into experience, and in the instance of one article, R. W. Hanning's paper on the Fall of Lucifer plays, the medieval distrust of mimesis is given very close attention. One paper represents the work of a practicing theater person: Natalie Crohn Schmitt's study of the "idea of a person" in the medieval moralities reasonably suggests a view of characterization that is highly antagonistic to views deriving from the modern realistic theater and contemporary expectations with regard to character, even as these expectations may have been modified by the sometimes perverse stage of Brecht.

With reference to the "evolution" of drama formerly assumed to have been the case in the growth of Elizabethan drama out of the medieval theater, the polemical paper of John Wasson presented below has special significance. We are reminded again that in studying drama the discontinuities count for as much as the continuities. Students of Renaissance drama still need to pay close attention to the medieval stage at the same time that they need to question clichés inevitably encountered in the older histories of drama. We now see that the medieval plays are distinguishable from the Renaissance drama in many ways, and yet of course we also need to recognize that both are distinctly premodern, for the modern age hardly began before the thought of Hobbes and Descartes and Newton attacked the core of medieval belief. Both also are very distinct from the work of the modern playwright except perhaps sometimes in cases of the manipulation of the purely recreative intent. Few competent modern playwrights have even dared to attempt serious handling of the cultic experiences associated with religion, and indeed even when they have done so their treatment of such experience has not usually resembled very deeply the effects possible on the medieval stage. Herein the Protestant Renaissance drama is important, for in it the cultic experience became a forbidden topic by law, though many earlier assumptions about the individual in relation to the cosmos remained intact. Hence it is often true that even when an early drama does not seem to participate in the cultic experiences of religion, it nevertheless functions in ways that are difficult to fathom today without the aid of historical scholarship to bridge its alterity.

There is no question, however, that the gap between medieval and modern can best be bridged by the actual performance of the plays, which, when informed by adequate knowledge of the early stage conditions and the social and religious milieu, are capable of being very effective theater. The medieval play, when it is based on a proper understanding of its structure and function, is able to come to life when it is played on a stage which breaks down the barriers between audience and actors. In that drama which is closer to ritual or which is even a part of it, time is transcended, and we are taken out of ourselves into the very scenes that are presented. As in the case of religious icons that insist on viewer participation with the prototype, the spectacle of the play draws the viewer into itself in order to achieve a transcendent experience. However, in the drama that depends more on the imagination than on ritual for its effect, the audience is drawn into the action in a different way. Here, the emotional effect of standing *as if* in the presence of the actual events becomes the standard by which the play is judged. On the other hand, secular drama with its mimicking of human foibles and human pride still pricks human pretentiousness today in ways that are surprisingly effective. The mirror held up by this secular and sacred drama is not a distant mirror, but one that appears as if held up among us for our immediate amusement and for our assistance in fleeing lives of trivia and despair.

— C. D.

NOTES

1. On the classification of medieval plays, see my comments in "The Concept of *Purpose* and Early Drama," *EDAM Newsletter,* 2, No. 2 (April 1980), 9–16.
2. For a survey of the condition of the glass in the cathedral, see David E. O'Connor and Jeremy Haselock, "The Stained and Painted Glass," in *A History of York Minster,* edited by G. E. Aylmer and Reginald Cant (Oxford: Clarendon Press, 1977), pp. 313–93. Some of the scenes in modern productions of the York plays are illustrated in J. S. Purvis, *From Minster to Market Place* (York: St. Anthony's Press, 1969), frontispiece and plates facing pp. 36, 37, 52, 53.
3. See especially Harold C. Gardiner, *Mysteries' End: An Investigation of the Last Days of the Medieval Religious Stage,* Yale Studies in English, 103 (New Haven: Yale Univ. Press, 1946). But the Counter-Reformation, in its zeal for purity of doctrine and liturgy, also proved hostile to liturgical drama and to some of the vernacular expressions of sacred drama.
4. See Ian Lancashire, "Medieval Drama," in *Editing Medieval Texts,* edited by A. G. Rigg (New York: Garland, 1977), pp. 58–85.
5. Robert Potter, *The English Morality Play* (London: Routledge and Kegan Paul, 1975), pp. 222–25; Lancashire, "Medieval Drama," p. 59.
6. Ibid., p. 59.
7. The critic is Tom Driver, writing a review of the York plays in the *Christian Century,* 78 (10 Aug. 1960), 927–28.
8. Hardin Craig, *English Religious Drama of the Middle Ages* (Oxford: Clarendon Press), 1955.
9. *English Institute Essays, 1950* (New York: Columbia Univ. Press, 1951), pp. 89–115.
10. *Selections from English Wycliffite Writings,* edited by Anne Hudson (Cambridge: Cambridge Univ. Press, 1978), p. 100.
11. Arnold Williams, "Typology and the Cycle Plays: Some Criteria," *Speculum,* 43 (1968), 677–84.
12. See the selected bibliography in my *Drama and Art: An Introduction to the Use of Evidence from the Visual Arts for the Study of Early Drama* (Kalamazoo: The Medieval Institute, 1977), pp. 162–65.

13. See ibid., *passim,* for comments on methodology. A recent introductory essay is by Pamela Sheingorn, "On Using Medieval Art in the Study of Medieval Drama: An Introduction to Methodology," *Research Opportunities in Renaissance Drama,* 22 (1979), 101–09; but see also Gail McMurray Gibson, "Long Melford Church, Suffolk: Some Suggestions for the Study of Visual Artifacts and Medieval Drama," *Research Opportunities in Renaissance Drama,* 21 (1978), 103–15.
14. David Bevington. "Discontinuity in Medieval Acting Traditions," in *The Elizabethan Theatre, V,* edited by G. R. Hibbard (Toronto: Macmillan, 1975), pp. 1–16.
15. William L. Smoldon. "The Melodies of the Medieval Church Dramas and Their Significance." *Comparative Drama,* 2 (1968), 185–209; rpt. with revisions in *Medieval English Drama,* edited by Jerome Taylor and Alan H. Nelson. Chicago: Univ. Chicago Press, 1972, pp. 64–80.
16. C. Clifford Flanigan. "The Roman Rite and the Origins of the Liturgical Drama," *University of Toronto Quarterly,* 43 (1974), 263–84; and "The Liturgical Context of the *Quem Queritis* Trope," *Comparative Drama,* 8, No. 1 [*Studies in Medieval Drama in Honor of William L. Smoldon on His 82nd Birthday*] (1974), 45–62.
17. See the surveys of Anna J. Mill and Sheila Lindenbaum in *A Manual of the Writings in Middle English,* ed. Albert E. Hartung (Hamden, Connecticut: Shoe String Press, 1975), and the review of research in liturgical drama prepared by C. Clifford Flanigan for *Research Opportunities in Renaissance Drama* in 1975 and 1976; the latter review of research is being expanded and updated for publication later this year by Medieval Institute Publications. See also Carl Stratman's revised *Bibliography of Medieval Drama* (New York: Ungar, 1972). Only the forthcoming work by Flanigan is up-to-date.

On the Dissemination of *Quem quaeritis* and the *Visitatio sepulchri* and the Chronology of Their Early Sources

David A. Bjork

The relation between the Easter dialogue *Quem quaeritis in sepulchro* and the dramatic resurrection ceremony *Visitatio sepulchri* has long been regarded as crucial for the history of European drama, since its oldest known example, the *Visitatio*, builds on the exchange between the three Marys seeking the body of Christ and the Angel keeping watch at the tomb:

INTERROGATIO: *Quem quaeritis in sepulchro, Christicolae?*
RESPONSIO: *Jhesum Nazarenum cruxifixum, o caelicolae.*
Non est hic; surrexit sicut praedixerat,
Ite nunciate quia surrexit de sepulchro.[1]

This dialogue was not always part of the Easter Play; at least it seems to have been independent at one time, when it was sung without dramatic elaboration at the beginning of Mass or just before it, in the simple version given above and in others not much longer. In some versions—most of the simpler ones—*Quem quaeritis* is a trope to *Resurrexi*, the Introit for Easter day. In others it is part of the festal procession preceding celebration of Mass. In the vast majority, however, it stands at the end of Easter Matins, just before the *Te Deum*, and in this position it is known as the *Visitatio sepulchri*, for here it achieved fuller dramatic development.[2]

In trying to clarify the relation between *Quem quaeritis* and the *Visitatio*, scholars have looked to the earliest sources to provide an answer. Once these were found and their chronology determined, it seemed perfectly clear that *Quem quaeritis* originated as a trope, and that it gradually assumed greater length and more dramatic form until becoming what could justifiably

1

be called the first play of medieval Europe (or, at least, the first that survived). Léon Gautier, in the course of his pioneering research on tropes, uncovered the connection: "L'histoire du *Quem quaeritis* n'est riens moins que l'histoire des origines du théâtre sacré, et nous allons essayer de le montrer en quelque lignes."3 This idea was elaborated by E. K. Chambers,4 then given definitive form by Karl Young.5 Stated concisely, the theory proposed by Young is the following:6

1. The *Visitatio sepulchri* developed from the *Quem quaeritis* dialogue by gradual accretion of other material.

2. In its original form, *Quem quaeritis* was a trope that stood before the Easter Introit *Resurrexi*.

3. The simplest version of *Quem quaeritis* is the earliest, and it appears first in a manuscript from St. Gall dating from the middle of the tenth century.

4. The one earlier manuscript source comes from St. Martial and dates from 923-34, but its version is slightly more elaborate than the one from St. Gall.

5. Thus it may be presumed that *Quem quaeritis* was written near the beginning of the tenth century, probably at St. Gall, and possibly by Tuotilo, the monk named by Ekkehard IV, in his history of that monastery, as a composer of tropes.7

6. The longer versions of the dialogue are assigned to other positions—some to a procession before Mass, but more of them to the end of Matins, where the most elaborate ones'—full-fledged plays—were performed.

7. The earliest version of the *Visitatio,* complete with directions for staging, comes from Winchester, in the *Regularis concordia* of c. 970; but it has its ultimate source in continental practice, perhaps that at Fleury or Ghent.

Young's theory has come under attack from several quarters. His contention that *Quem quaeritis* was written at St. Gall is no longer accepted as fact: Jacques Chailley and William Smoldon believe it was written at St. Martial;8 Helmut de Boor argues for a North Italian origin;9 others point toward the North of France or the Rhineland.10 And it is becoming increasingly common to admit that no deduction as to provenance can be drawn from the evidence.11 Two scholars have recently suggested that *Quem quaeritis* was not originally a trope at all. O. B. Hardison, Jr., has argued at great length against the assumption that simple forms preceded the elaborate; turning

Young's theory upside down, he sees the origin of the *Visitatio* in developed form as a ceremony connected with Easter Vigil, and the short dialogue used before Mass as a reduced version of it.12 Attacking straight on, Timothy McGee argues that *Quem quaeritis* was not a trope even where it seems most clearly to have been one; he contends that in connection with Mass the dialogue was always part of an elaborate procession known as a *collecta,* which took place at a station outside the church where Mass was to be celebrated.13 The date of the dialogue has been contested, too, especially in attempts to find contexts for the development of liturgical drama in something more cere-monious than a trope,14 and there is now general agreement that it was probably written before the end of the ninth century.

Something common to nearly all these arguments, as to those of Gautier, Chambers, and Young, is their assumption that the oldest pieces of evidence have special relevance to the search for the earliest versions of *Quem quaeritis* and the *Visi-tatio.* Whatever the tactic, proponents of one position or another turn to what is presumably the oldest source of all (the St. Martial troper Paris, Bibliothèque Nationale, lat. 1240) and to the next oldest (the St. Gall troper MS. 484),15 both of which treat the dialogue as a trope, and then go on to the earliest source for the *Visitatio* (the Winchester *Regularis con-cordia*). On these few fragile pieces of evidence are based the most disparate of claims. When supporting documents are drawn into the controversy, they tend to be likewise early, or even earlier, and the debate often focuses on whether their age may not give them special bearing on the subject, perhaps even more than the three sources cited above. It goes without saying, of course, that the earliest witnesses of a version provide its *terminus ante quem.* But it should not be forgotten that the nature of the *terminus* limits its significance. The witnesses merely document the existence of the version by a particular date. They reveal nothing about its age—and this is particularly true of chant books and customaries, which survive in only small number from the tenth century and, so far as we know, were not even copied much beforehand. The problem is that the various bits of evidence used in tracing the history of the Easter dialogue are often regarded as if their chronology re-vealed something about the sequence of the traditions they record.16

The purpose of this essay is to suggest that placing such emphasis on the chronology of the sources ´actually hinders our efforts at understanding the early history of *Quem quaeritis* and the *Visitatio*. Now that a proper catalogue of sources and edition of texts has been made available17 it is possible to pursue other lines of inquiry into the relation between the two forms. As it turns out, one can learn more from studying the geographical distribution of the various versions than from arranging their sources in chronological order. There should be no surprise in this, for it is true in other cases as well, of items added to the Roman liturgy by the Franks (in particular, the sequence and the trope). The results themselves, however, may be startling, even if only because they make the situation seem so clear. One of particular significance is the observation that the versions associated with Mass were confined to Italy, the South of France, and Catalonia, with but a few exceptions in Germany; and that ones intended for Matins were used across the North of France, in England, Lotharingia, and Germany. This configuration can be documented as far back as the tenth century, without encountering any indication that one placement is older than another. Thus the theory that *Quem quaeritis* was at origin a trope, and was only later transferred to the procession and to Matins, must be discarded unless other means of support can be found.

Laying aside the questions of what to call *Quem quaeritis* and what was its original use, let us consider how it corresponds to other chants in the Easter liturgy in terms of dissemination and style, which can tell us a great deal about its history. The Mass for Easter day was instituted at Rome sometime during the fifth or sixth century.18 (Previously the Mass of the Easter Vigil had been the one for that day; once celebrated at dawn to coincide with the hour of the Resurrection, it was gradually moved back to an earlier hour on the preceding day.19) The Proper of the new Mass (the series of lessons and chants assigned to it) might be presumed to date from that time, but regardless what change it may have undergone in the next few centuries, it had stabilized by the time the Franks imported the Roman rite and saw to its adoption throughout their realm. The earliest books containing chants of the Mass, from the eighth and ninth centuries, all show essentially the same items for Easter

day;20 these are the same ones found in the Vatican *Gradual*
except the eleventh-century sequence *Victimae paschali laudes*.
The proper chants, among them the Introit *Resurrexi*, are the
ones belonging to the repertory known as "Gregorian." One
distinction between them and chants added to the Mass during
Frankish times is their universal dissemination: the same five
items were known wherever the Roman rite was followed.
During the ninth and tenth centuries Frankish monks composed
many new chants for the Mass—tropes, sequences, and Ordinary
chants (settings of the Kyrie, Gloria, Sanctus, and Agnus
Dei)—and almost without exception they circulated within
narrower orbits, so that with regard to these items the liturgy
varied from one locale to another. At many centers there was
even some choice as to which trope or sequence would be sung,
and the selection may not have been the same every year. One
southern French manuscript includes thirteen tropes for *Resurrexi;* other sources more commonly give two or three.21 Where
Frankish chant is concerned, one source is never the same as
the next, and an individual piece often varies in shape and
detail more than its counterparts in the Gregorian repertory do.
A special problem is presented by the antiphons used in procession before Mass. They are sometimes found in *graduales* among
the fixed items of Mass—the Gregorian propers—but more
often in separate fascicles of manuscripts also containing sequences, tropes, or Ordinary chants—in other words, the non-
fixed items, chants composed during the ninth and tenth centuries. Like tropes, the processional antiphons assigned to
Easter, as to other feasts, vary from one source to another;
some were very widespread indeed, more than most tropes and
sequences, but they seldom acquired a stable position in the
liturgy. As a group they were far from having the universal
circulation and uniform assignment common to the largest part
of the Gregorian repertory.22 Certain of them may be very old,
but others probably go back only to the ninth or tenth century.
For Matins, the liturgy was never so fixed as it was for Mass,
yet it is probable that the most stable parts of this Office are
comparable in age to the Gregorian propers of Mass. The
several layers of chant for Mass and the Office differ enough
in style that it is possible to distinguish among them and to
judge, according to one characteristic or another, that a chant
is Gregorian, or Frankish, or representative of some other

period or style. Bruno Stäblein, for example, describes two of
the most widespread antiphons for the Easter procession, *Sedit
angelus* and *Christus resurgens,* as being *"ungregorianisch"* in
style, and suggests that they may be of Gallican origin; and
Michel Huglo singles out the Easter responsory *Et valde mane,*
on account of its style, as likely being of Frankish origin.23
Between Gregorian and Frankish chant there is, in other words,
enough stylistic discontinuity that pieces can generally be associated with one repertory or the other on the basis of their
resemblance to other pieces belonging to it. (Admittedly, the
difference between the two was for a long time overlooked or
underestimated; but its full significance has been clarified recently in an impressive way in the work of Richard Crocker.24)

It is a most peculiar fact that *Quem quaeritis* enjoyed nearly
universal circulation within the Frankish realm. The significance
of this fact has not been sufficiently underscored, nor has it been
well understood. Most tropers from the tenth and eleventh centuries include the dialogue: of the sixty-five inventoried for
*Corpus troporum,*25 all but sixteen include the piece; and in all
but two of these cases, its absence is proven immaterial by its
inclusion in other sources from the same locales. One of the
two, the St. Yrieix MS., is not an exception at all, for most of
its Easter tropes are now missing.26 In the sole remaining case,
a troper from St. Magloire (Paris), the absence of *Quem
quaeritis* seems to be a fluke, and the piece probably would
have found its place in an Office book.27 And the tropers by
no means exhaust the list of sources from the period. What this
implies is that the survival of another sixty-five, hundred, or
two hundred tropers from the same period but from other locales
would have demonstrated the presence of *Quem quaeritis* in a
proportionate additional number of monastic establishments.
The chant may not have been coextensive with Frankish rule
and its Roman rite, but it was certainly known in the vast
majority of monasteries and cathedrals of the realm, as well as
some others outside it. Only the limited number of tropers
prevents us from documenting its presence elsewhere during
this period. As it is, even the tenth-century witnesses are numerous and widespread; a list of sources dating from no later
than the first few years of the eleventh century would include
three from Winchester; one from Autun; three from St. Martial,
and three more from the South of France; one each from Mainz,

Prüm, Trier, and Echternach; one each from Reichenau, St. Emmeram, and Minden; one from St. Gall, and two more from the same vicinity; and one each from Verona, Mantua, Monza, and the Abruzzi or San Bartolomeo in Insula (see Table 1).

TABLE 1

EARLY SOURCES FOR *QUEM QUAERITIS*[a]

Sources	Lipphardt Edition No.	Provenance & Date
Southern French		
Paris, Bibl. Nat., lat. 1240	52	St. Martial, 923-36
Paris, Bibl. Nat., lat. 1120	53	St. Martial, XI early
Paris, Bibl. Nat., lat. 1121	54	St. Martial, XI early
Paris, Bibl. Nat., lat. 1084	44	South of France, X/XI
Paris, Bibl. Nat., lat. 1118	62	South of France, 987-96
Apt, Basilique-Ste-Anne, 18(4)	40	(?) Southeast France, X/XI
Northern French		
Paris, Bibl. de l'Arsenal, 1169	46	Autun, 996-1024
English		
Regularis concordia	394/395	Winchester, 965-75
Oxford, Bodl. 775	423	Winchester, XI middle[b]
Cambridge, Corpus Christi, 473	424	Winchester, c. 1000
Rhenish		
Vienna, Nationalbibl., 1888	76	St. Alban (Mainz), c. 1000
Paris, Bibl. Nat., lat. 9448	312	Prüm, 990-95
Paris, Bibl. Nat., lat. 9488	205	Echternach(?), 996-97
Wolfenbüttel, Herzog-August-Bibl., Helms. 1109	347	Trier, X/XI
German and Swiss		
St. Gall, Stiftsbibl., 484	79	Vicinity of St. Gall, c. 965
St. Gall, Stiftsbibl., 381	78	Vicinity of St. Gall, c. 965
St. Gall, Stiftsbibl., 391	80	St. Gall, 986-1011
Bamberg, Staatl. Bibl., Lit. 5	314	Reichenau, 1001
Bamberg, Staatl. Bibl., Lit. 6	319	St. Emmeram, c. 1000
Berlin, Staatsbibl., theol. lat. IV° 15	271	Minden, XI early
Italian		
Verona, Bibl. Cap., XC(85)	—[c]	(?)Verona or Monza, X mid
Verona, Bibl. Cap., CVII(100)	12	Mantua, XI first half
Rome, Bibl. Vat., lat. 4770	35	(?)Abruzzi or San Bartolomeo in Insula, X/XI
Monza, Bibl. Cap., c. 13/76	22	Monza, XI early

[a] Descriptions of the manuscripts and information pertaining to provenance and date can be found in Husmann, *Tropen- und Sequenzenhandschriften; Les sources,* Vol. 2 of *Le graduel romain* (Solesmes, 1957); Planchart, *The Repertory of Tropes*

at Winchester, II, 343-51; *Corpus troporum* I: 1, 46-50; and Lipphardt, *Lateinische Osterfeiern und Osterspiele;* regarding Apt 18(4), see Planchart's remarks in the *Journal of the American Musicological Society,* 32 (1979), 149. The reader is advised that the actual origin of many of these sources is unknown, and that the attributions and dates given here and in the sources cited are often only inferences or estimates. The customary of St. Vannes de Verdun (Lipphardt, no. 360) should perhaps be included in this list, if we can trust Martène's ascription of it to the tenth century (*De antiquis ecclesiae ritibus,* 2nd ed. [Antwerp, 1763-64], IV, 297); but according to Thomas Symons ("Sources of the *Regularis concordia,*" *Downside Review,* 59 [1941], 273n), Edmund Bishop believed it to date only from c.1030.

b This manuscript dates from the middle of the eleventh century but is included here as a copy of a tenth-century exemplar; see Planchart, *The Repertory of Tropes at Winchester,* I, 40-43.

c This source—one of the very oldest for *Quem quaeritis*—has been virtually ignored, although it has known since the citation of Hans Spanke in *Deutsche und französische Dichtung des Mittelalters* (Stuttgart, 1943), p. 33. For its text, see Planchart, *The Repertory of Tropes,* II, 39-40.

Already in the tenth century the piece was known throughout Europe; it is found in every extant troper from the period except one from Mainz (London, British Library MS. Add. 19768) and one from the St. Gall orbit (Vienna, Nationalbibliothek, 1609), both of which locales are represented by other sources nearly as old. Again, all that keeps us from demonstrating the presence of the piece in yet other places is that no more sources survive. It could be objected that the dialogue was not known—or, at least, that there are indications of its not being known—at certain monasteries, among them such important houses as Cluny, Fleury, and Gorze, whose early customaries make no mention of it.[28] But it should be remembered that most of the early sources are chant books, not sets of regulations governing liturgical practice; and that the latter, by their very nature, are selective in what they cover, while the former are not. (For example, Young points out that the earliest customary from Fleury [c.1000] says nothing about *Quem quaeritis;* but in fact, it says next to nothing about the Easter liturgy.[29]) What is particularly important is that none of these establishments have left any tropers, the one kind of book most likely to have contained the piece. Thus despite the total lack of evidence for *Quem quaeritis* at Cluny, for example, it is rash to presume that it was unknown there, as no troper from the abbey survives.[30] It should also be worth considering that the early customaries which can be counted as sources document the use of the *Visitatio* at Matins—not the use of *Quem quaeritis* at Mass. And insofar as Cluny and Fleury, in particular, are likely to have sung the piece at Mass rather than Matins, in

accordance with southern French usage, then it is only to be
expected that no traces of it should be found in their regulations. (Documents describing how *Quem quaeritis* or the *Visitatio sepulchri* were performed are much rarer than books
containing the chants themselves. What is unusual about the
Regularis concordia, the oldest one, is not so much its age as
its inclusion of detailed instructions for the representational
aspects of the ceremony, and—of course—its survival to the
present day. Its treatment of the *Visitatio* should probably be
taken as representative of a practice widespread on the continent—at least in the North—for half a century or more before this customary was drafted.)

Other lines of reasoning give us more indirect proof that the
dialogue was already widespread during the tenth century. Two
tropers of the same provenance but of different date typically
have nearly the same contents: the two Winchester tropers and
the lost prototype of one span a period of seventy years, and
yet agree closely; so do the two Nevers tropers (Paris, Bibliothèque Nationale, lat. 9449 and nouv. acq. lat. 1235), dating
from a century apart; likewise with similar pairs of manuscripts
from St. Martial or St. Gall. The later ones typically show a
slight reduction in the repertory, if anything; the number of
new pieces is small, and they are usually sequences or Ordinary
chants, not tropes to the Proper. Trope repertories appear to
have stabilized by the end of the tenth century, so that most of
what was sung in a monastery at the end of the eleventh had
been known there for more than a hundred years. Thus it can be
presumed that wherever the dialogue is documented in the
eleventh century, it was known already in the tenth. It can be
shown, moreover, that the very inclusion of *Quem quaeritis* in
any manuscript virtually guarantees its being known at other
establishments, from which no sources survive, by just as early
a date. The *Regularis concordia* draws from continental practice,
as does the Winchester Troper, but the tenth-century documents
which might have served as models have perished. The earliest
St. Martial troper shows signs of having been copied from a
northern French exemplar, but there is no prior source.[31] The
Apt troper MS. 18(4), too, shows signs of northern influence.[32]
The Reichenau troper Bamberg, Staatliche Bibliothek, Lit. 5, and
the Regensberg troper Kassel, Murhard'sche Bibliothek, theol.
IV° 15, alone of all the South German and Swiss manuscripts,

show peculiar affinities with Rhenish sources which imply derivation of their repertories from earlier ones in the North. The repertory of the mid-eleventh-century St. Vaast troper Cambrai, Bibliothèque Municipale, MS. 75(76) can be shown to be a century
older than the source by its inclusion, virtually entire, in the
Winchester Troper.33 The sole troper from Metz, reputedly one
of the foremost musical centers of the empire, dates from about
1100; yet its tradition is surely at least as old as the ones at
St. Martial, St. Gall, Mainz, and Winchester, where documen-
tation goes back another century and a half. This is not to say
that the chronology of individual sources is meaningless; rather,
that the date of the copying of a source implies far more than
it actually establishes.

The dissemination of *Quem quaeritis* does set it apart from
most tropes—indeed, from most Frankish chant. Still it should
not be taken to imply that the dialogue belongs to an older
repertory, for all signs suggest that it is a ninth-century creation
which simply happened to spread over an unusually wide territory. Even if it was almost as generally known as Gregorian
chant, it had none of the fixity associated with that repertory.
Both its form and context show manifold variation. Its position
in the liturgy was far from being uniform, and the shape it
took depended to a large extent on when it was used. Yet even
among the early versions for Matins, or for Mass, there could
be—and often was—considerable discrepancy from one to the
next. What one sees in them is a set of three lines that were
everywhere nearly the same, then several sets of items (mostly
antiphons and tropes, with the exact makeup of the set dependent upon liturgical position) that could be optionally drawn
upon to fill out the setting. This kind of variety in the liturgy
is associated with the innovations of the ninth and tenth centuries, in particular with tropes and sequences, but also with
processions and, to some extent, with the Office—just those
places, in fact, where *Quem quaeritis* came to be used. So far
as tenth- and eleventh-century sources are concerned, the chant
is found for the most part in tropers, or in *graduales* which
include tropes as well as Proper chant—not in collections of
processional antiphons, or in Office books, which survive only
in small number from this period. Those that place it at Matins,
if they are not customaries or ordinals dealing with the entire
spectrum of the liturgy, are primarily Mass books (particularly

tropers)[34] which set it apart with rubrics; for it was here that the newer chant was copied.

The style of the Easter dialogue is clearly Frankish. Its latinity displays the most obvious marks of the age—directness, emphasis on effect (assonance, refrain-like structure, large scale parallelism among the bipartite verses), and attempt at vividness and immediacy. It may paraphrase its biblical sources, but it is far removed from scriptural style; and when placed among antiphons or responsories whose texts are more literal borrowings, the difference is clear. The same can be said of its melody. However unusual the piece may seem to an historian of drama, anyone viewing it in the context of liturgical chant would be unlikely to think of it as being *sui generis;* and of the types of chant being written in the ninth and tenth centuries, the one to which this dialogue corresponds is the trope, being by far the most free of textual and musical constraint.[35] *Quem quaeritis* is a carefully balanced, self-contained little song three units long, which builds to a climax in the first half of phrase three (at the dramatic highpoint of the exchange *"Non est hic; surrexit sicut predixerat"*), then falls slowly to rest at the end (see Example 1). Anything coming before or afterward is extrinsic, and will sound that way whether it is a responsory or antiphon, another trope, or the *Te Deum* or *Resurrexi*. *Quem quaeritis* resembles other tropes on *D* far more than any of the items it is placed next to, whether it be the Easter Introit or some chant from Matins or the procession. Claims to the contrary notwithstanding,[36] the melody shows no sign of having been designed to complement *Resurrexi*. The other tropes to the Easter Introit all acknowledge in one way or another its *E* final; only *Quem quaeritis* does not. Even so, the dialogue need not have been intended for some other position, as tropes are often melodically independent of the chants they introduce. The syntactical independence and melodic closure of *Quem quaeritis,* however, can be used to explain its adaptability to a wide variety of contexts.

There is another possibility worth considering, one suggested by a northern French tradition of pieces comparable in style and scope to the version of the dialogue found in the Winchester tropers, without its processional antiphons. There are in these manuscripts six pieces, *versus ante officium,* versicles introducing Mass, for Christmas, Easter, Ascension, and the Feasts of St. Stephen, St. John the Evangelist, and the Holy Innocents.[37]

Example 1

Paris, Bibliothèque Nationale, lat. 909, fols. 21v-22

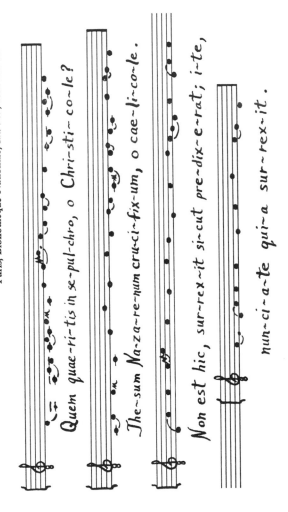

They are, as it were, tropes to the Mass, rather than to the Introit, and were presumably sung as part of (or, rather, at the end of) the procession before Mass, where the rubrics from the earliest North French sources place them;[38] only the piece for Easter, *Quem quaeritis in sepulchro,* is assigned to Matins. Elsewhere on the continent these pieces were treated as tropes, with the exception of *Quem quaeritis,* which was regarded as one in certain regions, but was generally kept in the same position it had at Winchester—i.e., at Matins before the *Te Deum.* They are hardly distinguishable from the vast majority of tropes; only their length makes them different. But their position before Mass was generally occupied by other kinds of pieces, most often processional antiphons. Being like tropes in style, rather than like processional antiphons, the pieces may have come to be treated as tropes wherever their special nature (or their special use at Winchester and in the North of France) was not recognized. Whether these *versus* were seen as coming before Mass, or in the procession before Mass, or just before the Introit, was immaterial, as all three positions are pretty much the same; and for all practical purpose, they are just a particular—if somewhat unusual—kind of trope.

Scholars of medieval chant now generally believe that trope composition began sometime about the middle of the ninth century—probably not too much before and certainly not very much afterward; so the lag between the composition of a piece and the copying of its oldest source could easily be a century or more. The activity is thought to have been centered at first in the great monastic houses of the North of France and the Rhineland, then to have spread gradually throughout the rest of Europe. The existence of a fairly clearcut division between East and West Frankish repertories of tropes and sequences has long been recognized. It is most obvious in the opposition of St. Martial and St. Gall or, more broadly, the South of France and the South of Germany: pieces from one region, by and large, did not move into the other. On the other hand, there was considerable overlap between northern and southern repertories. The opposition is less obvious in the North, because books from Lotharingia show a meeting of East and West; here there are next to each other chants from France and Germany, and some that were sung across the North of Europe. Otherwise it was unusual for pieces to be known on both sides of the Rhine.

The very few tropes and sequences circulating through all of
Frankish territory were anomalies. Their spread is no doubt a
measure of their popular appeal, but it also seems to have had
something to do with their age and provenance. They may well
belong to the oldest layer of Frankish composition; and if they
were written in the North, as most of them seem to have been,
they would have been well situated for dissemination in both
East and West. *Quem quaeritis* is one of these anomalies. Its
popularity is easy to understand, and its extraordinary circulation could be understood simply in relation to that. Yet the
evidence points beyond it, and all in the same direction—toward
the conclusion that the dialogue is a ninth-century composition,
written probably in the North of France or in the Rhineland.
One thing a study of the dissemination of Frankish chant can
tell us is that *Quem quaeritis* was not written at St. Gall or at
St. Martial or in northern Italy, for what characterizes the pieces
written there is that they seldom circulated outside their own
regions: except for the Notkerian cycle of sequences, pieces
from St. Gall were not readily accepted into the wider repertory;
pieces from St. Martial were seldom found outside Aquitania;
and there were virtually no instances of native Italian chant
circulating north of the Alps. The prevailing routes of transmission led from the North of France to the South; from the
Rhineland into Germany and Switzerland; across the North of
Europe; into England from the North of France; into Spain
from the South of France; and into Italy from the nearest quarter.[39] The pieces which, like *Quem quaeritis,* came to be most
widely known, appear to have originated in the North.

What remains to be considered is the varied placement of
Quem quaeritis in Mass, the procession before it, and Matins,
and the question of whether the chant was originally a trope,
a dialogue in a processional ceremony, or part of a fully developed ritual for the Easter Vigil. Among tenth- and eleventh-
century sources there is a split between those assigning *Quem
quaeritis* to Mass (or the procession before it)[40] and those
assigning it to Matins, but the division is not haphazard, nor is
it chronological.[41] It is geographic. The manuscripts of this
period are the first witnesses of local liturgical practice, at least
in those details that are not treated everywhere in strict uni-
formity. Whatever its date, the earliest troper from one monas-

tery is as significant a source as the earliest from another. Both
reveal what special items were used in these monasteries alongside the Gregorian propers for Mass (or in certain instances,
for Matins). The chronology of sources from this period is not
an important factor in comparing different practices, for the
manuscripts represent repertories which are, in the main, fifty
or a hundred years old, or even more. Once this is understood,
the distribution of books assigning *Quem quaeritis* to Matins
and Mass becomes clear. The dialogue was sung at Mass in the
South of France, in Catalonia, and in Italy; also, in a small
number of East Frankish locales—St. Gall and a few monasteries with closely related liturgical practices (among them,
Rheinau, Heidenheim, and Minden).[42] The dialogue was sung
at Matins across the North of Europe—in England, the North
of France, the Rhineland, and in most of East Frankish territory (see Table 2). The few German establishments which used
it at Mass seem to have moved it to Matins during the twelfth
century, as the later sources from St. Gall and Rheinau imply.[43]
What little evidence there is that *Quem quaeritis* was used as a
trope before being used in procession or at Matins is untrust-
worthy.[44] Most scholars have regarded treatment of the dialogue
as an Introit trope in the earliest St. Gall and St. Martial sources
as definitive proof of its origin as a trope. Yet the St. Martial
version is a conflation of two different pieces—one *(Psallite
regni magno),* an Introit trope, and the other *(Quem quaeritis),*
a piece that in the North was traditionally used at Matins.[45]
The St. Gall version is unrepresentative of the larger East
Frankish and Lotharingian tradition, and for that reason alone
should be regarded as suspect; it is also unrepresentative of the
type of trope written at St. Gall.[46] Chant scholars are slowly
reaching a consensus that neither St. Martial nor St. Gall (except in the instance of Notker's sequences) warrant their repu-
tations as the preeminent musical centers of Frankish civiliza-
tion: it is becoming clear that their fame rests largely on the
chance survival of large numbers of manuscripts, among them
the earliest integral sources for the East and West Frankish
repertories. A study of what was sung at the two monasteries
shows them to have been peripheral to the mainstream traditions
of the North. Representatives of Northern practice can be found
in sources from Mainz, Metz, Trier, Echternach, St. Vaast, and
Winchester (since Winchester practice was borrowed from the

TABLE 2

SOURCES INDICATING AN EARLY ASSIGNMENT OF
QUEM QUAERITIS TO MATINS[a]

Source	Lipphardt Edition No.	Provenance & Date
Regularis concordia	394/395	Winchester, 965-75
Oxford, Bodl. 775	423	Winchester, XI middle
Cambridge, Corpus Christi, 473	424	Winchester, c. 1000
Cambrai, Bibl. Mun., 75(76)	91	St. Vaast (Arras), XI middle
Cambrai, Bibl. Mun., 78(79)	—[b]	Cambrai, XI/XII
De officiis ecclesiasticis of Jean, Avranches	—[c]	Avranches, Rouen, 1060-67
Angers, Bibl. Mun., 96(88)	88	Angers, XII early
Paris, Bibl. Nat., lat. 9449	117	Nevers, c. 1060
Customary of St. Vannes de Verdun	360	Verdun, X/XI
Vienna, Nationalbibl., 1888[d]	76	St. Alban (Mainz), c. 1000
Paris, Bibl. Nat., lat. 9488	205	Echternach(?), 996-97
Paris, Bibl. Nat., lat. 10510	204	Echternach, XI/XII
Metz, Bibl. Mun., 452	267	Metz, XI/XII
Customary of Fulda	211	Fulda, before 1039
Wolfenbüttel, Herzog-August-Bibl., Helms. 1109	347	Trier, X/XI
Paris, Bibl. Nat., lat. 9448	312	Prüm, 990-95
Kassel, theol. IV° 25	334	Fritzlar or Seeon, XI 1st half
Bamberg, Staatl. Bibl., Lit. 6	319	St. Emmeram, c. 1000
Munich, Staatsbibl., clm 14083	321	St. Emmeram, 1031-37
Munich, Staatsbibl., clm 14845	320	St. Emmeram, XII
Bamberg, Staatl. Bibl., Lit. 5	314	Reichenau, 1001
Zurich, Zentralbibl., Rh. 65	337	Solothurn, XI

a For information regarding the manuscripts, see the sources listed in Table 1, fn. a.

b Text in Planchart, *The Repertory of Tropes,* II, 37-40.

c No text; see Dolan, *Le drame liturgique,* p. 50.

d The earliest Mainz source (Lipphardt, no. 76) should probably be understood as indicating placement at Matins, according to its use of the antiphon *Surrexit Dominus* (see fn. 42).

continent), and these show *Quem quaeritis* assigned to Matins. It would be possible to argue that this was the original placement for the dialogue, but it is not necessary or even desirable to do so. For in the end what the evidence shows is that as quickly as the piece spread through Europe, it came to be used in different contexts. In order to learn anything about the early history of *Quem quaeritis* it is first necessary to understand one important fact of medieval liturgical observance: insofar as non-Gregorian items of the Mass are concerned, there was no standard use, and to an astonishing extent the liturgy varied from one place to another. What was done at St. Gall and St. Martial was almost always different from what was done at Mainz, or Metz, or Tours, or Winchester. And it would be nonsense to pretend that only one of those traditions was right, proper, or authentic. It is far more reasonable to accept the diversity of medieval practice and to recognize that then as now, things were not everywhere the same.

As for Hardison's theory that the *Visitatio* originally belonged to the Easter Vigil, the most gracious response would be to ignore it, but as a corrective it may be worth pointing out the flaws in his argument. The Easter Vigil is among the most ancient of Christian ceremonies, a reflection of the earliest forms of liturgical worship in the Western Church; its peculiarities are due to its age and its refusal to accommodate change as the liturgy evolved into the more familiar forms of the Gregorian and Romano-Frankish rites. There is, in other words, no sign of the ceremony having changed much since the institution of the Mass for Easter day; whatever adjustments that caused, including those resulting from the gradual anticipation of the hour of the Vigil, had been settled long before the Roman rite was sent North.[47] There was, moreover, no place within its structure where a full-fledged *Visitatio* could have been fitted, and it is significant that tropes were never written for this Vigil, as it lacks the antiphonal chants to which they could be attached. The anticipation of the Vigil, on which so much of Hardison's case depends, had already resulted in celebration of its Mass in the early evening hours by the eighth century at latest[48]—in other words, far too early to have had any import for the *Visitatio*. The baptismal symbols which he finds in the *Visitatio* do not in themselves imply its use at Vigil, for the entire Easter octave is devoted to commemoration of the neophytes' first baptism and focuses on the intimate relation between the baptismal sacrament and the Resurrection; they seem, moreover, to be accretions rather than intrinsic elements of the dialogue. Perhaps most important is the shape of the *Visitatio* itself (any one of its shapes)—a hodgepodge of elements drawn from diverse styles and periods which could never have been conceived of as a uniform whole.

The argument presented here reviews the relation between

Quem quaeritis and the *Visitatio sepulchri* from the broadest possible perspective. It suggests that too narrow a focus on the earliest sources for the dialogue can be misleading. As a study of Lipphardt's edition shows, the geographical distribution of the various versions is the best key to understanding the relationships among them, particularly among the three main types associated respectively with Mass, the procession before it, and Matins. The danger of paying too much attention to the chronology of sources has been made abundantly clear by Hardison. Already in the tenth century the three types—trope, processional dialogue, and dramatic ceremony—were widespread. The version used at Matins can be shown to have existed just as early as the ones for Mass—so far back as the evidence goes—and over a much wider region. The versions associated with Mass were limited geographically to the South of Europe—particularly Italy, the South of France, and the Spanish march, but also a few locales within the St. Gall orbit. Thus the theory that *Quem quaeritis* was originally a trope, if it is to be justified, must be supported on other grounds. In order to get any closer to understanding the genesis and early history of the dialogue, there is nothing to do but fall back on logic and whatever critical methods there are for dealing with the history of liturgical chant.

We may never know exactly how *Quem quaeritis* was first used. The manuscript evidence is of little help. But it is worth considering circumstances which might account for its transfer from one liturgical position to another or, rather (since it is not really transfer that is concerned here), its varied liturgical use. If some ceremony involving the dialogue grew up in connection with the short Roman Office, the shift to Mass could have taken place wherever the regular observance was kept; this possibility does seem to be suggested by the evidence.[49] If the dialogue grew up within the procession—as a reworking, say, of one built entirely from antiphons[50]—a simple reordering of items could have left the dialogue just before the Introit, where it would appear to be just another trope. Such a ceremony could easily have been placed at Matins in order to preserve a procession already existing before Mass; for where the *Visitatio* was performed at Matins, there was also a procession before Mass. With both of the possibilities, but particularly with the latter, there remains one problem, and it involves the mixture of elements in the play and the procession. The difficulty is in imagining why an elaborate representational ceremony would have been simplified for performance as a trope. If *Quem quaeritis* began as a trope, on the other hand, its removal from proximity to the Introit would be easy to explain: whether another trope was added, or an antiphon inserted, the result would have been the same; and as there was virtually everywhere some kind of procession before Mass, the position of the dialogue could have been varied so as to coincide with arrival at whatever represented the Sepulchre (it was not always the altar).[51] Its transfer to Matins, too, could be easily understood as a means of preserving some of the other tropes to *Resurrexi,* which otherwise might never have been sung. But the particular attraction of this hypothesis is that the dialogue, unless it were truly *sui generis,* must have been intended as some kind of a trope. If it is to be identified as a particular kind of chant, what else could it be? The contrast between *Quem quaeritis* and the antiphons juxtaposed to it, and the manifold variation in its form and context, make it seem likely that Young was right after all. The three lines of the dialogue were written as a unit, and whatever else was sung with it was extrinsic and an accretion. The logical order of development outlined by Young may not represent or correspond to chronological development; he admitted as much himself. But his assumption that there must have been something orderly about the development is not arbitrary, as Hardison claims. It is only logical. Even if there remains some question as to how *Quem quaeritis* was first used, there can be no doubt that sometime in the ninth century a monk wrote its text and set it to music. What became of it in the next century is plain to see; but the intervening events unfortunately lie beyond our view.

NOTES

1 After St. Gall, Stiftsbibliothek, MS. 484, p. 111.

2 The sole instances of versions for Mass with elaborate rubrics explicitly calling for representational performance are the customary of Fruttuaria (c.1090) and a fifteenth-century ordinal from Brescia (Biblioteca Civica Queriniana, MS. 4686 [H. VI. II]). Yet it is important to remember that most sources assigning the dialogue to Mass or the procession before it are chant books in which rubrics of any sort are

exceedingly rare; the lack of them, in other words, implies nothing about the performance of the piece.

3 *Histoire de la poésie liturgique au moyen âge: Les tropes* (Paris, 1886), pp. 219-20.

4 *The Mediaeval Stage* (Oxford, 1903), II, 9-40.

5 "The Origin of the Easter Play," *PMLA*, 29 (1914), 1-58; and *The Drama of the Medieval Church* (Oxford, 1933), I, 201-450.

6 See especially *Drama*, I, 201-38.

7 *Casus sancti Galli*, in *Scriptores rerum sangalliensis*, ed. Idelfons von Arx [*Monumenta germaniae historica, scriptores*, 2] (Hannover, 1829), p. 101.

8 Chailley, "Le drame liturgique médiéval à Saint-Martial de Limoges," *Revue d'histoire du théâtre*, 7 (1955), 132; and *L'École musicale de Saint-Martial de Limoges jusqu'à la fin du XIe siècle* (Paris, 1960), p. 373. Smoldon, "The Origins of the *Quem quaeritis* and the Easter Sepulchre Music-Drama, as Demonstrated by Their Musical Settings," *The Medieval Drama: Papers of the Third Annual Conference of the Center for Medieval and Early Renaissance Studies, State University of New York at Binghamton, 3-4 May 1969*, ed. Sandro Sticca (Albany, 1972), pp. 142-43; and "The Melodies of the Medieval Church-Dramas and Their Significance," *Comparative Drama*, 2 (1968), 193.

9 *Die Textgeschichte der lateinischen Osterfeiern* [*Hermaea. Germanistische Forschungen, n. F.*, 22] (Tübingen, 1967), pp. 70-75.

10 Timothy J. McGee, "The Liturgical Placements of the *Quem quaeritis* Dialogue," *Journal of the American Musicological Society*, 29 (1976), 23-26; and Carol Heitz, *Recherches sur les rapports entre architecture et liturgie a l'époque carolingienne* [*Bibliothèque générale de l'école pratique des hautes études, vie section*] (Paris, 1963), pp. 220-21.

11 See, for example, Diane Dolan, *Le drame liturgique de Pâques en Normandie et en Angleterre au moyen-âge* [*Publications de l'Université de Poitiers. Lettres et sciences humaines*, 16] (Paris, 1975), pp. 32 and 35; Joseph Smits van Waesberghe *et al.*, "Liturgical and Secular Elements in Medieval Liturgical Drama," *Report of the Tenth Congress of the International Musicological Society, Ljubljana 1967*, ed. Dragotin Cvetko (Kassel and Basel, 1970), p. 272; and O. B. Hardison, Jr., *Christian Rite and Christian Drama in the Middle Ages* (Baltimore, 1965), p. 219. See also de Boor, *Textgeschichte*, p. 23.

12 *Christian Rite and Christian Drama*, pp. 178-227. This important book contains the most forceful and influential criticism of Young's work published to date, and offers interesting new perspectives on the *Visitatio*. Yet it should be pointed out that, whatever the value of Hardison's book, his use of evidence is surprisingly cavalier, and it is distressing to see this turned to account in making Young seem dogmatic and foolish, which he certainly was not. Young's *Drama of the Medieval Church* is of such high quality as to be nearly impeccable; he himself was an extraordinary scholar whose cautious reasoning and accurate control of detail have rarely been matched by his successors.

13 "The Liturgical Placements of the *Quem quaeritis* Dialogue." Terrence Bailey, *The Processions of Sarum and the Western Church* [*Pontifical Institute of Mediaeval Studies. Studies and Texts*, 21] (Toronto, 1971), provides a broader view of the Easter procession.

14 Hardison, *Christian Rite and Christian Drama*, pp. 187, 194, and "Gregorian Easter Vespers and Early Liturgical Drama," *The Medieval Drama and Its Claudelian Revival: Papers Presented at the Third Symposium in Comparative Literature held at the Catholic University of America, April 3 and 4, 1968*, ed. E. Catherine Dunn, Tatiana Fotitch, and Bernard M. Peebles (Washington, D. C., 1970), pp. 27-40; and McGee, "The Liturgical Placements," pp. 23-27. See also C. Clifford Flanigan, "The

Roman Rite and the Origins of the Liturgical Drama," *University of Toronto Quarterly*, 43 (1973-74), 263-84.

15 The early dates of these two manuscripts have been questioned by Chailley (*L'École musicale*, pp. 78-80), Heinrich Husmann (*Tropen- und Sequenzenhandschriften*, Vol. B V1 of *Répertoire international des sources musicales* [Munich, 1964], pp. 42-43, 47, 137-38), Kassius Hallinger ("Die Provenienz der Consuetudo Sigiberti," *Mediaevalia litteraria: Festschrift für Helmut de Boor zum 80. Geburtstag* [Munich, 1971], pp. 156-57), and de Boor (*Textgeschichte*, pp. 24, 31). Suffice it to say that the arguments of Chailley and Husmann have not been generally accepted by scholars who work regularly with the sources, and that the observations of Hallinger and de Boor are secondhand.

16 De Boor's work is almost alone is being free of this bias. Hardison's work is not, for after making a determined effort to show how confusing the evidence is when arranged in chronological order, he dismisses it all except the one early source useful for his argument, the Winchester *Visitatio;* virtually his entire case rests on this piece of evidence—and on his assumption that it belongs to the Easter Vigil. A more careful assessment of its liturgical position is given by Alejandro Planchart in *The Repertory of Tropes at Winchester* (Princeton, 1977), I, 239-40.

17 Walther Lipphardt, ed., *Lateinische Osterfeiern und Osterspiele* [*Ausgaben deutscher Literatur des XV. bis XVIII. Jahrhunderts, Reihe Drama* 5] (Berlin and New York, 1975-), 7 vols. See also Vol. 2 of *Corpus troporum, I: Tropes du propre de la messe* [*Studia latina stockholmiensia*, 21-] (Stockholm, 1975-), ed. Ritva Jonsson *et al.;* and the conspectus offered by Alejandro Planchart, *The Repertory of Tropes*, II, 37-42, an invaluable tool for understanding the material.

18 The details are obscure; but see C. Coebergh, "Les lectures de l'apôtre pour Pâques et leurs vicissitudes," *Revue bénédictine*, 77 (1967), 142-48.

19 Herman A. P. Schmidt, *Hebdomada sancta* (Rome and Freiburg im Br., 1957), II, 867-77; and Joseph A. Jungmann, "Die Vorverlegung der Ostervigil seit dem christlichen Altertum," *Liturgisches Jahrbuch*, 1 (1951), 48-54.

20 Réné-Jean Hesbert, *Antiphonale missarum sextuplex* (Brussels, 1935), pp. 100-01.

21 The Apt troper MS. 17(5), with thirteen, contains the largest number for the Easter Introit; see Lipphardt, II, 45-51, and Günther Weiss, ed., *Introitus-Tropen, I: Das Repertoire der südfranzösischen Tropare des 10. und 11. Jahrhunderts* [*Monumenta monodica medii aevi*, 3] (Kassel and Basel, 1970), pp. 232-51 and 412-15 (where, despite the lack of rubric, nos. 218, 225, and 227 are counted as separate tropes). The St. Martial troper Paris, B.N., lat. 1121 gives seven tropes for *Resurrexi*, including *Quem quaeritis;* see Lipphardt, II, 63-66, and Paul Evans, *The Early Trope Repertory of Saint Martial de Limoges* (Princeton, 1970), 155-61.

22 See Bailey, *Processions*, pp. 171-74; also Réné-Jean Hesbert, *Corpus antiphonalium officii* [*Rerum ecclesiasticarum documenta, series major, fontes* 7-11] (Rome, 1963-75), I, 176-84, and II, 320-31, 784-85.

23 Stäblein, *Schriftbild der einstimmigen Musik* [*Musikgeschichte in Bildern*, III, 4] (Leipzig, 1975), p. 116; Huglo, "L'Office du dimanche de Pâques dans les monastères bénédictins," *Revue grégorienne*, 30 (1951), 197.

24 See particularly "The Troping Hypothesis," *Musical Quarterly*, 52 (1966), 183-203; "The Sequence," in *Gattungen der Musik in Einzeldarstellungen: Gedenkschrift Leo Schrade*, I (Bern and Munich, 1973), 269-76; and *The Early Medieval Sequence* (Berkeley and Los Angeles, 1977), pp. 410-23.

25 Compare the table in Vol. I: 1, 46-50, with Planchart's list of sources for *Quem quaeritis* in *The Repertory of Tropes*, II, 39-41. For Kassel, Murhard'sche Bibliothek, theol. IV° 25, see Lipphardt, II, 442-43.

upon careful assessment of the repetory. That it does not stand up to close scrutiny is shown by Richard Crocker ("The Troping Hypothesis," pp. 183-91, and *The Early Medieval Sequence*, pp. 418-19) and Bruno Stäblein ("Zum verständnis des 'klassischen' Tropus," *Acta musicologica*, 35 [1963], 95), both of whom emphasize the formal and stylistic integrity of the trope. Following Crocker, and taking a similar stance, Planchart (*The Repertory of Tropes*, I, 67-68) chooses as his starting point the thirteenth-century definition of Bishop Durand: "A trope is a kind of versicle sung on important feasts before the Introit. . . ."

36 Smoldon, "The Origins of the *Quem quaeritis*," pp. 141-42, and "The Melodies," pp. 200-01.

37 Planchart, *The Repertory of Tropes*, I, 234-40, and II, 31-42.

38 Ibid., I, 236.

39 To date there is but one thorough study of a regional repertory and the patterns of transmission associated with it—Planchart's *The Repertory of Tropes at Winchester*. The reader interested in pursuing the matter on his own would do well to start there before moving on to the concordances for pieces found in vols. 47, 49, and 53 of *Analecta hymnica medii aevi*, ed. Guido Maria Dreves, Clemens Blume, and Henry Marriott Bannister (Leipzig, 1886-1922); *Corpus troporum*; Klaus Rönnau, *Die Tropen zum Gloria in excelsis Deo: Unter besonder Berücksichtigung des Repertoires der St. Martial-Handschriften* (Wiesbaden, 1967); and the author's "The Kyrie Trope," to be published in the *Journal of the American Musicological Society*, 33 (1980).

40 The number of sources clearly placing *Quem quaeritis* in the procession is small, much smaller than McGee would have us believe. Instances in which it is separated from the beginning of Mass by processional antiphons can be found only at Bologna, Monza, Heidenheim, St. Gall, and Minden (Lipphardt, nos. 7, 24-25, 75, 80-85, 271-73). Instances in which it comes at the end of the procession, after the altar has been reached—in other words, just before the Introit—can be found only at Monte Cassino, Benevento, San Juan de las Abadesos, Urgel, Vich, and Vienne (Lipphardt, nos. 14-19, 20-21, 59, 64-67a, 68-72, 74). The latter instances make it clear that there was no sharp division between the procession and Mass, so that it is difficult (perhaps even pointless) to distinguish placement at the end of processsion from placement at the beginning of Mass.

41 A major crux of Hardison's argument (*Christian Rite and Christian Drama*, pp. 187-91, 198) is his assertion that *Quem quaeritis* had no fixed place in the tenth century, "that it was not closely associated with any of the liturgical occasions where it later (in the eleventh and twelfth centuries) became conventional." The observation itself is incorrect: some sources give less information than others about where in the liturgy the dialogue was used, but whatever ambiguity remains in no way implies that the piece did not have its assigned place. What is wrong with his reasoning is the assumption that if chronological ordering of the sources does not produce a meaningful pattern of evidence, the diversity it does reveal must be random. But the traditional argument, that *Quem quaeritis* was first used at Mass and only afterward came to be associated with Matins, is just as misleading, as Hardison succeeds in demonstrating.

42 Lipphardt, nos. 1-85 (but not 30-31, 58, 73, or 76) and 271-73—simply too many to cite in tabular form. It is worth underscoring here a point made by McGee ("The Liturgical Placements," p. 15) that the chants accompanying *Quem quaeritis* are different at Mass and Matins. The antiphons, hymns, and responsories associated with the dialogue often reveal the context in which it was sung, when nothing else does. The *Te Deum*, for example, implies Matins, as does the antiphon *Surrexit Dominus de sepulchro*, which generally stands just before the *Te Deum* in early sources. The antiphons *Surrexit enim*, *In die resurrectionis*, *Vidi aquam*, *Sedit angelus*, and the hymn *Salva festa dies* imply the procession before Mass. Certain antiphons were sung in the Office as well as at Mass, but in most cases the association is much stronger with one than with the other. Thus the earliest Mainz *Visitatio* (no. 76)

upon careful assessment of the repetory. That it does not stand up to close scrutiny is shown by Richard Crocker ("The Troping Hypothesis," pp. 183-91, and *The Early Medieval Sequence*, pp. 418-19) and Bruno Stäblein ("Zum verständnis des 'klass-ischen' Tropus," *Acta musicologica*, 35 [1963], 95), both of whom emphasize the formal and stylistic integrity of the trope. Following Crocker, and taking a similar stance, Planchart (*The Repertory of Tropes*, I, 67-68) chooses as his starting point the thirteenth-century definition of Bishop Durand: "A trope is a kind of versicle sung on important feasts before the Introit. . . ."

36 Smoldon, "The Origins of the *Quem quaeritis*," pp. 141-42, and "The Melo-dies," pp. 200-01.

37 Planchart, *The Repertory of Tropes*, I, 234-40, and II, 31-42.

38 Ibid., I, 236.

39 To date there is but one thorough study of a regional repertory and the pat-terns of transmission associated with it—Planchart's *The Repertory of Tropes at Winchester*. The reader interested in pursuing the matter on his own would do well to start there before moving on to the concordances for pieces found in vols. 47, 49, and 53 of *Analecta hymnica medii aevi*, ed. Guido Maria Dreves, Clemens Blume, and Henry Marriott Bannister (Leipzig, 1886-1922); *Corpus troporum*; Klaus Rönnau, *Die Tropen zum Gloria in excelsis Deo: Unter besonder Berücksichtigung des Reper-toires der St. Martial-Handschriften* (Wiesbaden, 1967); and the author's "The Kyrie Trope," to be published in the *Journal of the American Musicological Society*, 33 (1980).

40 The number of sources clearly placing *Quem quaeritis* in the procession is small, much smaller than McGee would have us believe. Instances in which it is separated from the beginning of Mass by processional antiphons can be found only at Bologna, Monza, Heidenheim, St. Gall, and Minden (Lipphardt, nos. 7, 24-25, 75, 80-85, 271-73). Instances in which it comes at the end of the procession, after the altar has been reached—in other words, just before the Introit—can be found only at Monte Cassino, Benevento, San Juan de las Abadesos, Urgel, Vich, and Vienne (Lipphardt, nos. 14-19, 20-21, 59, 64-67a, 68-72, 74). The latter instances make it clear that there was no sharp division between the procession and Mass, so that it is difficult (perhaps even pointless) to distinguish placement at the end of processsion from placement at the beginning of Mass.

41 A major crux of Hardison's argument (*Christian Rite and Christian Drama*, pp. 187-91, 198) is his assertion that *Quem quaeritis* had no fixed place in the tenth century, "that it was not closely associated with any of the liturgical occasions where it later (in the eleventh and twelfth centuries) became conventional." The observation itself is incorrect: some sources give less information than others about where in the liturgy the dialogue was used, but whatever ambiguity remains in no way implies that the piece did not have its assigned place. What is wrong with his reasoning is the assumption that if chronological ordering of the sources does not produce a meaningful pattern of evidence, the diversity it does reveal must be random. But the traditional argument, that *Quem quaeritis* was first used at Mass and only afterward came to be associated with Matins, is just as misleading, as Hardison succeeds in demonstrating.

42 Lipphardt, nos. 1-85 (but not 30-31, 58, 73, or 76) and 271-73—simply too many to cite in tabular form. It is worth underscoring here a point made by McGee ("The Liturgical Placements," p. 15) that the chants accompanying *Quem quaeritis* are different at Mass and Matins. The antiphons, hymns, and responsories associated with the dialogue often reveal the context in which it was sung, when nothing else does. The *Te Deum*, for example, implies Matins, as does the antiphon *Surrexit Dominus de sepulchro*, which generally stands just before the *Te Deum* in early sources. The antiphons *Surrexit enim, In die resurrectionis, Vidi aquam, Sedit angelus,* and the hymn *Salva festa dies* imply the procession before Mass. Certain antiphons were sung in the Office as well as at Mass, but in most cases the association is much stronger with one than with the other. Thus the earliest Mainz *Visitatio* (no. 76)

should probably be placed with the others (nos. 251-63) as being intended for Matins, on account of its use of *Surrexit Dominus* (but the rubric and additional tropes *Alleluia, resurrexit dominus* and *Hodie resurrexit leo fortis* suggest Mass). Likewise, the Parma *Visitatio* belongs to Matins, as it uses both this antiphon and the *Te Deum*. On the other hand the rubrics and antiphons of the Minden sources (nos. 271-73) bespeak placement at Mass (and, besides, in many other details the manuscripts show their conformity with ones from St. Gall, where the dialogue was sung at Mass). In the Reichenau troper Bamberg, Staatliche Bibliothek, Lit. 5, *Surrexit enim* leads into the *Te Deum*, but this is a rare exception among early examples of the dialogue. Planchart (*The Repertory of Tropes*, I, 42) and Young (*Drama*, I, 244) are surely mistaken in associating *Surrexit enim* with Matins: with the single exception named, early sources using this antiphon (Lipphardt, nos. 75, 80-85) clearly indicate placement in the procession before Mass; only later does it come to be used in Matins (e.g., Lipphardt, nos. 178, 223, 248, 311a, 315a, 329, 379, 414, etc.), where it eventually became a common feature of second stage dramas (e.g., Lipphardt, nos. 694-715, 720). (The Echternach troper Paris, B.N., lat. 10510 has *Surrexit Dominus,* not *Surrexit enim.*)

43 Lipphardt, nos. 315-16, 327-32.

44 Cf. Stäblein, *Schriftbild*, p. 49. But the two cited sources from Mainz do not indeed establish the use of *Quem quaeritis* in procession: the first, *Le pontifical romano-germanique du dixième siècle,* ed. Cyrille Vogel and Reinhard Elze [*Studi e testi*, 226-27, 229] (Vatican City, 1963), II, 113-14, does not actually include the dialogue in its procession; and the second, Lipphardt, no. 76, may well belong to Matins rather than Mass (see fn. 42).

45 Planchart, *The Repertory of Tropes,* II, 154.

46 The pieces one can isolate as being confined to the St. Gall orbit are peculiar in style; they involve short melismas, melodies without texts, which usually alternate with syllabic settings of the same phrase. How different *Quem quaeritis* is from these tropes can be seen by comparing the layout in Lipphardt, I, 91-94, with the facsimiles in Gautier, *Les tropes,* especially pp. 214 and 216, but also 52-59 and 206-07. See also Smoldon, "The Origins," pp. 142-43.

47 Kenneth Levy, "The Italian Neophytes' Chants," *Journal of the American Musicological Society,* 23 (1970), 181-227, is perhaps the most comprehensive study on the subject, and a brilliant attempt at reconstructing the shape of the early Vigil Mass.

48 Schmidt, *Hebdomada sancta,* II, 867-77; see also Huglo, "L'Office du dimanche de Pâques," p. 192.

49 See fn. 30.

50 See, for example, the order for Easter Vespers in Hesbert, *Corpus antiphonalium officii,* I, 180-85, or the procession before Mass in the pontifical from Mainz, cited in fn. 44.

51 Young, *Drama,* II, 507-13; and Dunbar H. Ogden, "The Use of Architectural Space in Medieval Music-Drama," *Comparative Drama,* 8 (1974), 63-76.

Prophetic "Play" and Symbolist "Plot" in the Beauvais *Daniel*

Jerome Taylor

First composed and played by students at the cathedral school of St. Peter in Beauvais about 1140, and popular enough to have been carefully recopied nearly a hundred years later in the one manuscript of it remaining to us,[1] the *Danielis ludus* or "Play of Daniel" has become something more of a *pièce célèbre* for performing groups in our land and time than one suspects it ever quite became in its own. Text and music were first transcribed and edited by F. Danjou in the middle of the last century in his "Le Théâtre religieux et populaire au xiiie siècle: le Mystère de Daniel"[2] and slightly more than a decade later by Edouard de Coussemaker in his *Drames liturgiques du moyen âge*.[3] In our century, Karl Young, interested in the "evolution" of modern drama from "a spontaneous new birth and growth within the confines of Christian worship," as he thought, included the *Daniel,* but without the music, in his *Drama of the Medieval Church*.[4]

What gave the *Daniel* its popularity in our time, however, was its performance by the New York Pro Musica in January, 1958, "probably for the first time since the Middle Ages in the Romanesque Hall at The Cloisters, the medieval branch of the Metropolitan Museum of Art, in Fort Tryon Park, New York,"[5] the late Noah Greenberg being director, and Lincoln Kirstein producer. Brooks Atkinson in *The New York Times* called the production an "hour-long invocation to glory."[6] Within a year Oxford University Press issued a slim volume containing full transcription of the medieval music in modern notation, a Latin text of the libretto with English translation, essays and drawings on staging and costumes, and notes on correct Latin pronunciation.[7] In addition, a hi-fi stereophonic recording of the Pro

Musica performance appeared.8 These materials, together with numerous performances of the play by the Pro Musica in this country and abroad, have stimulated school groups, church groups, indeed academics in professional conclave, to attempt faithful reproduction of the play.9 They are not always sure that their reproductions are authentic, and, sometimes without having realized or intended it, are surprised to find that they have managed to evoke a moving religious experience for secular audiences—as if a moment from Christian Europe's cultural past had somehow come to life in an allegedly post-Christian world.

To be sure, authenticity of production and impact, religious or not, varies directly with the fidelity of producer and cast to the intent of the *Daniel's* art. Essentially the play is a multimedia vehicle for congregational *metanoia:* it offers the audience new grounds for faith in God, and, upon their discovery of these grounds, invites their reversal of any personal religious indifference or lukewarm passivity. The play terminates, perhaps one should say culminates, when the libretto, in its last words, confidently directs that the cantors will now intone the *Te Deum.* It is as if the whole assembly, actor-singers and audience, dropping their previous distinctness of role, will wish to break into this ancient hymn, a lyric outpouring of joyful praise and penitent petition, addressed in plainsong to the immediately present "Thou" of God, the expected consequence of the effect which the play is intended to produce upon all alike. This hypothesis concerning the intent of the play's art, an intent or goal which would have determined the instrumental nature and function of every part of the play, anticipates what one may well learn from analyzing the play's intrinsic form, its liturgical context, its materials and its setting, and from pondering modern productions which have seemed either remarkably or only relatively successful for reasons it is possible but not always easy to identify.

What becomes clear on reflection is that one does not discover or deliver the *Daniel's* intent simply through its words—the speeches and choruses and brief acting directions which Young was content to print. The speeches are skeletal, stylized, and afford no realistic development of thought or character. Dialogue, such as it is, will suddenly give way to third-person narrative, and the costumed chorus, at points, will unexpectedly cease to impersonate courtiers or warriors and will give voice, instead, to feelings programmed as the choristers' own. Nor can the intent of the play's art be found primarily in its music, though one appreciates the care of the retranscription which Greenberg commissioned and of his own editing and scoring of the music for voice and for attentively conjectured archaic instruments. Nor can a director "create" the art of the *Daniel* by coaching for finesse of elocution or fluidity or resonance or coloratura in voices, or by casting Balthasar as a towering *busso,* his queen as a dramatic soprano, and prophetic Daniel, ever youthful and wise beyond his years, as an athletic tenor. Not that these things are unimportant: they are part of the "language" of the play; but the message they are to carry originates outside them, just as the scenes in which they figure provide no realistic picture of life situations but, as symbols, bespeak things beyond themselves. In costume and staging, too, it is not fidelity to startling colors and clothing designs borrowed from manuscript miniatures, nor the reconstruction of a stray Romanesque arch or interesting fresco, which will bespeak the meaning of the play. The "language" assumed by the *Daniel* is rather the silent profundity of symbolic space in a cathedral apse, the symbolic order of persons in a monastic *statio* or solemn ecclesiastical procession, the known and expected sacramental value of sacred vessels, vestments, and gestures, and the Church Year itself—the Year of the Lord which, however vestigial it has become in the "A.D." still inserted in history-book dates today, once recycled annually a determined round of feasts and Scriptural readings by which the faith of the faithful was to be rejuvenated and redeemed from human fatigue and distraction and relapse. Within this Church Year and with these materials and this function, the *Daniel* was once given an expectable place, effective because then understood. Rediscovery, re-explanation, and recreation of that place are needed today if fidelity to the intent of the *Daniel's* art is to be fully achieved again.

Remembering Hardin Craig's insistence that Aristotelian "equipment" does not suit medieval religious drama,[10] one may nonetheless venture to approach the art and intent of the *Danielis ludus* of Beauvais with three sets of questions in mind: I. Is this *ludus,* or "play," a play at all, and if so, in what sense of the word? II. If indeed it is *a* play in some sense, and not simply juvenile play or pageantry, does it have a plot? Does the string of episodes, danced and sung and gesticulated, imitate an action of some sort? Does some principle of consequential choice or linear cause-and-effect, or perhaps some other art principle, endow this string of episodes with unity and hence with meaning? III. Finally, if one can discover plot here, and define its principle of unity and meaning, what precisely are the meaning and impact it is designed to deliver? The following observations, it is hoped, may contribute toward answers to these questions.

I

The first point to be made about the "Play of Daniel" is that it is not a play in the usual modern sense of the word. Neither is it simply "play" or "game" in the common sense of these words. The thirteenth-century manuscript title, *Danielis ludus* creates a problem, to be sure, but it is a philological and semantic problem that can be resolved. The Latin word *ludus* is properly translated as "play" or "game" and was used in Roman times of athletic contests, sports, children's games, jokes, diversions, tricks, trifles, playgrounds, training grounds, schools, and assorted exhibitions, and it was sometimes used of satires, or, with the addition of the word *scaenicus,* of comedies like those of Terence or Plautus. As Chambers indicates, the term was not used of para-liturgical dramatizations until relatively late in the Middle Ages, and then only rarely: churchmen regularly called such productions an *ordo, processio, officium, similitudo, exemplum, miraculum,* or *repraesentatio.* The term *ludus,* he suggests, "naturally came into use when the intention of recreation began to substitute itself for devotion"; it is "a generic term for 'amusement,' and the special sense of 'dramatic play' is only a secondary one."[11] When one learns that in the Egerton Manuscript the *Danielis ludus* is preceded by propers for the Feast of the Circumcision (January 1) and that these include the "Prose of the Ass," this fact, added to Chambers' surmise that the play "was perhaps intended for performance on the day of the *asinaria festa,*" later called the Feast of Fools,[12] may prompt the hasty inference that the *Daniel* is more sportive than serious, a youthful production (*inuenit hunc iuuentus,* 1. 4 of the text) the schoolboy authors of which can be forgiven for inept plotting, for stilted dialogue, even for circus costumes in which they may have played lions. But the inference is wrong.

V. A. Kolve, faced with the like problem of identifying the

dramatic quality of the English cycle plays in his notable book, *The Play Called Corpus Christi,* offers three significant conclusions.13 First, "play" and "game," as used in texts of Corpus Christi pageants, miracles, and moralities, points unmistakably to contemporary recognition that these productions were to be anything but realistic, were intentionally costumed but undisguised facsimiles, and belonged to what Kolve calls "a theater of game" or manifest make-believe, quite distinct from the realistic "theaters of illusion" which, familiar in modern times, pretend to hold up a scenic mirror to some slice of life, some everyday actuality from daily existence, past or present. "Theater of game," precisely because it was recognized as "a pleying of miraclis in sygne and not in dede," a "mechanical" and "adulterate" simulation of nature as a twelfth-century Master said of *theatrica,*14 cannot be interpreted or judged by the conventions or intent of the later realism or naturalism.

Second, though creating a game-world apart from the everyday world, "playing" in the Middle Ages was serious, not comic, in ultimate effect. That is, when the incongruous and ludicrous appeared in it as they necessarily did—for how, without humor could Noah build his ark in ten minutes, yet call it a hundred years? or how, without braying human speech, could Balaam's ass tell him he was a greater ass than his mount?—they were exploited for all the fun that was in them but not without loss of the seriousness of their context. A fresh sense of the serio-comic is required; the Middle English polarity between "ernest" and "game" or "play," even as Chaucer uses them,15 must be rethought: "ernest" comprehends the somber actuality of everyday moral action, of which the real consequences can be final, whereas "game" and "play" comprehend anything imitative, simulated, and sometimes funny or ridiculous, but not always. Whatever the humor in the matter or manner, however laughable it may immediately be, it acquires an edge of wryness upon reflection and a dimension of seriousness when all has been said and done.16

Third, Kolve cites Johan Huizinga's *Homo Ludens*17 in support of the view of play as being, in its visible forms, divorced from reality, yet intrinsically associated with serious values and portent, and profoundly related to the development of culture. The point that play, especially mythic play, is both the product of a culture and productive of that culture, bears upon one's

conception of the significance of the *Daniel* as serious play
and should be extended beyond Kolve's use of Huizinga.

Roger Caillois, in his *Les Jeux et les hommes,*[18] while taking
Homo Ludens as the stimulus for his own work, finds "most of
its premises debatable," yet at the same time praises Huizinga's
attempt "to clarify the role of play present in or animating the
essential aspects of all culture."[19] Caillois himself has been
praised for providing "probably the only work on the subject
that attempts a typology of play on the basis of which the characteristic games of a culture can be classified and its basic patterns understood."[20] Classifying the games of all cultures into
(1) games of competition (*agon*), (2) those of chance (*alea*),
(3) those of simulation (mimicry or *simulacre*), and (4) those
of vertigo (*ilinx*), and combinations of these, he further dis-
tributes games of all classes between two poles, the pole of *paidia*
(uncontrolled fantasy, frolicsomeness, or impulsive exuberance)
and the pole of *ludus* (a controlling set of rules that demand
skill, patience, and ingenuity).[21] Within Caillois' system, the
Daniel falls into category (3), simulation or mimicry, oriented
toward *ludus,* or controlling rules, not frolicsomeness.

Though Caillois provides a chapter "Towards a Sociology
Derived from Games,"[22] for illumination of the mythic dimension of the story of Daniel in the *Danielis ludus* one turns rather
to cultural anthropology and to the work of Bronislaw Malinowski, whose "Myth in Primitive Psychology" antedated Huizinga's
book by a dozen years.[23] Malinowski defines religious myths in
particular as a "special class of stories, regarded as sacred, embodied in ritual, morals, and social organization" and forming
"an integral part of culture," the "dogma backbone" of civiliza-
tion. He continues:

> These stories live not by idle interest, not as fictitious or even
> as true narratives, but are . . . a statement of a primeval, greater
> and more relevant reality, by which the present life, fates, and
> activities of mankind are determined, the knowledge of which
> supplies man with the motive for ritual and moral actions, as
> well as with indications as to how to perform them.[24]

While Malinowski's views of myth developed from his study of
primitive cultures, he is struck by the coincidence between the
mentality of such cultures and of modern ones, including our
own.[25] Francis Fergusson, when discussing Valéry as *symboliste*
in *The Human Image in Dramatic Literature,*[26] is impelled to

cite portions of the passage quoted above and to observe that "Malinowski's description [of religious myth] applies by analogy to the narrative in the Christian Creed, the basis of European social and cultural order, and of much European art, for a thousand years. And it applies also to what romantic poets seek vaguely, and more or less in vain, in the myths which they religiously invoke."

As sacred story within the Christian culture of the Middle Ages, the Book of Daniel enjoyed the special sanction of divine revelation and had a further special quality: prophetic. While not among the Prophets in the Hebrew Bible, Daniel stands among the four Major Prophets in Christian tradition—Isaiah, Jeremiah, Ezechiel, and Daniel. Jewish and Christian commentators go further. They find it unique in quality among the books of the Old Testament and comparable only to Revelation, or the Apocalypse, in the New. They find it prophetic in several respects: it confers upon Daniel the special wisdom of interpreting immediate dreams and symbols and delivering the warnings they portend; of prophesying the future birth and death of Christ, the destruction of Jerusalem and the Temple with its sacrifices (Dan. 9.21-27); and of foretelling the second coming of Christ (Dan. 7.13-14), the reign of Antichrist, the Last Judgment, and the end of the world (Dan., chaps. 8, 10-12). They find him, from his youth on, the epitome of fidelity to God amidst the snares of the world and, despite the threat of death, a "man of desires" who, pleading for the sins of his people and begging God's mercy, earns God's disclosure to him, through the angel Gabriel, that the advent of Christ is at hand (Dan. 9.1-23).

Christian exaltation of Daniel as prophet rests largely on Matt. 24.15-16, in which Jesus confirms his discourse on the destruction of Jerusalem and the world and on the Last Judgment by citing "Daniel the prophet." This passage from Matthew and Jerome's commentary on it conclude the Church Year on the last Sunday after Pentecost[27] before the season of Advent initiates the liturgical year anew. Advent begins between November 27 and December 3, on the Sunday nearest the Feast of St. Andrew (November 30) in any given year. In the first two weeks of November, just before Advent begins, readings from the prophet Ezechiel and patristic commentaries on them fill the first two nocturns of daily matins, succeeded in the third week of November by selections from Daniel and commentaries on them, including the passage adapted by the *Danielis ludus*.

During the four weeks of Advent, when the *Te Deum* and *Gloria* are silenced in the mood of penitential expectation of the long-awaited coming of the Messiah, messianic prophecies from Isaiah predominate at matins and throughout the liturgy of each day, but on Ember Saturday of the third week of Advent the Book of Daniel reappears. On this day, close upon Christmas itself, the fifth lesson and hymn for the Mass are taken from Daniel 3.47-56: the story of Daniel's three companions in exile, Sidrach, Misach, and Abdenago, who, when they heard "the sound of the trumpet, the flute, and the harp, of the sackbut, and the psaltery, of the symphony, and of all kind of music" (Dan. 3.5-15),28 refused to prostrate and adore the golden god of Nebuchadnezzar and were thrown into the fiery furnace for their fidelity to the God of their fathers. Their song, sung while they stood unharmed in the searing flames, terminated their confession of the past iniquities of their people and themselves and praised God for the multitude of his saving mercies and wondrous works (Dan. 3.24-90).

At this Mass, by general custom, youths were ordained to the four minor clerical orders (door-keeper, lector, exorcist, and acolyte), and older youths to the three major orders (subdeacon, deacon, and priest). The lesson and song from Daniel accompanied ordination of the subdeacons, who, in far fewer cathedrals than is widely supposed, were allowed to "rule" the office, by no means everywhere rowdy, of January 1. Their ordination terminated with the following *collecta* or prayer: "O God, who subdued the flames of fire for the three young men, mercifully grant that the flames of vice may not consume us, servants of your house" (*Deus, qui tribus pueris mitigasti flammas ignium, concede propitius ut nos famulos tuos non exurat flamma vitiorum*).

It would appear, then, that *ludus,* "play" or "game," as used of the *Danielis ludus,* is best understood in the sense which a cultural historian like Huizinga, a sociological analyst like Caillois, a cultural anthropologist like Malinowski, and an interpreter of medieval drama like Kolve have found it appropriate to give to these terms. Use made of the Book of Daniel in the liturgy preceding Christmas supports the view that "The Play of Daniel" found its place in a collective or communal activity symbolically designed to express and to re-affirm, through serious and reverently wrought imitation, the concepts and values which interpreted and judged life for its participants the source, the ideal norms, and the goal of their life in common.

If one is to define the "play" in this drama as "prophetic," however, one further effort toward precision may help. Prophesy, Thomas Aquinas proposes, is essentially a species of cognition or knowledge, residing only secondarily in the utterances in which such knowledge is communicated to others for their edification, and thirdly in the operation of miracles by which the truth of prophetic utterance is confirmed. Prophesy he divides into three types: comminatory or conditional prophesy warns that a particular consequence will follow if its cause, generally some form of behavior, is not amended; predestinal prophesy concerns good and desirable events which God will effect; and prescient prophesy concerns further acts, good or evil, perpetrated by the free will of men.29

Prophesy in all these senses is displayed in the "Play of Daniel." Daniel's recognition of the meaning of the handwriting on the wall, which the seers of Babylon could not read; his utterance of divine truth though it discountenanced Balthasar; the heaven-sent restraint of the lions which confounded his enemies and confirmed Darius's faith: these display prophesy as cognition, utterance, and miraculous act. King Balthasar's neglect of sufficient amendment, the foretold victory of Darius over him, and finally the prophesy of the coming of Christ and the termination of Temple and kingdom in Israel relate respectively to comminatory, prescient, and predestinal prophesy.

Reaching backward to the messianic and apocalyptic expectations of Advent and forward to the Christmas realization of Christ's birth, the "Play of Daniel" stands poised between the two liturgical seasons. It is difficult to avoid wondering whether the play was not designed for presentation after matins before the midnight Mass of Christmas, when the *Te Deum* was restored with joy for the first time since Advent had begun. It is even more difficult to comprehend Craig's statement (p. 66) that "The subject of the play is not prophetic; it is biographical and heroic," or Young's view (II, 305) that Daniel's climactic messianic prophesy "has no very close relationship with the dramatic action which precedes."30

The "Play of Daniel," a serious and mythic play reflecting the values of a Judaeo-Christian culture, is also a prophetic play.

II

Plot and meaning in the *Ludus Danielis* can now be considered together in a single concluding section, for meaning is a function of plot, whatever form plot takes.

Plot is generally regarded as a narrative sequence which provides a principle of unity in plays that imitate a human action. It rests upon a series of decisions made or of benefits received or sufferings undergone, each event except the first and last being linked to the one that precedes or follows in a cause-effect relationship. Such a plot of linear action is seen as providing the inductive grounds for a moral universal—that is, through its instances of individual human conduct, it invites the inference that certain kinds of act will universally give rise to misery and are blameworthy, whereas certain others will confer benefit and merit praise and imitation. Elder Olson, in his *Tragedy and the Theory of Drama*,[31] argues that all forms of plot, even those not based upon linear or consequential action, are "a system of actions of a determinate moral quality." We "feel different emotions at the sight of the fortunes or misfortunes of characters in a play," he concludes, "upon grounds of moral approval or disapproval."

Up to a point, it may be argued that the *Daniel* contains a plot of linear cause-and-effect action. Things begin to happen when Balthasar, in the midst of a drunken revel with his court, orders that sacred vessels taken as booty from the Temple in Jerusalem be brought in to serve his debauch. If Balthasar had not thus profaned the vessels of God, the hand of God would not have written his doom on the wall. If God had not so written, Balthasar would not have discovered the incompetence of the worldlywise sages whom he asked to interpret the handwriting on the wall. If such sagacity had not proven wanting, the perceptive Queen would not have directed Balthasar's attention to Daniel, "learned in the oracles of prophesy," and Daniel's God-fearing wisdom would not have been displayed, honored, and envied. If Daniel's comminatory prophesy had not failed to produce any response from Balthasar beyond his conferring upon Daniel an honor Daniel did not want, the unregenerate Balthasar would not have been slain by Darius, and Darius's counselors would not have arrived to envy Daniel's superiority to them and to seek his execution. If, out of envy, the counselors had not devised a legal trick by which Daniel was doomed to the lions' pit against Darius's will, there would have been no climactic occasion for the miracle of Daniel's salvation, no consequent confirmation of Darius's faith in Daniel's God, no spread of that faith throughout his kingdom, and no condemnation of the calculating counselors to the very death they had intended for Daniel.

Stated in such fashion, the story of this *ludus* is "a system of actions of determinate moral quality." One sees the overthrow of foolish pride, the folly of presumption, the temerity of profaning what is sacred, the vanity of human counsel, the just deserts of envy, the ultimate value of fidelity which confers truth in knowledge, speech, and action: and one is led to make the proper inference. What must be conceded, however, is that these moments of moral value and their concatenation in cause-and-effect relationship, while they are latent in the play, do not emerge from the representation programmed by the text. They do not emerge as they would if the play had been written along the lines of realistic theater. By intention, the text provides no naturalistically projected slice of life, no play of manners, no dark comedy, no history play, but rather a set of living tableaux, of symbolic moving-pictures, almost like a set of cartoons laid out in a strip, in which each cartoon or picture delivers its message or meaning by selecting and positioning a limited number of exaggerated features and protracting them momentarily before the stylized movement continues. The narrative matter of the story is subordinated to the representational manner of the play, and what results may be called a symbolist plot.

This play, this solemn and symbolic reaffirmation of religious concepts and life-values, is made not for presentation on a stage but for celebration in a church, indeed in the former Carolingian apse of St. Peter's cathedral, Beauvais.[32] The setting assumed by the text, therefore, is the site of the highly symbolic or sacramental Church ritual of a medieval cathedral, the symbolic architecture of which has been well explained in Otto von Simson's *The Gothic Cathedral*.[33] The windows of the apse, facing east as does the chevet of every medieval cathedral, catch the first light of the dawning sun, image of the Sun of

Justice, the *Lux ex oriente,* celebrated in the "O" antiphons of Advent.34 The episcopal chair or throne, the *cathedra* itself, was placed square at the head of the apse, the very head of the Church, above and behind the altar: it was properly the throne of the bishop or head pastor, his rod and his staff being a shepherd's crook, his crown a mitre, and he himself a substitute or vicar for Christ, the Good Shepherd, the divine King of Kings. In front of this seat of authority, teaching, and judgment was the altar-table of Christ, the divine Wisdom became man, the Good Pastor eternally giving his life for his sheep and selflessly validating his right to be known as Love and Light and Life and King.

Into this symbolic setting came the visual spectacle of "The Play of Daniel." The first four-line verse of the play is no part of an imitated action. It is a salute to Christ, as gladiators saluted Caesar in the amphitheater before the games began, for this is, in effect, the amphitheater of spiritual combat and these are Christ's players, and the episcopal throne is his. The salute is almost a shout before the players presume to enter and move from the western portal and up the nave:

> Ad honorem tui, Christe,
> Danielis ludus iste!
> In Belvaco est inventus
> Et invenit hunc iuventus!

> To your honor, O Christ,
> This Play of Daniel!
> In Beauvais was it made,
> Invention of our youth!

The next verses (lines 5-34 in Young's text) are the entrance song proper, and they form no part of the imitated action either. It is true that the actors have their courtiers' costumes on, and they are ushering in the crowned and robed Balthasar, who brings up the end of the procession in the place where one would expect the bishop, vicar of Christ. But the chorus at this point affects no impersonation. The "throng of older youths and crowd of boys" (*turba virilis et puerilis contio*) sing in their own proper identity. They sing that they applaud the Almighty (*cunctipotenti plaudit*) because they hear how Daniel, ever faithful, underwent many things and bore them without flinching (*audit Danielem multa fidelem subiisse atque tulisse firmiter*). They summarize selected moments of the Daniel story, those which will carry the basic themes and meaning of the play once it begins, including the interpolated episode of Habacuc, who brought Daniel food from heaven. Called a *conductus* or conducting song, it is like the *introitus* or entry-song with which the servers and ministers conduct the priest or bishop to his seat at the beginning of a solemn eucharist or liturgy while they sing the instructional themes of the Mass to come. The words and narrative voice-structure of this *conductus,* the verbal facts at this point, are non-dramatic; the visual facts, however, are something else. The costumes of the choristers and King reverse all that is expected of an ecclesiastical procession advancing down the center of a nave, and Balthasar, silent, may have begun to pomp his part.

The fully dramatic action begins precisely when, not a priest, not the bishop, but the personified Balthasar is enthroned in the *cathedra,* where he does not belong. The moment he is seated, another acclamation or salute, this time imitative and fraught with irony and heard repeatedly throughout the play, is sounded: choristers, now courtiers, cry *Rex, in aeternum vive!*—"Oh King, live into eternity!" But Balthasar is not capable of sustaining his kingship, and he is not capable of living eternally in his regal posturing, as one is fast to see. The violent distortion of reality that his enthronement and this acclamation perpetrate becomes clear against the realities of the place and the incongruity of the appearances delivered in it.

The action next to be mimed is described in the play's source, Dan. 5.1-2:

> Balthasar the king made a great feast for a thousand of his nobles: and every one drank according to his age. And being now drunk he commanded that they should bring the vessels of gold and silver which Nabuchodonosor his father had brought away out of the temple that was in Jerusalem, that the king and his nobles, and his wives and his concubines, might drink in them.

In heavy decasyllabic verses, one musical note scored for each syllable, Balthasar sings for the sacred vessels, which will be brought from sacristy to altar not for the eucharistic banquet but for feigned profanation. And then follows the silly song of the satraps, high-pitched and jingly, its effeminate stupidities skipping metrically along as the satraps, mincing with the meter one supposes, move to fetch the vessels. They style themselves as a merry bunch, plucking stringed instruments, clapping hands, singing a thousand tunes (*jocunda turba, citharizent, plaudant manus, mille sonent modis*). They have nothing but praise for the King who has clothed them in purple and scarlet (*suos perornavit purpura et ostro*); they misapply to him the attributes of God—*Iste potens, iste fortis, iste gloriosus,* with the *iste* suggesting that gesticulating arms point toward Balthasar each time the term is uttered. The terms of divine praise receive bathetic reduction when suddenly followed by *Iste probus, curialis, decens et formosus!*—power, strength, and glory are succeeded by "upstanding he is, courtly, beautifully dressed, and handsome"—praise fit for a fop.

It is in this manner that the representation proceeds. To follow it through in detail would be inappropriate here; the principles are clear. Not all the lines of the text are dramatic play: like the initial *conductus,* some are non-imitative statements made narratively or interpretively about the matter of the play, or are direct addresses to Christ or the congregation and made by the players *in propria persona.* The choral *conductus* escorting the Queen to the "stage" is one such. The *conductus* escorting Daniel first before Balthasar, later before Darius, are others. In the latter, addressing itself literally to the occasion and its intended impact, the choristers sing:

> Rejoicing together, let us celebrate the solemnities
> of Christmas!
> Now has the Wisdom of God redeemed us from death.
> Born he is as man in flesh, he who created all,
> The new-born One foretold of old by utterance prophetic.
> . . . On this natal day, O Daniel, with joy
> This throng to you its praises gives! (11. 270-78)

Even such literal and direct addresses, however, though verbally non-dramatic, carry further meaning by the spectacle they afford in costume, gesture, the setting of church, sanctuary, *cathedra,* altar, and the season of the liturgical year.

When the lines are impersonational speeches in dramatic scenes, the scenes themselves, in their multi-media dress, are symbols of thought both within and beyond the immediate meaning of word and action. They provide the literal-historical grounds for moral inferences regarding presumption, envy, fidelity, and the like, as has been said; but because the spectacle predominates, one is led, for example, to reflect upon Balthasar's debauch as an emblem of man's profanation of himself, a vessel of God, when he gives way to pride and sensuality. One is led to see the Queen as the wise woman, who appears in many guises and roles in Scripture, and would bring man back from his senses to his reason and to listen, if he but will, to prophetic admonition. One is led to remember that envy is a beast seeking power in its pride, a roaring lion seeking whom it may devour, but conquered by the prophet's resurrection from the pit and, in the end, devouring the envious by their own device.

Not to be ignored is the pictorial symbolism of the tableaux at beginning and end of the play: Balthasar who sits pomping in the seat of God, from which he falls, at the outset; and in the closing tableau, Darius a figure of Power, Daniel a figure of Wisdom at the right hand of Power, and the Angel above them with the Nativity message of Love. Power, Wisdom, Love—analogical terms for Father, Son, and Spirit[35]—pose in picture familiar enough in medieval iconography, there in the cathedral apse, as the *Te Deum* is about to begin.

Symbol energizes the manner and meaning which govern what is therefore the "symbolist" plot of the Beauvais *Daniel*.

It is hardly necessary that the modern producer of the play acquire a cathedral, ordain his actor-singers to clerical status, or play the play at a midnight liturgy ushering in Christmas. These may have been the place, the players, and the hour that gave meaning to the original medieval production. But all that is required of the modern producer, director, and players is that they understand what they are simulating and, entering into the spirit and spirituality of the play with fidelity, imitate the medieval imitators well. Any further fidelity which the play were to prompt in anyone at all would be the work of grace, not of man.

NOTES

1 The *Danielis ludus* is uniquely found in British Library MS. Egerton 2615, in which it is preceded by all the propers, first vespers through second, for the Feast of the Lord's Circumcision (January 1, octave of Christmas) and followed by a note specifying the correct Gospel for Easter ("In Pascha Domini euangelium ad Missam secundum Marchum"). The note "Iste liber est beati Petri beluacensis" appears on the MS. The MS. itself has been dated between 1227 and 1234, but the play about 1140. Dates and description reported by E. K. Chambers, *The Mediaeval Stage* (New York: Oxford Univ. Press, 1903), I, 284, n. 2, and 285, n. 1, citing the *Catalogue of Additions to MSS. in the British Museum, 1882-87,* p. 336, but correcting the latter by independent inspection of the MS. Karl Young, *The Drama of the Medieval Church* (Oxford: Clarendon Press, 1933), II, 290, nn. 4-5, and II, 486, *s.v.* "Page 290, note 5" adds no new information. Note the *lapsus calami* in Young's statement, "The MS was written during the first half of the twelfth [read "thirteenth"] century, and probably within the period 1227-34."

2 In *Revue de la musique religieuse populaire et classique,* IV (1846); see pp. 65-78 and, after p. 96, the separately numbered pp. 1-32.

3 (Paris, 1861), pp. 49-82. Separate edition, Rennes, 1860.

4 Text of *Daniel* and brief critical discussion, II, 290-306. Quoted statement appears in Young's Preface, II, vii. Criticism of Young's espousal of the hypothesis that drama "evolved" out of the liturgy of the medieval church in O. B. Hardison, Jr., *Christian Rite and Christian Drama in the Middle Ages* (Baltimore: Johns Hopkins Press, 1965), pp. 1ff.

5 See Margaret B. Freeman, "The Play of Daniel at The Cloisters," an essay that appears on p. 12 of Album DL 79402, Decca Records, Gold Label Series.

6 Cited by Freeman in essay noted above, n. 5.

7 *The Play of Daniel: A Thirteenth-Century Musical Drama Edited for Modern Performance by Noah Greenberg* (New York: Oxford Univ. Press, 1959).

8 See above, n. 5.

9 Thus, the play was produced by the *Collegium Musicum* of the Southern Baptist Theological Seminary, Jay Wilkey, Director, at The Second Annual Medieval Conference sponsored jointly by the Seminary and The University of Louisville, February 15-16, 1974, in Louisville, Ky. An abbreviated form of this essay was presented at the conference just before the *Daniel* was played.

10 *English Religious Drama of the Middle Ages* (1955; rpt. Oxford: Clarendon Press, 1964), pp. 4-5. Craig must not be misunderstood. He does not deny that medieval para-liturgical drama is drama, but rightly insists that it is drama and dramatic in its own terms. He errs, however, in charging Aristotle's *Poetics* with supplying "a body of criteria" on "the techniques of the drama," like those of Horace or Renaissance interpreters of Aristotle and Horace. Aristotle's philosophic discrimination among material means, dramatic manner, object or action imitated, plot as imitative form, and effect achieved, supplies not a set of normative criteria but a set of tools for philosophic analysis applicable to disparate forms of drama. See Elder Olson, "The Poetic Method of Aristotle: Its Power and Limitations," *English Institute Essays, 1952* (New York, 1952), pp. 70-94; reprinted in *Aristotle's "Poetics" and English Literature* (Chicago: Univ. of Chicago Press, 1965), pp. 175-91. Cf. Jerome Taylor and Alan H. Nelson, *Medieval English Drama: Essays Critical and Contextual* (Chicago: Univ. of Chicago Press, 1972), pp. 11-12, and p. 12, n. 19.

11 *Mediaeval Stage,* II, 104. Cf. V. A. Kolve, *The Play Called Corpus Christi* (Stanford: Stanford Univ. Press. 1966), p. 12.

12 Brief description of contents of MS. above, n. 1. MS. discussed in relation to the Feast of Fools in *Mediaeval Stage,* I, 284-86; Chambers' surmise that the Daniel

was played on this "feast," actually the Circumcision, January 1, ibid., II, 60. Young (II, 303) reports this surmise but rightly observes that "we have no certainty of it." See lines 270-73 and 388-92 in Young's text of the play for evidence that it was intended for Christmastide, that is, for one of the twelve days of Christmas from December 25 up to January 6, or Epiphany, but with no indication which day.

13 See especially pp. 8-32. *Danielis ludus* and term *ludus* mentioned on p. 12; medieval English plays describing their representations as "play" and "game" treated on pp. 13-17; the meaning of "play" and "game" in contrast with the meaning of "ernest" on pp. 17-19.

14 See Hugh of Saint-Victor, *Didascalicon,* II, 27, on "theatrica" as one of the seven "mechanical" arts, and I, 9, on the artificiality of all "mechanical" arts, imitations of nature. "Adulteration" of nature in the "mechanical" arts touched upon in II, 20. English translation of the work in Jerome Taylor, *The Didascalicon of Hugh of Saint Victor: A Medieval Guide to the Arts* (New York: Columbia Univ. Press, 1961), pp. 79, 55-56, and 74-75.

15 The narrator of the *Canterbury Tales,* respectful of moral seriousness, warns any who might be scandalized by the bawdry of the Miller's Tale to "Turne over the leef and chese another tale," but in any case to absolve him from "yvel entente" and put him "out of blame" for recording "harlotrie" in the tale of a "cherl" with the fidelity or truth required of art: "men shal nat maken ernest of game" (I, 3170-86). Implied is the thesis that the moral seriousness of life ("ernest") is one thing and the gaminess of "game" another, and that the latter causes no harm or scandal if the game-perspective of art is kept clearly in mind. The principle that corrective truth is effected even by obscene "play" and "game" is maintained by Harry Bailie, of all persons, when he concludes his estimate of the Monk's sexual prowess and "lust" with the admonition: "But be nat wrooth, my lord, though that I pleye./ Ful ofte in game a sooth I have herd seye!" (VII, 1963-64).

16 Of exceptional value in this connection are two chapters in Kolve, pp. 124-74. The thirteenth-century *Carmina Burana* contains a *"Play"* of the Passion" *(Ludus breviter de Passione);* see the treatment of wry humor in English dramatizations of Christ's suffering in Kolve, chap. 8, "The Passion and Resurrection in Play and Game," pp. 175-205.

17 Subtitled *A Study of the Play Element in Culture;* most recently published by Harper and Row, 1970. Quoted and discussed by Kolve, pp. 19-20.

18 Paris: Librairie Gallimard, 1958. Trans. by Meyer Barash as *Man, Play, and Games* (New York: Free Press, 1969). Quotations are from the Barash translation.

19 Ibid., p. 3.

20 Barash's evaluation, ibid., Translator's Introduction, p. vii.

21 Caillois faults Huizinga for regarding the "spirit of play" as the exclusive source of culture without sufficient regard for cultural institutions, including liturgies, as being themselves the sources of particular games or plays. Similarly, he finds reductivism in Huizinga's failure to attend to formal differences between play and reality. See esp. pp. 64: ". . . to explain games as derived from laws, customs, and liturgies, or in reverse to explain jurisprudence, liturgy, and the rules for strategy, syllogisms, or esthetics as a derivation of play, are complementary, equally fruitful operations provided they are not regarded as mutually exclusive. The structures of play and reality are often identical, but the respective activities that they subsume are not reducible to each other in time or place. . . . It is obvious that trying to define a culture by deriving it from games alone would be a rash and probably fallacious undertaking."

22 Chap. V, pp. 93-109 in the French edition.

23 In Bronislaw Malinowski, *Magic, Science, and Religion and Other Essays* (Garden City, New York: Doubleday, 1955), p 93-148.

24 Ibid., p. 108.

25 Ibid., p. 145.

26 Garden City, New York: 1957. Malinowski quoted and discussed, pp. 166-67.

27 Matth. 24.15-35 is the Gospel pericope in the Mass for the twenty-fourth Sunday after Pentecost; the pericope and Jerome's commentary appear in the third nocturn of that Sunday's matins in the Roman breviary.

28 The instruments here mentioned, or their medieval and Renaissance equivalents, were introduced by Greenberg into the *Pro Musica Daniel.*

29 *ST* II-II, 171.1, "Utrum prophetia pertineat ad cognitionem," and 174.1, "Utrum convenienter dividatur prophetia in prophetiam praedestinationis, praescientiae, et comminationis" (Rome: Marietti, 1948), pp. 792 and 809-10.

30 Craig, p. 66, similarly says: "It is perhaps not significant that at the end of the play, which is a life of Daniel, the prophet should have uttered the prophecy associated with him in his role as a prophet." Craig also remarks that the Beauvais *Daniel* "was not gathered up with the plays of the Pentateuch into the group of Old Testament plays of the older tradition found in the vernacular cycles." This is true, but the use of Daniel in Chester XXII, "de prophetis prophetantibus de Die novissime," etc., and in Towneley VII, the *Processus Prophetarum*, should be remembered for the persistence of Daniel's prophetic function in vernacular drama.

31 Detroit: Wayne State Univ. Press, 1966, pp. 37-38.

32 The Carolingian apse has been replaced by a late Gothic chevet, known in the countryside as "le lanterne de Beauvais," its towering windows being visible at night for miles around when services are being held within. For architectural details and photographs see Jean Desmarest, *Dictionnaire des églises de France, Belgique, Luxembourg, Suisse* (Paris: Robert Laffont, 1966-), tome IV: France (Ouest et Ile-de-France), section IVD, pp. 12-15: Cathédrale S. Pierre.

33 New York, 1956.

34 The "O" antiphons precede the Magnificat at Vespers from Dec. 17 through Dec. 23. That for Dec. 21 is: "O Dawn of the East, Splendor of the Light Eternal and Sun of Justice, come and enlighten those who sit in darkness and the shadow of death" *(O Oriens, Splendor Lucis Aeternae et Sol Justitiae, veni et illumina sedentes in tenebris et umbra mortis).* That for Dec. 17 begins *O Sapientia,* that for Dec. 22 begins *O Rex gentium,* and that for Dec. 23, *O Emmanuel, Rex et Legifer noster.* The reason for the name "O" antiphons is obvious.

35 See Roy J. Deferrari, trans., *Hugh of Saint Victor On the Sacraments of the Christian Faith* (Cambridge, Mass.: Mediaeval Academy of America, 1951), Bk. I, Part Three, Chap. XXVI: "Why power is attributed to the Father, wisdom to the Son, goodness or benignity to the Holy Ghost," pp. 53ff.

On the Uses of Iconographic Study: The Example of the *Sponsus* From St. Martial of Limoges

Clifford Davidson

The great advantage of the study of iconography in relation to early drama is that it ruptures the usual self-contained structures that literary criticism has consistently attempted to impose on individual plays and on quasi-dramatic forms. Careful and systematic study of the iconography quickly determines that the dramatic structures being observed are not at all self-contained, and that instead they involve a careful focusing of our attention that paradoxically denies the unity of the dramatic action. Indeed, the concept of unity, which is still being applied to such plays by some American critics, is surely the most inaccurate conception that could possibly be utilized as a device to describe the "action" of early drama, which was never intended to be viewed as a self-sufficient art form. The religious plays in particular have their roots in cultic experience, and are deeply influenced by the manner in which the cult looks at religious scenes in the visual arts as well as in imagination. When we turn specifically to the medieval religious music drama as well as to the quasi-dramatic rituals to which it was so closely related, the *purpose* of the spectacle is quite easily distinguished; in the words of Dom Odo Casel appropriately quoted by C. Clifford Flanigan in a study of the *Quem queritis* trope, "God has made it possible for us, even in this life, to enter into the divine present."[1] Iconography therefore leads quite naturally to phenomenology and the recognition that perceived experience and observable structures need to be the focus of our attention as we attempt to place the individual medieval play, in this case the *Sponsus* from St. Martial of Limoges, into its proper critical context.

Iconographic study itself, of course, needs to be disciplined and careful if it is to provide the kind of convincing information that will illuminate plays and create the groundwork for similarly meticulous work on the phenomenology of dramatic forms. This is particularly important at this time because of the methodological crisis that the study of drama as *literature* is now experiencing. Some recent studies of texts have unfortunately tended to violate their integrity, to cut them off from attention to their original purpose, and to exploit them for political and other purposes.[2] Therefore our work of scholarship and criticism needs to take the greatest care with regard to its approach to the many diverse aspects of even an individual scene, and indeed these aspects include much that can never be known through texts at all. Thus contemporary illustrations in the visual arts will be seen to contain crucial information that is very difficult to reduce to verbal equivalents. There are very specific ways in which the designs, for example, of manuscript illuminations from St. Martial of Limoges which are contemporary with the *Sponsus* would throw light on the way the scenes of the play were visualized.[3]

At the same time, of course, texts must not be neglected, for they are capable of providing the necessary linkage of ideas that will piece together for us the meaning of a particular fragment of spectacle. Our methodology will avoid merely the tracing of iconographic ideas apart from their hermeneutic context, for it is true that iconographic configurations may have different meanings in different periods and different settings. We also need carefully to avoid neat schema of causes and effects, of assumptions ultimately based on rather simplistic notions about literary and dramatic sources. Hence it would seem appropriate to examine first the work of an influential critic, Émile Mâle, who has previously considered the *Sponsus* not in terms of its structure *as play* or in terms of its *purpose*, but in terms of finding missing links between examples in the arts and their presumed sources.[4] Indeed, Mâle's attempts to trace the widespread iconography of the Wise and Foolish Virgins in an entire region in France to the play at St. Martial would seem to place the *Sponsus* somewhat in the untenable position of the Piltdown man. Only when we rescue the play from such a critical view can we turn to the genuinely important matter of the drama studied in terms of the perceived experience implied by the spectacle presented before early audiences.

Mâle's comments on the *Sponsus* appear in a well-known and influential chapter of his study of twelfth-century art in France written more than half a century ago and designed to set forth some principles of "enrichment" by which the visual arts were allegedly augmented iconographically by the liturgical drama.5 Only recently translated into English, Mâle's study has had immense impact in spite of its controversial claims concerning the relationship between early drama and art,6 but it is now clear that his understanding of the liturgical drama was imprecise and that much which he attributed to the influence of the drama may as easily be explained through other causes. In the case of the *Sponsus* from St. Martial, therefore, his assumption that the play must antedate examples from the visual arts and that it "must have been performed throughout southwestern France, for in the twelfth century, the artists of this region frequently represented the Wise and Foolish Virgins"7 can only be demonstrated to rest on very inadequate logic. Extant art in France does not represent the entire corpus of eleventh-century art, and there is no means of proving that the local popularity of the theme did not antedate its presentation in the play. Futhermore, we have no proof that the visual artists were in fact influenced by the play, especially since the latter would involve a very ephemeral art form and not one that was broadly popular in its appeal to lay audiences. Finally, the extensive production of the *Sponsus* or other plays on the same theme throughout the region remains entirely hypothetical. There is even doubt concerning the likelihood that the extant *Sponsus* would have been in fact performed at St. Martial of Limoges since the Provençal dialect points to a location some fifty miles away,8 and dramatic records as yet uncovered do not record any productions at all in the area. Indeed, the only presentation of a play on the Wise and Foolish Virgins which would appear to have been recorded was a German *Ludus de decem virginibus* noted at Eisenach on 4 May 1321.9

Nevertheless, in spite of his unfortunate biases, Mâle was entirely right in the important matter of bracketing together drama and art as a means of illuminating both. His principal error was perhaps his obsession with cause and effect, with the evolution of realistic and dramatic details in the visual arts. Such an attempt at scientific study of the origins of iconography must be looked upon with as much suspicion as the now discredited evolutionary approach to early drama—an approach thoroughly annihilated by O. B. Hardison, Jr., in his *Christian Rite and Christian Drama in the Middle Ages* (1965). But liturgical drama is *iconic,* as Mary Marshall has argued;[10] hence its close association with the visual arts can hardly be doubted.

Like paintings and sculpture, therefore, the medieval music-drama had as its intent the presentation of scenes before the eyes of the beholders. Its use of text and music provided a liturgical or quasi-liturgical context, and also extended verbally the visual tableaux. The design of this drama was to break down the temporal distance separating the audience from the event being depicted and to make the audience participate directly in the sacred mysteries. *Sponsus,* closely related to liturgical drama but also associated with vernacular poetic and musical traditions,[11] is, however, different from the usual liturgical drama. First, it is written in a mixture of Latin and Provençal rather than the Latin that would have been strictly used in plays designed only for presentation in a monastery. Additionally, it takes as its subject one of Christ's parables—a parable reflecting eschatological realities—and utilizes it as a model illustrating visual/verbal experience. Iconographically, therefore, the play utilizes an allegorical structure in which the literal level appears to exist only as a vehicle for a didactic lesson. Nevertheless it is a didactic lesson that directly reflects the order of Christian life as lived by members of the audience/congregation in the late eleventh century when the play along with its music was copied into the manuscript, Bibliothèque Nationale MS. lat. 1139, fols 53-55ᵛ.

It is certain that the dramatization of the parable of the Wise and Foolish Virgins in the *Sponsus* was regarded as a gloss on the account of the Last Judgment which appears in the same chapter of St. Matthew's Gospel. Since the account of the Last Day in this Gospel account emphasized the role of specific works of mercy as a test in the judgment of souls, St. Augustine in his comment on the parable had identified the lamps of the virgins as indicative of good works warmed by love. Of the Wise Virgins, he writes as follows: "No coldness of love then crept over them, in them love did not wax cold; but preserves its glow even unto the end. And because it glows even unto the end, therefore are the gates of the Bridegroom opened to them; therefore are they told to enter in, as that excellent servant, 'Enter thou into the joy of thy Lord'."12 Much emphasis in the play from St. Martial of Limoges therefore is also rightly placed on watchfulness which derives from a motive quite different than mere duty. Thus the motive of the watchfulness enjoined by Gabriel must be devotion to the incarnation and suffering of Christ, whose vigil they are keeping. In a rather real sense, therefore, the virgins need to remain in an aroused state, desiring access to the banquet with the Bridegroom above all things. They are possessed by the divine *eros,* which echoes the holy passion of the *Song of Songs.* The *Song of Songs,* of course, was in spite of its originally controversial nature crucial as the basis of the New Testament emphasis on the desire of the soul for union with God, whose role is that of the Bridegroom.13

From the time of the Church Fathers, *eros* had been associated with chastity when the former was focused on a holy contemplation of the divine and on desire for union with God.14 Through *eros,* the soul is directed upward even as the flames of the lamps of the Wise Virgins reach up, in contrast to the seductive forces that lead the Foolish Virgins to drop their lamps downward—a motif always present in medieval examples in the visual arts15—in indication of their love being inclined away from the highest Good.16 The use of the parable of the Wise and Foolish Virgins, therefore, seems indicative also of the warmer and more emotional religion which would characterize the later Middle Ages.

Yet the focus of the play and of most representations in the visual arts from the Middle Ages is upon the *failure* of fully half the virgins to maintain their watchfulness against the reality of a late-arriving Bridegroom. Modern commentators on the *Sponsus* have sometimes assumed that all the virgins, both wise and foolish, go to sleep.17 This would be consistent with the biblical account, of course. However, as Karl Young points out, the most likely interpretation of the play would insist that "the wise virgins obey precisely the injunction *vigilate,* and that only the *fatuae* sleep at all."18 Axton furthermore finds a "relevant link" between the *Sponsus* and the Easter vigil, especially in a Northern Spanish rite; he quotes the following words of the deacon to the congregation:

It is fitting that the congregation of the faithful should wait up

for the advent of the radiant bridegroom with lights ready
kindled; lest at the wedding feast he refuse the company of
those he finds sleeping beneath the shadow of old sins . . . let
us therefore be like the wise virgins and not like those foolish
ones.19

While the parable of the Wise and Foolish Virgins has never
been tied very closely to Easter,20 the echo in the play of the
Easter vigil nevertheless is significant here, for thus we may
assume the likelihood that the Wise Virgins strictly kept watch
in order to guard their lamps and to make proper preparation
for the arrival no matter how late of the Bridegroom. A statement by a Patristic writer is appropriate here for the manner
in which it connects the parable with the Easter vigil:

The lamps that you will light are the sacrament *(mysterion)* of
the resplendent procession of heaven with which we will go before the Bridegroom, souls virginal and respendent, with burning lamps of faith. Let us not allow ourselves by negligence to
become drowsy, so as to let Him for Whom we are waiting go
by us when He comes unexpectedly, and let us not remain
without sustenance and without oil, for fear of being excluded
from the bridal chamber. There is no room there for the man
who is proud and negligent, nor for him who is clad in a
stained garment and not in a wedding-robe.21

But the Foolish Virgins, who represent careless souls of both
men and women, are "proud and negligent" in their behavior,
for they not only fall asleep as a group but they also allow their
oil to be wasted. Their subsequent despair is therefore rooted in
their failure with regard to the watchfulness that has been
demanded of them.

The deadly sleep of the Foolish Virgins, though it is of
crucial importance to the play, is not to my knowledge represented in contemporary or near-contemporary art. Yet such
graphic use of posture in drama must have been seen as the
key to the meaning of the drama. In contrast to the Wise Virgins
whose vigil does not deflect their desire from the Bridegroom,
the Foolish Virgins literally decline from the upright posture
which their chastity ought to demand. Through their posture,
they repeat the Fall, which has been noted through mention of
its feminine participant—Eve—in the second stanza of the
choral introduction to the play. As Erwin W. Strauss notes in
his perceptive paper on "The Upright Posture,"

> In sleep, we do not withdraw our interest from the world so
> much as we surrender ourselves completely to it. We abandon
> ourselves to the world, relinquishing our individuality.22

Succumbing in this way is precisely what characterizes the
Foolish Virgins. In late twelfth-century illuminations illustrating the text of Joinville's *Credo* (Bibliothèque Nationale MS.
4509, fols. 12-12ᵛ), the Foolish Virgins are appropriately vain,
wearing elaborate headdresses which sharply contrast with the
plain hair of the Wise Virgins, who, like pilgrims bound for a
sacred place, carry palms as well as their lamps. The Foolish
Virgins, however, are not pilgrims, but souls who have lost their
proper sense of orientation. They know they are lost, as their
body postures, hand gestures, and random glances show.23

Now it should be clear why the *Sponsus* opens with a series
of choral stanzas announcing not only the coming of the Bridegroom but also explaining his nature as the *second Adam* who
has rectified what the first Adam abrogated in the Garden of
Eden. The traditional idea of Christ as the second Adam—and
of the Blessed Virgin as the second Eve—indeed is here of
utmost significance, for as through the indulgence of the one
person mankind found itself doomed, so through the submission
of the other to the cross the same mankind became the potential
recipient of salvation. Thus through Christ's sacrifice—a sacrifice reflected first among the sacraments in baptism—men have
their sins *washed away,* while the power of the great Enemy of
man no longer necessarily has ultimate power over them. Before
the first advent of Christ, all were therefore in bondage to
demons; following this event, freedom was given to do good
works and to receive the ultimate reward of participation in the
heavenly banquet. Purity of heart is not something innate, but
rather it is something that must be achieved through the gift
of grace. The virgins, both wise and foolish, thus embody an
initial break with the fallen condition: they are the baptized
ones who have put aside their past as if it had not existed. For
this reason, the Wise Virgins especially have a curious connection with the figure of Mary Magdalene, who likewise in the
Middle Ages was regarded as an exemplar of the Church motivated by devotion of the strongest kind—i.e., by *eros.*

It may not be inappropriate to call attention to the iconography of the Hortulanus scene as it appears in liturgical drama
and in medieval art. In the Type III *Visitatio Sepulchri*24 as in

examples in the visual arts, the disappearance of the body at the tomb and the announcement of the angel to the holy women is eventually followed by this scene in which the risen Christ is mistaken for a gardener by Mary Magdalene. In the art and surely also in the play, he in fact does appear in the garments of a gardener holding a spade along with the vexillum which announces his Resurrection. Iconographically, he is indeed the second Adam announcing his victory over death in the most graphic way possible. The first Adam was normally shown after the Fall in two ways: first, as the father of the race being expelled from the Garden of Eden, and, second, as the penitent whose spiritual condition was reflected in his appearance as a gardener with a mattock or spade. Thus Adam is portrayed with the tools of the gardener's trade in the famous panel in the glass of Canterbury Cathedral.25 Appearing in the *Visitatio* from the Fleury Playbook "in similitudinem Hortulani,"26 Christ thus proclaims his identification with the race descended from Adam. He is the second Adam who has now completed his soteriological work for the benefit of the descendants of the first Adam.

Upon recognition of Christ's identity in the *Hortulanus* scene, therefore, Mary Magdalene cries, "Raboni!" and throws herself prostrate at his feet. The appearance of Christ in the Fleury example of the Type III *Visitatio* is first of all an answer to her prayer immediately preceding: "My heart is burning with desire to see my Lord; I seek and I cannot discover where they have laid him, alleluia."27 The echo of the seeking and separation of the *Song of Songs* should be obvious here,28 and surely the absent lover theme could hardly be introduced more appropriately. The Magdalen, who in the Middle Ages was a composite of three presumably separate biblical women,29 is here the exemplar of eroticism reformed, rechanneled, and purified; the prostitute has turned away from the world and become the perfect model of contemplative Christianity with its longing for the *Christ-Eros* identified in the Patristic era by Origen.30 Her posture upon seeing the risen Christ—i.e., the object of her highest desire—seems to oppose precisely the posture of the upright Wise Virgins; yet the meaning is the same, for only by humbling herself at Christ's feet and by submitting herself to her ardent love for him can her former submission to earthly pleasures be perfectly overcome. Hence according to her legend, the final period of Mary Magdalene's life will be spent in Provence in retirement from the world; this will be a time when she is enabled even to break her dependence upon earthly sustenance, for she will be fed heavenly food each day by angels.31 In the account of this event in the Digby play, the food which she receives is identical in appearance with the Eucharistic host.32 On this side of death, therefore, she is able to participate miraculously in the heavenly banquet—a feast to which the Wise Virgins have also been invited. In the Fleury *Visitatio,* the conclusion of the drama also flows directly from the Hortulanus scene with the angels' announcement of the completion of the Resurrection and the Harrowing, with the consequence that for all the just the entrance to heaven has been opened.

It is an entrance into bliss that will be denied to the Foolish Virgins, however, for like the medieval representations of Synagoga (as opposed to Ecclesia), they ultimately fail in the living of their spiritual lives. Their deep sleep is a blindness that may be compared to the blindfold worn by later representations of Synagoga in the visual arts, and their empty lamps are comparable to the broken pilgrim's staff which she commonly carries.33 This comparison is corroborated by medieval explanations of the meaning of the number *five* for the Foolish Virgins: *five* is the number of the senses, and therefore these characters in the play as in the visual arts must represent the five senses.34 They represent the means by which human beings find access to the world and through which the world in return casts its spell upon them. For the world as seen through the senses is not reality but shadow—a distraction which is potentially fatal for those who would take such shadow for true substance.35 To achieve true knowledge, therefore, the mind is required to turn itself to the *five spiritual senses,* which are represented by the five Wise Virgins.36 Thus only can the bondage to things earthly be broken and the vision of love established in order that the spiritual life might be sustained in charitable works without lapse.

The banquet to which the Wise Virgins are invited therefore, while it preserves the normal iconography of Communion, points beyond the earthly signs to the heavenly substance which is signified. The symbolism is actually similar to that of the Marriage Supper of the Lamb, illustrating *Revelation* 19.7-9, which in a thirteenth-century miniature in the Leningrad Breviary provides a vision of the Church as Ecclesia or Sponsa with the Lamb who, standing with his hind feet on the table, kisses her.37 Upon the table are containers and small circles with crosses in their center—presumably hosts. Several crowned figures with hands joined in adoration look on from each side, and angel musicians play fidels, a psaltery, and a harp while another waves a censer above. *Christ-Eros* thus appears as the Lamb, the Agnus Dei of early Christian iconography, in what clearly signifies the rite of the Mass at the same time that it reveals the heavenly mysteries foreshadowed by the earthly liturgy. The lower part of the page in this Breviary, which originally was prepared for use in Rheims, shows the Last Judgment, with the archangel Michael before the Judge separating the good souls from the evil ones with his sword. Beyond the Judgment, the souls of the righteous will encounter the mystical marriage of the Sponsus and Sponsa, who suggest the consummation of the desires of the congregation of believers. The separation between the Bridegroom and his beloved—a separation lamented in the Song of Songs—may be partly healed in the Eucharist, but the ritual nevertheless points forward to a permanent union beyond the end of time.

In a twelfth-century miniature from Bury St. Edmunds in a manuscript now in the Pierpont Morgan Library,38 the Wise Virgins, still holding their lighted lamps, appear crowned at the table with the Sponsus and the Sponsa, who also wear crowns. A server is holding toward him a chalice, which the Bridegroom is signing with his blessing. On the table also is a circle with a cross in the center—presumably a large host. The Virgins have been admitted to the Wedding Feast which is also the heavenly banquet, the eschatological marriage celebration. On the central portal representing the Last Judgment on the West facade at St. Denis, a Wise Virgin stands at the gate to heaven while a Foolish Virgin is at the entrance to hell.39 The Bury St. Edmunds miniature thus shows the scene of joy following admission to the gate of bliss—a gate which can be reached only by passing through the less comfortable scene of the Last Judgment.

For the Foolish Virgins, the Last Judgment is indeed a scene of extreme discomfort. Already in the fourth-century representations in the catacombs at Rome, the visual effect was to emphasize the tragedy of those without oil for their lamps. In the damaged lunette of the catacomb of St. Cyriaca, the Bridegroom turns away from the Foolish Virgins on his left and toward the ones with the lighted torches on his right. Indeed, his hand is raised in a greeting to the virgins who will be accepted into his feast.40 The effect is even stronger in the sixth-century Rossano Gospels, which show the Foolish Virgins behind a set of closed doors at the left; inside Christ holds up his hand in denial of entrance and presumably speaks the words recorded at *Matthew* 25.12. In the *Sponsus* from St. Martial of Limoges, he additionally consigns them to the everlasting bonfire in words adapted from the description of the Last Judgment at verses 41 and 46 of the same chapter of St. Matthew's Gospel. Arriving in the play at a moment of intense despair for the Foolish Virgins—they have failed to arrange a purchase of fuel for their lamps from the oil merchants, and know that they are fated not to enter into the feast—the Bridegroom without pity releases them to hell and its demons. Indeed, the demons here make their first appearance in extant Western religious drama when they appear in the play in order to receive the Foolish Virgins and to throw them into the mouth of hell. In the production of the drama, these demons cannot be seen as merely grotesque or comic; they are an extension of human fears that are quite normal, and must be played with grim seriousness so as not to provoke laughter. The entire effect of the play depends upon a right conception of the iconography of the end of the Foolish Virgins; the great power of the drama must not be dissipated finally.

Sponsus, of course, antedates the portal at St. Denis, which Mâle insisted set the pattern for so many imitations, especially in France.41 Without claiming that primacy with regard to time indicates anything about source and influence, the sculpture nevertheless does illustrate rather exactly the connection between the parable and the meaning of the Judgment theme which these ten young ladies help to illuminate. Suger's placement of the Judgment scene over the doorway at the center of the West façade—a position not unrelated to the placing of wall paintings of the Doom over the chancel arch in English parish churches such as the Church of St. Thomas of Canterbury in Salisbury42 —is indicative of the orientation of the individual worshipper in relation to the divine realities as these are made visible to him within the structure of the church. The direction of life's journey may be thought of as properly from West to East, for it is in the East that the second advent of Christ is believed to be scheduled.43 Hence prayers are spoken with the priest and people facing the East.44 Entry into the church from the world is therefore most clearly represented through the door at the center of the West façade, and surely it must be recognized that as one approaches the high altar he comes closer and closer to the table on which the mysteries are performed and the banquet is set forth for Christ's people. Anagogically, the approach to the celestial banquet must be through the doors of heaven which are metonymically related to the doors of the church, for without the earthly rites performed inside the building—especially the sacraments of baptism and the Eucharist—there can be no hope of salvation.

Naturally the iconographic arrangement in actual church buildings was often less rigidly "correct" than at St. Denis. For example, the influence of Suger's church and its ornaments meant that the Judgment Porch tympanum of c.1280 at Lincoln Cathedral treats the subject of the second advent and includes the Wise and Foolish Virgins. But the location of the sculpture at Lincoln is over the south doorway rather than on the façade at the West of the building.45 At each side of the tympanum also are mutilated figures of Ecclesia and Synagogue carved in stone46—indications of the binary division of the race at the Last Judgment when the final separation shall be effected between the saved and the damned, the followers of Abel and of Cain, of Peter and Judas. At Lincoln, Ecclesia had very likely been originally crowned as in the banquet scene in the Pierpont Morgan manuscript cited above, and she continues to hold a model of a church in her left hand. Synagogue, in addition to her other attribute noted above, also probably held the tables of the law, which she was dropping from her hand.47 At Chartres, the Wise and Foolish Virgins make one of their appearances on the portal on the North façade where they are illustrated in association with the Incarnation—i.e., scenes of the Nativity, Annunciation to the Shepherds, the Adoration of the Magi, and their dream warning them to return to their homes by another way.48 The inclusion of the Wise and Foolish Virgins here, however, underlines their character as elsewhere defined if we see them as imitators of the Virgin Mary. Adolf Katzenellenbogen calls attention to the importance of Pseudo-Jerome for the design of this portal: "Yet there are wise and foolish virgins. Therefore, my beloved, imitate the blessed and glorious Virgin

whom you love and whose feast you celebrate today on earth."49
Salvation or damnation in fact depends upon the degree to
which the virgins, who are clearly again linked to the Church or
Ecclesia, are willing to imitate the Blessed Virgin Mary, who
was honored as the second Eve or the gate through which divinity was able to come into the world to save it.

The iconography of the Wise and Foolish Virgins thus points
to a more important spatial orientation of considerable potential
significance for early productions of the *Sponsus*. This involves
the division of space into *right* and *left*. Phenomenologically
right and *left* have fairly established meanings which have been
corroborated through anthropological study.50 *Right* is associated with nourishment, growth, life, and hope; *left* points to the
opposite—death, decay, filth, and despair. So it is that the
account of the Last Judgment in *Matthew* 25 separates the good
(sheep, light in color) on the Judge's right, and the evil (goats,
dark in color) on his left (vv. 32-33). Examination of the
iconography of the Wise and Foolish Virgins in the visual arts
indeed shows great sensitivity to *right* and *left* symbolism in
most cases. As early as the Rossano Gospels (sixth century)
the Foolish Virgins, excluded from the wedding feast, are placed
at the viewer's left—a psychologically important factor which
suggests the existential orientation of the scene in relation to
the viewer's own spiritual condition. The placing of the Foolish
Virgins at the left is very frequently repeated and is obviously
a deliberate attempt to illustrate the point that they have placed
themselves incorrectly in relation to the divine realities. Hence
we again and again see the Foolish Virgins at the left side, as
in the Pierpont Morgan manuscript cited above, on a capital
from St. Etienne,51 and in illustrations designed to illustrate
the text of Joinville's *Credo*.52 A similar effect would appear
to be achieved in the fourteenth-century *Speculum humanae
salvationis* (Munich, Bayerische Staatsbibliothek, Clm. 146, fol.
43) which shows the Wise *above* and the Foolish *below*.53 The
Foolish Virgins are representative of all those souls who, while
having received the benefit of baptism, nevertheless in the end
decline from the Marian pattern of perfection and bcome
spiritually closed in—i.e., cut off from the sources of light and
life. Hence in the end they are placed among those who are
separated among the accursed *on the left hand* at the Last
Day.54 Thereafter, as the stage directions at the conclusion of

the *Sponsus* indicate, they will be forced to tumble *downward* into the pit of hell.

The Wise Virgins at the right, however, enter into the banquet associated with life, nourishment, and joy without ending. Curiously, in the Rossano Gospels the Wise Virgins instead of being seated at a table for the Wedding Feast are standing with their torches still flaming before an arbor which contains trees with fruit on their branches. Not only is this an appropriate symbol of nourishment, but it is also indicative of the manner in which the parable actually describes the return to the enclosed garden or *hortus conclusus* of Eden. For the Wise Virgins, the conclusion is a return to the beginning of time—to the joyful innocence which was abrogated by the first Eve but corrected through the function of the second Eve and her Son, whose Incarnation and Passion release mankind from time and its effects. In the Leningrad Breviary, the thirteenth-century miniature designed to illustrate Joinville's *Credo* even more clearly distinguishes between the fate of the Wise and the Foolish Virgins.[55] As noted above, the Foolish Virgins are at the left, excluded by locked doors for which they have no key (i.e., they do not possess the "key of David" or Christ, who only could give them admission) and hence placed *in darkness*. Their lamps having been extinguished through their carelessness and lack of watchfulness, they are now experiencing the terror of the outer darkness. The Bridegroom's rejection of them is expressed through his hand gesture and through his words, inscribed as follows: "Amen dico uobis: nescio vos." On the other hand, the Wise Virgins, still holding their lamps, move in the light and presumably airy garden at the right among vines and leaves illustrative of the fruitfulness of the place.

It may not be irrelevant at this point to ask why more than half of the lines of the *Sponsus* and an even larger proportion of its action are devoted to a scene in which the Foolish Virgins attempt to refill their lamps either from stock borrowed from the Wise Virgins or from oil merchants. The tension herein dramatized surely gives the play much of its intensity, building up to the point of terror when the Foolish Virgins are rejected by the Bridegroom. The point is not merely didactic—a learning experience on the part of the audience. The spiritual *dryness* or *acedia*—the term is one that was commonly associated with despair in the Middle Ages[56]—experienced by the virgins lacking oil to burn in their lamps is something that cannot be alleviated by borrowing or buying; while it can be shared by individuals, grace cannot be purchased with money or passed mechanically from one person to another. For the Foolish Virgins, their seduction by the world and the flesh ultimately cuts them off from the very sources of spiritual fruitfulness. They therefore lose their desire to be watchful, and succumb to a blindness which will separate them from all hope. Hence they become lost souls, unhappy and despairing. Martin Schongauer's engravings of the Wise and Foolish Virgins[57] should illustrate the point. The Wise Virgins, all wearing laurel wreaths on their heads and moving decorously toward the right, are distinctly contrasted with the Foolish ones, who take various postures and, while tending to look toward the left, show evidence of no consistency of direction. In each case, the laurel wreath is at the feet of the despairing virgin.

As imitators of perfect womanhood of the kind represented by the Blessed Virgin, the Foolish Virgins are progressively defective following their submission to the shadows of worldly success in preference to the substance of heavenly hope. But as reflections of the actual religious experiences encountered by members of the audience, the Foolish Virgins express more exactly the imperfection of human devotion to the ultimate realities. The ideal is the Wise Virgin who is perfectly centered on *Christ-Eros* and who overcomes the weaknesses of Eve. Normal souls, however, are not able to accomplish all that is demanded of them by the ideals of cultic behavior. It is this recognition of imperfection, which the members of the audience identify in themselves, that makes the focus upon watchfulness (and especially watchfulness as presented in terms of failure) so existentially viable in the *Sponsus*.

When we regard the *Sponsus* as like a game, the nature of the play's structure also becomes more clear to us. There may be danger in this analogy, but it is one that was constantly being made in the Middle Ages.[58] The actors, presumably clerics acting before audiences which included the laity, were divided into two groups arbitrarily—i.e., not on the basis of the actors' natural inclinations! (No principles of casting would have suggested assigning the roles of the most wicked to the worst persons, or of the least wicked to the most pious.) Once assigned, the text, the music, and the demands of the *tableaux* as visual statement would have determined the direction of the action as it was staged in the church building. As in any game, the spatial organization of this action must have been very important. Though it may seem very gauche to mention such a less-than-polite modern game as baseball, the spatial organization of that game may serve as a test of what happens in *Sponsus,* which also of course involves a *contest* that requires watchfulness of a sort. The difference is that in the *Sponsus* the element of chance is eliminated, of course. The game is all set in advance when, during rehearsals, the demands of the text, music, and *tableaux* are imposed on the individual *players* who have been chosen to represent the various characters. The demands of the game thus presented will determine that the scenes have their own integrity—and that the scenes reflect the structure of life more accurately than normally didactic sermon or treatise or even static art object. The *ludus* becomes a window through which the working of the divine order and the nature of human participation in it may be observed.

As Heidegger would have it, the play becomes a means by which reality is deconcealed so that Being is able to shine through.[59] The spectator too becomes a participant in this spectacle, for it is in fact the interaction between *play* and those looking on it as spectators that is the essence of the production. In the case of the *Sponsus,* it is the profundity of the drama that makes its plot and outward structure incapable of being reduced to mere critical description. Like the devotional image,[60] the iconic art of the *Sponsus* is not intended to provide realistic reflections of outward events; instead, the object is to open up a window to the divine, whose workings are more wondrous than we might ever have expected.

The hermeneutic lesson of the *Sponsus* from St. Martial of Limoges is therefore quite clear. Through the play, the audience is enabled to come to terms with its own shortcomings as played out by the Foolish Virgins, but ultimately the drama has as its major purpose the task of bringing the audience "into the divine present." In a sense, through the presentation of the play as the movement of the Wise Virgins is into the banquet chamber, so the spectators too are able to look beyond the unreality of that which is seen by means of the earthly sense of sight. Indeed, the *Sponsus* is a carefully structured work of theatrical art which may be approached through its iconography, but ultimately it must be seen as a lesson in phenomenological hermeneutics. As a drama originally played by mortal actors, the play for the watchers looking on will illuminate not only Being but also that eternity which is beyond time.61

NOTES

1 Odo Casel, *The Mystery of Christian Worship*, trans. Charles Davis (Westminster, Md.: Newman Press, 1962), p. 142, as quoted by C. Clifford Flanigan, "The Liturgical Context of the *Quem Queritis* Trope," *Comparative Drama*, 8 (1974), 50 (rpt. under title *Studies in Medieval Drama in Honor of William L. Smoldon*, ed. Clifford Davidson [Kalamazoo, 1974]).

2 I am thinking particularly of studies that claim to be "Brechtian" or that play unwarranted semiotic games with texts. One of the most notorious focuses on Shakespeare (J. Kott's *Shakespeare Our Contemporary*), but earlier drama also is very vulnerable to such exasperating "modernization." The cavalier treatment of texts *among critics who also focus on texts to the exclusion of other evidence* is particularly annoying.

3 See D. Gaborit-Chopin, *La Décoration des manuscrits à Saint-Martial de Limoges et en Limousin du IXe au XIIe siècle* (Paris and Geneva: Droz, 1969).

4 Émile Mâle, *Religious Art in France*, trans. Marthiel Matthews and ed. Harry Bober, Bollingen ser., 90, 1 (Princeton: Princeton Univ. Press, 1978), pp. 151-53; this book was originally published in 1922 under the title *L'Art religieux du XIIe siècle en France*.

5 *Religious Art in France*, pp. 126-53.

6 See, for example, Otto Pächt, *The Rise of Pictorial Narrative in Twelfth-Century England* (Oxford: Clarendon Press, 1962), but Mâle's arrguments have also been adopted by those who see similar and more advanced influence of the vernacular drama—e.g., W. L. Hildburgh, "English Alabaster Carvings as Records of the Medieval Religious Drama," *Archaeologia*, 93 (1949), 51-101, and M. D. Anderson, *Drama and Imagery in English Medieval Churches* (Cambridge: Cambridge Univ. Press, 1963). Careful criticism of Mâle's argument has been widespread; for convenience, see my *Drama and Art* (Kalamazoo: Medieval Institute Publications, 1977), pp. 1-14, and A. M. Nagler, *The Medieval Religious Stage* (New Haven: Yale Univ. Press, 1976), pp. 89-105. Very influential has been F. P. Pickering, *Literature and Art in the Middle Ages* (Coral Gables: Univ. of Miami Press, 1970), *passim*.

7 Mâle, *Religious Art in France*, p. 154.

8 See Karl Young, *The Drama of the Medieval Church* (Oxford: Clarendon Press, 1933), II, 361n.

9 Grace Frank, *The Medieval French Drama* (Oxford: Clarendon Press, 1954), p. 62; Richard Axton, *European Drama of the Early Middle Ages* (London: Hutchinson, 1974), p. 104. The date of the *Sponsus* from St. Martial has been established as 1096-99; see Jacques Chailley, *L'Ecole musicale de St-Martial de Limoges* (Paris, 1960), p. 114. Claims for a Spanish play on the Wise and Foolish Virgins during the next century in Catalonia are, unfortunately, based entirely on the existence of murals from Sant Quirze de Pedret which are now in the Museum of Barcelona; see Richard B. Donovan, *The Liturgical Drama in Medieval Spain* (Toronto: Pontifical Institute of Mediaeval Studies, 1958), p. 161.

10 Mary H. Marshall, "Aesthetic Values of the Liturgical Drama," *English Institute Essays, 1950,* rpt. in *Medieval English Drama,* ed. Jerome Taylor and Alan H. Nelson (Chicago: Univ. of Chicago Press, 1972), pp. 28-43.

11 See the comments of Gustave Reese, *Music in the Middle Ages* (New York: Norton, 1940), p. 197. The music of the *Sponsus* was first edited by E. de Coussemaker, *Drames liturgiques du moyen age* (1860), pp. 1-6 (text, pp. 7-10), and more recently by Raffaello Monterosso in *Sponsus: Dramma delle Vergini Prudenti e delle Vergini Stolte* (Milan and Naples: Riccardo Ricciardi, 1965), pp. 123ff (text edited by D'Arco Silvio Avalle, pp. 71-81; facsimile appended). Performing editions of the play have been provided by William L. Smoldon, *Sponsus* (London: Oxford Univ. Press, n.d.), and Fletcher Collins, Jr., *Medieval Church Music-Dramas: A Repertory of Complete Plays* (Charlottesville: Univ. Press of Virginia, 1976), pp. 261-79. The text is also edited by Young, II, 362-64.

12 St. Augustine, Sermon 93 (Caput V); trans. in *A Select Library of the Nicene and Post-Nicene Fathers,* ed. Philip Schaff (rpt. Grand Rapids, Mich.: Eerdmans, 1956), p. 403; see Migne, *PL,* 38, 576, for Latin text. The influence of the writings of St. Augustine on the Eisenach *Ludus de decem virginibus* was noted in the contemporary account of the play; see Axton, p. 104.

13 See especially *John* 3.29 and *Revelation* 19.7-9.

14 See Anders Nygren, *Agape and Eros,* trans. Philip S. Watson (1953; rpt. New York: Harper and Row, 1969), p. 415. Bishop Nygren is specifically making reference to the thought of Methodius of Olympus and his treatment of this topic in his *Symposium.*

15 Medieval illustrations normally include lamps which are of medieval design, quite different from the torches of the early Christian artists. But the torches remain in the mural from Sant Quirze de Pedret; see Josep Pijoan, *Les Pintures murals romàniques de Catalunga,* Monumenta Cataloniae, 4 (Barcelona, 1948), Pls. 77-78

16 See Nygren, p. 485.

17 Frank, p. 59; cf. Young, II, 366.

18 Ibid., II, 365. See, however, Walter Lehmann, *Die Parabel von den klugen und törichten Jungfrauen* (Berlin, 1916), p. 23.

19 Quoted (in translation) by Axton, p. 101, from St. Isidore's Missal, *PL,* 85, 441.

20 The parable is not one of the readings for the Easter vigil, however, nor indeed has the *Sponsus* been identified as belonging to a particular feast day. For association with matins on All Saints' Day in the Sarum Breviary, see Young, II, 496. Rosemary Woolf (*The English Mystery Plays* [Berkeley and Los Angeles: Univ. of California Press, 1972], p. 45), is among those who see the play as appropriate for the first Sunday in Advent. The text is, however, closely associated with the reading for the feast of a virgin martyr.

21 Gregory of Nazianzen, *In Pent.,* 3; Migne, *PG,* 36, 429, as quoted (in translation) by Jean Daniélou, *The Bible and the Liturgy* (Notre Dame, Ind.: Univ. of Notre Dame Press, 1956). pp. 218-19.

22 Erwin W. Straus, "The Upright Posture," in *Essays in Phenomenology,* ed. Maurice Natanson (The Hague: Martin Nijhoff, 1969), p. 168.

23 Lionel J. Friedman, *Text and Iconography for Joinville's Credo* (Cambridge, Mass.: Mediaeval Academy, 1958), pp. 48-49.

24 See Young, I, 369-410.

25 Madeline Harrison Caviness, *The Early Stained Glass of Canterbury Cathedral* (Princeton: Princeton Univ. Press, 1977), fig. 6.

26 Young, I, 395; cf. ibid., I, 409.

[27] Young, I, 395, as translated by David Bevington in *Medieval Drama* (Boston: Houghton Mifflin, 1975), p. 42.

[28] Cf. Axton, p. 69; and see also Rainer Warning, "On the Alterity of Medieval Religious Drama," *New Literary History*, 10 (1979), 270-78.

[29] See Anselm Hufstader, "Lafèvre d'Étaples and the Magdalen," *Studies in the Renaissance*, 16 (1969), 31-35; Marjorie M. Malvern, *Venus in Sackcloth: The Magdalen's Origins and Metamorphoses* (Carbondale and Edwardsville: Southern Illinois Univ. Press, 1975), pp. 16-29.

[30] See ibid., p. 61; Origen, *The Song of Songs, Commentary, and Homilies*, trans. R. P. Lawson, Ancient Christian Writers, 26 (Westminister, Md.: Newman Press, 1957), pp. 21-24, 79.

[31] See Jacobus de Voragine, *The Golden Legend*, trans. William Caxton (London, 1493), fol. clxxxvii, and the commentary in my article "The Digby *Mary Magdalene* and the Magdalene Cult of the Middle Ages," *Annuale Mediaevale*, 13 (1972), 84-86.

[32] The "Gostly fode" which the Magdalen receives is indeed even identified as *"an oble"* or host (1. 2027 and s.d. at 1. 2019). See the edition of the play in Bevington, *Medieval Drama*, p. 749.

[33] See the late thirteenth-century example in the Chapter House Vestibule glass at York Minster (Clifford Davidson and David E. O'Connor, *York Art* [Kalamazoo: Medieval Institute Publications, 1978], p. 182). But cf. Émile Mâle, *The Gothic Image*, trans. Dora Nussy (1913; rpt. New York: Harper and Row, 1958), pp. 18-90.

[34] *Glossa ordinaria, PL*, 114, 164. See also the discussion in Mâle, *Gothic Image*, p. 198.

[35] Understanding the world as encountered through the senses in terms of "shadow" will be recognized as part of the legacy of Neoplatonism. See St. Augustine, *Soliloquia*, I. xiv, 24, as quoted in translation by Erich Przywara, *An Augustine Synthesis* (New York: Harper and Row, 1958), p. 1.

[36] *Glossa ordinaria, PL*, 114, 164; cf. Mâle, *Gothic Image*, p. 198.

[37] *Joinville's Credo*, Pl. XXII; cf. Walter Lowrie, *Art in the Early Church*, revised ed. (1947; rpt. New York: Norton, 1969), pp. 51-53.

[38] Fletcher Collins, Jr., *The Production of Medieval Church Music-Drama* (Charlottsville: Univ. Press of Virginia, 1972), fig. 48.

[39] This portal has been heavily restored; see Mâle, *Religious Art*, p. 181, fig. 152.

[40] Joseph Wilpert, *Die Malereien der Katakomben Roms* (Freiburg im Breisgau: Herder, 1903), II, Pl. 241.

[41] See Mâle, *Relilgious Art*, pp. 181ff.

[42] M. D. Anderson, *The Imagery of British Churches* (London: John Murray, 1955), p. 68, Pl. 1; for more detailed discussion of the Salisbury wall painting, see Albert Hollaender, "The Doom Painting of St. Thomas of Canterbury, Salisbury," *Wiltshire Archaeology and Natural History Magazine*, 50 (1942), 351-70.

[43] See Durandus, *The Symbolism of Churches and Church Ornaments*, trans. John Mason Neale and Benjamin Webb (London, 1893), pp. 177-79, and, on the idea of life as a journey, Gerhart B. Ladner, "Homo Viator: Mediaeval Ideas on Alienation and Order," *Speculum*, 42 (1967), 233-59.

[44] Louis Bouyer, *Rite and Man* (Notre Dame, Ind.: Univ. of Notre Dame Press, 1963), pp. 175-76.

[45] Arthur Gardner, *English Medieval Sculpture*, revised ed. (1951; rpt. New York: Hacker, 1973), pp. 145-47, figs. 274-75.

46 Ibid., figs. 277-78.

47 Ibid., p. 147.

48 Adolf Katzenellenbogen, *The Sculptural Programs of Chartres Cathedral* (1959; rpt. New York: 1964), p. 53.

49 *PL*, 30, 140, as quoted (in translation) by Katzenellenbogen, p. 67.

50 Robert Hertz, "The Pre-eminence of the Right Hand: A Study in Religious Polarity," in *Right and Left: Essays on Dual Symbolic Classification*, ed. Rodney Needham (Chicago: Univ. of Chicago Press, 1973), pp. 3-31.

51 Mâle, *Religious Art*, Pl. 133.

52 *Joinville's* Credo, Pls. III, XXI.

53 *Speculum Humanae Salvationis*, ed. J. Lutz and P. Perdrizet (Leipzig, 1907), Pl. 80. The association of *up* with *right* is quite universal, and is nicely recognized in the Swedish language which uses the word *högra*—i.e., *higher*—for the right hand.

54 See *Matthew* 25.41.

55 *Joinville's* Credo, Pl. XXI.

56 Susan Snyder, "The Left Hand of God: Despair in Medieval and Renaissance Tradition," *Studies in the Renaissance*, 12 (1965), 44-46; Morton W. Bloomfield, *The Seven Deadly Sins* (East Lansing: Michigan State Univ. Press, 1967), *passim*. We may compare the conclusion of Macbeth's career in Shakespeare's play; see my *Primrose Way: A Study of Shakespeare's* Macbeth (Conesville, Iowa: Westburg, 1970), pp. 73-76.

57 Charles I. Minott, *Martin Schongauer* (New York: Collectors Editions, 1971), Pls. 76-86.

58 See V. A. Kolve, *The Play Called Corpus Christi* (Stanford: Stanford Univ. Press, 1966), pp. 8-32, though this discussion introduces some controversial and doubtful ideas concerning the understanding of drama as *play*. Everyone interested in this matter will need to consult the seminal work by Hans-Georg Gadamer, *Truth and Method* (New York: Seabury, 1975), pp. 91-119.

59 Martin Heidegger, "The Origin of the Work of Art," in *Poetry, Language, Thought*, trans. Albert Hofstadter (New York: Harper and Row, 1971), pp. 17-78. See also Gadamer, pp. 91ff, for the argument that play may be "the clue to onto-logical explanation."

60 See especially Sixten Ringbom, "Devotional Images and Imaginative Devotions," *Gazette des Beaux-Arts*, 111 (1969), 159-70.

61 Research for this paper was supported by a Faculty Research Fellowship and a Grant from Western Michigan University.

The First Perugian Passion Play:
Aspects of Structure

Kathleen Falvey

One of the most valuable documents for studying the origins and development of vernacular drama in Italy and in all of western Europe is the fourteenth century *laudario* of the Confraternity of St. Andrew in Perugia. The *laude* in this collection were sung by members of the lay society when they gathered in their oratory to meditate on the passion of Christ, administer their works of charity, and practice self-flagellation in common. Similar groups of lay men and women, called *disciplinati* because of the adoption of the *disciplina,* or small scourge, into their devotional ritual, sprang up all over Europe after the movement initiated by Raniero Fasani had spread out from Perugia in the spring of 1260 in a chain-reaction of penitential processions that reached as far as Poland.[1] In marked contrast to the enthusiastic excesses of the movement's origin, the numerous confraternities founded in its wake were notable for their conservatism and orthodoxy, especially in their early years. And, for reasons yet to be fully explained, within the circle of these lay confraternities vernacular drama began to flourish in late medieval Italy. The *laudarî* that have survived well document this theatrical tradition.

A typical *laudario* might contain both lyric and dramatic *laude,* the former being, generally speaking, vernacular hymns of praise to God, the Virgin Mary, or a saint. A dramatic *lauda,* on the other hand, could be anything from a simple narrative in dialogue form sung during the private gatherings of the confraternity, to a complex musical drama performed publicly. Such dramatic works were composed in either of two characteristic verse stanzas: the *sestina semplice,* whose verses numbered eight or nine syllables and rimed *ababcc,* was employed for penitential

63

occurrences and sung *ad modum passionalem;* the *ballata maggiore* stanza of alternating septenaries and hendecasyllables riming *aBaBbCcX* was sung *ad modum paschalem* on Sundays and joyous feasts. The Latin phrases indicating passional or paschal mode are generally considered to refer to the melodies, perhaps of liturgical origin, to which the stanzas were sung. These melodies have not survived.

The St. Andrew *laudario* contains the fullest, most authentic selection of extant dramatic *laude*. In its present state it forms the second part of MS. 955 (già Giustizia 5) of the Biblioteca Augusta in Perugia, the first part consisting of the Confraternity's statutes dated 1374. The *laudario* proper was transcribed around 1350,[2] although some works give evidence of having been composed a good deal earlier.[3] Its 76 parchment leaves contain 117 lyric and dramatic *laude,* five of which are repeated for a total of 122 texts. The first 109 compositions take their subject matter from and are arranged according to the occurrences of the liturgical year, beginning with Christmas Day and ending with the Vigil of Christmas. Usually, lyric *laude* are shorter than dramatic ones; a lyric work can have as few as 24 verses, a dramatic one as many as 468. The former are generally assigned to lesser occurrences, the latter to Sundays and important feasts. Every day of Lent has its own dramatic *lauda* which follows closely the gospel of the day; many of these are brief, but as Holy Week approaches they lengthen and become fully "theatricalized." *Laude* 110-20, all lyric, are for the dead, and 121 seems to fit no category at all; it concerns the Perugians whose punishment seems imminent because of their sins. A fragment concludes the codex.

The two Good Friday plays in this collection represent the first fully developed vernacular passion plays in Italy. The first of these deserves special attention, being the longest work in the St. Andrew *laudario* and among the most complex. It not only exhibits many interesting traits characteristic of this early drama, but also blends together scriptural, devotional, lyrical, and, perhaps, liturgical influences with conscious artistic purpose. The anonymous author's careful combination of literary modes and his use of a skillful and complex transitional passage contribute to the play's structural and aesthetic unity.

The first passion play is entitled *Singnore scribe* from its opening words addressed to the "Honorable scribes," probably by a pharisee, but the text does not make this clear.4 It dramatizes events from Holy Thursday evening when Judas is shown making his bargain with the priests, to late Good Friday morning when Christ sets out for Calvary. Unlike the two notable passion plays possibly related to it within the Italian tradition, the earlier Latin Montecassino *Passion* and the later Roman work spectacularly presented in the Colosseum, this Perugian *lauda* portrays neither Christ's crucifixion nor his death. It is followed in the manuscript by *Quista vesta,* the second passion play in the St. Andrew collection, which opens with the scene of the three soldiers casting lots for Christ's garments at the foot of the cross where he hangs already dead.

Singnore scribe exhibits a most important characteristic of the earliest Perugian drama: while the action of the play achieves full dramatic development, it nevertheless maintains a close fidelity to the gospel narrative. Ignazio Baldelli observes that the play, "proprio per il suo procedere evangelico . . . da una parte, e dall'altra per la sua struttura tutta teatralizzata, si riconnette a quella parte del laudario perugino più assolutamente originale"5 ("precisely because its action proceeds as in the gospel accounts . . . on the one hand, and on the other because of its fully theatricalized structure, belongs to that part of the Perugian *laudario* most genuinely original"). Elsewhere in the same article Baldelli affirms that the play follows step by step the gospel of the day, that is, the Passion according to John assigned to the liturgy of Good Friday; and, that even the ordering of the dramatic episodes is scriptural.6 Now, while these things are so for the greater number of scenes, there are notable exceptions. For example, incidents from John's account are omitted, and some are borrowed from other evangelists, such as the payment of thirty coins to Judas (vv. 31-34) alluded to by the three synoptics (*Mt* 26.15; *Mc* 14.11; *Lc* 22.5), and Christ before Herod (vv. 253-64, from *Lc* 23.8-12).7 Because of dramatic need events are at times portrayed in violation of scriptural chronology and sequence. Verses 1-54, for example, represent a satisfying compression of events that take place in the gospels at different times shortly before the Passover, depicting as they do the plotting of the chief priests and pharisees to bring about Christ's death, and Judas' pact with them. In the play all this occurs on Thursday evening. In the play, furthermore, Peter denies Christ near the court of Pilate during the scourging, while all four evangelists record the denial as taking place in Caiaphas' courtyard when Christ is first brought before the Chief Priest (*Mt* 26.69; *Mc* 14.66; *Lc* 22.55; *Jn* 18.18). Since *Singnore scribe* does not include the agony of Christ on the cross, and since significant events of great dramatic potential happened during that time, such events are portrayed, but out of scriptural sequence. So, for example, Christ recommends his mother to John while they are still at Pilate's court (vv. 391-96).

Singnore scribe divides into two parts, the first consisting of rather straightforward enactment of the scriptural narrative; scenes are often brief, three of them composed of only twelve verses. Dramatic action, at times hurried and violent, moves urgently from *sedes* to *sedes:* the courts of Caiaphas, Annas, Pilate, and Herod, all possibly indicated by simple thrones; the Cenacle where the women are gathered; and Mt. Olivet. Pilate's court and movement toward and away from it account for 192 verses of the play, more than any other location. A pillar is located near this *sedes,* as is the fire near which Peter will warm himself. It usually takes a strophe or less of dialogue, at times no dialogue at all, for characters to get from one place to another, and such movement affords ample opportunity for silent mime. The frequent use of the verbs *menare* and *ducere* in both text and stage directions, especially in the first part, stresses the processional quality of the play which concludes as Christ sets out for Calvary. In the second part of the play, one relatively long scene stretches out for 120 verses, containing very little action, filled instead with the lyric lamentation of Christ himself, Mary, John, Magdalen, and the Sisters. Scriptural drama blends here with influences from the devotional *Meditations on the Life of Christ* attributed to St. Bonaventure,[8] and from the vernacular tradition of the lyric lament.

The first part of the play contains three Latin passages, two of which occur also in the Montecassino *Passion,* and suggest the possibility of a slight textual relationship. The first passage occurs only in the St. Andrew play, but is recalled here for purposes of comparison: as Christ begins his agonized prayer on Mt. Olivet, at verse 72, he repeats the "Tristis est anima mea usque ad mortem;/ Sustinete hic et vigilate mecum" recorded by both Matthew and Mark (26.38; 14.34). Later in the same scene, at verse 127, Christ asks the Jews who have come for his capture, first in the Perugian dialect: "Cuie andate voie cercando?" When they answer—"Quil Iesu ch'è messo en bando"—he declares: "Io so' esso." This exchange is then immediately repeated in the Latin of *Jn* 18.4-5, all the Jews having fallen to the ground at Christ's first questioning: "Christus eis: 'Quem queritis?' Et Iudei: 'Iesum Nazarenum.' Christus: 'Ego sum'." Concerning this *Quem queritis* passage, Baldelli observes the following: "La lauda *Segnore scribe* serve anche a precisare i rapporti della lauda drammatica dci flagellanti col teatro liturgico medievale, in quanto vi troviamo inserite al loro luogo evangelico . . . le battute: *Quem queritis? Ihesum Nazarenum. Ego sum.* Il tropo famoso, come è noto, è stato desunto da questo punto della Scrittura ed applicato alla *Visitatio sepulcri:* comunque, l'inserzione, sia pure al loro posto evangelico, di quelle battute potrebbe essere suggerita dal ricordo del *Quem queritis* del tropo del sepolcro."[9] Now, while it is very possible that the passage may have been suggested to the author of the vernacular *lauda* by its occurrence in an Easter sepulchre trope where it replaces the angel's unanswerable "Quid quaeritis viventem cum mortuis?" recorded by Luke alone (24.5), it is also possible that the suggestion came from or was influenced by an analogous use of the phrase "quem quaeritis" that appears in the Montecassino *Passion* in the Mt. Olivet capture scene where Christ says to the *loricati:* "Venientes cum lanternis/ armis fustibus lucernis/ dicite quem quaeritis" (vv. 43-45).[10]

The third Latin phrase in *Singnore scribe* opens the scene depicting Peter's denial, somewhere near Pilate's court during Christ's scourging. The stage direction reads: "Iudei ligantes Iesum ad colupnam; tunc dicit ancilla ad Petrum sedentem ad ignem" (stage direction after v. 276). The Jews bind Christ to the column, and attention is abruptly directed to a nearby scene which gives no evidence of its being in view of the scourging. Peter sits near a fire and a servant girl declares: "Tu cum Iesu Galileo/ Giù nell'orto stave ier sera" (vv. 277-78). The first phrase is Latin, the second vernacular, although both form part of the same sentence. The exact Latin phrase occurs in the Montecassino *Passion* at verse 103, where Peter's denial takes place in proper scriptural order near Caiaphas' court much before Christ's scourging. The servant girl cries out against Peter and says: "Tu cum Iesu galileo/ eras [inqua]m tu cum eo/ [vi]di sine dubio" (vv. 103-05). There are no close verbal echoes in the remainder of the two analogous scenes, however, and both authors may well have independently remembered the phrase from *Mt* 26.69: "Et tu cum Iesu Galilaeo eras." Then too, the more one studies the phrase in the context of the vernacular *Singnore scribe,* the more one feels moved to interpret what appears to be a Latin phrase from the Vulgate as a vernacular phrase in the fourteenth century Perugian dialect, containing two Latinisms, one common, *Iesu,* one not unknown, *cum,* and an uninflected proper adjective, *Galileo.* Especially since the two clearly Latin passages are extra-stanzaic, and the phrase in question is incorporated into the metrics and rime scheme of the vernacular stanza, does this seem so.

The question of the relationship between *Singnore scribe* and the Montecassino *Passion* is not, of course, limited to a consideration of such verbal parallels; much larger issues extend beyond the scope of this study. And, however interesting it is to ascertain the vernacular play's ties with such an illustrious predecessor, so much more important is it to discover and appreciate the skill whereby the anonymous Perugian author combined the influences of the varying traditions he drew upon into one artistic whole. Nowhere in the play can we better discover this than in the transitional sequence that begins with the stage direction recalled above. Pilate has just given the command: "Frustatel forte a la colonda/ Desfin ch'el sangue a terra 'bonda" (vv. 275-76). The stage direction follows: "Iudei ligantes Iesum ad colupnam; tunc dicit ancilla ad Petrum sedentem ad ignem." It can justly be supposed that, once having bound Christ to the column, the Jews then execute Pilate's command to scourge him. But no stage direction indicates this, no "scene" depicts the scourging, no dialogue reveals that it is being carried out. Valuable information concerning the staging of this scene is, however, furnished by the inventories of theatrical furnishings possessed by the Confraternity of St. Dominic,[11] considered one of the three "great" Perugian confraternities together with those of St. Francis and St. Augustine. The proximity of these three prestigious groups, their early foundation dates between 1317 and 1320,[12] and the homogeneity of the early Perugian dramatic tradition allow one justly to assume their direct influence on such smaller local confraternities as St. Andrew's, to whom they may well have lent props, costumes, and other furnishings, perhaps even playbooks. The earliest entries in the

St. Dominic inventories pertinent to the scourging scene are for the year 1339: items 78 and 79 mention "una colonda penta" and "doie fruste," respectively. More specific information is given for the year 1386 where item 58 reads: "Ancho una colonda, a la quale se lega Cristo al tempo de la sua passione, e doie fruste," and item 41: "Ancho una vesta encarnata de cuoio da Cristo e colle calze de cuoio encarnate." The garment and stockings of flesh-colored leather provided not only for the theatrical violence of the scourging scene, but also for the nudity of the main character. Whoever informs Mary of her son's capture stresses the fact that Pilate has had him stripped *nudo nudo* for the scourging (v. 311). Magdalen, too, twice laments the nudity of Christ in her speech "O maestro mio cortese" (vv. 379-90) soon after the scourging has taken place.

The Perugian tradition, then, clearly gave careful attention to the scourging scene when it staged the passion, and this was surely the case in the St. Andrew play under consideration. Yet, immediately after Pilate gives his command "Frustatel forte . . ." attention is drawn to a quick succession of three brief scenes that take place elsewhere in the acting area: Peter denies Christ and goes off weeping, exclaiming that he wants to "get on [his] horse and go away"; Judas returns the silver pieces to the priests and, despairing, goes off to hang himself. Then follows a scene reminiscent of that described in Chapter LXXV of the *Meditations on the Life of Christ*: "someone" goes to the place where Mary and the Sisters are gathered, probably the cenacle from which Christ and his disciples departed to go to Mt. Olivet in Scene ii, and tells her that her son *has been* captured and *is now being* scourged:

> Maria, ch'el tuo figluolo è preso,
> E Giuda gle fe' 'l trademento.
> Da capo a piei è tucto aliso,
> Tanto gl'òn dato tormento;
> E nudo nudo el fe' spoglare
> Pilato, e fa 'l forte frustare.

> (Mary, your son has been taken;/ Judas betrayed him./ From head to foot he is all torn,/so badly have they tormented him./ Pilate had him stripped all naked,/ and is having him cruelly scourged.)   (vv. 307-12)

Mary and the Sisters move toward Pilate's court, meeting John

along the way, lamenting together. Mary draws near the court
and sees her son:

> Chi me t'à tolto, o figluol mio,
> Ch'iersera a casa non tornaste?
> De te tradir co' s'ardio
> Quil con cuie pur ier cenaste?
> Giuda, el tuo apetito avaro
> A la dolente costa caro.

> (Who has taken you away from me, O my son,/ so that
> you did not come home last night?/ How did that man dare
> betray you,/ who only yesterday had supper with you?/
> Judas, your hunger for money/ costs the Sorrowful One
> dearly.)   (vv. 349-54)

Christ seems to hear his mother's voice before he is able to see
her, probably because of the unruly crowd clustered around him:

> Or, nonn è la mate mia,
> Quilla che me pare udire?
> Priegove per cortesia
> Che la lassiate a me venire.
> Più me duol del suo lamento
> Che de tucto el mio tormento.

> (Is it not my mother/ that I seem to hear now?/ I beg
> you, please,/ let her come to me./ Her lament grieves me/
> more than all my torment.)   (vv. 355-60)

Mary pushes her way through the crowd with painful difficulty,
for the "hungry people" throw themselves on her, knock her
about. When she is finally near enough to see him, Christ laments to her about the scourging and other torments he has
already endured:

> Co' tu me vede, madre, stare,
> Così gram parte de la nocte
> Nonn òn posato me frustare,
> Chi de puine, chi d'altre bocte,
> Chi me sputa per lo viso,
> Chi me fiere el capo arciso.

> (As you see me now, mother,/ so for a great part of the
> night/ they have not stopped scourging me;/ some punched
> me, some dealt me other blows./ Some spit in my face,/
> others strike my bleeding wounded head.)   (vv. 367-72)

A satisfying way to explain this use of the past tense in
reference to the scourging is to say that it has been taking place
in mime simultaneously with the three brief scenes just des-

cribed, and that it ceases shortly before Mary nears Pilate's court. The playwright again takes liberties with the gospel text: he has the scourging sequence indicate the transition from Thursday night to Friday morning, fusing the torment ordered by Pilate with the nocturnal mocking of Christ in the house of Caiaphas recorded by Luke (22.63-65). The rest of the play consists, for the most part, of the lamenting of Mary, Magdalen, the Sisters, and John over the sufferings they see Christ experiencing until he sets out for Calvary bearing a great cross, and the play ends.

What we have then, in the scourging sequence, is a carefully choreographed transition between the two parts of the play that are distinguishable mainly by differences in mode. This transition employs mime, repetition and variation, final exits and first entrances of main characters, movement away from and back to a central *sedes* where all the while Christ is being scourged. Now, where the first part of the play, before Christ is bound to the column, presents a relatively straightforward dramatization of the gospel narrative with events compressed or rearranged to meet artistic needs, the introduction of "someone telling Mary about the passion of her son" marks the beginning of the second division, with the narration in dialogue of events already enacted or presently taking place somewhere else. Against the background of the mimed scourging, such narration serves to introduce Mary, the Sisters, and John, and to add the dimension of their anguished compassion to these events. Verses 307-30 seem to fold back over the strict scriptural dramatization of the preceding scenes, reiterating them, but this time in the lyric mode. Then, at verse 335 as Mary leaves the cenacle and begins to approach Pilate's court, dramatic action moves forward again, now wholly suffused with elements of lyric lament. This second mode is maintained until the end of the play.

The stanza beginning with verse 307, where the lyric mode is introduced, bears close examination. Mary is told that her son has been arrested; Judas betrayed him. So badly have the soldiers tormented him that he is all torn from head to foot. Pilate has had him stripped naked and is having him cruelly scourged. Although a scene similar to this is described in *Meditations* LXXV, where Christ stands bound to a column, not for the scourging, but to be kept during the night, left to the insults and assaults of the guards, a more immediate source can

surely be found in the opening verses of Jacopone da Todi's
only fully dialogued *lauda,* his "Donna de Paradiso,"13 a composition often considered a very early example, if not the ancestor, of the dramatic Umbrian *lauda:*

> Donna de Paradiso,
> lo tuo figliolo è preso,
> Iesù Cristo beato.
> Accurre, donna, e vide
> che la gente l'allide:
> credo che lo s'occide,
> tanto l'ho flagellato.
>
> (Lady of Paradise,/ your son has been taken,/ blessed
> Jesus Christ./ Run, lady, and see/ that the people tear
> him;/ I think they will kill him,/ they have scourged him
> so.)   (vv. 1-7)

As *Singnore scribe* proceeds, other echoes of Jacopone and the
vernacular tradition he represents, that of the lyric lamentation,
are clearly heard. We are far from the spare biblical dramatization of the play's first part, with its three Latin insertions.

Assistance in understanding both the bipartite structure
and modal variety of *Singnore scribe* may be found by examining
a parallel work contained in an Assisian *laudario* coeval with
and closely related to the Perugian collection. The *laudario* attributed to the Confraternity of St. Peter in Assisi contains sixteen compositions,14 among them three laments of the Virgin15
and a shorter version of *Singnore scribe*. This shorter version
closely parallels the first part of the hybrid Perugian play, but
ends with the scene of Judas' despair, just before the lyric element would be introduced—that is, just before "someone" tells
Mary about the passion of her son. This abrupt ending of the
Assisian play can be considered purposeful, since it affords a
proper occasion for the intonation of one of the many dramatic
laments of the Virgin known to Umbrian tradition, three of
which are contained in the same manuscript, or, perhaps even
Jacopone's "Donna de Paradiso" which picks up the action just
where the Assisian passion play leaves off and carries it through
to Christ's death. It is interesting to consider just how aptly
"Donna" would serve this purpose, for the dialogue of its introductory stanzas narrates the capture and scourging as having
already happened, as indeed they have in the Assisian play; yet,
as Mary nears Pilate's court, the tense shifts to the present and

the rest of Jacopone's *lauda* either narrates or presents in dialogue the on-going experiences of Christ, Mary, and John. If such a dramatic lament were added on to a brief passion play, stanza form and melody would have to change, but a somewhat similar "polyphonic" treatment exists in the Perugian Harrowing of Hell play where, just as Christ leads Adam out of Limbo, stanza form and melody change with a flourish from passional to paschal.16 It seems possible, then, that the Assisian author composed his play in an abbreviated form with the intention of completing the presentation of the passion with the addition of a well-known dialogued lament. Such a combination of forms may also represent an earlier version of the related Perugian play, so intimately were the two traditions allied.

Devotion to the passion of Christ was central to the religious concerns of the fourteenth century *disciplinati,* so it is no wonder that the longest play in the prestigious St. Andrew collection should portray the initial scenes of that passion with a highly developed artistry and a theatrical skill not attained by many of the other works accompanying it. Nowhere are these qualities more evident than in the transitional sequence wherein the anonymous author begins to fuse elements of the traditional lyric lament with the on-going scriptural dramatization of the second part of his play, a transitional sequence that employs one of the earliest notable examples of simultaneous staging in Italian vernacular drama. And, it is interesting to consider that this sequence is presented against the background of a mimed presentation of just that aspect of the passion that the confraternities sought to imitate in their characteristic penitential ritual: the scourging of Christ .

NOTES

1 See Pier Lorenzo Meloni, "Topografia, diffusione, e aspetti delle confraternite dei disciplinati," in *Risultati e prospettive della ricerca sul movimento dei disciplinati,* Convegno Internazionale di Studio, Perugia, 5-7 decembre 1969 (Perugia: Deputazione di Storia Patria per l'Umbria: Centro di Documentazione sul Movimento dei Disciplinati, 1972), pp. 15-98.

2 See Anna Maria Vinti, "Precisazioni sul movimento del flagellanti e sui maggiori laudari perugini," *Studi di Filologia Italiana,* 8 (1950), 316-19.

3 See Ignazio Baldelli, "La lauda e i disciplinati," reprinted in his *Medioevo volgare da Montecassino all'Umbria* (Bari: Adriatica Editrice, 1971), p. 348.

4 All quotations from *Singnore scribe* are from my "Scriptural Plays from Perugia," Diss. State University of New York at Stony Brook (1974), pp. 50-103.

5 "La lauda," p. 345.

6 Ibid., p. 343.

7 Scriptural references in my text are to *Biblia Vulgata*, 4th ed., ed. Alberto Colunga and Laurentio Turrado (Madrid: Biblioteca de Autores Cristianos, 1965).

8 References in my text are to the *Meditations on the Life of Christ: An Illustrated Manuscript of the Fourteenth Century; Paris, Bibl. Nat. MS. Ital. 115*, trans. Isa Ragusa and Rosalie B. Green (Princeton: Princeton Univ. Press, 1961).

9 "La lauda," pp. 345-46. This passage may be translated as follows: "The *lauda Segnore scribe* serves, too, to make clear the relationship of the dramatic *lauda* of the flagellants with the medieval liturgical theater, for we find . . . inserted into its proper place according to the gospel account the passage: *Quem queritis? Ihesum Nazarenum. Ego sum.* The famous trope, as is well known, was taken from this place in the scripture and applied to the *Visitatio sepulcri;* nevertheless, the insertion of this passage, albeit into its proper scriptural place, could have been suggested by the remembrance of the *Quem queritis* of the sepulchre trope."

10 Quotations from the Montecassino *Passion* are from the edition of D. M. Inguanez, "Un dramma della Passione del secolo XII," *Miscellanea Cassinese*, 17 (1939), 7-55; reprinted by Sandro Sticca in *The Latin Passion Play: Its Origins and Development* (Albany: State Univ. of New York Press, 1970), pp. 66-78, to which I refer.

11 These valuable inventories, destroyed in an anti-fascist uprising at the end of World War II, were partially edited by Ernesto Monaci in his "Appunti per la storia del teatro italiano: Uffizj drammatici dei disciplinati dell'Umbria," *Rivista di Filologia Romanza*, 1 (1872), 257-60.

12 See Anna Maria Jemma, "Le confraternite disciplinate di S. Fiorenzo e di S. Simone in Perugia," Diss. Università degli Studi, Perugia 1969, pp. 62-69.

13 Gianfranco Contini, ed., *Poeti del duecento* (Milano: Riccardo Ricciardi Editore, 1960), II, 119.

14 MS. Vittorio Emanuele 478 (già Frondini), Biblioteca Nazionale Vittorio Emanuele, Roma.

15 "Or ve piaccia d'ascoltare," "Venete a piangere con Maria," and "O Die, gente, or que remore," on ff. 11, 18v, and 23.

16 See the Holy Saturday play *Quiste lume* in my "Scriptural Plays," pp. 184-86.

The Trinity in Medieval Drama

Lynette R· Muir

Although drama has been closely associated with religious rites in many ages and in many parts of the world, only Christianity of all the great world religions has produced a drama that can truly be called a theophany and that at only one period of its history: the high Middle Ages. For medieval drama does not only put God on the stage as a *deus ex machina* or part of a ritual enactment; it portrays in most intimate and revealing detail every aspect of the history of God's relationship with Man, from the Creation to the Incarnation and beyond to the end of the world. In order to do this, the dramatists go far beyond the limits of mere dramatization of biblical stories: with a sublime *naiveté* that robs their work of blasphemy, they lift the veil and show us the very innermost councils of the divine Trinity.

It might truly be said that in this as in all things God had been the first to act, for the theophany of God in Christ was the starting point for the growth of Christianity and it was from the ritual re-enactment of this revelation of God in the liturgy of the Church that medieval religious drama developed. It is not surprising, therefore, that the person of the Trinity most commonly found in the plays should be the Second Person, the *Logos,* the *Salvator,* Christ Jesus, the Lord. Not until late in the Middle Ages did the First and Third Persons of the Trinity tread the boards, and Father, Son, and Spirit together "justify the ways of God to man."

The earliest play based on the Gospels is of course the Greek *Paschon Christi,* dating probably from the fourth century. In form it is closely akin to the classical tragedy, but its subject matter makes it a fairly conventional Passion play with the major role for the Virgin Mary and a smaller but definitely dramatic and not liturgical role for Christ. However it was

75

staged, and we have no information at all on this point, it would
have been impossible to avoid some kind of Crucifixion scene
since this is explicitly required by the dialogue. The Passion was
not to be staged again for nearly a thousand years.

The two commonest subjects for early medieval Latin
music-dramas were the Visit to the Sepulchre and the Adoration
of the Magi.1 Numerous plays on both subjects are extant in
manuscripts that date from the tenth century onwards. However, as Young (I, 369) points out, there is no manuscript older
than the "latter part of the twelfth century" that contains a scene
showing the Risen Christ in person.2 In fact, of all the texts
quoted by Young for these versions of the *Visitatio* play, only
one manuscript is described as twelfth-thirteenth century and all
the others are thirteenth century or later, and it is in the plays
of this period that we find the first real attempts to portray God
on the stage in liturgical drama, though at least one vernacular
play of the twelfth century, the Anglo-Norman *Adam,* had already done so.

The Risen Christ is shown in a number of different ways in
the music-drama. He appears to Mary Magdalene, the other
Maries, and the disciples. He is variously referred to as *Deus,
Jhesus, dominica persona, in persona domini.* Quite often a costume is prescribed: he may appear to Mary Magdalene *in habitu
ortolani,* then change his gardener's clothes and appear in a
white dalmatic or a silk cope with perhaps a gold crown or a
white headdress, carrying a banner, a golden book, or a cross.
So attired, and often accompanied by angels, Christ may harrow
Hell; but the dramatic possibilities of this liturgically common
ritual seem to have been generally rather neglected in the early
dramas, though occasional thirteenth-century examples are to
be found.

The incomplete Monte Cassino Passion (*Miscellanea Cassinese,* XII, 1939), is probably late twelfth century, but Passion
plays elsewhere appear no earlier than the thirteenth century. It
has sometimes been suggested that the rarity of these plays was
due to a reluctance to stage the Crucifixion, but it seems more
probable, if we accept that the Latin music-drama was created
from a superabundance of liturgical joy and worship overflowing
the limits of the Christmas and Easter Sunday rejoicings, that the
events of Good Friday and the emotions they aroused found their
expression in the elaborate and prolonged Good Friday liturgy

and Veneration of the Cross. The thirteenth-century Passion plays both come from the same source: the famous thirteenth-century *Carmina Burana* manuscript from the Benediktbeuern monastery. In this manuscript we have one of the most important of Latin drama collections: the Christmas play includes Prophets, the Nativity with Shepherds and Magi, a Slaughter of the Innocents, and Flight into Egypt. The longer of the two Passion plays begins with the Ministry of Jesus, and includes events of Holy Week before the Passion and Death of Christ; there is also an incomplete Resurrection play. Young has pointed out that the manuscript has "evidence of a still more impressive innovation. In the upper margin of the third page (fol. vi^r) are entries indicating that when the angels sing the passage *Alleluia resurrexit victor ab inferis,* Christ himself comes forth from the tomb and takes a speaking part in the action" (Young, I, 438). This innovation becomes a commonplace of German vernacular Resurrection plays which very often have a sequence of the angel or angels coming to the tomb and singing *Exurge, domine,* followed by a German text on the same theme. Christ then appears and sings either *Resurrexi* or *Dormivi* ("I laid me down and slept and rose up again," Ps. 3.6), followed by a German elaboration of the Latin.[3]

These early Passion plays, even when they stage the Crucifixion, do so ritually and liturgically, with no attempt to harrow the feelings of the audience through an emphasis on the physical sufferings of Christ. This is the case though the grief of the Virgin Mary and other onlookers is freely expressed, and the *Planctus* or lament of the Virgin is a commonly found set-piece even without the Passion play context. An interesting curiosity among the early Latin texts is a semi-dramatic version of the Visit to the Sepulchre from the convent of Origny in France: in this ceremony, which formed part of the Vespers of Easter, women not only played the three Maries but also Christ, as is quite clear from the rubric: "celle qui fait Dieu" (Young, I, 689). This is probably a unique instance of a woman's taking the part of God.

A final group of early Latin dramas which must be mentioned are the *Peregrinus* plays, dramatizing the story of the appearance of Christ to the disciples on the way to Emmaus. This was a popular subject and many examples survive, some of them from the twelfth century.[4] It is perhaps significant that in these texts, as the name implies, Christ is never presented as God or the Lord. He is simply the pilgrim, the *Peregrinus*. Hence these plays do not really contradict the assertion made about the comparative lateness of plays in which Christ himself appears. A similar example of an early symbolic rather than personal portrayal is the role of the bridegroom or *Sponsus* in the play of the Wise and Foolish Virgins. It was normally accepted exegesis that the bridegroom in the parable was Christ, but this does not really put the *Sponsus* in the same category as an Easter play.

Although the combination of Incarnational theology and liturgical precedent was strong enough to make the dramatic presentation of God in Christ acceptable to all but a few medieval Christians, the representation of God the Father was a very different matter. The Deuteronomic prohibition against graven images was taken over and restated in Christian terms by the early Church, with the added dimension of the impropriety of seeking to portray God other than as he had chosen to reveal himself in the Incarnation: "He that has seen me hath seen the Father; and how sayest thou then, show us the Father?" (*John* 14.9). It is significant that Christian art before the thirteenth century almost never shows the Father. Old Testament paintings and carvings regularly show the Creator in a cruciform halo, or young and beardless, clearly implying that it is the *Logos,* the creative Word of God. There are a few interesting exceptions to this rule. One is the Baptism of Christ on the font at Liège in Belgium, where an explicitly named *Deus Pater* looks down benignly as the Spirit-Dove hovers over the Son. Another example is a Crucifixion from Hildersheim, Germany, in which the Father supports the Son's arms on the Cross while the Spirit, in his dove form, proceeds out of the mouth of the Father and touches the head of the Son. Both these Trinitarian groupings are found in later plays.5 This reluctance to portray the Father is almost certainly the reason for the appearance of God as the Savior in the only early Creation play, the Anglo-Norman *Adam.* The opening rubric tells us that *tunc veniat Salvator,* and for the rest of the play He is referred to as *Figura,* which almost certainly implies the Son as the Figure of the Father: *Figura substantiae eius (Hebrews* 2.3).6 It is interesting to note that this play is one of the very earliest in which God appears at all, and provides certainly by far the most elaborate role for the actor playing him of any play written before the fifteenth century. The dominant tone in the pre-Fall scenes is one of kindly didacticism with a feudal rather than paternal choice of images; after the Fall there is a strong strain of irony in the questioning of Adam and Eve, very reminiscent of the Book of Job.

Despite the steady growth and spread of Latin dramas in the twelfth and thirteenth centuries, the great age of vernacular biblical plays is of course the fifteenth century, with a few scattered examples from the fourteenth. God appears as a judge or *deus ex machina* in saints' plays and miracles of the Virgin from the fourteenth century onwards, but an attempt to analyze these texts would necessitate introducing the Virgin Mary into this study since it is in their relationship with her that the Persons of the Trinity are mainly significant in these plays. I have, therefore, deliberately omitted this whole range of plays though they include many interesting scenes, especially in the French *Miracles de la Vierge* where the Virgin almost forces her son to do her will by the application of a form of emotional blackmail.[7] These earlier vernacular plays, the French *Passion de Palatinus* (ed. Grace Frank, 1922), the German Frankfurt play preserved in the famous producer's copy, the *Dirigierrolle* (ed. R. Froning, in *Das Drama des Mittelalters,* 1895), and the Italian *Laude drammatiche* have in common their close adherence to the Bible and liturgy. The original treatment of biblical material in *Adam* and to a lesser degree the *Seinte Resurrexion*[8] is not found again until the fifteenth century, and then only in certain works. The majority of Italian plays, both *Laude* and *Sacre Rappresentazioni,* retain a formal structure and characterization: in the Old Testament texts, such as plays of Abraham, the words of God are usually communicated to Abraham by an angel, and in the New Testament texts the words of Christ are mainly biblical or liturgical. There is, however, a considerable elaboration of the Creation scene in the Bologna *Rappresentazione ciclica* (ed. V. de Bartholomaeis, 1943, in *Laude Drammatiche e Rappresentazioni Sacre,* III) with a corresponding increase in the role of *Dio Padre*. It is an unusual feature of the Bologna play that after the Trial in Heaven the Son of God, not the Father, dispatches Gabriel to announce the tidings of the Incarnation to Mary. His commission to Gabriel includes the statement that He is and ever will be God and is to be incarnate for love of man: "per salvar l'uomo . . . vuo prender carne per suo grande amore" (p. 224). Spain and Portugal have comparatively few medieval biblical plays, and those few are not of particular interest in their presentation of the Trinity.

In the fifteenth century a distinctive feature of the very substantial number of surviving medieval biblical plays in German vernacular is their extensive use of Latin liturgical material. It is the rule rather than the exception for speeches to be sung in Latin and then spoken in vernacular; in addition, it is notable that the plays are mainly Christmas and Passion plays with comparatively few Old Testament episodes. Often the plays that do include Old Testament scenes, such as the Corpus Christi plays from Eger (ed. G. Milchsack, 1881) or Künzelsau (ed. Dona B. Reeves, Univ. of Texas diss., 1963), refer to God as *Salvator* throughout, and this title is regularly used also in the Passion plays, sometimes varied with *Christus* or Jesus. This raises an interesting question in connection with the Heidelberg Passion play (ed. G. Milchsack, 1880) which has no Old Testament *Vorspiel* but a number of scenes or *Prefiguraciones* of episodes of the Ministry and Passion intercalated in the New Testament. These scenes include Abraham and Isaac, Moses and the Brazen Serpent, and Jonah and the Whale, in all of which God speaks as *Der himmlische Vater*. In the play of Job, however, which is a prefiguration of the flagellation, the words of God are spoken by the *Salvator*. Now during this scene we are told that *Jesus bleybtt siczenn verbundenn.* Do we therefore assume that the actor playing Jesus, sitting there bound, also plays the *Salvator?* It would fit the stage directions satisfactorily since both Satan and Job go to the Savior and no direction is given for the *Salvator* to move. If this is indeed how it was intended, the dramatic effect of such an arrangement must have been most striking and original.

Another very unusual presentation of God in the German plays is in the *Hessische Weihnachtsspiel* (ed. R. Froning, 1895), which is the only Christmas play I have ever read which has a dancing, singing, and speaking part for the Christ child! At the Nativity, which is attended by many singing angels and virgins (bilingual in Latin and German), we have the direction:

> Et puer dicit:
>   Eya, eya, virgo deum genuit.

A little further on we read:

> Joseph et servus corisant cum puero et canunt:
> En trinitatis speculum.

After this song and dance, the servant welcomes the *puer* in German; so far it might be possible to see the *puer* as merely a boy, but his next words are conclusive:

> Et puer dicit:
>> Eya, eya, Maria liebe mutter myn
>> Sal ich von de Ioden liten grosse pin?
> Maria dicit:
>> Swige, libes kindelin Ihesu Crist
>> beweyn diner marteil nicht zu disser frist.
>
>> Ah! Ah! Mary, my dear mother,
>> Shall I suffer great torment from the Jews?
> Mary answers:
>> Hush, Jesus Christ, dear little one
>> Do not bewail your sufferings at this time.

This dialogue with its foreknowledge of the Passion expressed in terms suited to a child and his mother could have been very moving when acted. The action then passes to the Adoration of the Shepherds.

There are a number of plays in German which, like those from England and France, depict Old Testament stories of Noah, Moses, and Abraham in which God has a speaking part, or New Testament scenes such as the Baptism or Transfiguration of Christ in which at least the voice of the Father is dramatically necessary. The attitudes of different playwrights in different countries vary considerably, but there are certainly many examples in the fifteenth century of *Deus Pater* being quite explicitly represented. Considerable pains were taken to make these appearances as reverent and impressive as possible. Music often accompanies or introduces these scenes, and angels escort the Father if he has occasion to move about the *platea*.[9] The costumes, when mentioned, are always rich, and sometimes a gold mask is suggested. Heaven itself is hung with silk curtains and contains a throne.[10] The outward forms of the representation of the Father thus form an even more glaring contrast with the increasingly sordid and brutal presentation of the Passion of the Son.

In Chester, no distinction of Persons is made. *Deus* creates the world and talks to the Patriarchs; he also lives among the disciples and Jews in the New Testament (only occasionally in the latter is a speech ascribed to Jesus or *Christus*). There is no Baptism or Transfiguration in this cycle, and the same actor could well have played God throughout (apart from the requirements of pageant staging). Even for the Entry into Heaven, which has a dialogue between God and the angels based on the text "who is this coming from Edam, from Bozrah in garments stained with crimson" *(Isaiah* 63.1), there is no Father in Heaven to welcome the Triumphant Son. (This stands in contrast to the more developed scene in the Cornish plays.) The sole instance of two Persons together as God in the Chester cycle is in the Pentecost play where *Lyttle God* asks *Deus* to send the Holy Spirit to the Apostles as had been promised; this is done *in spetie ignis*. Fire or doves are the commonest manifestations of the Spirit in medieval drama. Special machinery for this is indicated in the Lucerne production details, which require a special person *(leitter)* for the Star and the Holy Ghost.[11]

Apart from Personification, the Trinitarian theology in the plays is achieved in two ways. Sometimes a sermon is used, or an expositor includes a reference or explanation on the nature of the Trinity. In some of the French plays, especially the *Passions* of Greban and Michel, this descriptive technique is helped by various devices of appearance and language. In Michel's *Passion* (ed. Jodogne, 1959), God the Father declares his intention, at the Baptism of Christ, of manifesting himself in Trinity; then he speaks the biblical words "this is my beloved Son" and a dove descends. The direction notes that *Dieu le Père* may here speak in three voices, high, middle, and low: "hault desus, une hault contre et une basse contre bien accordees" (p. 26). A similar situation obtains for the Transfiguration (a stage direction demands: "Icy parle Dieu le Pere en troys voix ainsi comme il fist au baptesme de Jesus," p. 128), but the most original part of the treatment in this play is the verbal intervention of the Father at the Passion. He not only sends angels to comfort Christ on the Mount of Olives, but to accompany him on the Road to Calvary and to remain with him throughout the Crucifixion. Thus the visual effect would be similar to the many Crucifixion carvings and paintings with angels mingling with the humans round the Cross. This stress on the divine Sonship counterbalances the emphasis on the human nature of Christ. In a number of plays, including N-Town, Greban's *Passion*, and the Rome *Passione*, a separate character, *Anima Christi*, is introduced to harrow Hell, before the Christ is taken down from the Cross.

Although the Trinity is occasionally presented visually or verbally in these ways, it is rare for the *Third* Person to have a speaking part. The personified Holy Ghost appears exceptionally in the Norwich Grocers' play. After the Fall when Adam and Eve have been in the grip of Misery and Dolor, the Holy Ghost, the Comforter, comes to them with the promise of eventual salvation: "Then cumyth in the Holy Ghost comforting Man" (*Non-Cycle Plays and Fragments,* ed. N. Davis, p. 17).

The only examples of all three Persons speaking together are in the Trial or Parliament in Heaven Scenes. This sequence, in which the Daughters of God—Mercy, Justice, Truth, and Peace—debate together and with the Deity about the Redemption of Man, occurs before the New Testament scenes in many different versions and as many languages. It is most common in French but is also found in Dutch and Flemish, Low German, English, and Italian.12 The French version is often literally a Trial, with Mercy pleading for Man's Redemption, Justice opposing her and Peace and Truth trying to bring about a settlement. In Greban's *Passion* (ed. O. Jodogne, 1965), it is a very long scene, about 4,000 lines, and includes much theological information, imparted by Wisdom, on the nature of the Trinity. The role of *Deus Pater* is virtually limited to accepting the conclusions of the court and implementing them, though with reluctance. From time to time during the Ministry and Passion of Christ the discussion in Heaven is renewed, and after the Ascension Peace is restored to the Heavenly Court, whereupon Mercy and Justice kiss one another.

Although in these scenes the playwrights tell us much about the Trinity, they are not truly a dramatic representation of God but only a dramatized explanation of certain theological arguments.13 The Semur *Passion* (ed. P. T. Durbin, Univ. of Leeds thesis, 1973) has a more truly dramatic variation, in which God, appealed to by Charity and Hope, asks them how He can have pity on Man:

> Conbien que puisse tout despecier et tout faire,
> Cy ne me pui ge pas de moy mesme deffaire.

Je, quil suis verité, mentir je ne pouroie,
Ce j'estoie menteur, Dieu pas je ne seroie. (1758-61)

Although I can destroy all and create all,
I cannot free myself from myself.
I, who am truth, could not lie,
For if I lied, I would not be God.

God cannot, therefore, break his own condemnation of Adam
and hence must find another way to help Man. This he does
through his wisdom:

Puis qu'il vous plait, mes filles, que le monde repaire,
Je le vuilz sans destruire tout de novel reffaire.
Ung paradix terrestre de novel reffairé,
C'est le corps de la vierge ouquel je descendray. . . . (1784-87)

Since it is your wish, my daughters, that I restore the world,
I will make all things new without destroying it.
I will make a new earthly Paradise,
It is the body of the Virgin into which I shall descend.

In this new Paradise, i.e., the Eucharist, God himself will be
planted and bear fruit of eternal life which can be given to
man.14

Here, then, God actually discusses the problem and its solution with his interlocutors. In two other plays, however, this
debate is carried a step further. In the Flemish *First Joy of Mary
(Die eerste bliscap van Maria,* ed W. H. Beuken, 1973) and the
English Parlement of Heaven from the N-Town plays *(Ludus
Coventriae,* Play XI), we have scenes where the debate is between the three Persons of the Godhead, so that we have before
us on the stage an attempt to show the Trinity as a self-contained, non-allegorical Unity. The Flemish and the English texts
show marked resemblances of content and approach, though
there are important differences of language and detail.

The Flemish text is longer than the English.15 God asks his
Son for advice on how to reconcile Charity and Justice:

Hoe salict maken, en stoerder eene?
Want alle beide moeticker plegen.
Dadict niet, sone, hoert wies ic meene:
Ic ginge miere hoger godheit tegen.
Dies wilt mi tesen avise gewegen. (1212-15)

How shall I proceed without displeasing one of them?
For I have to take both into account.

> If I did not do so, Son, hear what I mean:
> I would run counter to my own High Majesty.
> Therefore advise me in this consideration!

God's Son reminds his Father that:

> Wi en mogen niet bat, noch ghi noch icke,
> Dan trecht in hout van desen sticke (1219-20)

> We cannot do more, neither you nor I,
> than what the Law holds in this case

and recommends asking Law and Truth for their advice. The Holy Spirit joins in and urges the Father to settle the matter:

> Wes u behaecht, gelieft ons beyen,
> Als u ende me, sonder mestermen;
> Want doch ons proper es ontfermen. (1228-30)

> Whatever may please you, will please both of us,
> namely you and me without discord;
> For having pity is natural with us.

Truth's verdict is that:

> Sal den mensce sorcoers gescien,
> Dat wort bi rechte van uwen sone; (1238-39)

> If Men are to receive salvation,
> this will be given, properly, by your Son.

God then appeals to the Son to do so: "If you felt so much love towards them" (1266), and after some hesitation (and more than a hint of a *Why me?* attitude, to which God answers: "You are the middle Person in the Godhead . . . so you are obliged . . . to be a mediator in this matter") the Son finally agrees, willingly, because:

> Dat mi Ontfermicheit heeft ontstaect
> Vierich dorscoten mijn hert, mijn sinnen,
> Ende metten strale van minnen geraect. (1342-44)

> . . . Charity has kindled me
> run through with fire my heart and my senses,
> and hit it with the arrow of love.

In contrast to this scene, the English version of the Council of the Trinity itself is very brief: just three quatrains. The Father declares that Man was made by Wisdom and tempted by it, so the *sone, sapyens* must see "how of man may be Salvacion." The

Son says it must be done by one who is *both God and Man* and announces himself *redy to do this dede;* the Holy Ghost concludes the council of the Trinity:

> I the holy gost of yow tweyn do procede
> this charge I wole take on me
> I love to your lover ȝal you lede
> this is the Assent of oure unyte. (181-84)

In the Flemish play, then, the Virtues and the Persons of the Trinity mingle together in a general debate, while in the English version the Virtues conclude their vain attempt first and then appeal to the Trinity as to a higher but separate court. The former is more "human" in its characterization, the latter more formal, more divine. Both truly put the Trinity on the stage.

St. John Chrysostom declared that "he insults God who seeks to apprehend his essential being," and on another occasion claimed that it "is an impertinence to say that He who is beyond the apprehension of even the higher Powers can be comprehended by us earthworms."16 The medieval dramatists thought differently, and in all humility asked pardon:

> se riens avons dit ou escript
> ou mal fait ou mal ordonné (Greban, 34409-10)

and invited the audience at the end of yet another "earth worm's eye view" of

> . . . chose si inestimable
> si parfaicte, si transcendente
> infinie incomprehensible (Michel, 332-35)

to join in rendering "graces a Dieu le pere, chantans Te Deum laudamus" (Greban, 34428-29).

NOTES

1 The principal source of the texts of Latin music-dramas is Karl Young, *The Drama of the Medieval Church* (Oxford: Clarendon Press, 1933), 2 vols. A number of additional pieces are to be found in R. Donovan, *The Liturgical Drama of Medieval Spain* (Toronto, 1958). Unfortunately, neither of these includes the music of the plays.

2 Young arranges his texts by subject matter, not by the date of the manuscripts. The latter information has to be distinterred from the footnotes.

3 For example, Christ sings *Resurrexi* in the Redentin, Alsfeld, Augsburg, and

Innsbruck plays, and *Dormivi* in the plays from Eger, the Tyrol, and Donaueschingen (German text only). The scene makes only a rare French appearance in the *Passion du Palatinus* (French text only). There is a similar scene, without Latin text, in the Rome *Passione*.

4 See Young, I, 451-83.

5 In representations of Old Testament scenes, God the Father may be depicted in symbolic form: a Hand, a Star with one long, pointed ray in Eastern European art, or a Burning Bush. This last is the only one to recur in drama—for example, in the York play of Moses.

6 For a discussion of the *Figura* in *Adam*, see Lynette R. Muir, *Liturgy and Drama in the Anglo-Norman Adam*, Medium Aevum Monographs, 3 (Oxford, 1973), pp. 15-16.

7 The role of God and the Virgin has been examined by Helen Taylor in *A Study of the Supernatural Element in the Miracles de Nostre Dame par personnages*, University of Leeds thesis (M.A.), 1975.

8 The twelfth-century Anglo-Norman *Seinte Resurrexion* play has what is possibly the earliest surviving scene of Christ on the cross in medieval drama. Longinus thrusts his spear into Christ's side and is healed of his blindness, before the Deposition and Entombment.

9 For the role of music as indicating heavenly harmony and order in the plays, see John Stevens, "Music in Medieval Drama," *Proceedings of the Royal Musical Association*, 84 (1958), 81-95. For music in the French plays, see G. Cohen, *La mise en scène dans le théâtre religieux français du moyen âge* (Paris, 1926), pp. 134-41.

10 Details for French plays are given in G. Cohen, *La Mise en scène*, pp. 220-32. In the *Abregié de la Passion joué à Mons*, the stage direction for the Transfiguration requires Jesus to put on "une face et les mains d'or bruni" (ed. Cohen, p. 177). This suggests that a gold mask and gloves are part of the image of God. Further support is provided by the note of the "diademe with a veserne gilted" for God in the Endenture of the York Mercers Company; see Alexandra F. Johnston and Margaret Dorrell, "The Doomsday Pageant of the York Mercers, 1433," *Leeds Studies in English*, n.s. 5 (1971), 29-30. The Norwich Grocers' Play accounts include "A face and heare for the Father" (*Non-Cycle Plays and Fragments*, ed. Norman Davis, EETS, s.s. 1 [1970], p. xxxv). The Lucerne Passion Play records do not require a mask for *Pater Aeternus*, but they do specify the usual (*gwonlich*) diadem and "beautiful patriarchal gray long hair and beard" ("schön allt vätterisch graw lang Har und Bart"). The detailed accounts and production notes for this play have been described and partially edited in *The Passion Play of Lucerne* by M. Blakemore Evans (New York, 1943).

11 The *Stern und Heiliggeist Leiter* was stationed in an upstairs room of one of the houses at the end of the square where the play was staged. He was responsible for letting down the Star for the Kings and a live dove (*lebenden Tuben*) for the Annunciation and Baptism. A reminder to him to test his equipment is included: *Item, das der Stern und Heiliggeist Leyteer sin rüstung probiere* (Evans, *Passion Play of Lucerne*, p. 199).

12 For a discussion of these Trial Scenes in relation to the different doctrines of the Atonement, see Lynette R. Muir, "The Fall of Man in the Drama of Medieval Europe," forthcoming in *Studies in Medieval Culture*, 10 (1976).

13 The Spanish *Dialogo del Nascimiento* by Torres Naharro is principally a dialogue between two pilgrims on their way to Rome. Among the subjects they discuss is "the reason" why the Son was chosen as a Redeemer instead of some other person of the Trinity" (J. P. W. Crawford, *Spanish Drama before Lope de Vega* [Philadelphia, 1922], p. 47). This same question is explained by Sapience in the Greban *Procés au Paradis* and by the Father in the Flemish play (See *Die eerste bliscap van Maria en Die sevenste bliscap van Onser Vrouwen*, ed. W. H. Beuken [Culemborg, 1973], p. 12).

14 The Semur Passion owes much to the *Pélérinage de l'âme de Guillaume de Deguilleville*, ed. J.-J. Stürzinger (London: Roxburghe Club, 1895).

15 I am deeply grateful to my colleague Professor W. P. Gerritsen of Utrecht for sending me a translation of this lengthy scene. In the Revello *Passione* (ed. V. Promis [Turin, 1888], p. 35) the Father and Son only appear, and Domina Providentia speaks for the Holy Spirit. A similar device is used in the *Actes des Apôtres* of 1536, when the direction calls for the Holy Spirit to speak "par la bouche d'ung seraphim" (fol. CLI).

16 *Discourses on the Incomprehensibility of God,* as quoted in Rudolph Otto, *The Idea of the Holy* (rpt. Oxford: Oxford University Press, 1973), pp. 179-80.

Metaphorical Obscenity in French Farce, 1460-1560

Barbara C. Bowen

The plays usually referred to by French critics as "l'ancienne farce" are at last being thoroughly studied.[1] There are about 150 of them (definitions differ), but the only one well known to most students of literature is *Maistre Pierre Pathelin,* probably written about 1464. They are all in verse, most usually in octosyllabic rhyming couplets, and most of them are anonymous. Unlike the contemporary *sotties,* which use personification and allegory, often for satirical purposes, the farces are about real people: husbands and wives, cobblers, policemen and fishmongers. Though quite short (between 10 and 40 minutes' acting time), farces have plots, often very similar to the plots of *fabliau* and *conte,* which show human folly in action in specific circumstances. And there is plenty of action—farce characters engage in trade and chicanery, disguise themselves, chase and beat each other, eat, drink and urinate, hide in cages and privies, seduce each others' wives, confess to priests and go to law.

These plays have attracted a good deal of critical attention in recent years, but two aspects of them have never been thoroughly examined. The first is the scatological, which will not be dealt with here but which is undoubtedly worth study,[2] and the second is the sexual. European critics, in an interesting survival of nineteenth century attitudes, remain profoundly shocked by sexual expressions, and particularly by the farces in which sexual intercourse apparently takes place on stage. Their assumption, often openly stated,[3] is that plays which deal with sex are crude, primitive, unsophisticated, and unfunny. It is odd that this prejudice, highly understandable in the 1920's, should persist into the 1970's. My intention in this paper is to examine some uses of sexual terminology in the farces, to see whether or not this prejudice is justified.

We can tell, from our general knowledge of Renaissance literature, that both social and theatrical taboos operated then very much as they do today. In good society, it was perfectly acceptable to make jokes and insinuations about sex; it was not acceptable to use anatomical terms. On the comic stage any kind of language was acceptable, but copulation certainly was not. If the *farceurs* wanted deliberately to transgress these taboos, we should expect them to do so brutally, especially if, in Bakhtine's terms, the authors were lower-class men seeking revenge against the social hierarchy which had imposed the taboos. But this is not what we find. Crudity and brutality in the farces occur, not in the talk about sex, but in the insults, gibes and swear-words exchanged by characters quarrelling or fighting. If a cobbler shouts at his wife: "Bren pour toy!" she will reply: "Merde emmy tes joues!" He will retort: "Mais vieux ort cul, cabas breneux!"4 and so on indefinitely. These grotesquely descriptive insults are violent, and substitute for the wished-for physical violence which would be both condemned by society and hard to manage on stage. But when we look for a similar violence in the longer obscene passages, or for anything like the cynical brutality of some French Renaissance poetry, we do not find it.

What we do find is a remarkable fascination with metaphor. A penis may be referred to as an instrument, a stick, a sword, a candle, a syringe, a hoe, a spade, a spit, a chimney-brush, a spur, a needle, a horse, a musical instrument, or a billiard cue. A vagina may be a lantern, a basket, a shoe, a basin, a packsaddle, a vineyard, a cooking-pot, a shell, or a cupboard. What the man does to (with) the woman can be explained as planting, digging, bending a bow, doing the laundry, mending a pot, polishing armor, sifting flour, chimney-sweeping, firing an arrow, playing at *jeu de paume,* bearing a lance, singing, sewing, hitting the mark, measuring cloth, weaving, dancing, playing music, riding a horse, fencing, playing billiards, climbing a tree, or declining nouns. Is this crude? Surely it is rather highly imaginative, poetic, and comic. Many of these metaphors can be found in other literary genres, but there is no other, to my knowledge, which uses them all. They cover a very broad range of human activity, suggesting that to the *farceurs* sex is an essential human pastime like the activities of farmers, craftsmen, and artists. There are, it is true, a few disagreeable metaphors, usually related to medical treatment, but they are in a small minority. All the rest present activities which are natural, necessary, and often joyous.

So far are we from an atmosphere of brutality that most of the metaphors in question arc not even anti-feminist. It is true that some of these actions are normally performed, in their literal as well as their metaphorical sense, by men: digging, firing an arrow, polishing armour, or bearing a lance. But some of them pertain to either sex (singing, dancing, riding) and some more plausibly to women (doing the laundry, sewing, weaving). Is a man whose sexual activity is described by a female metaphor being accused of lack of masculinity? Apparently not, especially as some of the images in question are sexually interchangeable. *Engin,* a general word for "instrument" as well as for "intelligence" (from *ingenium*) can designate a penis or a vagina, and so can *cas,* while the horse-riding metaphor can be used by the man or the woman. Nor is the woman generally considered an object. Whereas in some cases a highly energetic male symbol encounters a very passive female one (digging, hitting the mark, or playing billiards), in other cases both symbols are active (dancing, fencing, or singing in harmony). Moreover, the attitude of the partners is in general the same; both are experienced, and they are looking not for romantic love but for physical satisfaction.

The metaphors I have quoted are scattered throughout more than half of the extant farces. There is no general correlation between scabrous subject and obscene treatment. There are plays whose plot concerns an adulterous affair but whose language is perfectly "clean," and plays not concerned with sex which use one or two sexual metaphors in passing. But the most interesting farces, both dramatically and poetically, are those in which sexual metaphor provides the plot and/or action. There are by my definition 15 such plays[5] in which these metaphors can be used for different purposes, and I propose to examine here three of these purposes in some detail. First, there are the plays which are all talk about sex, usually either the recollection of sexual exploits or the discussion of sexual capacity. Secondly, in some farces sexual metaphor is used as a weapon by one sex to browbeat or humiliate the other. And finally, in some of the most entertaining plays, metaphor is a means of depicting sexual intercourse on stage.

I

Discussion of sex on stage. The two commonest strategies here are confession and debate. For instance, *La Confession Margot* is a dialogue between Margot and a priest. She confesses various sexual acts committed with members of the clergy, to which he invariably replies that good deeds done to churchmen are deserving of salvation. Margot describes how: "Il me le fit troys foys ou quatre Sans descendre"; how the bed fell over as a result of their efforts, and how her lover put his knees between her legs. One encounter does receive more graphic treatment, and here she describes in detail the appearance of a penis (but she calls it a sausage—*une endoille)* before and after. Before, it stood up proudly, with a red head, a cape, and two little bells which sounded a delightful song. (This is much more poetic than Rabelais' similar description in the Prologue to the *Quart Livre.)* Afterwards it is soft and small and weeps, so that she feels quite remorseful. This is both explicit (although no ana-tomical terms are used) and poetic, and while the author's aim is no doubt to titillate the audience, he does it with considerable wit.

Several plays are debates over the relative sexual merits of different men. *Ragot, Musarde et Babille* is an entertaining variation on the perennial debate between the active and the contemplative life. Is it better to love a churchman or an aristo-crat? Gentlemen, says Musarde, are always boasting about their attributes: "Je l'ay si grant, j'en ay autant." But when it comes to the actual measuring *(aulner,* the tailor's term for measuring cloth), their boasted *quatier* turns out to be *ung petit doy.*

Similarly, in *Le Proces d'un jeune moine et d'ung viel gendarme,*6 a girl appeals to Cupid to find her a lover. The six-teenth century poet gives the medieval *topos* a nice ironic twist; a *young* monk and an *old* soldier each plead their fitness to be the girl's lover, and she of course chooses the monk, traditional representative of the contemplative life, precisely because he is better equipped for the action she has in mind. There are several conventional erotic expressions: "l'apoinctement," "fourrer le pelisson," two metaphors from jousting—"presenter le bois" and "frapper a la quintaine"—and a sizeable passage based entirely on music metaphors. Cupid proposes that they sing a song before continuing the argument. The girl's answer to this is:

> Si vous voulés que je sostienne
> Le bas, si baillés bon dessus,
> Car aucunesfois sans dessus
> Mauvais chantre est par ung desol.

The soldier admits: "Je ne chante que de bemol [flat]," while the monk boasts:

> Et moy je chante de becare [sharp],
> Hault et gros comme une barre,
> Quant j'ay un dessoubz de nature [natural].

Not only is the soldier less well furnished by nature; his technique is also less to the girl's liking:

> Je ne chante que de mesure,
> Tout bellement sans me haster.

She does not take long to decide for the monk, who is "fourni comme ung marchant" with "instrumens organistes Gros et ouvers pour ung plain chant," and who describes his technique thus:

> une foy que je rencontre
> Unicum en ma chanterie
> C'est une droicte melodie
> Et plaisant que m'escouter.

He and the girl celebrate their agreement by singing a two-part song.

There are several variations on the debate technique. In *Le Ramonneur* the chimney-sweep boasts of his sexual prowess, and his wife on the contrary complains of his incapacity, using various technical terms related to the sweeping of chimneys: *lever le boys du ramon, ma gaulle ploye,* as well as other obscene metaphors—including *avoir le bont, darder la flesche, être à ses declinaisons,* and *sec et mast.* In *Le Faulconnier de Ville* there are two separate debates. The first is between the *faulconnier champestre,* who hunts wild game, and the *faulconnier de ville,* who chases girls. The fun is in the contrast between the literal and metaphorical uses of the same terminology: each has a stick, a ferret, and a horse. Furthermore, they use the same verbs: *abatre beste, frapper d'estoc et de taille,* and so forth. The *faulconnier de ville* does point out that they are different, because he whistles to attract his prey, while his companion blows his horn in order to terrify his. The second debate is a dispute between the *faulconnier de ville* and a local aristocrat over the girl whom the former has attracted by whistling. Here the terminology is related mainly to the cutting-up of game after the kill.

There are three different strategies for discussing sex in *Frère Guillebert,* which has a conventional cuckoldry plot: wife complains of husband's impotence and allows herself to be seduced by the friar. But nothing actually happens; as he is getting into bed with her the husband returns, having forgotten his shopping-bag. The friar hides, and the husband mistakes his pants for the bag and goes off with them. The obscenity is conveyed in three ways. Friar Guillebert opens the play with a burlesque sermon full of thinly disguised obscene latinisms: "Foullando in calibistris Intravit per boucham ventris." When he is hiding from the husband he is terrified of castration and says so in some detail; and when convinced of his fate he makes a burlesque will regretting his sexual exploits. Unusually, the word *vit* ("penis") is used once, but all other anatomical references are metaphorical: *outil, baston, coquille, instrument,* and so on. There are at least nineteen different metaphors in French, some of which have never been satisfactorily explained linguistically,7 as well as the obvious obscenities in pseudo-Latin. The French metaphors are comic first by their very profusion—one way of underlining the fact that a friar ought not to be making love at all—and then because several of them are socially quite unsuited to a priest, such as larding a rabbit, polishing a hauberk, digging a field, or charging with a lance.

Even in the farces where sex is merely recalled or discussed, then, there is an astonishing variety of metaphor, ingeniously chosen and poetically developed.

II

Sexual metaphors as weapons. In only one of these plays, *Le Ramonneur,* could we say that sexual metaphors are used with cruel intention. The poor, old, tired chimney-sweep is despised by his wife because he is not good at his (metaphorical) trade any more. In the other plays examined so far the intent is entertainment, not attack, and this is true of most of the farces. But in a small number of cases sexual metaphors are used as weapons in the battle of the sexes.

Many farces are structured round an idiom or metaphorical expression, which a character ignorant of the conventions of language takes literally and puts into action. *Le Pasté* is one of two farces based on the idiom *chauffer la cire,* "to heat wax," which means, roughly "to twiddle one's thumbs." (Cotgrave's definition is: "To attend long for a promised good turne"). In both plays wife and lover have a rendez-vous, and to get the husband out of the way they order him to go heat wax. In *Le Pasté* they call for water to wash their hands, but the husband says he cannot bring any because the bowl (*cuvier*) is cracked (*fendu*). The lover, who is the local priest, suggests fixing it with wax, upon which the husband bursts out in a tirade against the bowl, which is really a denunciation of his wife's vagina:

> Si souvent a esté feru,
> Bouté, rebouté et pressé
> Qu'il est trestout despetassé.

The *curé* then gives him two candles to melt—candles which had been given to him by a parishioner to burn in church. And while the wife and *curé* eat the pie of the title and drink their fill, the furious husband sits melting the candles which are the symbol of his virility in order to patch a leak in his wife's bowl. The harshness of this humiliation points the moral: it is the man's duty to be master in his house, and when he fails no punishment is too severe.[8]

In the well-known farce *Le Cuvier* a bowl is presumably also a sexual symbol. Here it is much bigger—a tub of some kind for washing clothes—and the shrewish wife who has been dictating menial tasks to her husband falls into it. She is not able to get out by herself: in the longest scene of the play she struggles helplessly inside it while her husband deliberately reads through the list (*rolet*) of household chores she had given him to see if helping her out of the *cuvier* is included. When he finds that "cela n'est point à mon rolet" he refuses to help her until she promises that from henceforth he shall be master of the household. The wife's confinement inside a female sexual symbol has brought home to her what she should have known all along —that it is the man's place to give orders and the woman's to obey them.

One of the best of the "metaphorical" farces is *L'Arbalète* (the cross-bow). The plot is very simple: wife bullies husband until finally he has had enough and takes his revenge. The ostensible subject is folly: the wife's name is Sibile, "Sybil," which means "wise"—a reference to the Sybils of antiquity— and she begins by lamenting her husband's stupidity. The play is divided into five episodes, each of which is a "proverb in action." The husband demonstrates his folly by taking literally the idioms used by the wife. First she tells him that he has a green head which needs ripening: "Y vous la fault faire murir." So he puts on a little straw hat like the ones farmers put over fruit to ripen it faster. The other episodes are similar. When she urges him to educate himself and asserts that the best way is to chew over Scripture and taste its meaning, he naturally begins to munch on a book.

Finally the wife repeats an idiom she had used at the beginning, that in order to be wise one must "parler à traict," which Cotgrave translates thus: "To speake leasurely, soberly, softly, by pauses, without hast." But *un traict,* literally, is an arrow, so the poor husband begins to talk to the arrow of his crossbow. However, he now decides that he has had enough of all this humiliating instruction, and turns the tables by forcing his wife to talk to the crossbow itself and the individual parts of it. The moral, spoken by the husband, is that wives should not undertake to criticise their husbands in public. The apparent fool, as so often, has turned the tables on the apparently wise.

The obvious male symbol of the crossbow adds a good deal to the effectiveness of this play. The husband loses patience at the moment when the symbol is to hand, and uses it to force his wife to submit to him, thereby taking a double revenge on her. He shows her that her boasted intellectual superiority was illusory, since it depended on a simple manipulation of language of which he is just as capable as she; and he comments decisively on the relation between words and action. A crossbow is a symbol of male superiority because it stands for two different kinds of action, and men are naturally superior to women because they act, both on the battlefield and in bed. Talking about wisdom is irrelevant to this basic situation. The woman's proper rôle is to be as passive in life generally as she allegedly is in sexual intercourse. Like the wife of the *Cuvier,* this one has been put in her place by a sexual symbol.

III

Presenting sex on stage. The plays in which actual sexual intercourse apparently takes place on stage raise the question: how were they performed? We know that theatrical convention would have excluded a realistic staging, and that sex was, in the etymological sense, ob-scene—it must take place off stage, in the wings. There are several farces in which wife and lover ostentatiously leave the stage in order to make love, and none in which they make love in front of the audience. How, then, were the sexual-action farces staged?

The technique is very simple. Take for instance *Les Chambrières,*9 for which the full title is: *The maids who go to 5 a.m. Mass to get holy water*. This play contains both obscene conversation (the maids gossip about the sexual habits of their masters) and obscene action, whose main metaphor is the obvious one of the *aspergillium* or sprinkler containing holy water. The two maids and the nurse stand in front of the priest to receive the water. Quite innocuous, apparently. But the conversation throughout is nothing but *double-entendre*. The priest says: "You mustn't think my water ever runs dry" and "Come closer, I can't deal with you all at once" (the verb is *fournir,* often used in sexual contexts). The women say, for example: "Do it harder, your sprinkler is too short!" and "Be careful! If you broke his instrument it would be a shame." The action as seen is harmless, but the extended use of an obvious metaphor makes it clear that a quite different action is to be understood. And the ecclesiastical context serves to emphasize the circumvention of a taboo.

In *Les Femmes qui font rembourrer leur bas* the basic metaphor is from saddlery: *rembourrer* means "to stuff," and *bas* denotes a pack-saddle or anything else that is low down. The two women complain that their saddles need re-stuffing, the two men claim to be saddlers, and the action then consists of the insertion of tools, measuring, sewing, stretching leather with the teeth, enlarging openings, and so on. Presumably the actors used real saddles and tools while accentuating the joke with rhythm as well as gesture. The whole farce is witty and light-hearted. The women begin by complaining that they lack entertainment (*esbatement,* which is a pun on *bas*), and end by granting a farewell kiss. One of the men is careful to point out in his *envoi* that no reference is intended to *good* women.

Les Femmes qui font écurer leur chaudron is structurally very similar. Two women complain of sexual frustration, then welcome the tinker who offers to fix their leaky cooking-pots. A cauldron or *marmite* as a sexual metaphor goes back at least to Plautus, so the audience knows what to expect from the title.

When the tinker enters, the women ask him if it is his pleasure (ambiguous) to serve them (ambiguous). He replies: Certainly, but first I need to see: "L'oeuvre où voulez que je besogne"— another ambiguous verb. The first woman assures him:

> Vous n'aurez point vieille besogne,
> Ne qui soit forte à esclarcir

and the second warns him to harden his *broche* so that it doesn't get bent sideways "en nostre ouvraige." (*Broche* must be a specific technical term here, since it usually means "spit.") The tinker is quite offended and says that his *broche* never bends. The second woman, who is more of a fault-finder than the first, warns the tinker not to put in such a small nail that it doesn't stop the hole properly.

The tinker then sets to work on each *chaudron* in turn, encouraged by both women, who cry "Frappez fort!" at intervals. When he's finished with one he remarks that he's sweating and almost out of breath, but then goes on to attend to the other. After that, all three sit down for a friendly drink, while the tinker complacently asks for, and gets, compliments on his workmanship. The play ends after they have agreed to meet again.

This farce must have been more difficult to stage than those mentioned so far. The tinker has more tools at his disposal than the priest or the saddler, and more varied actions to perform: heating, de-rusting, hammering, riveting, polishing. The fun, from the actors' point of view, must be in varying the gestures while keeping them obviously sexual. The taboo-breaking aspect is emphasized here as in other plays by the fact that one man is attending to several women at once, running to and fro, getting tired and breathless. The author was a wit; in his *envoi* the tinker says farewell to the audience "d'amour polie," which means both "polite, noble love" and "polished love," polishing being one of his recent activities with the cooking-pot.

Perhaps the best sexual-action play, *Raoullet Ployart,* was written by the poet Gringoire. Some of the other farces may never have been performed, but this one presumably was, on Shrove Tuesday 1512, with his much more famous *Jeu du Prince des Sotz.* The basic pattern is again the same, but Gringoire was clever enough to find a metaphor which had far more interesting possibilities than saddlery or ironmongery.

The wife, Doublette, begins by complaining that her vineyard is in bad shape. As in all the farces cited here, there is no coy attempt to disguise what the metaphor means. Her husband Raoullet (whose surname Ployart means "bending") replies at once that he worked very hard in it once upon a time. Now, however, if he hoes in it one day his back hurts for the next three, which, says his wife, is the fault of poor tools. She asks that he allow the servant, Mausecret, to work there since he can't. Mausecret says the earth would have to be very thick for *his* spade not to get to the bottom of it, to which Raoullet replies that no one else is going to plant vine-poles (*fischer eschallatz*) except himself. Mausecret then pleads that Doublette needs a workman who can turn over the earth thoroughly. We already have a considerable variety of male metaphors, while the female metaphor remains constant. Mausecret now changes his metaphor startlingly, and exclaims: "You should see how she squeezes the grapes in the wine-press!" (literally, between the cheeks of the wine-press). The metaphors continue to change thus throughout the play. Sexual activity is described as hoeing, digging, planting, putting in poles, layering the vine, working the wine-press, and so forth, since vineyards have to be dug, planted, maintained, and harvested. The interaction of these metaphors is worthy of careful study; sometimes the male symbol changes, sometimes the female, and sometimes both. As in all the sexual farces the male symbols are both more varied and more aggressive than the female. And a few delightfully mixed metaphors add to the comedy, as when Raoullet complains that his spade is bending ("ma besche ploye") or Doublette longs for workmen with eager spades ("des besches friandes").

This was already an excellent comic device, but Gringoire's ingenuity is not exhausted. As well as the vineyard allegory he gives us another in the persons of the two men, Dire and Faire (Saying and Doing), who come to work in it. They first appear talking about the effect of bad weather on the vines. After Raoullet leaves, Doublette agrees to try their skill. She first tries Dire, but he talks all the time and does nothing. Faire, of course, then goes to work and pleases her mightily. He even performs three times, but runs away when Raoullet returns. The end of the play is dramatically disappointing; husband and wife appeal to the Seigneur de Balletreu (another obscene name) who decides that Doublette is in the right. But the association of a familiar expression—"Doing is better than Saying"—with the sexual activity which is the subject of the play is both comic and interesting. Whereas in the farce about the crossbow a comment on words and action was at the same time a statement about male and female rôles, here the jokes about saying and doing have no moral import. Doublette is certainly amoral, but she is using her sexual metaphors for her own satisfaction, not as a weapon against her husband. He is undoubtedly annoyed at the situation, but he is not humiliated or mistreated by the successful "actors."

Indeed, the tone of all these sexual-action plays is very similar. There are no exploiters and no victims (as there are in many of the sexual *fabliaux*, for instance). We can appreciate the naughtiness involved in the breaking of a social taboo, but this naughtiness is mild and witty, not satirical or savage. The authors are making fun of the traditional sexual insatiability of women, but the fun is kind, not cruel. In sharp contrast to the farces which use sexual metaphors as weapons, these plays leave us with the impression that sex is harmless, entertaining, and even good.

IV

The three uses of metaphor discussed here are not fundamentally different. Whether it enables farce characters to discuss recalled or anticipated sex, to win a battle in the war of the sexes, or to simulate sexual intercourse on stage, obscene metaphor serves the same two basic purposes: to circumvent a social and dramatic taboo, and to make the audience laugh. The *farceurs* accomplished both with remarkable skill. The audience was certainly never in doubt about the meaning of the metaphors, and the sexual action farces consequently are hilarious.

In some of these plays (e.g., *La Confession Margot* and *Le Faulconnier de ville*) the author's only aim is to talk about sex with impunity. But in a majority of them, he has other aims in view. *Ragot, Musarde et Babille,* and *Le Proces d'un jeune moine* are literary jokes—parodies of the often serious debate over the active or contemplative life. Most of the sexual-action farces seem to be saying that it is natural for women to be frustrated and natural for them to find satisfaction wherever they can. In the sex-war plays there is a stern moral, although not the traditional Christian one. Family life (and hence society) cannot function unless male and female fulfill the rôles assigned to them.

Most interesting, perhaps, to a modern critic are the sexual metaphors leading to conclusions about action and words, *res* and *verba*. Doublette, like the young girl appealing to Cupid and indeed most of the frustrated women, prefers doing to saying in a specific practical context, but Sibile has made a fundamental mistake about doing and saying. She thought that wisdom meant the action of improving her husband. He first mocks her desire for action by taking her metaphors literally and acting them out, and then shows her that the desire for action is in her case misplaced—women are made for saying, not doing.

Much more critical attention needs to be given to these farces, but it has been the purpose of this brief analysis at least to make clear how very rich and varied they are. Their authors' imaginative manipulation and choice of metaphor show them to be experienced dramatists and poets, very far from the crude and unsophisticated versifiers which they have been claimed to be in the common critical opinion.[10]

NOTES

1 The most recent general work is Halina Lewicka, *Etudes sur l'ancienne farce Française* (Paris: Klincksieck, 1974), which contains a complete list of farces and provides their location (pp. 136-47). A somewhat different list can be found in B. C. Bowen, *Les Caractéristiques essentielles de la farce française, et leur survivance dans les années 1550-1620* (Urbana: University of Illinois Press, 1964), pp. 195-202. All the necessary bibliographic information can be found in these two works.

2 John Velz has discussed the scriptural implications of scatology on *Gammer Gurton's Needle*, in a paper delivered at the Ninth Conference on Medieval Studies at Kalamazoo in 1974. Analogous work on the farce is badly needed.

3 To give a recent example, A. Hindley, the editor of *Ragot, Musarde et Babille* in *RHTh*, 19 (1967), 7-23, apologizes for "son tort le plus grand—l'obscénité," and claims some merits for the play, "si imparfaite ou grossière qu'elle soit."

4 *Le Savetier Audin.*

5 *Les Queues troussées, Les Femmes qui font rembourrer leur bas, Les Femmes qui vendent amourettes, Le Faulconnier de Ville, La Femme à qui son voisin baille un clistoire, La Bragarde et la Goriere, Les Femmes qui font écurer leurs chaudrons, Le Ramonneur, Frere Guillebert, Les Chambrières I, Ragot, Musarde et Babille, Raoullet Ployart, Frere Philibert, Le Proces d'un jeune moine et d'un vieux gendarme,* and *La Confession Margot.*

6 There are several different versions of this play. My quotations are taken from the Recueil Trepperel text.

7 Some are analyzed by E. Philipot, "Notice sur la farce de *Frere Guillebert*," in *Mélanges Mario Roques,* I, 237-41.

8 Heywood imitated this farce in *John-John the Husband,* but the linguistic joke is necessarily lost in English.

9 There are two farces whose titles begin thus. I am quoting the one in the British Library, sensibly designated by Lewicka *Les Chambrières I.*

10 A shorter version of this paper was presented to the Special Session on Fabliau and Farce at the MLA annual meeting in December 1976. I am grateful to the Center for Advanced Study of the University of Illinois for the released time which made the necessary research possible.

Techniques of Transcendence
in Medieval Drama

Robert Edwards

Criticism of medieval drama has for the most part been Aristotelian. The categories of the *Poetics* as well as the structure Aristotle creates for them have shaped the manner in which not only scholars but the general audience view the plays. Implicit in E. K. Chambers' *The Mediaeval Stage* (1903) and Karl Young's *The Drama of the Medieval Church* (1933) is a belief that the plays imitate action and character, and even so radical a study as O. B. Hardison, Jr.'s *Christian Rite and Christian Drama in the Middle Ages* (1965) recurs to Aristotelian bases. Hardison maintains that "in the ninth century the boundary . . . between religious ritual (the services of the Church) and drama did not exist. Religious ritual *was* the drama of the early Middle Ages and had been ever since the decline of the classical theater." As the Mass comes to be viewed as a drama by commentators from the ninth century onwards, the framework of liturgy also becomes dramatic so that "in one sense, at least, the Easter liturgy is a transitional phase between the sacred drama of the Mass and liturgical drama." "Its descending action begins with Lent. The point of crisis is reached on Good Friday, and Holy Saturday and Easter Sunday are devoted to the entombment and Resurrection, respectively." The model for this larger structure is Gilbert Murray's concept of the ritual form of Greek tragedy whose Aristotelian orientation Hardison calls "obvious from its terms."[1]

Although Hardison does not go so far as to break down his study into such parts as plot, character, thought, diction, music, and spectacle, these Aristotelian elements are consistently apparent in the book. He tends to accept Aristotle's notion of tragedy as the imitation of an action which is "serious, complete, and of a certain magnitude" as well as what was believed to be Aris-

103

totle's history of the development of tragedy. At the time Hardison's study was published, Gerald Else's *The Origin and Early Form of Greek Tragedy* (1967) was questioning the authenticity and accuracy of that development. Classical scholarship has moved away from the notion of tragedy's having arisen from ritual, and this reversal should be a caution to one's uncritical acceptance of the view that medieval drama arose directly from Church ritual. For Else, Greek tragedy arises out of certain social conditions and the genius of two playwrights—Thespis and Aeschylus. Else does not question the notion of mimesis in tragedy and only implicitly, on historical grounds, does he question the hierarchy of the six elements of tragedy. His acceptance of the new date for the writing of *The Suppliant Maidens* (467 B.C.) counteracts the importance which Aristotle gives to character and conversely stresses the importance of music and spectacle.[2] This reversal is even more apparent in what is thought to be an even later play, *Prometheus Bound*. Aristotle relegates this play to the fourth and lowest category of tragedy, the tragedy of spectacle. "The interest of such a play," Hardison rightly notes in his commentary on the *Poetics,* "is its appeal, written or performed, to the visual imagination."[3] Critics of medieval drama who must deal with the unique event of redemption through Christ's death and resurrection are forced to go beyond Else's questioning of the development of drama. They must question drama as an exclusively mimetic form and reconsider the place which Aristotle gives to spectacle. In so doing, it will pay them to view drama along the lines suggested by both phenomenology and structuralism. The absence of expressly articulated theories makes these approaches necessary to understand the affective and intrinsic features of the form.

I

The drama Aristotle outlines is based upon the belief that the action being imitated can be repeated. His tragedy develops according to the laws of necessity and probability, and its shape follows the demands of credibility rather than veracity. Logical syllogism takes the place of revealed truth as the measure of a work. One might find these terms acceptable for an art that wishes to remain secular, but for medieval drama the view has generally been that the art aims at transcendence. Such an aim

is apparent in the stress early medieval drama places on spectacle and music in its directions for the visual and aural features
of the plays. The notion of transcendence in a form which at no
time completely relinquishes mimetic character suggests that
critics look for a basis for drama in something that allows imitated action to move beyond time. But in pursuing that suggestion which is primarily phenomenological, one should always
keep clear a distinction between the dramatic and drama. The
dramatic deals with tension between two forces, and its effect is
to elicit the kind of interest Murray finds in the *agon* of the
ritual form. Drama is a sophisticated art form whose diverse elements presumably contribute to a single, overall impression.
Foremost among its elements is a sense of the dramatic, but this
sense in isolation does not add up to the complexity of the form
any more than impersonation defines the totality of drama.
Young's notion that drama begins with "impersonation" is
guilty of mistaking a part for the whole. Impersonation, for
example, exists in the rhetorical practices of the *suasoriae* or
speeches where students assume roles in order to persuade usually famous men from taking the historical actions they did; it
continues in the advocate role that is part of ecclesiastical as well
as civil courts. Yet no one would argue that any of these impersonations adds up to drama.

Nor should one abandon for the moment the value of Aristotle's definition of a play as an action complete of itself, having
beginning, middle, and end, dealing with human beings, and
involving some change in state. Even when the characters are
gods, angels, abstractions, or animals, they are presented in
humanized forms. One should, however, qualify this definition
with Else's view that the degeneration of one form does not lead
into the consummation of a second. Drama is created by an
artist. James Joyce's *A Portrait of the Artist as a Young Man*
(1914) asserts that for such an artist "the dramatic form is
reached when the vitality which has flowed and eddied round
each person fills every person with such vital force that he or
she assumes a proper and intangible esthetic life. . . . The artist,
like the God of the creation, remains within or behind or beyond
or above his handiwork, invisible, refined out of existence, indifferent, paring his fingernails."4 Earlier, Friedrich Nietzsche's
The Birth of Tragedy (1872) had made drama the product of
the writer's ability to contemplate: "At bottom the esthetic

phenomenon is simple: if a man merely has the faculty of seeing perpetual vitality around him, of living continually surrounded by hosts of spirits, he will be a poet. If he but feels the impulse to transform himself and to speak from out the bodies and souls of others, he will be a dramatist."5

But if this is the case for the artist, the case for his audience is somewhat different. The audience reacts to drama by recognizing its form. If ritualistic elements are present in early medieval drama, they may be present because the dramatist hinges the acceptance of his drama to the recognition of these elements and not because drama represented a disintegration of these elements from another form. The intent of drama differs from that of liturgy just as it differs from the intent of several other art forms. One must also bear in mind that medieval drama is not a nascent genre. Drama had existed before, and it is clear from the writings of the Church Fathers that they had some acquaintance with its texts if not its performance. The history of drama, however, does seem to preclude an awareness on the audience's part of drama as a genre; for, although there remains a language for drama, theater disappears at the end of the classical period and reemerges only in the tenth and eleventh centuries. Rosemary Woolf's *The English Mystery Plays* (1972) shows that "spectacle" is a viable concept from St. Paul through St. Bernard. Paul speaks of martyrdom as a spectacle for the heavenly audience, while Tertullian redirects the notion so that spectacle focuses on the torments of the damned. Rabanus Maurus follows this tradition, whereas Bernard speaks of a *bonus ludus* for heavenly spectators.6 E. R. Curtius' *European Literature and the Latin Middle Ages* (1948) demonstrates that the theatrical metaphor "reached the Middle Ages from pagan Antiquity and the Christian writers. Both sources mingled in late Antiquity" and are revived and developed by John of Salisbury's *Policraticus* in the twelfth century.7 Along with this tradition of viewing spiritual life as spectacle, there is a use of classical dramatists such as Plautus and Terence as stylistic models in the Middle Ages. St. Jerome affirms that reading Plautus made the Hebrew prophets seem crude,8 and this continuing possibility of speaking in dramatic terms permits the medieval dramatist the recognition and acceptance of his form.

One of the commonplaces of medieval thought was Augustine's belief that knowledge of God was innate in one's memory

(*Confessions*, Bk. 8), and the issue of memory emerges as one of the avenues introduced into the theories of medieval drama. In this connection three books will prove useful: Frances Yates' *The Art of Memory* (1966), Boethius' *De institutione musica* (A.D. 525), and Gaston Bachelard's *The Poetics of Reverie* (1960). Miss Yates discusses memory techniques as they evolved in the ancient world and continued through the Renaissance. Central to her discussion is the parable of Simonides which Cicero and Quintillian relate. Simonides was commissioned to write a poem for a banquet. The poem digressed into praise of Castor and Pollux, and Simonides was given half the sum originally agreed upon and told to collect the balance from the twin gods. Later, during the banquet he was summoned outdoors by two young men who wished to see him. As soon as he passed the threshold, the roof collapsed. The bodies of the guests inside were so maimed that they could not be identified for proper burial. However, Simonides remembered where each guest sat in relation to the other and so was able to identify them. Miss Yates neglects to point out that Castor and Pollux, the twin gods united in love, symbolize the joining of the divine to the worldly. Yet in observing that memory techniques can reduce action occurring in time to an image or sequence of fixed images, she touches on a major concern for Christian drama. In order to achieve transcendence, the drama must move past time and reorder the flow of narrative which in itself establishes a kind of time scheme. In mnemonics this reordering would be visual. The worldly image dissolves into the Eternal form. A scene like the Betrayal of Christ set in historical time is meant to evoke the sacred or transhistorical through the same kind of leap that bound Castor and Pollux. From a sequence of these images a sense of Christian history develops, and its memory techniques do not work against the principles of Aristotelian imitation so much as adapt the imitation to new purposes. In this regard, one will find useful Hardison's suggestion that a drama based on spectacle would be episodic rather than continuous, a series of discrete dissolutions whose impact would be cumulative reinforcement. The images of memory underlie those episodes in the way iconic scenes underlie the miniature cycles of Christian art. Much as this art uses the devices of condensation, conflation, and omission to create its scenes yet retains a sense of narrative development, the drama relies on the fixed images of memory to add a vertical dimension to the horizontal movement of mimesis.

Many of these images, as early dramas suggest, evolve from painting. The Montecassino Passion, for example, uses models from the visual arts for such scenes as the betrayal, Peter's denial, the trial before Pilate, and Judas' repentance.9 Fletcher Collins' *The Production of Medieval Church Music-Drama* (1972) indicates similar ties between the dramas and iconography of the twelfth and thirteenth centuries in regard to character, costume, and the division of scenes. He concludes of a work like the Rouen shepherds' play that "there was tacit agreement among graphic artists and playwrights as to major episodes of a story."10 Painting itself was looked upon as having *verba-res* connections, and the defenses of the pictorial arts against its various detractors stressed both mimetic and mnemonic functions for painting. These defenses saw the mimetic level of icons giving way to symbolic levels in a series of transcendences which culminates in anagogic truth. By imitating Christian history, painting served the purpose of educating the illiterate and enforcing orthodoxy. At the same time, icons could effect changes which were not mimetic. These changes were recollective of Divine immanence. In popular devotion, icons became associated with miracles and the "pictorial rendering of the living form was able to inherit the virtues of the relic and to gain an equal, and eventually more than equal, importance." Such importance derives in large part from the rationale of Pseudo-Dionysus for whom "the entire world of the senses in all its variety reflects the world of the spirit. Contemplation of the former serves as a means to elevate ourselves toward the latter."11

Closely related to this view of mnemonics and its transcendence would be the medieval view of music. Derived generally from Boethius' *De institutione musica,* the view emphasizes music as a *speculum* or mirror of the universal order. It divided music among three kinds: *in instrumentis constitua, musica humana,* and *musica mundana.* By a kind of sympathetic vibration based on numbers, man would be tied to a reaction which, in the first instance, is to the harmony of sounds; in the second, to the harmony of relationships like body and soul; and in the last, the *musica mundana,* to a harmony with the entire universe. Thus, as medieval drama incorporated music in its structure, it did so also as a means of possible transcendence through numbers. This transcendence through *ratio* would parallel that essayed by the mnemonic tokens and complement the hierarchy of meanings given to language in *verba-res* treatises, just as the interpretation of the words could be on a literal, moral, or anagogic level. Again, since the highest music was not to be considered mimetic, the inclusion of music as it essayed the universal would be a nonmimetic device.

The medieval dramatist in writing for an audience inexperienced in such forms would be moved by knowledge of prior dramas to rely on widely accessible "dramatic" analogues like dream, reverie, and liturgy in translating his vision into drama. None of these analogues is exactly identical to drama. For instance, in dream, as in drama, an action is projected before a subject. In both, this action is "a virtual present, an order of direct apparition."12 Scenes shift, time shifts but always in anticipation and never in logical sequence. The dreamer is central but he is a passive observer rather than a participant. Conversely in reverie, as in drama, there is activity on the part of the dreamer. There is a willing suspension of disbelief and a willingness to change scenes and time as needed. Bachelard's *Poetics of Reverie* distinguishes reverie from dream by arguing that the images of reverie are directed toward the future rather than simply determined by the past. Reverie, like drama, allows speculation in areas where dreams can be only psycho-therapeutic. "Imagination attempts to have a future," Bachelard iterates. "There is *futurism* in any dreamed universe." Cosmic reveries "situate us in a world and not in a society. The cosmic reverie possesses a sort of stability or tranquility. It helps us escape time. It is a *state*."13 The Harrowing of Hell plays adumbrate one aspect of cosmic reverie by showing how one can attain, in Bachelard's phrase, "a world in which we should like to live." In creating the possibility of this world, reverie establishes a positive psychology through the drama.

Most criticism of medieval drama has substituted dogma for such a psychology of the plays and contented itself with mentioning the awe and terror that scenes from Christian history must have aroused in the medieval audience. Yet reverie is not drama, for drama has a complete action whereas reverie's action need not be complete; drama involves human beings and requires a change in state while reverie does not necessarily involve either. The character and action of drama are made up and controlled by the dramatist not the dreamer. As reverie approaches these qualities, it approaches drama. Moreover, one suspects from Bachelard's study that an audience would have reacted to pieces like the Harrowing of Hell plays in a somewhat different fashion and that their response would have to do with specific intentions for the drama. Christian drama in the Middle Ages brings to the exterior those memories of God which Augustine finds innate in man and it organizes the narrative of Christian history around transcending images. The drama aims to resolve the dialectic of inner and outer lives and of the worldly and the divine by permitting a closure that sacralizes action and language in the world. In sacralizing action and language, much as monastic life attempts to sanctify time, early medieval drama reflects the differing situations of the classical and the Christian playwright. The classical dramatist must create plot, character, and thought and give them the kind of logical form which Sophocles gives to the Oedipus myth; the Christian dramatist receives these elements from his history, and his work consequently tends toward spectacle that expresses mystery rather than rational demonstration. Yet, however much it expresses mystery, such a drama would have to be mimetic of previous forms in order to be recognized and responded to.

The unity which drama attains distinguishes it as well from liturgy. As Romano Guardini maintains in "The Spirit of the Liturgy" (1935), Church ritual is an autonomous form which enlists faith but is not created or validated by successive acts of belief. The liturgy offers a world, "rich in types and symbols," which is timeless, whereas drama has a time-centered world which it aims to escape. Theorists who would see Christian drama deriving from liturgy by the use of liturgical elements in early medieval drama both argue against the fundamental nature of liturgy and ignore the possibility that the dramatist may be using liturgy as a device to introduce dramatic structures to an audience which had little or no experience of them. This second reason would account for the disappearance of liturgical elements as dramatists could expect experience of previous dramas from their audiences. Here one can see the wisdom of Else's proposition that a disintegrating form does not lead into a second form.

II

Just as one kind of transcendence in medieval drama is

achieved through spectacle, a second kind is achieved through action. This kind of transcendence is perhaps best interpreted through structural analysis. The twelfth-century *Jeu d'Adam* contains in its primal scene a model for the action of transcendence in the later mystery cycles. This transcendence centers on the breakdown of human kinship systems which would replace divinely instituted ones. As Erich Auerbach noted in his essay on "Adam and Eve," the kinship between Adam and Eve is ordained, and Eve would break the tie which united her to Adam and both of them to God. The intervention of the serpent and his advice to Eve "upset the order of things established by God, it makes the woman the man's master, and so leads both to ruin."[14] Adam acknowledges this break with divine kinship when he accepts the apple from Eve and says to her, "tu es ma per." His subsequent anger and deeper understanding of the break come to reveal the impossibility of establishing a human counterpart to divine order:

> Ne me ferat ja nul aïe
> For le filz que istra de Marie.
> Ne sai de nus prendre conroi,
> Quant a Deu ne portames foi.

("No one will help me now except the Son who will come forth from Mary. To no one can I turn for protection, since in God we kept no faith.")[15] Adam's speech, which first appears to be a dramatic anachronism, defines the terms of transcendence. The de-creation of kinship in human ties which parallels the dissolution of literal levels in spectacle permits the analogous transcendence.

Nevertheless, the de-creation of kinship in the action of medieval drama must occur within the framework of a second, viable system of kinship. In illustrating the problematics and repeated collapses of human institutions, the playwright has to preserve his own co-eval kinship with his audience. Language provides a means for this preservation. As anthropologists like Claude Lévi-Strauss assert, language systems are based on an original incest prohibition which occurs when the self and the Other are differentiated and a need for mediation begins. In theological terms, this original condition of undifferentiated Creator/created exists between Deity and man and collapses with original sin. Its restoration is possible only through Christ,

the Logos. In the exchange systems of language, objects which
are intended as tokens must be distinguished from the objects
themselves. Tokens are displaced images and their values de-
rive from recalling the sources of the image. Their purpose is to
maintain a relationship between exchangers rather than accumu-
late objects. Therefore, the actual possession of what tokens
represent would violate the nature of their mediating function,
for possession precludes exchange.

The syntax of such tokens as either sentences or art forms
based on linguistic building is agreed upon by playwright and
audience. To this extent, the syntax has a social rather than
biological basis. In medieval drama, such social agreements within the kinship of language permit in cycle plays what normally
might be unthinkable—the dissolution of the Christian polity.
In visualizing this dissolution, the playwright undertakes to
appease the expectations of his audience in regard to closure.
If he does not, a violation preventing communication might
result. In an Aristotelian poetics, closure would involve the
completion of an action and a change in the situation of the
drama, but for the medieval dramatist, the movement has to do
with an accepted psychological return rather than a syllogistic
progression. The dissolving of human ties returns man to pre-
history and a recollection of his primal undifferentiated state.
The demise of language becomes the expression of this return,
and the systems of silence that such a demise adumbrates preserve
the union of audience and playwright. In order to achieve this
silence, the playwright has to dissolve what is the normal boundary between the spaces of art and life, much as more recently
cubism has essayed a similar dissolution. As Clement Greenberg's "Collage" (1959) points out of synthetic cubism, the
art form must retain its two dimensional qualities while extending itself into space. Such intrusion by art into life space is precisely the intrusion intended by religious drama into the lives
of its audience.[16]

In dissolving boundaries and retaining a sense of artificiality
and convention, medieval drama breaks the limits necessary for
imitation and raises the possibility of infinite enlargement to
counter what Bachelard terms "Platonic dialectics of large and
small." In place of such dialectics, art and the drama of the
Middle Ages create "external" and "internal" situations. "Le
propre du théâtre," Paul Zumthor argues in his *Essai de poétique*

médiévale (1972), "est d'accentuer fortement la 'situation externe' du texte, résultant des rapports qui s'établissent entre celui-ci et l'auditeur-spectateur: à la limite, la 'situation interne' produite par les références propres du texte, pourrait n'être plus perçue. D'où l'équivocité du théâtre, à la fois plus 'réel' que la poésie narrative, et plus évidemment fonctionnel puisque la réalité perçue du matériau (espace, personnes) tend à effacer l'impression de réalité provoquée par le texte: ce double caractère (qu'avaient senti les rhétoriciens antiques lorsqu'ils distinguaient entre les degrés d'immédiateté de l'action) explique peut-être le fait que l'opposition chant *vs* nonchant soit neutralisée dans le 'théâtre'."17 This double character, again, lies at the basis of a non-Aristotelian poetics in the drama and reflects its mnemonic features. The internal situation created by the text is the source of imitation for plot, character, and thought. Yet it is once more in the external situation of diction, music, and spectacle that language makes its full connections. There the drama moves past the limitations of mimesis and relates to the larger expectations and memory of the audience.

As Greenberg suggests of synthetic cubist art, once the boundaries of internal and external have been destroyed the possibility of infinite repetition exists. Medieval cycle plays, at least in theme, make use of this possibility. The repetition of various kinds of kinship dissolutions often becomes a connecting thread between segments and establishes a typological unity in the cycles. The killing of Abel as he performs sacrifice in a system of exchange with God illustrates the continuing Fall of man from Divine will and the dissolution of familial bonds. The Isaac plays deal with a similar, though sublimated, violence which is avoided only by God's intervention; the plays further subvert the structure of human kinship in identifying Abraham with God and Isaac with Christ. Noah's wife recapitulates Eve in her refusal to accept the delegated authority of her husband. God's monologue in the Towneley Noah play emphasizes the inherent contradiction of human kinship. He says, "I haue maide all thyng that is liffand, / Duke, emperour, and kyng with myne awne hand" and so "Man must luf me paramoure, / by reson, and repent."18 His speech distinguishes the roles these figures play in institutions from the bond which they must establish with God as men. Thus when Noah emerges from the ark, he notices immediately that the implements of a culture founded on kinship and the castles and towns have been swept away. The dissolution of human polity is even more apparent in the plays about the slaughter of the Innocents where the power of the state and its king is directed against its children.

The Jacob play from the Towneley cycle deals specifically with the issues of kinship and exchange. The first scene focuses on the relation of man to God mediated by language and exchange, and God's appearance to Jacob in sleep is evidence of the implicit distance between Creator and created as well as the singular relation between them. Even God's promise, "I shall thi seede multiply" (v. 19), refers to the singular bond which Jacob hopes to maintain by exchanging tokens. "This stone," he says when he awakes, "I rayse in sygne to day/ shall I hold holy kirk for ay" (vv. 55-6). The later wrestling reaffirms the bond of Deity, and Jacob is told, "In tokynyng that thou spekis with me,/ I shall toche now thi thee" (vv. 89-90). The reaffirmation of this bond provides the context for the play's subsequent scenes. Jacob in effect exchanges Rachel when he sends her to the rear company of his forces for safety, much as he had earlier exchanged presents with Esau. Yet it is only after the kinship with God has been established by mutual tokens that Jacob is able to find reconciliation with Esau. In these terms, the bonds of family are a consequence of Jacob's bond with God, rather than an inducement to it.[19]

Rosemary Woolf offers one view about the cycle plays when she maintains, "It is clear that the main principle was historical, not typological: that is the events were chosen for their importance in a historical sequence, and not in the first place because they foreshadow the Redemption" (p. 61). Though the plays do establish some typological connections with each other, these links and the historical principle behind the selection of plays suggest the concept of cycle is itself problematic. Christian history is linear rather than cyclical. "Its central doctrine of the Crucifixion," says G. J. Whitrow in *The Nature of Time* (1972), "was regarded as a unique event in time not subject to repetition, and so implied that time must be linear and not cyclic."[20] The redemption may rectify original sin but it cannot deny the fact of original sin and the subsequent break between man and Deity which leads to the differentiation of the self and the Other. Thus history moves from the Fall to the Last Judgment and from the emergence of a secular world to transcendence to a divine world. Jerome Taylor sees the plays imitating "the history of God's wonders, that is, of his responses, specifically, to man's defections from the divine Monarchy and Law to man's consequent social, familial, and personal disintegrity."21 This progression would admit only one variety of kinship—the relation of the soul to God whose terms Dante's *Paradiso* (III.85) specifies in saying, "la sua volontate è nostra pace." In this manner, the direction of the plays explains what Miss Woolf calls the "oddity of Corpus Christi cycles ending with the Last Judgment. . . . The Last Judgment is a penitential theme which arouses fear not delight" (p. 71). In ending with the dissolution of the secular world and its kinships, the sequence of dramas in the later Middle Ages carries out in its action the separate dissolutions of spectacle in the dramatic form itself.

Such a drama modifies the notion of completion in an Aristotelian poetics. If one sees the discrete episodes of the Corpus Christi play reverberating to a culmination, much as Hardison suggests drama based on spectacle would, and interprets the build-up in musical rather than logical structures, one can see how Taylor's position of recurrent themes will resolve in an action which is completed by transcending the possibility of further recurrence. The Last Judgment, which ends history and thereby the possibility of recurrence, does not allow repetition. In a medieval Passion play, Christ the man transcends by means of his sacrifice into the second person of the Trinity. In some plays, a final mystical song, usually liturgical in origin, amplifies the movement from the internal to the external situation of the drama and provides the shift from temporal to eternal. Once out of time, each event is continuous rather than discrete and exists in a universe of harmony that has no need of syntax or linguistic building. This is the nature of action in medieval drama, as it had been the purpose of spectacle. Like symbol, spectacle and action dissolve into meaning.

One must therefore qualify the sense of integrity conveyed by Aristotle's definition of drama and bring it nearer the definition of unity in art that John Dewey proposes in *Art as Experience* (1934). Aristotelian categories maintain a separation between the internal and external elements of drama, and the confounding of these elements by medieval drama makes necessary the search for a different basis of unity. Dewey softens the rigidly formal elements and proposes that unity in art results

from various fusions, including those of "fringe" elements outside the art work. This unity of internal and external terminates
only with the presence of a problematic situation that forces a
break by creating a discontinuous counter quality of discrimination or analysis. In medieval drama, the break often comes with
a reversal of rhythms as the momentum of man's action forcing
back upon itself a reception of God's judgment recovers from its
passive state and embarks upon new action. This post-history
of grace or punishment marks the closure of the art form. Thus
the audience of the *Jeu d'Adam,* having been put in awe by
God's judgment and received the promise of redemption of his
Prophets, concludes the play by dissociating itself from Adam's
fate and deciding on their own ordinary actions.

NOTES

1 (Baltimore: Johns Hopkins Press, 1965), pp. viii, 82, 83, 285.

2 Martin Classical Lectures, XX (Cambridge, Mass.: Harvard Univ. Press, 1967).

3 *Aristotle's Poetics,* ed. Leon Golden and O. B. Hardison, Jr. (Englewood
Cliffs: Prentice-Hall, 1968), p. 236. Stephen Orgel explores the relation of visual
image to language in Renaissance theories in "The Poetics of Spectacle," *New
Literary History,* 2 (1971), 367-89.

4 (New York: Viking, 1964), p. 215.

5 *The Birth of Tragedy from the Spirit of Music,* tr. Clifton Fadiman, in *The
Philosophy of Nietzsche,* ed. Willard H. Wright (New York: Modern Library, 1927),
p. 988. I have chosen the Fadiman translation over the translation by Walter Kauf-
mann (*The Birth of Tragedy and the Case of Wagner* [New York: Vintage Books,
1967]) because Fadiman echoes Joyce's language.

6 (Berkeley and Los Angeles: Univ. of California Press), p. 31.

7 Tr. Willard R. Trask (1953; rpt. New York: Harper and Row, 1963), pp.
138-39.

8 See A. H. M. Jones, "The Social Background of the Struggle between Paganism and Christianity," in *The Conflict between Paganism and Christianity in the
Fourth Century,* ed. Arnaldo Momigliano (Oxford: Clarendon Press, 1963), pp.
17-37.

9 See Robert Edwards, "Iconography and the Montecassino Passion," *Comparative Drama,* 6 (1972), 274-93.

10 (Charlottesville: University Press of Virginia), p. 10.

11 Ernst Kitzinger, "The Cult of Images in the Age before Iconoclasm,"
Dumbarton Oaks Papers, no. 8 (1954), pp. 116, 121.

12 Susanne Langer, "A Note on the Film," in *Film: A Montage of Theories,*
ed. Richard Dyer McCann (New York: Dutton, 1966), p. 201.

13 Tr. Daniel Russell (Boston: Beacon Press, 1969), pp. 8, 14.

14 In *Mimesis: The Representation of Reality in Western Literature,* tr. Willard R. Trask (Garden City: Doubleday, 1957), p. 130.

15 *Le Jeu d'Adam (Ordo representacionis Ade),* ed. Willem Noomen, CFMA, no. 99 (Paris: Champion, 1971), vv. 313, 381-84. The translation is the same as Trask's (p. 137).

16 A comparable link between analytic cubism and medieval art is suggested in Georges Lemaitre, *From Cubism to Surrealism in French Literature* (Cambridge, Mass.: Harvard Univ. Press, 1947): "The simultaneous juxtaposition in the same picture of aspects which can only be perceived successively in time was not altogether an innovation in the history of painting. During the Middle Ages it was not unusual to behold, all in one composition, illustrating, for instance, the life of a saint, first perhaps the spectacle of the saint undergoing picturesque maceration in solitude, then the scene of his trial before a wicked judge, and then the gruesome display of his martyrdom; he might even sometimes be shown performing a few edifying miracles after his death" (p. 83).

17 (Paris: Editions du Seuil), p. 431.

18 *The Towneley Plays,* ed. George England, EETS, e.s., 71 (1897; rpt. Oxford: Oxford Univ. Press, 1966), p. 25, vv. 73-81.

19 The wounding of Jacob's thigh, the emphasis on names, and the alternating bonds with God and a family structure suggest certain parallels with the Oedipus myth discussed in Lévi-Strauss' *Structural Anthropology,* tr. Claire Jacobson and Brooke Grundfest Schoepf (Garden City: Doubleday, 1967), pp. 202-28.

20 (New York: Holt, Rinehart, and Winston), p. 14.

21 "The Dramatic Structure of the Middle English Corpus Christi, or Cycle, Plays," in Bernice Slote, ed., *Literature and Society* (Lincoln: University of Nebraska Press, 1964); rpt. in *Medieval English Drama: Essays Critical and Contextual,* ed. Jerome Taylor and Alan H. Nelson, Patterns of Literary Criticism, 11 (Chicago: Univ. of Chicago Press, 1972), p. 153.

Narrative Bible Cycles in Medieval Art and Drama

Patrick J. Collins

In order to account for the distinctive selection and arrangement of episodes in the Corpus Christi cycles, critics have usually turned to the general liturgy of the church, to the corpus of Latin liturgical drama, to the ecclesiastical documents promoting the establishment of Corpus Christi as an official church holiday, or to the liturgy with which the feast is celebrated. In this paper I want to propose that it is the traditional selection of biblical episodes in the pictorial art of the Middle Ages which best accounts for the subject matter and chronological pattern of the later English mystery cycles.

There are four major extant mystery cycles: the plays of York, Chester, Wakefield, and N-town. The four cycles are characterized by a selection of episodes which recount events from the books of Genesis and Exodus, from the Nativity and Passion periods of Christ's life, from the post-Resurrection miracles, and from the prophesied events of the Doom. The cycles are further characterized by the chronological order in which the biblical scenes are dramatized. It cannot be said, however, that there is any rigid "Corpus Christi" format to which each cycle subscribes, for while the cycles are similar in their selection of episodes, they are not isomorphic. The N-town cycle alone includes a large number of plays dealing with the apocryphal life of Mary; Chester, in its treatment of the public ministry, lacks a play of the Baptism of Christ, although it is the only cycle to stage the Cleansing of the Temple; Towneley has a more richly developed Old Testament prologue than the York cycle, but stages far fewer New Testament episodes. Even the length of the cycles varies from city to city: Chester's cycle consists of twenty-four pageants; York stages forty-eight; Wakefield, thirty-two; and the N-town cycle contains forty-two pageants. Moreover, in all four cycles there are episodes with only marginal dramatic value (the Visitation or the Purification), while Biblical episodes with great potential dramatic interest (the Old Testament tales of Joseph or Job) are never dramatized. Thus any description of the subject matter within the four major English cycles must take into account the consistent presence of certain episodes as well as the consistent absence of others. It must recognize that the cycle form includes a great deal of variation among the extant cycles with regard to selection of episodes, treatment of themes, and number of plays.

The evidence which this study will present demonstrates that the Creation-to-Doom format of the vernacular drama was not a child of the Corpus Christi feast, nor of the liturgy which surrounded it.[1] Rather, it had its roots in pictorial representations of the significant events in the history of man's salvation. Although the late medieval playmakers needed a pattern with which to shape their dramatic pageants, it is misleading to maintain that they adopted patterns of liturgical drama similar to the display recorded at Cividale in the beginning of the fourteenth century.[2] The entire force of the evidence indicates that the pictorial scenes in the wall-paintings and in the manuscripts of thirteenth- and fourteenth-century England provide a pattern which is both analogous to and prior to the earliest cycles of either Latin or vernacular drama. More than this, it is reasonable to conclude that the Creation-to-Doom depictions of Bible history embodied in art schemes throughout England engendered a conception of world history which subsequently permeated the mind of medieval man. The narrative pictorial model provided the medieval communities with a traditional outline of biblical events upon which their dramatic craftsmen could readily draw. We shall see that the forces which shaped the pictorial tradition account for standardization as well as variation of subject matter, inclusion as well as exclusion, intensive development as well as a widespread distribution.

In proposing this relationship I am reversing the more usual claim that the influence is one of drama on art. Many studies by art historians call attention to the impact of medieval drama upon the iconography of the contemporary art; and the studies of Émile Mâle, in particular, focus upon shifts in contemporary iconography which are attributable to the popularity of theatrical

activities.3 Recently Professor Otto Pächt, in a series of essays
particularly relevant to this present study, has again raised the
question of the drama's influence upon medieval art. Through
an analysis of the full-page miniatures of the St. Albans Psalter
(c. 1120), executed by an artist of exceptional talent known as
the Alexis Master, Pächt argues that the sudden revival in
England of large, pictorial cycles illustrating the highlights of
salvation history was prompted by the growing popularity of
dramatic representations of biblical episodes in the liturgical
plays of the Christmas and Easter seasons.4 The impulse for the
twelfth-century revival of pictorial story-telling—the arrangement of a sequence of biblical episodes into a coherent narrative—derives from the expanding story lines of contemporary
Latin drama:

> the revival of story-telling in the twelfth century started
> with an enactment of spoken narrative in visual form and
> . . . it is only later that we find pictorial narrative gradually
> proceeding from the literal transcription of words to the
> visual realization of scenes and actions.5

The "literal transcription of words" accounts for the marked
changes in iconographic formulas; but Pächt also argues that
the re-emergence of a style of pictorial narrative was decisively
influenced by the church's presentation of Bible history as a
staged drama.

While conceding the probability that Pächt's thesis is correct, this study will nevertheless argue that the Middle English
Corpus Christi cycles were heavily influenced by the accom-
plishments of the pictorial tradition. It is quite reasonable to
assume that the medieval artists attempted to duplicate what
they witnessed in the plays; but it is just as reasonable to assume
that the sponsors of the dramatic and processional activities of
the Middle Ages imitated pictorial patterns found in countless
manuscripts, murals, and sculptures. This study reverses the
common assumption of dramatic influence on art, and argues
that in the selection and arrangement of biblical episodes it was
the art which had the decisive influence upon the drama.

Pächt's studies note that the twelfth-century pictorial cycles
represent a revival rather than an entirely new phenomenon.
Although there is compelling evidence indicating the influence
of the Latin liturgical plays, it is important to note that Pächt

limits the influence of the church drama to a certain few scenes in the Easter cycle and, more tentatively, to a few episodes in the Epiphany cycle. The St. Albans cycle as a whole, with its selection of biblical material ranging from the creation to the post-Resurrection events, cannot be attributed to the influence of contemporary drama. As Pächt himself conceded: "it would be risky to embark on a hypothesis which would attempt to explain the whole miniature cycle in terms of the mystery plays."[6] We know that the extant liturgical dramas of the twelfth-century period fail to provide anything near the comprehensive model of creation-to-doom scope. In any one geographic area the corpus of liturgical plays was severely limited,[7] and even if it had been possible for the Alexis Master to travel the length and breadth of the European continent in order to view each type of twelfth-century church drama, he would still lack theatrical models for the greater part of the pictorial cycle. The entire repertoire of Latin drama, whether in a single location or throughout the continent, cannot account for the selection of episodes which appear in the St. Albans Psalter's pictorial cycle. That selection, as we shall see, was a tradition that pre-dated the rise of church drama.

I

The decoration of the St. Albans Psalter, commissioned for the anchoress Christina of Markyate, includes forty full-page miniatures, depicting the following biblical scenes:

> The Fall
> The Expulsion from Paradise
> The Annunciation
> The Visitation
> The Nativity
> The Annunciation to the Shepherds
> The Magi before Herod
> The Magi guided by the star
> The Adoration of the Magi
> The Dream of the Magi
> The Return of the Magi
> The Presentation in the Temple
> The Flight into Egypt
> The Massacre of the Innocents
> The Return from Egypt
> The Baptism
> The First Temptation

The Second Temptation
The Third Temptation
Christ in the House of Simon the Pharisee
The Entry into Jerusalem
The Washing of the Feet
Christ in the Garden of Gethsemane
Christ and the Sleeping Apostles
The Last Supper
The Betrayal
The Mocking
The Flagellation
Pilate washes his Hands
The Carrying of the Cross
The Descent from the Cross
The Entombment
The Harrowing of Hell
The Three Maries at the Sepulchre
Mary Magdalene announces the Resurrection to the Apostles
The Incredulity of St. Thomas
The Legend of St. Martin in two scenes
The Ascension
Pentecost
David as a Musician

The full-page miniatures are followed by a series of tinted drawings:

Scenes from the Life of St. Alexis
Christ on the Road to Emmaus
Christ Breaking Bread at Emmaus
Christ Disappearing from the Table
Two Knights locked in a combat symbolising the allegorical
   struggle between good and evil[8]

The Alexis Master's prefatory cycle can be seen as a part of the general twelfth-century intellectual renaissance with its enlargement of vision and revival of learning. Although it is true that the Ottonian schools of the tenth and eleventh centuries executed series of manuscript illuminations in a monumental style which drew upon early Christian cycles of biblical stories, the Ottonian painting is, nevertheless, characterized by an almost total concentration on New Testament episodes, especially those with great liturgical significance. The English revival of pictorial cycles in the twelfth-century, by contrast, produced several examples of prefatory cycles comprised of Old and New Testament episodes; and, because of the fresh interest in the drama of Christ's life, the cycles included episodes of little liturgical import.[9]

Several features of the St. Albans picture cycle warrant attention. The custom of placing a series of Bible illustrations before the text of the psalms seems to be English in origin.[10] The earliest extant example of a Psalter with preliminary Bible pictures is the British manuscript B.M. MS. Cotton C. VI, a work which is considerably older than the St. Albans Psalter, and which we must soon examine in greater detail. The combination of both Old and New Testament scenes within the St. Albans Psalter results in a sequence which tells the story of man's fall and of his subsequent redemption. Indeed, the subject of the last full-page miniature—David as a Musician—alludes by means of its iconography to the events surrounding the Last Judgment. The St. Albans Psalter's portrayal of David as a musician (a variation on a pictorial convention used in Latin Psalters from the eighth to eleventh centuries)[11] incorporates the iconographic symbols of the blessed and the damned—a sheep and a goat—into the scene. The animals allude to the bibical prophecy concerning the Last Judgment, and they are analogous to the allegorical clash between good and evil represented by the two armed knights. As Pächt confirms:

> A picture which, though not actually representing the Last Judgment, contains at least a reference to it, would also be well suited to terminate the pictorial account of the story of redemption.[12]

Thus, the Alexis Master is able to achieve a pictorial narrative ranging from the events surrounding man's fall to the events surrounding the Doomsday. This achievement, coming at the beginning of the twelfth-century Renaissance, provided a style of pictorial narrative which influenced works throughout the twelfth, thirteenth, and fourteenth centuries.

The St. Albans Psalter itself, however, belongs to an already well-developed insular tradition of manuscript illumination. This tradition, which we will now examine, predates the rise of either vernacular or liturgical dramatic cycles; establishes the custom of joining Old and New Testament materials into a pictorial narrative, episodic in nature, which highlights the events of salvation history; and achieves a selectivity in its choice of episodes which enables the artist to span great spaces of historical time with coherence and economy.

B.M. MS. Cotton Tiberius C. VI—the earliest extant exam-

ple of an English psalter prefaced by a pictorial cycle13—has
been dated about the mid-eleventh century on the basis of both
stylistic and palaeographic evidence.14 Unlike other early English Psalters which intermingle pictures and text, and which
choose the subjects for the pictures directly from the words of
the Psalms (see, for example, the English copy of the Utrecht
Psalter, B.M. MS. Lat. 8846), the Tiberius C. VI psalter
prefaces the Psalms with a history cycle of Old and New Testament material.15 The opening illustration in the Tiberius C. VI
cycle, for example, is based not on the Psalter text, but rather
on the description of the heavenly Creator in Isaiah 11.12. The
Creation scene therefore introduces an uninterrupted, episodic
world-history cycle of twenty-four drawings executed in colored-
outline technique. Tiberius C. VI represents a pre-Conquest,
insular tradition of manuscript illumination which stressed the
attachment of a series of Bible miniatures to the beginning of
the text.

In addition to the Creation, the subject matter of the drawings can be divided into two cycles: a life of David consisting of
five episodes, and a life of Christ in eleven scenes:

> The Creation
> David seizing a lamb from the lion's mouth
> David with sling (above) / David kills Goliath with
>   Goliath's own sword (below)
> Goliath with shield and spear raised against David
> The Anointing of David
> David with a harp
> The Third Temptation
> The Entry into Jerusalem
> The Washing of the Feet
> The Betrayal of Christ
> Christ before Pilate
> Christ Crucified
> The Women at the Sepulchre
> The Harrowing of Hell
> St. Thomas touches the side of the Lord
> The Ascension
> The Descent of the Holy Spirit
> St. Michael and the Dragon16

The component parts of Tiberius C. VI's world-history cycle
may be traced to even earlier prototypes. Examples of earlier
Anglo-Saxon Christological cycles may be found in the Bene-
dictional of St. Aethelwold and in the Missal of Robert of

Jumièges.[17] A cycle of David pictures was extant in England by the eighth century (see the initials in B.M. MS. Cotton Vespasian A.1), although the ultimate source of the Tiberius C. VI's David cycle may have been a Byzantine sequence of David episodes.[18] Scenes from the Infancy period in the life of Christ, although absent from the Tiberius cycle, were included in earlier English psalters (B.M. MS. Cotton Galba A. XVIII, dated between 925 and 940).[19] Once a Creation episode is joined to cycles of Old and New Testament events, however, we have the formation of an episodic world-history cycle. Like the placement of a picture cycle at the beginning of the text, the addition of Old Testament to New Testament material is a characteristic of English Psalter illumination. All the known examples of early psalters with Old Testament scenes are English.[20] The combination of the Old and New Covenants outlines the large-scale plan of Salvation from the Creation to the Last Judgment. The Tiberius C. VI manuscript is at the very beginning of the characteristically English tradition which prefaced the psalter text with such a pictorial cycle.

We have seen how the pre-Conquest tradition of English manuscript illumination developed the combination of biblical history cycles into full-scale pictorial narratives of salvation history. There is, however, a complementary development of great significance which must be mentioned. The very early, "late-antique" illustrated Bibles (for example the fifth-century Greek manuscript known as the Cotton Genesis) have a full, explicit, and continuous series of pictures which are supplementary to virtually every detail of the text. The pictures form a continuous as opposed to episodic or selective narrative. By the time of the ninth century, however, this continuous pictorial narrative was abbreviated by a growing tendency to select only the most significant scenes. The great pictorial chronicles of biblical events were pared down through a double process of subordination for minor episodes and emphasis for significant events. A principle of selectivity is at work which, generally, emphasizes the scenes from the Passion period of Christ's life, and subordinates the public ministry miracles. In the following survey of English art we shall note how this selectivity operates, and we shall see its relevance for the choice of episodes in the late, vernacular mystery plays.

Other twelfth-century manuscripts which manifest stylistic

affinities with the St. Albans Psalter also reflect many of the characteristics of the pre-conquest tradition of narrative art. A good example is a set of four leaves from an English Psalter. Located in various museums, they are catalogued as B.M. MS. Add. 37472; Victoria and Albert MS. 661; and Pierpont Morgan MSS. 521 and 724. The figure style of the leaves is related to the St. Albans Psalter style, and the scene of the Deposition from the Cross is based directly on the St. Albans miniature.[21] The organization and comprehensive range of the cycle, however, indicate a strong debt to early Christian Bible cycles.[22] The episodes, identified in a study by M. R. James,[23] comprise a long narrative of Old Testament history as well as the Infancy, Ministry, and Passion periods in the life of Christ. Each of the four leaves is divided into twelve compartments or spaces. A hierarchy of significant events within the cycle is established through the allotting of either a half space or full space to the Bible episodes. In this case, the artist highlights particular events from the Old Testament, Nativity, and Passion cycles, while de-emphasizing the Public Ministry scenes.

The English revival of pictorial narrative which continued into the latter part of the twelfth century resulted in an illuminated psalter which has been termed "the most characteristic work of the High Romanesque phase of English art"[24]—the manuscript Cottonian Nero C. IV. The manuscript is preceded by a cycle of thirty-eight full-page miniatures, divided, for the most part, into two zones. The full psalter cycle contains a sequence of Old Testament history beginning with the story of Adam and Eve and continuing to the time of King David; scenes from the apocryphal early life of Mary; the Infancy and Passion episodes in the life of Christ; and an elaborate series of Doomsday scenes. The effect of the miniatures' successful fusion of the agitated, linear line of the native English tradition with the classical spaciousness of the High Romanesque style is to create a dramatic mood for the substantial figures. As one historian has remarked:

> The scenes of the Passion have an intensity of emotion
> that is at times almost painful: every line tells in the
> violent agitated pattern: the emaciated Christ, swaying
> under the blows, is sharply contrasted with the grinning,
> robust tormentors. Had we any knowledge of passion
> plays performed at so early a date, it would be natural to
> discern here the influence of theatrical performances.[25]

We know, however, that the drama of the medieval church did not employ a Creation-to-Doom framework until several centuries later. But this framework had been attained in the pictorial medium by the twelfth century, and as the twelfth-century revival of pictorial narrative progressed beyond the bounds of the Albani Psalter school, the Creation-to-Doom format became established as a viable program for other schools of illumination throughout England.

The revival of pictorial story-telling spread from the Canterbury workshops in Southern England to the Northern Augustine ateliers. Throughout the country the revival reflected not only the selection of episodes achieved by the masters of Early Christian art, but also the new learning and theology of the twelfth-century schools. The Infancy and Passion of Christ, together with the life of the Blessed Virgin, commanded the interest and sympathies of the people.[26] These incidents, as well as incidents from the lives of important local saints, were often emphasized at the expense of the public ministry scenes. By the end of the century most English psalters which contained prefatory cycles had eliminated all but a few traditional scenes of Christ's public life.[27]

The custom of pictorial selection is continued throughout the thirteenth and fourteenth centuries and was still popular at the very time when the Corpus Christi cycles originated.[28] Such thirteenth-century manuscripts as B.M. MS. Arundel 157, Leyden University MS. 76 A, B.M. MS. Roy. I. D. X, and the three manuscripts Chantilly MS. 1695, B.M. MS. Royal 2A. XXII, and B.M. MS. Harley 5102, which are stylistically related, participate in the custom of prefixing a miniature Bible history cycle to the Psalter text.

The fourteenth century continued to follow the time-honored traditions of English manuscript illumination while developing a new style of painting known as the East Anglian style. A well-known example of this style is the forty-two leaf Holkham Bible Picture Book (B.M. MS. Add. 47682) which is divided into three sections: Old Testament history (scenes from Genesis), New Testament life of Christ (scenes of the Nativity, Public Ministry, and Passion), and scenes depicting the events surrounding the Doom.[29] The work, prefaced by the statement "so I will, and if God grant me life, you will never see a better book than mine," was never completed.[30] The unfinished state of the manuscript, however, indicates which scenes the artist considered most important. The episodes from the middle leaves, namely the scenes of the Public Ministry, are incomplete and in some cases there is a blank on the manuscript folio. Earlier and later scenes illustrating the childhood and Passion of Christ, as well as the events surrounding his second coming, are fully drawn. The artist seems to have skipped from section to section in an attempt to illustrate the most important episodes of world history before filling in the remaining scenes.31

Although the costumes and scenery have led some historians to see a direct connection between the artist's visualization of scene and the staging of early world history cycles in England, the evidence for this is uncertain.32 The presence of stage-like details in any given illustration does not necessarily argue for the existence of a comprehensive, Creation-to-Doom cycle of drama. But the most telling argument against considering the Holkham Bible Picture Book as a pictorial record of an early English drama cycle is the gap which exists between the date of the manuscript and the earliest records of English cycle drama. Thirteen eighty-four is the first year for which we have a record of large-scale dramatic activity in England. In that year, a *ludus valde sumptuosus* was presented in London over a period of five days. In 1385 there was a proclamation made by the civic officials forbidding the play which took place at Skynners Well. As the fourteenth century drew to a close there are numerous references to the London dramatic activities which, by 1411, had expanded into an activity which "lastyd vij dayes contynually."33 On the other hand, the Holkham Bible Picture Book is dated c. 1325,34 or at least a full half-century before the earliest reference to the London dramatic presentations. On the basis of dating and other evidence it seems best to view the London drama as a late fourteenth-century phenomenon which was organized according to the *prior* principles of selection used in the Holkham manuscript and in other pictorial works.

By the opening of the fourteenth century, English art had a two-fold tradition of manuscript decoration. Many manuscripts, especially Psalters, contained a reduced amount of Bible material spanning the time of the Creation to the Last Judgment. Others, especially the great illustrated Bibles, contained hundreds of episodes drawn from the entire history of Biblical and Apocryphal writings. The point to notice is that whenever such

a large-scale presentation of biblical history was not possible,
the manuscript illuminators traditionally focused on a select
range of material from Genesis, Exodus, the Nativity, and the
Passion of Christ. Public Ministry episodes as well as the stories
of David, Solomon, and other noteworthy Hebrew leaders,
sometimes appear within the pictorial cycles, but the illustrations rarely emphasize them. As Otto Pächt has remarked:

> The Middle Ages knew, roughly speaking, two types of
> Bible illustration and especially Old Testament illustration.
> The one follows the events of the text in a continuous nar-
> rative, aiming at nothing but a pictured chronicle; the other
> represents only the salient points of the story, the selection
> being guided by more or less rigid principles.[35]

The propriety of presenting a select and traditional group
of scenes from the Old and New Testaments was thus established
at least several hundred years before the earliest recorded mystery cycles. The art of manuscript illumination transmitted the
traditional thematic structure of biblical narration throughout
the fourteenth century, and it is this tradition of pictorial selection and arrangement which may best account for the inclusions,
exclusions, and variations found in the cycles of medieval Bible
drama. With regard to the establishment of a chronological pattern of significant events of salvation history, it seems clear that
the pictorial arts were far in advance of their theatrical counterparts. The pictorial tradition had developed a format which was
readily adaptable by various sized cities throughout medieval
England for dramatic and processional purposes.

One further aspect of the manuscript pictorial cycles which
reinforces their analogous relationship to the dramatic cycles is
that they are subject to a limitation of space. The miniaturist
must decide how best to fill a limited space with a program of
decoration expressive of the major aspects of his theme. Whereas the dramatist is limited by such factors as the number of
guilds, time for production, and so forth, the artist is often
limited by the number of available leaves left blank for him,
and by the monetary support of his patron. Thus, although our
survey of twelfth- and thirteenth-century illumination covers a
field so large as to make it impossible even to mention some of
the more important developments, the material which is most
profitable to investigate is the illuminated manuscripts which attempt to reduce Old and New Testament history into a smaller,

traditional format. The artist's selection of episodes in the face of limited space is analogous to the limitations in the number of guilds within a medieval city.36 Given these similar restrictions, and given the vast amount of material of a biblical, religious, or devotional nature, it seems more than coincidental that the artists and playwrights chose the *same* episodes. Thus, the tradition of English pictorial narrative art—especially the customary selection of episodes which forms an episodic history of the world—provides a most opportune pattern for the dramatic endeavors of the trade guilds.

II

The developments of medieval English manuscript illumination, however, did not take place in an artistic vacuum. The advances in the art of the miniaturist often were incorporated into the art of the mural painter. The channels of influence between the wall painter and the miniaturist were numerous and the effects of innovations flowed in both directions.37

Medieval wall painting is "vernacular" in a way that miniature painting is not. Illuminated manuscripts were produced for, and exclusively owned by, the wealthy, and it was rare for ordinary medieval tradesmen to encounter the art of the miniaturist.38 Such, however, was not the case for the art of wall painting which from the twelfth through the fifteenth centuries was both widespread and intensively developed.39 The work of the mural artist was a revelation of Christian history open to all people of the parish, literate or otherwise; and the subjects and format of church mural series became a model for the way the viewers conceptualized the significant events of salvation history.

Reformation damage to medieval mural paintings, especially in the Northernmost counties of England, was very severe. Where once there were large-scale programs of decorative art, there remain only isolated, often undecipherable, fragments. As many as fifty or more separate scenes may have been integrated into an outline of salvation history encompassing both Old and New Testament events within a single church.40 The scenes from the life of Christ and the life of His Mother follow a pattern of selection and arrangement which is markedly similar to many of the sequences of manuscript illuminations. Generally speaking, the episodes are grouped into Infancy and Passion sequences, with the Public Ministry seldom appearing on the church walls. The groups often were executed in conjunction with each other thus forming a comprehensive series of Bible history for all to see on the walls of the parish church.41

In the next few pages I want to examine closely three decorative mural programs—one dating from the twelfth century, and the remaining two from the fourteenth. The twelfth-century mural scheme is strikingly similar to the Creation-to-Doom framework of the English dramatic cycles in both the selection and arrangement of episodes. The important point, however, is that the mural program provides additional evidence that the form which characterizes the drama cycles existed long before the cycles of Latin or vernacular plays, and that the Creation-to-Doom pattern of salvation history was an established part of the cultural heritage of medieval communities.

The twelfth-century cycle of paintings which approaches the extensive range of material in many of the extant dramatic cycles is displayed on the walls of St. Botolph Church in Hardham, Sussex. In addition to Old Testament scenes from Genesis, episodes from the Infancy and Passion of Christ, and a group of scenes from the Last Judgment, the mural scheme depicts the life of Saint George and the Gospel parable of Dives and Lazarus. This extensive set of mural paintings was discovered about 1866; unfortunately, work on cleaning, varnishing, and preserving did not commence in earnest until 1900, and during the interval many scenes were badly mutilated and much detail was lost. On the upper tiers of the nave, on the east side of the chancel arch, and on the lower tiers of the north and south walls of the chancel, are scenes from the life of Christ. Episodes from the Last Judgment are depicted on the west wall of the nave, above the chancel arch, and on the east, north, and south walls of the chancel. On the southern part of the west chancel wall is the scene of the Fall of Man; and there are traces of a second painting directly beneath, which may have represented the shame of our first parents. On the west wall of the chancel the series continues with a painting of Adam cultivating the earth for food and Eve tending an animal after their expulsion from the Garden. In several tiers around the nave of the church are the incidents from the early life of Christ. The pictures of the Annunciation and Visitation begin on the east wall of the nave, and bear the inscription "Virgo salutatur, sterilis fecunda probatur" above them. On the south wall are the often fragmentary remains of the Nativity with shepherds, the appearance of the star to the Magi, the Journey of the Magi, and the court of Herod. The north wall continues with the Adoration of the Magi, the Dreams of Joseph and of the Magi, the Flight into Egypt, the Fall of the Idols, the Massacre of the Innocents, and the remains of what may have once been a Presentation in the Temple. On either side of the chancel arch are paintings of Christ among the Doctors and of the Baptism by John in the river Jordan. The subjects on the lower tiers of the chancel walls, although in a very fragmentary condition, comprise a history of Christ's Passion. The scenes which can now be identified include the Last Supper, the Betrayal of Christ by Judas, the Resurrection, and the Marys at the tomb. In the church of St. Botolph, therefore, we find a rather comprehensive cycle of painting which puts forth the main episodes of Christian history on a scale comparable to many of the contemporary illuminated manuscripts and to the later cycles of biblical drama which were eventually to comprise an important part of medieval English theater.42

Although there are numerous series of mural paintings executed in the twelfth, thirteenth, and fourteenth centuries which parallel the selection and arrangement of episodes found in the late medieval mystery plays, we may, for the purposes of brevity, limit our inquiry to two fourteenth-century decorative programs. The first is the series of paintings located in the Church of Croughton, Northamptonshire. The paintings cover both of the nave walls, with the south being divided into three rows of biblical events, while the north is arranged in a double tier. An extensive life of the Virgin, including many scenes from the early life of Christ, decorates the southern wall. On the north is a Passion cycle ending with the episodes of the Ascension and Pentecost which as now destroyed. Two further scenes—St. Anne and the Virgin and an Annunciation—are associated with the Lady Chapel's altar. The series was discovered in 1921, and dates from the early fourteenth century.43 It is executed in the East Anglian style and bears strong resemblances to several well-known illuminated manuscripts. The arrangement of scenes parallels certain illustrations from the Psalter of Robert de Lisle (Arundel MS. 83), while the drawing of the human physiognomy resembles the miniatures of the Holkham Bible Picture Book or the Queen Mary's Psalter (B.M. MS. Royal 2. B. VII).44 If the style of the mural is contemporary with the advances in medieval miniature painting, the subject matter draws from a long tradition of narrative pictorial cycles. Correspondences between the subject matter of the twelfth-century capital frieze of Chartres Cathedral's west front, the Psalter Nero C. IV, the series of wall paintings at All Saints' Church in Witley, and the Croughton paintings, have been noted.45 In addition, the striking resemblance of the subject matter of the Croughton church murals with the N-town mystery cycle has been recorded by art historians.46 It is important, however, to note that the Croughton series was executed some hundred and fifty years before the existing manuscript of the N-town plays was composed, c. 1315 as opposed to 1468.

The second scheme of mural paintings which bears close examination is slightly later than the Croughton series. The paintings in Chalgrove church date from the beginning of the second quarter of the fourteenth century, and like Croughton, are executed in the manner of the East Anglian school of illumination.47 The scheme, discovered in 1858, is located on the interior of the chancel. The murals are arranged in three tiers of about twelve and one-half feet in height, with the individual figures varying in height from three to four feet. Integrated into the continuous series formed by the rows of painted murals are individual figures of about six feet in height painted on the splays of the windows.48

The pictorial narrative of New Testament events begins with a large Jesse Tree. Over the Tree stands the Blessed Virgin with Child; and, on the side tendrils, is a group of four prophets each holding his scroll. The splays of the first window contain large-scale figures of Gabriel and the Virgin and thus comprise an Annunciation scene. The series continues with the Nativity, Adoration of the Magi, Slaughter of the Innocents, and the Presentation in the Temple. In the upper row the murals depict the Betrayal of Christ with Peter striking off the ear of Malchus, Christ before Pilate, the Mocking of Christ, the Scourging, the Carrying of the Cross, the Crucifixion, the Descent from the Cross, and the Entombment. St. Helena and another female saint (Mary Magdalene?) occupy the space on the window splays. The scheme continues on the east wall with the Harrowing of Hell, the Resurrection, the Ascension, and two Saints (Peter and Paul) on the window splays. At the west end of the south wall the artist depicted the General Resurrection and Last

SCHEME OF WALL PAINTINGS IN THE CHURCH OF CROUGHTON, NORTHAMPTONSHIRE.

SOUTH WALL OF NAVE

Joachim's offering rejected	Angel and Anne	Anne and Joachim meet	Birth of Virgin	Entrance of Joachim	Presentation of Virgin	Virgin leaves Home	Espousals
Annunciation (*lost*)	Visitation	Nativity	Angels and Shepherds	Magi and Herod	Adoration of Magi	Massacre of Innocents	Flight into Egypt
Presentation of Christ	Palm given to the Virgin	Virgin gives palm to John	Virgin meets Apostles	Death of Virgin	Miracle of the Jews	Burial of the Virgin	Assumption

NORTH WALL OF NAVE

Entry into Jerusalem	Last Supper	Betrayal	Christ before Caiaphas	Mocking of Christ	Scourging of Christ	Christ bearing the Cross	Crucifixion
Deposition	Burial	Harrowing of Hell	Resurrection	Ascension (*lost*)	Pentecost (*lost*)	St. Anne teaching the Virgin	Annunciation

Judgment. Saints Bartholomew and Lawrence are within the jambs of the window. A second series of subjects commences with the narrative of the final days of the Virgin. The first scene is the presentation of the heavenly palm to Mary. This is followed by a destroyed and hence unidentifiable subject. The remainder of the series, however, includes the gathering of the Apostles, the Death of Mary, the Funeral Procession with the Apostles carrying the bier, the miracle of the Jewish high priest, the Burial of the Virgin, the Assumption (placed on the eastern wall in conjunction with the scene of the Resurrection), the presentation of the girdle to St. Thomas, a destroyed subject, and finally the Coronation of the Blessed Virgin in Heaven. The figures of St. John the Evangelist holding a palm-branch and of St. John the Baptist occupy the window jambs. The Chalgrove series thus represents a very extensive pictorial narrative of New Testament events which embraces the early life and Passion of Christ, as well as the Doom and apocryphal episodes of Marian history.

The subject matter, identified by some as unique to the Corpus Christi occasion, occurred in the pictorial arts at least a century before the earliest recorded English cycle drama. In medieval churches, products of an entire community's cooperative efforts, were the pictorial and sculptural models for the episodes of the world history drama. The principles of inclusion and exclusion had been determined over the course of several centuries by a more or less rigid pictorial tradition. The availability of this pattern, the desire of the communities to develop appropriate forms of holiday celebrations, and the recognition of the importance of religion both to the individual and to the medieval social structure, influenced the creation and shape of the English mystery plays.

The audiences of the mystery cycles generally knew beforehand what they were about to see simply because, from their day to day acquaintance with the decorative schemes in their churches, they were able to form a clear conception of the appropriate subject matter for a world history, a Nativity, or a Passion. The cycles partake of these traditional patterns and their authors never radically rearranged or reinterpreted what their heritage provided. This largely explains why the cycles exclude a wide range of Old and New Testament stories which might have provided dramatically appropriate conflict or suspense.49 Conversely, it provides an explanation for the inclusion in the cycles of episodes which contain little dramatic tension. The purely representational forms of pictorial arts were simply not concerned with selection on the basis of the dramatic qualities of an event. Rather, the pictorial arts expressed the fundamental Christian awareness that a series of important events occurred, and that these events decisively influenced the entire course of Salvation history.

III

The implications of this brief inquiry into the narrative Bible cycles of medieval art and drama for the study of the English mystery cycles are several. It demonstrates that a study of medieval drama must encompass much more than a philological inquiry into a manuscript tradition. The authors of the late vernacular cycles were drawing their material from a long-standing tradition which can best be characterized as communal, pictorial, and anonymous. It is important to realize that to a great extent, the medieval audience understood the dramatic pageants as a review of their cultural and spiritual heritage. The overall, episodic, narrative structure of the cycles cannot be explained in terms of the structure of liturgical ceremonies, devotional treatises, doctrinal schemes, scholastic patterns, or mystical revelations. Any attempt to fit the mystery cycles into a mold which is alien to their nature can only blur critical insight. Quite simply, the authors of the medieval mystery plays sought to present an entertaining, public, dramatic reaffirmation of the major events of Bible history. If, in this reaffirmation of the Christian heritage, authors such as the Wakefield Master delighted the audience by blending contemporary references, humor, and realism with the traditional material, surely this does not represent a deep concern with a sophisticated cosmology of historical events or with an abstract scheme of conflated time. On the contrary, it is a fit artistic device for professing the continued relevance of the events in far-away Palestine for the social and spiritual health of the fifteenth-century English community. The mystery cycles drew from the traditional written and pictorial resources of the community, and, in turn, served to revitalize these materials.

NOTES

1 Both Jerome Taylor, "The Dramatic Structure of the Middle English Corpus Christi, or Cycle, Plays," *Literature and Society*, ed. Bernice Slote (Lincoln, 1964), 175-86, and V. A. Kolve, *The Play Called Corpus Christi* (Stanford, 1966), pp. 48-49, attempt to link the subject matter of the English cycles to the ecclesiastical documents which pertain to the Corpus Christi feastday.

2 Hardin Craig, *English Religious Drama of the Middle Ages* (Oxford, 1955), pp. 131-32.

3 Émile Mâle, "Le Renouvellement De L'Art par les 'Mystères' à la fin du Moyen Age," *Gazette des Beaux-Arts*, 4 (1904), 89-106, 213-30, 284-301, 379-94; and *L'Art réligieux du XIIIe siècle en France*, trans. into English under the title *The Gothic Image* by Dora Nussey (New York, 1913). For a discussion of the various revisions of Mâle's thesis see Otto Pächt, *The Rise of Pictorial Narrative in Twelfth-Century England* (Oxford, 1962), p. 33.

4 Otto Pächt, C. R. Dodwell, Francis Wormald, eds., *The St. Albans Psalter (Albani Psalter)* (London, 1960), p. 171.

5 Pächt, *Rise of Pictorial Narrative*, p. 59.

6 Pächt, *St. Albans Psalter*, p. 77.

7 Kolve, p. 39; F. K. Chambers, *English Literature at the Close of the Middle Ages* (Oxford, 1947), p. 8; Virginia Shull, "Clerical Drama in Lincoln Cathedral, 1318 to 1561," *PMLA*, 52 (1937), 948-66; and Alan H. Nelson, *The Medieval English Stage* (Chicago, 1974), pp. 101-04.

8 For dating and identification of illumination see Pächt, *St. Albans Psalter*, pp. 5-7; for general description of contents see T. S. R. Boase, *English Art, 1100-1216*, The Oxford History of English Art, III (Oxford, 1953), pp. 101-02.

9 John Beckwith, *Early Medieval Art* (New York, 1964), p. 194; Pächt, *St. Albans Psalter*, p. 57.

10 George Henderson, *Early Medieval* (Baltimore, 1972), p. 105.

11 Pächt, *St. Albans Psalter*, p. 51.

12 Ibid., p. 51.

13 M. Rickert, *Painting in Britain: The Middle Ages* (London, 1966), p. 68.

14 Francis Wormald, "An English Eleventh-Century Psalter With Pictures, British Museum, Cotton MS. Tiberius C. vi," *The Walpole Society*, 38 (1960-62), 6.

15 M. R. James, "On Fine Art as Applied to the Illustration of the Bible in the Ninth and Five Following Centuries, Exemplified Chiefly by Cambridge MSS.," *Proceedings of the Cambridge Antiquarian Society*, n.s. 1 (1888-89), 39-40.

16 Wormald, "An English Eleventh-Century Psalter," pp. 8-11.

17 Ibid., p. 6.

18 Ibid., p. 5.

19 Mary Ann Farley and Francis Wormald, "Three Related English Romanesque Manuscripts," *The Art Bulletin*, 22 (1940), 158.

20 Pächt, *St. Albans Psalter*, pp. 51-52.

21 Boase, pp. 109-10.

22 The Psalter leaves bear a strong resemblance to the scenes in the Cambridge,

Corpus Christi College MS. 286—a late-antique cycle of Bible illustrations brought to England by the beginning of the eighth century. See Francis Wormald, ed., *The Miniatures in the Gospels of St. Augustine* (Cambridge, 1954).

23 M. R. James, "Four Leaves of an English Psalter 12th Century," *The Walpole Society*, 25 (1936-37), 1-23.

24 Boase, p. 172; C. R. Dodwell, *The Canterbury School of Illumination 1066-1200* (Cambridge, 1954), p. 56.

25 Boase, p. 173; see also Francis Wormald, *The Winchester Psalter* (London, 1973).

26 James, "On Fine Art," pp. 46-47.

27 Isa Ragusa, "An Illustrated Psalter from Lyre Abbey," *Speculum*, 46 (1971), 280.

28 The recent review of dramatic records by Nelson, *Medieval English Stage*, pp. 11-14 and passim, has established the following chronology of Corpus Christi events: 1350-1400 for pageant processions; 1400 and later for dramatic cycle plays in the provinces; and 1384 for cycle drama in London.

29 W. O. Hassall, *The Holkham Bible Picture Book* (London, 1954), pp. vi-vii.

30 Rickert, p. 135.

31 Hassall, *Holkham Bible Picture Book*, pp. 6, 29.

32 Rosemary Woolf, *The English Mystery Plays* (Berkeley and Los Angeles, 1972), p. 58.

33 W. O. Hassall, "Plays at Clerkenwell," MLR, 33 (1938), 564-65.

34 Hassall, *Holkham Bible Picture Book*, p. 27; Rickert, p. 135.

35 Otto Pächt, "A Giottesque Episode in English Mediaeval Art," *Journal of the Warburg and Courtauld Institutes*, 6 (1943), 60.

36 Arthur Brown, "York and its Plays in the Middle Ages," *Chaucer und Seine Zeit*, ed. Arno Esch (Tübingen, 1968), p. 417. See also Woolf, *The English Mystery Plays*, p. 62.

37 E. W. Tristram, *English Medieval Wall Painting: The Thirteenth Century* (Oxford, 1950), p. 378.

38 H. J. Chaytor, *From Script to Print: An Introduction to Medieval Vernacular Literature* (New York, 1966), p. 108.

39 Tancred Borenius and E. W. Tristram, *English Medieval Painting* (New York, 1926), p. 17.

40 Tristram, *Thirteenth Century*, pp. 33-34.

41 W. A. Pantin, *The English Church in the Fourteenth Century* (Notre Dame, 1962), pp. 240-41; Tristram, *Thirteenth Century*, p. 46.

42 Philip Mainwaring Johnston, "Hardham Church, and Its Early Paintings," *Sussex Archaeological Collections*, 44 (1901), 73-112; Rickert, *Painting in Britain*, pp. 75-76; J. Lewis André, C. E. Keyser, *et. al.*, "Mural Paintings in Sussex Churches," *Sussex Archaeological Collections*, 43 (1900), 235; E. W. Tristram, *English Medieval Wall Painting: The Twelfth Century* (Oxford, 1944), pp. 128-32; Clive Bell, *Twelfth Century Paintings At Hardham and Clayton* (Lewes, Sussex, 1947), plates. Rickert dates the murals c. 1125. André chooses the period between 1150 and 1200. Johnston favors a date of c. 1100, while Tristram dates them "early twelfth century."

43 Borenius and Tristram, *English Medieval Painting*, p. 20; Rickert, *Painting in Britain*, pp. 140-41.

44 E. W. Tristram and M. R. James, "Wall-Paintings in Croughton Church, Northamptonshire," *Archaeologia*, 26 (1927), 183.

45 Tristram and James, "Wall-Paintings in Croughton Church," p. 197. On the capital freize of Chartres see Adelheid Heimann, "The Capital Frieze and Pilasters of the Portail Royal, Chartres," *Journal of the Warburg and Courtauld Institutes*, 31 (1968), 73-102. On the paintings at All Saint's Church in Witley see Tristram, *Twelfth Century*, pp. 29, 153-54.

46 M. D. Anderson, *Drama and Imagery in English Medieval Churches* (Cambridge, 1963), pp. 113-14; Tristram and James, "Wall-Paintings in Croughton Church," pp. 198-99.

47 William Burges, "On Mural Paintings in Chalgrove Church, Oxfordshire," *Archaeologia*, 38 (1860), 435.

48 Burges, "Paintings in Chalgrove Church," pp. 431-38; Rickert, pp. 140-41.

49 Beryl Smalley, *The Study of the Bible in the Middle Ages* (Notre Dame, 1964), p. 24, records that "the *Rule* of St. Benedict forbids that the books of Kings and the Heptateuch should be read in the evening, in case they might over-excite the hearers."

"You Have Begun a Parlous Pleye": The Nature and Limits of Dramatic Mimesis as a Theme in Four Middle English 'Fall of Lucifer' Cycle Plays

R. W. Hanning

This essay can perhaps best be characterized as an extended footnote to V. A. Kolve's brilliant and epoch-making study of the Middle English cycle plays, *The Play Called Corpus Christi*.[1] In the second chapter, "The Drama as Play and Game" (pp. 8-31), Kolve considers the implications of the designation of these cycles by those who created them as *plays, games,* or *pageants.* As distinct from the Latin liturgical drama, for which the usual nomenclature was *representatio*,[2] the popular, vernacular cycles were clearly identified by means of a terminology which stressed the play-element of the drama—the creation of a self-contained world with its own rules, intended to entertain and instruct, but not able to be confused with or taken for "reality."[3] The reason, in part, for this definition of the drama as play and game was, according to Kolve, the desire to avoid the danger of blasphemy inherent in any attempt by men to impersonate God—i.e., to imitate the Inimitable and thereby confuse the created with the Creator.[4] One way to eliminate this danger was to stress the "game" as opposed to the "earnest" nature of the dramatic representation.[5] That the danger existed Kolve documents by referring to the Wycliffite attacks, in late fourteenth-century religious tracts, on the popular Corpus Christi drama as blasphemous, and to attempts made to avoid the difficulty by various means in liturgical drama.[6]

In urging that the problem of the mimesis of God was a real one for the dramatists of the Corpus Christi cycles, Kolve points out that "Lucifer, [medievals] believed, fell because he imitated God. By sitting on God's throne and demanding the forms of adoration due to God alone, he sinned in pride and was condemned to hell" (p. 9). Kolve adds that "the Chester cycle stages this very action," and asks, "Might it not be analogous to the Corpus Christi dramatic endeavor?" It is the purpose of this essay to urge that Kolve's question be answered with a decided affirmative. The playwrights of the Corpus Christi cycles perceived the analogy between Satan's mimesis of God and their own mimetic art, and they addressed themselves in the opening plays of several cycles (not only the Chester cycle) to offering a self-conscious explanation of the significance, *and* the limits, of the analogy. The plays in question have as their historical matter (in Christian terms) the creation of the angels and the fall of Lucifer, the brightest angel, who became the Devil when God banished him to hell for his sin. But they are also plays about the origin and nature of drama as a peculiar feature of the fallen universe. By placing the mimetic-dramatic impulse within a hierarchy of responses to the divine providence—a hierarchy which includes as well impulses to praise God and to declare his power—the cycle dramatists indicate that they know the limits of their art, and thus differentiate the intent of their mimesis, which is to glorify God by showing his dealings with men, especially through his Son, from the subversive and delusory intent of Lucifer's imitation of his Maker. I will examine the "Fall of Lucifer" plays of the N. Town, Wakefield, Chester, and York cycles, to see how they raise the problem of the dangerous imitation of God by his creatures—and how they set it to rest.

I

As a necessary prelude to analyzing the "Fall of Lucifer" plays, I must say a few words about the significance of the action they represent. The Corpus Christi Cycles begin with the creation of the universe since, as Kolve indicates, the sacrifice of Christ, and its recreation in the eucharist which the feast of Corpus Christi celebrates, are only comprehensible by Christians within the context of the entire history of salvation.[7] The canonic story (or more precisely stories) of the Creation in Genesis comprises two parts, corresponding to the so-called Priestly and Jahwist narratives; of these, only the second, recounting the temptation of Eve by the serpent and the eating of the forbidden fruit, contains real dramatic possibilities: conflict between characters, crucial and symbolic action, and dramatic irony (i.e., the audience's awareness of the true effects of man's disobedience, as opposed to the serpent's representation of those effects in tempting the woman). In addition, the concept of mimesis could be seen as implicit in the serpent's telling the woman that eating the forbidden fruit will make her and the man become like gods (Gen. 3.5).[8] By contrast, the Genesis account of the creation of the universe by God lacks any dramatic element (or even any explicit element of praise), consisting as it does of a progressive ordering and categorizing of the matter of creation by the omnipotent and unchallenged creator.[9]

However, in the course of the development of Christian beliefs during the first centuries after Jesus, the idea took form that there had been an earlier fall in the course of creation: Lucifer, the brightest and most powerful angel, defied and challenged the power of God, and was cast into hell to become the devil who later tempted the first man and woman to *their* fall. The evolution of this belief resulted from the combination of a tradition of fallen angels, whom God cast into dark pits for misconduct with mortals, with the exegesis of a passage in Isaiah (14.12-15), in conjunction with the account of the battle between Michael and the dragon (the latter identified as the devil, and thrown down with his angels from heaven to earth) in Revelation 12.7-9.[10] The Isaiah passage is as follows:

> Quomodo cecidisti de caelo lucifer, qui mane oriebaris? Corruisti in terram, qui vulnerabas gentes, qui dicebas in corde tuo: In caelum conscendam, super astra Dei exaltabo solium meum, sedebo in monte testamenti in lateribus aquilonis; ascendam super altitudinem nubium, similis ero Altissimo. Verumtamen ad infernum detraheris, in profundum laci.[11]

Within the context of Isaiah's prophecies, it is directed against a proud king of Babylon, but once it became associated in patristic interpretation with the devil, it assumed a dramatic potential which the Corpus Christi plays were ultimately to exploit. Two points are especially germane to this discussion: 1) Lucifer is portrayed as planning to set up his throne *(solium)* illicitly in God's special enclave *(in monte testamenti);* 2) he declares that he will be like the Most High *(similis ero Altissimo),* a statement easily taken as an echo of the serpent's promise to Eve in Genesis and, in conjunction with the reference to intruding his throne into God's territory, as the suggestion of a program of false impersonation of the Deity.

Paraphrases of the Isaiah passage in *Piers Plowman,*[12] Gower's *Confessio Amantis,*[13] Chaucer's *Monk's Tale,*[14] and *Purity*[15] provide a random sample of its familiarity to English poets at the time when the Corpus Christi cycles were becoming widespread (the last half of the fourteenth century).[16] Of these, the example in *Purity* is especially useful for present purposes in linking the references to the throne and similitude to God with a statement of Lucifer's narcissistic abandonment of his Creator:

> He seȝ noȝt bot hym self how semly he were,
> Bot his souerayn he forsoke & sade þyse wordeȝ:
> "I schal telde up my trone in þe tramountayne,
> & by lyke to þat lorde þat þe lyft made."　　(11. 209-12)

On the one hand, this passage provides a useful comparison with the dramatic presentation of Lucifer's narcissism in the York play;[17] on the other, it points us toward the patristic treatment of Lucifer's fall which was most influential in the Middle Ages and therefore in the formation of the plays here under discussion: the protracted analysis in Augustine's *On the City of God* of how the disobedience and fall of the evil angels brought into being the two cities (the *civitas Dei* and the *civitas terrena*) into which mankind is divided here on earth.[18]

Augustine makes much of this first moment of disharmony in God's universe because it signifies the origin of the evil will, i.e., the deficient will which turns away from adoration of a higher good (God), to a lower good (itself—in this case, Lucifer's created beauty, which is in fact a further tribute to the power of God, and therefore should be a further inducement to adore him); in so turning, the will becomes wicked.[19] The issue is clearly drawn here, for, unlike Adam and Eve who are tempted by the serpent, the devil is tempted by no outside agent—there is, says Augustine, no ultimate efficient cause of the evil will, for otherwise it would not be a free will.[20] Lucifer, in his pride, became enamored of his own (lesser) beauty and power; the fault lay not with God, nor with the beauty and power itself, nor, as Augustine's *bête noir,* Manicheeism, would claim, with some deliberately created evil principle—but with the proud will itself.[21]

Augustine, then, traces the conflict between creature and

Creator, which has forever lost part of mankind to the city of God, back beyond tempted man to Lucifer who acts autonomously. Such a view makes it possible to read drama into the account of the creation itself, as is shown by allegorization of God's separating the light from the darkness in Genesis 1.4: this passage, he says, refers to the separation of good from bad angels and the sending of the latter to hell.22 But the play of contraries here discovered in the apparently calm and triumphal text of the Priestly creation account appeals to Augustine primarily on aesthetic rather than dramatic grounds.

> For God would never have created any, I do not say angel, but even man, whose future wickedness He foreknew, unless He had equally known to what uses in behalf of the good He could turn him, thus embellishing the course of the ages, as it were an exquisite poem set off with antitheses.23

One cannot, therefore, simply say that the "Fall of Lucifer" plays are staged versions of Augustinian theology. Augustine knew the Isaiah passage which the early Church interpreted as describing the devil's fall—he refers to it in xi.1524—but does not mention the throne of Lucifer nor the angel's intent to make himself like God. False mimesis *per se* forms no part of his analysis of this first denial of God's lordship. It is the originality of the opening plays of the Corpus Christi cycles—an originality which Kolve does not sufficiently stress, since it has, to my knowledge, few if any medieval antecedents—to present Augustine's exegesis as a discrete dramatic action, in which an improper act of mimesis—Lucifer's seating himself in God's throne —expresses the corruption of the angel's will, its fateful turning toward a lower rather than a higher object of adoration.25

II

Each of the four plays here under discussion offers its own special approach to a shared goal, viz., the combination of an Augustinian interpretation (however popularized) of Lucifer's fall with an adaptation of the events alluded to in Isaiah 14.12-15 into a self-conscious drama raising the issue of the permissible limits of mimesis. Before proceeding to an analysis of each play separately, I will try to indicate how, as a group, they share features of plot and structure which direct the audience's attention at the beginning of the Corpus Christi cycle to what the cycle is and is not trying to do, i.e., which condition the audience's response to the following plays.

The basic plot of the "Fall of Lucifer" play comprises four sections—though, as we shall see, one of the four examples I am using omits the last part, and there is wide variation among the plays as to the relative weight and development afforded each constituent part. Part I is a speech by God declaring his nature, his power, and his role as uncreated creator of the universe. This speech, which is addressed to the audience in a tone of serene and triumphant confidence, calls forth from the angels, the highest forms of created life, a response of praise, i.e., a thankful affirmation of the facts which God has just asserted about himself. In Part II, Lucifer, the brightest angel, assumes an adversary role, claiming for himself the veneration due God; his usurpation, which focuses on his sitting in God's temporarily vacated throne, creates conflict in heaven among the angels, some praising and some condemning Lucifer's action. Part II becomes Part III at the moment of peripateia, when Lucifer's rebellion issues in a symbolic action which results in God's reasserting his authority and banishing the rebel and his accomplices to hell. Part III shows the angels-become-devils in their new home and newly characteristic behavior. Part IV consists of heavenly comment on the foregoing crisis, and/or transition to the next act of the drama of providential history, the creation and fall of man.

The movement of this first Corpus Christi play is, then, from declaration (God) to acquiescence and acclamation (angels) to counter-assertion (Lucifer), and then to conflicting voices reacting to the counter-assertion. The verbal conflict builds to a summary action, an immediate reversal, and final statements which at once place what we have seen into perspective, look back to the matter and manner of the play's opening, and look forward, establishing continuity between this play and its successor. We see, then, that the play is constructed around a contrast between non-dramatic (i.e., declarative, audience-directed, acclamatory) and dramatic (i.e., character-to-character, argumentative, ironic) discourse, with the dramatic element strengthened by being focused on the play's one crucial action (Lucifer sitting on God's throne), but also effectively contained within an envelope of opening and closing declarative, non-dramatic statements. This structure does much to determine the play's

overall effect as a self-conscious statement about the Corpus
Christi dramatic enterprise.

That the opening of the "Fall of Lucifer" plays is quin-
tessentially non-dramatic is no accident. By defining God (or letting God define himself) in terms of his absolute power,26 the
first speech denies all possibility of doubt, meaningful conflict,
dramatic irony, tragic failure. The angels confirm God's statement, and do so, moreover, in song—presumably the *Te Deum*27
—thereby pushing the play at this point far in the direction of
a liturgical celebration, both in medium and in content.28 For
drama to begin in such a situation, God must create the possibility for it. This he does by vacating his throne (from which,
presumably, he has delivered the play's first speech) and, as
Chester makes explicit while the other versions imply, leaving
the scene of dramatic action.29 The logical impossibility of God
"leaving" any place makes it clear we are not to take this
action literally; rather, it is a symbolic statement, acceptable
as such by the audience, creating or defining a *dramatic space,*
i.e., a place which is the locational equivalent of the metaphysi-
cal state of not-being-God (and therefore not being in full control of one's world and all else that exists in it). With the with-
drawal of God, we are asked to imagine the world not as it appears to the eye of faith—a place of order, testifying to God's
rule, eliciting songs of praise—but as it is experienced by its
creatures, as a place presenting opportunities and challenges to
control it as much as we can, as a place moreover in which to
attempt to realize ourselves as fully as possible. In such a place
agon, irony, suspense, and *peripateia* become available to the
dramatist—and the spectator—as they are not in heaven with
God in residence.

The sudden shift from quasi-liturgy to incipient drama, in
combination with the reverse movement from drama back to
declaration after Lucifer and his followers have become devils
in hell, also defines a shape for a dramatic action often used
by medieval dramatists: the play opens and closes with statements that prompt and explain the intervening drama, made by
characters outside the action proper, but who control or understand it thanks to power or knowledge beyond that available
to the audience or characters.30 In fact, one effect of this "envelope" structure is to push the characters into closer identity with
the audience—in other words, to allow the characters of the

"inner drama" to function as audience surrogates vis-a-vis the "Other"-figures whose powers (of action and comprehension) set them apart from normal human experience.[31] Even more importantly, the shape of the play suggests that life, as therein imitated, carries on in God's "absence"—i.e., without man's having God's control over the world and knowledge of its future—yet still within the framework (perceived through faith and the biblical record) of God's presence and ultimate, absolute authority.

Drama, then, as a form peculiarly belongs to God's creatures, not to their creator. It issues from and characterizes the difference (specifically the difference in power) between God's creatures and God himself, and its stimulus lies in the conflict between the properly and the improperly directed will of the creature. To return to the "fall of Lucifer" drama, God's absence sets the stage for dramatic conflict between good and evil angels, which in turn leads to history's first specific dramatic performance, i.e., the imitation of one being by another. Lucifer, imitating God's authority, voice, and claim to adoration by the creation,[32] is not just mimicking; he is setting his will against God's, as the faithful angels realize.[33] Satan's mimesis culminates in an act of impersonation, involving God's throne and thus fulfilling the dramatic potential of Lucifer's speech sarcastically reported in Isaiah 14: *super astra Dei exaltabo solium meum, sedebo in monte testamenti . . . similis ero Altissimo.* Satan not only pretends to be God, but, because his will is now self- instead of God-directed, he believes in his imitation. This is the cause of the doom which is the immediate (indeed the simultaneous) result of his completed impersonation.[34] At the level of physical staging, God's absence is necessary to have the throne vacant for Lucifer's ultimate mimetic act and its immediate consequence of his physical banishment, i.e., to set up an exciting, dramatically successful sequence of actions illustrating the peripateia which is the *raison d'être* of the "fall of Lucifer" play. At the metaphorical level, God's absence and the advantage Satan takes of it to sit in the divine throne provide a paradigm of how the created will, turning away from the proper goal of its aspiration—its creator—and thereby declaring, in effect, the absence of any such obligation to an object external to itself, sets itself up instead as its own God. Believing in its counterfeit deity, the created will condemns itself (as we shall see illustrated in the last section of the "Fall of Lucifer" plays) to proving by its subsequent misery and deprivation that God is indeed the source of all power and authority and therefore the only legitimate object of the will's desire.

The "Fall of Lucifer" plays thus dramatize a choice between loving God "undramatically"—the good angels' devotion, issuing in liturgical acclamation in which the individual will is subordinated to God and partakes of undifferentiated unity among his creatures—and indulging in the perverse imitation of God, to use another Augustinian phrase,[35] leading to double conflict—between creature and creature, between creature and creator—and finally to the deeply ironic affirmation of God's inimitability. Only within this context can we understand the implications of Kolve's recognition that Lucifer's act of illicit mimesis is an apt parallel to the representation of the Deity (and his purposes) in the Corpus Christi drama. The parallel betrays the same self-awareness about the religious dramatic enterprise and its dangers in a believing community which Kolve finds in the game-play vocabulary used by the cycle plays about themselves. Unlike the latter instance, the "Fall of Lucifer" plays bring the danger of the enterprise into the open by establishing the ancestry of mimesis as one leading back to the very first sin. This recognition that without conflict there can be no drama, and that the impulse to mimetic action is a uniquely apt symbol and consequence of man's (like Lucifer's) willed alienation from God—i.e., of his fallen state—allows the cycle plays at their best to exploit the theme of false imitation and illusion in some memorable characterizations of villains who are particularly Lucifer's mimetic progeny.[36]

But the Corpus Christi drama can also turn its awareness of the danger of imitating God to advantage in avoiding the danger itself. The "Fall of Lucifer" plays carry within themselves no implicit defiance of God; God, not Satan, is their hero, and they are of the latter's party neither by accident nor design. By showing how God controls the forces of disorder (and therefore of drama) in "coming back" and expelling Satan, and then proceeding calmly with his foreordained plan of creation, these plays establish a dramatic-historic paradigm in which, as I have already suggested, invincible power and providence envelop the forces of disharmony and sin. Satan, without meaning to, proves by his rebellion the might of God, which is merely stated by God at the beginning of the play. Drama, although inextricably linked to fallen nature, becomes in the right hands an even more effective instrument for praising and revealing God's ways than other, less exciting media (e.g., liturgy, historical narrative). By representing the full story of the divine providence, the Corpus Christi drama rises above the limitations inherent in Lucifer's impercipient mimesis, and shows that it knows its place, as Lucifer did not, as part of the universe's testimony to the greatness of its creator. By enveloping its portraits of sins, from Lucifer's though Adam's to the crucifixion, within the providential continuum of which the gift of *Corpus Christi* (comprehending the nativity, the resurrection, and the eucharistic sacrament) is the high point, the cycles place the exciting chronicle of fallen man within an envelope of celebration —the celebration of God's rule over and love for even his fallen ones.

III

I will now proceed to examine each "Fall of Lucifer" play as a separate treatment of the themes and issues discussed thus far, in order to see how, operating within a common awareness of the function to be performed by the opening play of an immense cycle, the individual playwright could create an autonomous work of drama with its own emphases of theme and character. The order of the discussion corresponds to what I believe to be the progressively fuller exploitation of the dramatic possibilities inherent in the *mythos* of Lucifer's fall in each successive play.

The briefest "Fall of Lucifer" play is the 82-line version in the N. Towne cycle.[37] According to the division outlined above, Part I (God's declaration) comprises thirty-nine lines, and ends with the angels, newly created as God's servants and worshippers (11. 33-39), chanting at least part of the *Te Deum*.[38] In Part II (11. 40-65) Lucifer makes his counterclaim to the praise of the angels; the good angels refuse to comply, reasserting their duty, but after the usurper has seated himself in God's seat (11. 56-57)[39] bad angels do worship him. Immediately, God banishes Lucifer, whose reply to his Maker's command ratifies his subordinate position:

> At thy byddyng þi wyl I werke

and pas fro joy to peyne smerte
now I am a devyl ful derke
þat was An Aungell bryht.   (11. 75-78)

The rest of Part III, which concludes the play, consists of a
brief lament by the devil for the life he faces in hell. (The place
of Part IV, in this case, is taken by the beginning of the following play in the cycle, in which God calmly proceeds through the
days of creation.)40

In the N. Towne "Fall of Lucifer," Lucifer's act of mimesis,
seeming to displace God, only serves to show how all must bow
to the creator. The irony of the devil's usurpation as a confirmation of God's power is simply but dramatically expressed in the
play's pivotal words and action: at 1. 66, the bad angels pay
obeisance to their new lord, "and ffalle down at þi ffete"—presumably matching the words with the deed. At once God replies:
"Thu lucyfere ffor þi mekyl pryde/ I bydde þe ffalle from hefne
to helle . . ." (11. 67-68). God's reaction gives to the word
(and deed) *fall* a meaning which mocks its misguided use by
Lucifer and his followers, and establishes the real meaning (and
end) of Lucifer's mimetic career. Something similar happens
in the last two lines of the play, spoken by Lucifer as he leaves
for hell: "Ffor fere of fyre a fart I crake/ In helle donjoon myn
dene is dyth" (11. 82-83). As the once-brightest angel becomes
the devil, he brings low comedy into existence (presumably
fitting deed to word), and the playwright makes a common
medieval connection between anality and the devil.41 But he is
also defining such comedy, and the fallen world it represents, as
something confirming, through fear, God's irresistible might.

Other "Fall of Lucifer" plays, as we shall shortly see, introduce comedy into the action (and, in effect, into the universe)
once Lucifer has fallen into hell with his accomplices, and carry the comic impulse further, into comic dialogue and slap-
stick, than the brief compass of the N. Towne version permits.
In all these instances, the intent is the same, viz., to establish
vividly and experientially42 a universe with two "spaces" within
which the rest of the cycle plays will move, and the interaction
between which the dramatist will be able to exploit. One space
is heaven—the place, from now on, of unruffled power, of stasis,
affirmation, celebration, and above all, of control. The other
space is non-heaven—in this case, hell, but later, the audience's
world in all its variety—the place where the behavior of crea-

tures stands on the brink of movement at any moment toward uproar, comic chaos, calamity, i.e., the lively representation of the fallen state of willed alienation from the source of order and harmony in the universe.43 Each space is also metaphoric, of course, expressing tropologically or anagogically the moral significance and ultimate consequences of loving or not loving God. But because heaven will continue to exist for a fallen world, and will continue to send its representatives (culminating in Christ) into the other space, the Corpus Christi dramatist can allow the comic impulse toward chaos and disruption to play itself out, and still demonstrate in his plays the reality and finality of heaven's control of non-heavenly space, just as he can indulge to the fullest his mimetic impulse in portraying salvation history and still claim in good conscience to be praising God as much as do the angels who sing the *Te Deum* in heaven. In sum, the devil is the father of comedy as he is the father of lies; but his offspring ultimately honor their God-father more than their natural one.

IV

The Wakefield cycle's treatment of the "Fall of Lucifer" episode is actually part of a larger dramatic unit, which includes also the creation and fall of man.44 (The Wakefield cycle is unique among extant cycles in this respect.) This linking of episodes means that the sins of Lucifer and Adam are made to seem two parts of the same action, more so than in other cycles, while that action is made to depend for its effect, more than in the analogous plays elsewhere, on a balancing of false mimesis and the true work of creation carried out by God. The first sixty lines of the play, God's speech, not only describe his power, but also recount the first five days of creation.45 Part I ends with a speech by the Cherubim (11. 61-76), whose praise of their creator focuses specifically on his achievement in making Lucifer so bright and beautiful. The angels' speech (which in this play alone replaces the *Te Deum*) is intended as a paradigm of proper appreciation of created greatness (i.e., appreciation which refers all glory back to the creator), and therefore as a contrast to Lucifer's improper response to his own beauty (11. 77-107) which opens Part II. Lucifer's pride issues in his sitting in God's vacant throne, and asking his fellow angels for their opinion of his deed.

This schematic juxtaposition of speeches of proper and improper reaction to the beauties of creation, summed up in Lucifer, is unique to the Wakefield play, as is the next stage of the drama: the more direct but equally schematic juxtaposing of voices in actual debate (11. 108-28) between the good and bad angels over whether or not Lucifer belongs on God's throne, i.e., whether the usurper's mimesis of God is seemly or blasphemous.[46] Rejecting the warning of the good angels, Lucifer now proposes a new symbolic action: he will take flight to demonstrate that he is above correction or reproof (11. 129-31). As he tries to rise, however, he falls to hell instead, with the other bad angels; the speeches of regret by two angels form a brief Part III, and God proceeds at once, without commenting on Lucifer's fall, to the sixth day of creation and the making of Adam (11. 132-61; God creates living things at 1. 162 and man at 1. 165).

The absence of any reaction by God to Lucifer's sin means that, in this play above all, the sequence of Lucifer's actions (sitting in the throne, rising above it, falling to hell) imparts meaning to the drama, but is also most thoroughly subordinated to the forward movement of creation, and becomes, as it were, a small incident in heaven somewhere between the fifth and sixth days of creation.[47] Moreover, the deeds of the rebellious angel function here as their own ironic and explanatory commentary. Lucifer's seeking to rise, and in fact falling, provides an exegesis, acted rather than verbal, of his mimetic act of sitting in the throne; in rising against God (and above his place in the hierarchy of creator-created) he has fallen from God's grace. The physical recreation of the motion of a monarch on fortune's wheel implicit in Lucifer's movements recalls the treatment of Lucifer in Chaucer's *Monk's Tale,*[48] but also dramatizes the futility of his deed and demonstrates how God controls all movement in the universe for his own ends. Finally, the bewailing by the new-made devils of the "pride in thoght" (1. 152) by which they lost heaven accords with the Wakefield dramatist's desire (seen in the balancing speeches, debates, and paired rising-falling actions) to clarify all the issues inherent in Lucifer's false mimesis. The angel's perverse imitation of his creator is a denial of the order of creation, an attempt to rise above one's place, which leads to his own fall to the lowest place of all, but does not interfere with the invincible progress of creation forward toward man and later his redeemer.

<h2 style="text-align:center">V</h2>

Alone among the "Fall of Lucifer" plays, the Chester version presents the first sin as a "back formation" from, and therefore preview of, the fall of man in Paradise, which furnishes the plot of the next play in the cycle. By this device the play gains in clarity of motivation and in suspense. Lucifer, like Adam, is given authority over all other creatures by God, who also warns him not to sit in God's throne while the creator is absent, lest he lose his power and beauty. Thus Lucifer is punished not only for pride but for the even more comprehensible sin of disobedience to a divine command. To motivate the disobedience, the playwright creates a henchman-doublet of Lucifer, Lightborne (cf. Lucifer, meaning light-bearing), whose subordination to Lucifer reduplicates the latter's subordination to God.49 Lightborne encourages his master to rebel, as the serpent does Eve, and accompanies Lucifer to hell.50 How this articulation of motive is accompanied by the conscious cultivation of suspense will become clear from a brief summary of the action of the play.

In Part I of the Chester play, God, as usual, speaks first, declaring his greatness and power in long lines of pompous and aureate verse—an attempt to fit manner to matter unique among the opening sections of the "Fall of Lucifer" plays here under discussion.51 He then creates the angels and promises them happiness in their task of praising him (11. 1-28). The play then moves at once from declaration to dialogue—the only one of those here under discussion to do so at a pre-lapsarian stage of the action—as, in conversation with God, Lucifer and the other angels express their agreement with, subordination to, and praise of the plan of their maker (11. 29-84). This section, together with God's speech of encouragement and warning before he leaves for a brief tour of his creation (11. 85-104),52 makes of Part I an expression of the proper hierarchy of wills corresponding to a hierarchy of power. God explains the system: "Eche one of you kepe well his place,/ And, Lucifer, I make the Governour" (11. 91-92). The guarantee and reward of "my order,"

as God calls it (1. 94), is God's beauty, the physical attribute
of his omnipotence, and the promise of its continuance:

> Behold the beames of my bright face,
> Which ever was and shall endure! . . .
> Here will I bide now in this place,
> for to be Angels Comfortour. . . .
>   (11. 95-96, 101-102)

In other words, God knows, and will remain in, his place and
expects his creatures, who benefit from his constancy, to be as
constant themselves. In Lucifer's case this means that, while he
is God's governor, he must not pretend to be God:

> Now sithe I haue formed you so fayre
> and exalted yow so exellent,
> and here I sett you next my Chayre,
> my loue to you is so fervent,
> Looke, ye fall not in no dispayre,
> touche not my trone by non assent.   (11.65-70)

This concrete visualization of Lucifer's greatness and the limits
of it which he must recognize (expressed more generally at 11.
47-48 and 87-88) sets the stage for the climactic role of the
throne in Part II of the play, and allows the dramatist to create
suspense by portraying Lucifer moving slowly toward the moment of disobedience in which he will sit in the throne.

While God is still present, Lucifer declares his dread and
obedience of his maker (11. 73-80), and Lightborne echoes
his speech of subordination (11. 81-84). As in the other plays,
the angels add their voices in quasi-liturgical affirmation:

> . . . hym for to thanke with somp solace,
> A songe now let us singe in feare.   (11. 63-64)

The Chester playwright, however, goes further than any other to
have his characters articulate their roles in a specific heavenly
order circumscribed and, as it were, rationalized in time and
space by means of God's prohibition concerning the throne, his
announced departure from the scene, and the arrangement of
God, a uniquely "good" Lucifer, and Lightborne into a function-
ing hierarchy.

As soon as God leaves, Part II begins: the dialogue suddenly becomes dramatic, i.e., it becomes an exchange in which
different characters express sharply differing points of view.
Lucifer's earlier declarations of his brightness (e.g., 11. 37-40)

become boasts that he is as bright as, nay brighter than, God (11. 105-08, 163-64). He decides that, were he to sit in God's throne, he would be as wise as well (another echo of the serpent's temptation of Eve; 11. 109-10). The various orders of angels reject Lucifer's contention and stigmatize his pride; only the exaggerated flattery and parasitic self-interest of Lightborne urge the would-be rebel on.[53] Finally deciding to defy (and become) God, Lucifer sits in the throne (11. 189-92); at once God re-appears, condemns the over-reacher, and orders him to fall into hell (11. 193-208).

To balance the heavy and explicit emphasis on obedience to an established order in the first part of the Chester play,[54] its second part presents the rejection of that order by Lucifer—his progress from obedient governor to defiant rebel—as a kind of dramatic *psychomachia* building suspense out of the pull between the promptings of the good angels toward continuing in God's absence the hierarchy he created and the urgings of Lightborne to violate the hierarchy. We may, indeed, see this section as a para-digmatic externalization of the impulses within any creature toward the proper and improper use of the will. The debate here is much longer than that in the Wakefield play (84 lines against 25), and only in the Chester version does it take place before Lucifer is on the throne, thereby representing the background, as it were, of Lucifer's perverse imitation of God, and not just comments on a sin of false mimesis already committed. The Chester playwright's procedure, by creating and exploiting sus-pense—i.e., by deliberately postponing, but keeping before us, an act which we know must eventually take place[55]—heightens the impact of Lucifer's central symbolic deed, and of the peripateia which immediately follows it. God's reappearance, and the exer-cise of his power to banish Lucifer, is cast in the form of a speech contrasting the favor shown the rebel and his betrayal of it:

> Lucifer, who set thee here, when I was goe?
> what haue I offended unto thee?
> I made thee my frende, thou art my foe!
> whie hast thou trespassed thus to me?
> Aboue all Angels there were no mo
> that sate so nighe the maiestye.
> I charge yow fall tyll I byd: 'Noe!'
> to the pitt of hell, evermore to be!   (201-08)

The antitheses of the speech underscore the ironies which attend

false mimesis in all the "Fall of Lucifer" plays: Lucifer has
screwed his courage to the point, not of triumph, but of disaster.
He has lost all he had, and gained only pain, in passing from
the "frende" which God made him to the "foe" he has made himself in trying to act God's role in the universe.56 Equally important for the drama (and unique to this play) is God's injured
tone—"what haue I offended unto thee?"—which further hu-
manizes the events in heaven, bringing them into the low mimetic
world of the audience's experience and further suggesting that
Lucifer's sin is recreated each time we behave selfishly toward
another who deserves better of us.

The self-consciousness with which the cycle playwrights related the central point of all the "Fall of Lucifer" plays—that the
success of perverse mimesis is its failure, because to pretend to
be God when one is not is to call forth from God a response
which proves the inimitability and irresistibility of the divine
power—to their enterprise also finds unique expression in the
Chester play. The good angels issue a warning to Lucifer, just
before his fateful act, which they couch in the same metaphor
used by the Corpus Christi drama to describe and protect itself:

> Goe to your seates and wend hence [from the throne]!
> Yow haue begun a parlous pleye.   (11. 185-86)

This language can be applied to the playwright as well, of
course; he, too, has begun a "parlous pleye." But the final two
sections of the Chester play again show the dramatist avoiding
peril by demonstrating his grasp on the larger implications of
Satan's (and his own) mimesis. Part III (11. 209-52), in which
the fallen angels bemoan their fate in hell, mingles reproach
and comedy and suggests a more sophisticated dramatic awareness than does the N. Towne play of how to exploit the base
while simultaneously using it to exalt the holy.57 The devils accuse each other of the responsibility for their fall, and their rejection of each other echoes, at a lower level, Lucifer's sinful
rejection of God. The comic animus with which they abuse each
other—"the Devill may spede thy stinking face!" (1. 216)—
is but another facet of the penchant for insubordination which
now leads them to plan the overthrow of soon-to-be-created man
(11.233-44). Thus justified, fallen comedy can be given a large
role in making the Corpus Christi cycle succeed as drama and
entertainment, without subverting the cycle's high purpose.

God's final speech (Part IV of the play) shows the Deity pondering, again in very human fashion, the effects of pride.58 He mourns the loss of Lucifer, warns the angels that "pride is your foe," and, filled with sorrow, turns nonetheless to the next step of creation, dividing night from day. The play ends with his pronounced blessing (11. 277-80). The effect of this fourth part is the opposite of the passage in the Wakefield play following the lament of the fallen angels. There, we recall, God takes no notice of Lucifer's crushed rebellion; the creation is already well along and no mere sinner can ruffle its serene architect. Here, by contrast, God is all attention and all regret; his lament for his creatures gone astray and solicitude for the remaining angels, that they not repeat Lucifer's mistake (11. 259-60), opts for pathos and humanity, in a fashion we can identify with some central tendencies of late medieval sentimental piety.59 God's paternal benevolence is no mere sop to contemporary religious feeling, however, but rather the other half of the play's last dramatic contrast. He reiterates his love for his creation, and looks forward to making man:

> And thoughe they have broken my Commaundment,
> me ruethe yt sore full soveraynelye;
> never the less, I will have myne Intent:
> what I first thought, yet so will I.
> I and 2 parsons are at one assent,
> a solemne matter for to trye.
> A full fayre Image we have I-ment,
> that this same stydd shall multeply.   (11. 261-68)

The devil, meanwhile, is plotting to betray man, as we have seen. Fallen, dramatic man will be the devil's victim but never his triumph, for God's loving favor will never be denied to his creation. The dramatist realizes this, Satan does not: therein lies the saving difference between the effect of the former's mimesis— to glorify God—and the latter's—to expose his own futility.

VI

While the York "Fall of Lucifer" play is in some respects a less attractive drama than the Chester version, with its sophisticated use of suspense and humanization of God, a case can be made that the York play most sucessfully fulfills the dramatic potential of this opening *mythos* of the Corpus Christi cycle.60

It does this by finding for each of the four clearly articulated
sections of the play a kind of discourse appropriate to itself and
supportive of the section's meaning within the overall dramatic
development of the play. In Part I, as usual, God declares his
power, and creates the angels, who establish one pole of the
play's intent by praising God via the *Te Deum* (11. 1-24). God
then creates earth and hell, and declares that his faithful creatures shall enjoy heaven, but those who are not "stabill in
thoghte" (1. 30) shall suffer below. Next comes the creation of
Lucifer, whom God names "merour of my myghte" (1. 34),
and to whom he promises "al welth in youre weledyng,/ Ay
whils yhe ar buxomly berande" (11. 39-40). With maximum
economy, the York playwright has established heaven as the
place of order and praise, but also suggested the alternatives
which Lucifer's career, and the punishment it earns, will bring
into the *play* to make of it a *drama*.

Further singing of the *Te Deum* marks the end of Part I;
taken as a whole it is what God creates Lucifer especially to
be: a mirror of his might, i.e., a reflection of the creator's power, and as such naturally calling forth praise and worship from
all creatures. Now, however, into the chorus of praise (which
has become words spoken by an individual angel, 1. 41f.)
Lucifer injects a new voice: that of narcissism, finding expression
in a distortion of the mirror image applied by God to his brightest angel, as quoted above: "I so semely in syghte my selfe
now I se . . ." (1. 51). Lucifer, that is, discovers in himself not
the reflection of God's power, but his own. There ensues a new
level of discourse which is neither choric praise, formal debate
(as in the Wakefield play at this point), nor real dialogue with
tendencies toward realism (as in the Chester play). The angels
continue to praise God hieratically and serenely (11. 57-64, 73-
80) while Lucifer praises himself in the excited voice of
discovery:

> O what! I am fetys and fayre and fygured full fytt!
> The forme of all fayrehede apon me es feste,
> All welth in my weelde es, I wete be my wytte,
> The bemes of my brighthede are bygged with the beste.
>   (11. 65-68)

These two radically different voices talk past rather than to each
other in a kind of "pre-dialogue" which only the audience, from
its position of knowing the consequences of Lucifer's new voice,

can evaluate properly, and which is the verbal analogue of the "pre-dramatic" state of the action. Drama becomes possible once different voices, representing different reactions to, and estimates of, reality, appear; drama actually exists when an action is found which focuses the voices and reveals the implications of their opposition.

Lucifer's discovery of his own beauty leads him to decide that he has power as well ("I am so mightyly made my mirth may noghte mys," 1. 83), sufficient that he can make a place for himself "on heghte in the hyeste of hevvwn" (1. 88). Paraphrasing Isaiah 14 more closely than any other playwright, the York dramatist does not allude to God's throne, but has Lucifer resolve:

> Ther [i.e., in the highest part of heaven] sall
>   I set my selfe, full semly to seyghte,
> To ressayve my reverence thorowe right o renowne,
> I sall be lyke unto hym that es hyeste on heghte;
> Owe! what I am derworth and defte.—Owe! dewes!
>   all goes downe!   (11. 89-92)

The mention of Lucifer's seating himself, and of being "lyke unto" God, and the sudden reversal, which finds him falling to hell without warning a moment later, suggests a sequence much like that of the Wakefield play, and leads me to believe that, although it is not mentioned, God's throne serves as the focus for the stage business here, and that the crucial act is once again the angel's sitting in his creator's place in order to complete his announced plan of mimesis.[61]

The fact that God does not return to cause Lucifer's fall means that the York play moves from the "pre-dialogue" of Part II directly into the full, racily comic dialogue of Part III, spoken by the devils in hell, without the intervention of God's authoritative voice to recall the declarative mode of the play's first part. Lucifer bemoans his fallen state and is abused by the angels whom he has led astray (11. 97-112); he denies any responsibility for others' pain:

> Walaway! wa es me now, nowe is war thane it was.
> Unthryvandely threpe yhe, I sayde but a thoghte.
>   (11. 113-14)[62]

In a peculiar way, he is almost justified, for unlike the other "Fall of Lucifer" plays, the York version includes no appeals by Lucifer for allegiance from other angels. He is so intoxicated by his narcissistic contemplation that, as we have seen, he makes no contact with anyone else in heaven—not even the negative contact of argument. Only here, in the new, fallen space of the dramatic world, does dialogue become possible, but it is the dialogue of quarrel, of attack and defense, issuing in a physical melee which the only kind of interaction possible among creatures each of whom has set out to pretend to be his own God. Since, of course, the devils are not God, and also, thanks to their own narcissistic folly, no longer part of his heavenly choir, their comic uproar is a gross parody and logical conclusion of Lucifer's removal of himself from the social harmony which reflects creation's glad subordination of itself to its creator. This is life at the court of the God that failed:

> *Second Devil*:   Owte! owte! I go wode for wo, my wytte
>   es all wente nowe
> All oure fode es but filth, we fynde
>   us beforn. . . .
> Owte! on the Lucifer, lurdan! oure
>   lyghte has thu lorne.
> Thi dedes to this dole nowe has dyghte us,
> To spille us thu was oure spedar. . . .
> We! lurdane, thu lost us.
> *Lucifer*:   Yhe ly, owte! allas!
> I wyste noghte this wo sculde be wroghte.
> Owte on yhow! lurdans, yhe smore me
>   in smoke. . . .
> *Second Devil*:   Thou lyes, and that sall thu by.
> We! lurdans, have at yowe, lat loke.
>
> (11. 105-20) [63]

The separation of the individual from the group makes possible drama, but when the separation is one of defiance issuing in false mimesis, its final and most bitter fruit is strife among creatures, at once horrifying and ridiculous to those who can see the evil. The York dramatist here shows dramatic skill neatly combined with (and justified by) theological insight.

The final section of the York play contrasts hell's dialogue with an equally new, but completely dissimilar, dialogue in heaven. The good angel praises God for having punished Lucifer, and reveals that he has learned something of the Lord's ways in watching the drama unfold:

> Thi rightwysnes redes to rewarde on rowe
> Ilke warke eftyr it is wroghte.
> Thorowe grace of thi mercyfull myghte
> The cause I se itt in syghte,
> Wharefore to bale he [Lucifer] es broghte.   (11. 124-28)

God confirms the angel's insight, promises continuance in bliss to those who obey him, and, having decided to replace the fallen angels by a new creature, man, sets about preparing the world for him.64 In other words, Lucifer's fall has left its mark in heaven, not as a legacy of strife, but as a means of further clarifying the nature of God's power and wisdom, and as a stimulus to continue the work of creation. The York play's God is neither the unnoticing victor of Wakefield nor the hurt parent of Chester, but a teacher commenting on his method and plans to an obedient pupil who perceives them with new understanding. Thus the York dramatist is able to give to each section of his 160-line play an atmosphere distinct from all the others: the words and actions fully express and support the dramatic and doctrinal point being made at that stage of the action. Such mastery over his material, rendering it at once entertaining and revealing, is the York playwright's best argument against the charge of being like Lucifer, whose mimesis shows neither control over its chosen action nor, until too late, awareness of the realities of its world.

VII

My examination of these four plays has hopefully demonstrated that each has its own strategies for making an effective didactic drama out of the tradition of Lucifer's fall. In addition, the issue of false mimesis or perverse imitation—the blasphemous confusion between creator and creature—is dealt with self-consciously in all the plays, with the dramatist able by his awareness and presentation of the issue to distinguish between his own enterprise and Lucifer's. In the "Fall of Lucifer" plays, Lucifer's act of defiance becomes, through the playwright's skill and understanding, a means to glorify God. Equally important, these plays try to define God's relationship to the world in which the dramatist works and finds his material—a world fallen (and thus dramatic) as seen through the eyes of experience, yet redeemed (and thus celebrating God and his sacramental presence in the *Corpus Christi*) as seen through the eyes of faith. By encompassing within his larger, celebratory dramatic intent the deliberate representation of Lucifer as a practitioner of false mimesis, the Corpus Christi dramatist himself transcends the level of such naive and self-destructive pretense, and thus hopes to lay to rest the charge of blasphemy levelled against his art.

NOTES

1 Stanford, 1965. I am also indebted to the students of my senior seminar in medieval literature in Columbia College, 1971-72, whose enthusiasm for the medieval drama was as stimulating as their perceptions were helpful.

2 See Kolve, pp. 11-12; on the terminology of the Latin plays, see K. Young, *The Drama of the Medieval Church* (Oxford, 1933), II, 407-10. Young says, "Probably the most normal term for a dramatic performance is *repraesentatio*. . . . Occasionally one finds the word *ludus*, a designation rendered generally ambiguous through its common association with popular revelling . . ." (p. 408). For a distinction between the concept of representation and the basic liturgical form, ritual, see O. B. Hardison, Jr., *Christian Rite and Christian Drama in the Middle Ages* (Baltimore, 1965), pp. 67-68, 230-32.

3 See Kolve, p. 32: "The aim of the Corpus Christi drama was to celebrate and elucidate, never, not even temporarily, to deceive. It played action in 'game'— not in 'ernest'—within a world set apart, established by convention, and obeying rules of its own. A lie designed to tell the truth about reality, the drama was understood as significant play."

4 See Kolve, p. 9: "If the Corpus Christi plays had been concerned merely with human beings—Adam and Eve, knights and Jews, midwives and thieves—the range of dramatis personae would have presented no real difficulty. But medieval men believed that human history could not be explained in purely human terms, and therefore in their drama, a mimesis and interpretation of that history, they could not restrict themselves to the representation of human characters. God the Father must appear, God the Son in his human form. . . . Here a crucial difficulty arises [for] the image and its referent are so different in kind that blasphemy or sacrilege may be involved. The actor's human nature risks defiling the most awesome of Christian images; man is not God, and God will not be mocked."

5 See Kolve, pp. 17-18 on the antithesis of game and earnest as a type of topos in late Middle English literature; as Kolve says (p. 19), "there was little fundamental distinction made between drama and other forms of men's playing" at that time. The most famous example of this point, and of the game-earnest theme brilliantly treated as a literary theme, is of course *Gawain and the Green Knight*, in which the opening scene at King Arthur's court shows the courtiers playing Christmas games (see especially 11. 37-49, 64-71). As the court sits down for dinner, the Green Knight bursts in, and, despite the strength of his body ("Hit semed as no mon myȝt/ Vnder his dyntteȝ dryȝe," 11. 201-02) and the menacing quality of his axe (11. 208-13), and the brusqueness of his address (" 'Wher is,' he sayd,/ 'Þe gouernour of þis gyng," 11. 224-225), he tells the astonished courtiers that he has come looking for a partner in a game (ll. 272-74, 283; cf. his comment on the court's reputation as a place full of people "Preue for to play wyth in oþer pure laykeȝ," 1. 262)! Of course, the game turns out to be an earnest, life-and-death matter for Gawain—or so at least it appears until the very end of the poem, by which time we are not sure where game stops and earnest begins. King Arthur, after the departure of the Green Knight, head in hand, tells the apparently terrified Queen, "Wel bycommes such craft vpon Cristmasse,/ Laykyng of enterludeȝ, to laȝe and to syng. . . ." (11. 471-72). "Enterludeȝ" refers, of course, to a play-type entertainment; see E. K. Chambers, *The Medieval Stage* (Oxford, 1903), II, 178-226. One can even think of events at Bertilak's castle as a play designed with a leading role for Gawain. See further M. Stevens, "Laughter and Game in Sir Gawain and the Green Knight," *Speculum*, 47 (1972), 65-78.

6 See Kolve, p. 10; further support for Kolve's contention that there was uneasiness about the representation of God on stage can be drawn from sixteenth-century documents relating to the suppression of the cycle plays by ecclesiastical authorities in a now officially Protestant England. One such document shows that the York Diocesan Court of High Commission, in suppressing the annual performance of the Wakefield cycle, forbade that "the Majesty of God the Father, God

the Son, or God the Holy Ghost . . . be counterfeited or represented" in any play—
a prohibition which, by design, made the performance of many of the individual
plays, including the central Passion group, impossible. See M. Rose, ed., *The Wakefield Mystery Plays* [a modernized acting version] (New York, 1961), Introduction,
pp. 17-18, from which I have quoted this passage.

7 See Kolve, ch. 3.

8 E. A. Speiser, in his translation of Genesis (The Anchor Bible; New York,
1964), translates the passage, "The moment you eat of it your eyes will be opened
and you will be the same as God in telling good from bad" (p. 21). And the
Vulgate version known to the Corpus Christi playwrights (or their advisers), says,
". . . in quocumque die comederitis ex eo, aperientur oculi vestri, et eritis sicut
dii scientes bonum et malum" (*Biblia Sacra Vulgatae Editionis . . . cura et studio
monachorum Abbatiae Pontificiae Sancti Hieronymi in urbe . . .* [Rome, 1959], p. 2).

9 For a discussion of the different provenance and outlook of the various
traditions combined in Genesis, see Speiser, pp. xx-xxxvii. Speiser's specific comments on the first, or "Priestly," creation account in Genesis appear on pp. 8-13
of his translation, where he demonstrates how this account is based on the Meso-
potamian creation epic, *Enuma Elish*. In the latter, however, the polytheistic myth
makes possible conflict and tension absent from the Genesis adaptation. As Speiser
puts it, "The Babylonian creation story features a succession of various rival deities.
The biblical version, on the other hand, is dominated by the monotheistic concept
in the absolute sense of the term." On *Enuma Elish*, see the perceptive analysis of
G. R. Levy, *The Sword from the Rock* (London, 1953), pp. 99-119. The story of
the Fall of Lucifer (see below, and next note) introduces into the Genesis account
a note of conflict which, interestingly enough, renders its impact closer to that of
the Babylonian epic.

10 The tradition of the fallen angels, traceable ultimately to Genesis 6. 1-4, and
elaborated in the late Old Testament pseudepigrapha, the First Book of Enoch, is
referred to in 2 Peter 2.4 and Jude 6. See B. Reicke, ed. and trans., The Epistles
of James, Peter, and Jude (The Anchor Bible; New York, 1964), pp. 164, 199.
(According to Reicke, the early Christians regarded the Book of Enoch as an early
and inspired text.) The patristic tradition, building on these references, began quite
early to speak of Lucifer's fall as a specific and important event. As W. W. Skeat
says in his note to Chaucer's reference in the *Monk's Tale* to Lucifer's fall, "St.
Jerome, Tertullian, St. Gregory and other Fathers supposed [Isaiah 14, 12f] to
apply to the fall of Satan" (*The Complete Works of Geoffrey Chaucer*, 2nd ed.
[Oxford, 1900], V, 227-28). He adds that it was "a favorite topic for writers both
in prose and verse" in the Middle Ages. H. Craig, *English Religious Drama of the
Middle Ages* (Oxford, 1955), p. 183, notes that the fall of Lucifer "was not liturgical and indeed was relatively new" at the time the Corpus Christi cycles came
into existence, by which he appears to mean only recently had the "fact" of Lucifer's fall been embroidered so that "there was a cult that gave names, characteristics, and classification to evil angels as well as good." Such expansion is not, as
we shall see, very important for the impact of the "Fall of Lucifer" cycle plays.

11 Vulgate, p. 766.

12 A Text, Passus I.109-13; B Text, Passus I.111-21; C Text, Passus I.107-22.
The C Text raises the issue of mimesis most explicitly (11. 10-11), and concen-
trates on the symbolic fact of Satan sitting where he should not, but does not say,
as do the plays, that he sat in God's throne.

13 Book V.1701f. Lucifer's fall is also considered in Book I.3299f; Book VIII.
1-23. Actually, Gower is less interested in the circumstances of the fall, than in the
consequences of sin to the sinner—that is, his is a homiletic, not a narrative approach, and Lucifer is an exemplum of how terrible it is to cut oneself off from
God. Hence Gower's dwelling on the horrors of hell (in a manner recalling, for
example, the Middle English homily *Sawles Warde*) in the passage from Book VIII,
mentioned above. See also note 21, below.

14 *Canterbury Tales,* VII.1999-2006 (Fragment B, 11. 3189-96). On the Monk's formulation of Lucifer's fall as an exceptional instance of a Fortune tragedy, in relation to the Wakefield "Fall of Lucifer" play, see below.

15 L1. 205f.

16 On questions of dating see Craig, *English Religious Drama,* pp. 129-33; he says, "We may believe, then, that the Corpus Christi play was set up, probably on the model of an inclusive dramatic form invented on the Continent, about the end of the first quarter of the fourteenth century at some place probably in the north of England, and spread thence to other places in the island" (p. 133). The earliest record of a Corpus Christi play dates from 1376, in York, and G. Wickham, *Early English Stages* (London, 1959), I, 125, argues that "performance [of religious plays] in English and by laymen is a development of the last quarter of the four-teenth century. . . ." Kolve, pp. 37-39, offers pictorial evidence supporting a date nearer Craig's than Wickham's. See also D. Mills, "Approaches to Medieval Drama," *Leeds Studies in English,* n.s. 3 (1969), 47-61, for a consideration of how the forma-tion of the cycles, and the specific incidents they dramatized, were influenced by a tradition of narrative and didactic religious poetry covering the whole salvation history, e.g., *Cursor Mundi.* See especially pp. 51-55.

17 See below.

18 I use the translation of M. Dods (rpt. New York, 1950). See XI.9, 11, 13-15, 17, 19-20, 33-34; XII.1-2, 6-8.

19 See *City* XII.6: "When the evil will abandons what is above itself, and turns to what is lower, it becomes evil—not because that is evil to which it turns but because the turning itself is wicked. Therefore it is not an inferior thing which has made the will evil, but it is itself which has become so by wickedly and inordinately desiring an inferior thing" (p. 386).

20 See *City* XII.7 (p. 387).

21 As Gower puts it, in the *Confessio Amantis,* Book I, "For Lucifer, with them that felle,/ Bor pride with him into helle./ Ther was pride of to grete cost,/ When he for pride hath heven lost" (11. 3299-3302; see G. C. Macaulay, ed., *The English Works of John Gower* [Oxford, 1900], p. 125). W. E. Meyers, in his study of the Wakefield cycle, *A Figure Given* (Pittsburgh, 1970) points out (pp. 41-43) that Augustine (*City* XIV.13) unequivocally states that pride—love of self—resulted in the founding of the *civitas terrena;* Meyers then connects this statement and the presentation of the proud Lucifer in the opening play of the Wakefield cycle. But his analysis of this play does not proceed further in the direction which interests me in this paper, i.e., the relation between self-love and its symbolic expression as the mimesis of God. On the Manichees' interpretation of the origin of evil in the devil's innate sinfulness, and Augustine's rebuttal, see *City* XI.15 (p. 359).

22 *City* XI.9, 18, 19.

23 *City* XI.18 (p. 361). Augustine's aesthetic appreciation of the contraries im-plicit in typological pairings and the earliest Christian catechesis is very interesting. Cf. the neat opposition of the old and new Adams in Romans 5, or the elaborate balancing of the tree of man's Fall and the rood-tree of his redemption. On the latter, see, for instance, L. H. Leiter, *"The Dream of the Rood:* Patterns of Trans-formation," in R. P. Creed, ed., *Old English Poetry* (Providence, 1967), pp. 98-102.

24 P. 359 (of the Manichees): "And how do they answer the prophetic proofs— either what Isaiah says when he represents the devil under the person of the king of Babylon, 'How art thou fallen, O Lucifer, son of the morning!' or what Ezekiel says, etc."

25 The homiletic approach of Gower, mentioned in note 13, above, is a much more common one, as, by the late fourteenth century, it was the method which cate-gorized the fallen angels and fitted them into a scholastic analysis of evil (see Craig, *English Religious Drama,* p. 183, as mentioned in note 10, above).

26 See, for example, the N. Towne version:

> . . . And all þat evyr xal haue beynge
> it is closyd in my mende
> whan it is made at my lykyng
> I may it saue I may it shende
> After my plesawns
> So gret of myth is my pouste
> All thyng xal be wrowth be me. . . .   (11. 5-11)

All references to this play use the text in K. S. Block, ed., *Ludus Conventriae* [Oxford, 1922], pp. 16-19.) Cf. Wakefield version, 11. 13-18; Chester version, 11. 11-13; York version, 11. 1-4.

27 Wakefield is the exception to this statement; its angels praise God in speech (11, 61-76). The *Te Deum* is specifically quoted in the N. Towne and York stage directions.

28 The *Te Deum* is, of course, a paraliturgical rather than a liturgical hymn. On its origin and function in the early Church, see J. A. Jungmann, *The Mass of the Roman Rite,* tr. F. A. Brunner (New York, 1950), I, 346-50, 356.

29 See Chester version, 11. 89-104.

30 A good example of this structure is found in the Chester "Deluge," another in the most famous morality play, *Everyman.* Interestingly enough, the structure of *Gawain and the Green Knight* corresponds to this dramatic form much more than to the episodic form of the French chivalric romances which inspired its content. The Green Knight sets up the conditions of Gawain's testing at the beginning of the romance, and then disappears, allowing Gawain to undergo temptations of various kinds, only to "return" (or, more accurately, to be rediscovered by the questing Gawain) at the end to explain the significance of all that has happened. Like God, the Green Knight has actually controlled all the events which Gawain has undergone at Bertilak's castle, ignorant of their initiator.

31 Cf. Kolve's remark concerning the portrayal of evil in the cycle plays: "In my view, the Corpus Christi drama succeeds best in its characterization of evil when it is showing the energy, the wiles, the playfulness and moral simplicity of ordinary men at their most instinctive and creaturely" (pp. 235-36). The whole of Kolve's chapter ix, "Natural Man and Evil," is apposite to my point, though differently focused, and so is chapter v, "Medieval Time and English Place," discussing "what manner of address this drama makes to *present* time" (p. 101, italics Kolve's).

32 Cf., for example, in the York version, 1. 2 (spoken by God): "I am maker unmade, all mighte es in me," and 1. 49 (spoken by Lucifer): "All the myrth that es made es markide in me." In the Chester version, Lucifer demands homage from the other angels, as though he were God, with special insistence; see 11. 121-24, 157-60, 169-72.

33 Their warnings and rebukes to Lucifer and his partisans is especially marked in the Chester version, 11. 117-88 *passim.* On the use of language self-consciously naming the danger of mimesis when the angels warn Lucifer, see below.

34 On the symbolic value of sitting in the king's throne, see the interesting parallel to these plays in the seventh book of Herodotus' *Histories,* where Xerxes, the Persian king, stages an impersonation of himself by his relative, Artebanus, who is to wear the king's robes and sit on the king's throne in order to have the dream, urging him to invade Greece, which has repeatedly troubled Xerxes. The point of this incident seems to be that Artebanus, who has urged moderation on Xerxes and opposed war, places the king in a position of false mimesis of himself, i.e., of accepting the trappings of kingship but refusing its heroic destiny of seeking conquest. (Such, at least, is Herodotus' view of the barbarian ideal of leadership.)

35 See Augustine's *Confessions* II.6 (trans. R. S. Pine-Coffin [Baltimore, 1961],

p. 50), where, after considering how men's sins disguise themselves as virtues which God possesses in infinitely greater quantity, Augustine exclaims to God: "So the soul defiles itself with unchaste love when it turns away from you and looks elsewhere for things which it cannot find pure and unsullied except by returning to you. All who desert you and set themselves up against you merely copy you in a perverse way; but by this very act of imitation they only show that you are the Creator of all nature and, consequently, that there is no place wherever where man may hide away from you." This statement offers, I believe, a remarkably accurate and complete explication of the message of the "Fall of Lucifer" plays here under discussion. Cf. this description of pride, which is Lucifer's sin in the plays and in the tradition of exegesis of the Isaiah 14 passage: "pride . . . which is a pretence of superiority, imitating yours, for you alone are God, supreme over all . . ." (*Confessions* II.6, p. 49).

36 See especially the plays of the so-called "Wakefield Master," who is throughout aware of the problematic nature of mimesis. Thus Cain, in the *"Mactacio Abel"* play, after killing his brother, pretends to be bailiff announcing the king's peace for himself and his *garcio*—an ironic comment on the fact that he has just earned the enmity of the heavenly King—while the *garcio* imitates and mocks Cain in sarcastic asides; cf. also Mak, the wily actor-thief of the "Second Shepherd's Play," and Herod, in *"Magnus Herodes,"* who closes his play with a speech in which he promises to 'com agayn" to distribute rewards and punishments, i.e., he imitates Christ's apocalyptic message as king of all creation. (See 11. 483-513; the parallels in this play between Herod's boasting words and images in Apocalypse are indicated by Meyers, *A Figure Given*, pp. 71-72. Meyers sees the relationship between Lucifer and the great villains of the cycle plays as a typological one, and says little about their mimetic propensities, except that "Herod has committed the sin of Lucifer, taking the honors of God to himself" (p. 71). See his third chapter, "Diabolical Typology" (pp. 37-55).

37 Also called the *Ludus Coventriae* or the Hegge plays. See note 26, above.

38 See the stage direction after 1. 39, p. 17.

39 "I wyl go syttyn in goodys se/ Above sunne and mone and sterrys on sky[.]/ I am now set as ȝe may se . . ." (11. 56-58); note the echoes of Isaiah 14.13, with the precise difference that it is "goddys se," not a rival throne of his own, that Lucifer sits in.

40 See the first stanza of the next play (p. 19, 11. 83-91). God does not refer to Lucifer directly, saying only, "Now hevyn is made ffor Aungell sake/ þe fyrst day and þe fyrst nyth . . ." (11. 83-84), suggesting perhaps that the dramatist is thinking of Augustine's allegory of the separation of the light from the darkness (see above).

41 Cf., for example, the story told against friars in the *Summoner's Prologue* of the *Canterbury Tales,* and the famous signal of Malacoda at the end of *Inferno* XXI. Anality is also central to the humor of the *"Mactacio Abel,"* and is sometimes linked to the devil, e.g., 11. 63, 266.

42 In the Chester "Fall of Lucifer," God creates hell before Lucifer's fall (11. 50-51), and similarly in the York version (11. 25-32), but in both cases it takes on no dramatic reality until Lucifer is thrust into it.

43 For a brilliant discussion of "fallen comedy" and the uses made of it in the Corpus Christi plays see Kolve, chapters vi and vii. See also H. Schless, "The Comic Element in the Wakefield Noah," in M. Leach, ed., *Studies in Medieval Literature* (Philadelphia, 1961), pp. 229-43, on the relationship between comedy and human disorder.

44 The edition I use is G. England and A. W. Pollard, eds., *The Towneley Plays* (Oxford, 1897), pp. 1-9; the manuscript breaks off after Lucifer, now in hell, has promised to have Adam and Eve, newly created, expelled from paradise (1. 267), and the editors (p. 9) believe that twelve leaves are missing from the text. See also

Martin Stevens, "The Missing Parts of the Towneley Cycle," *Speculum*, 45 (1970), 256-57.

45 By contrast, in the other versions the fall of Lucifer comes after the first day (N. Towne) or before the first day (Chester and York, which are clearly related in their treatment, as is shown by the structural and verbal parallels at the beginning and ending of the plays; cf. especially Chester 11. 269-280 and York 11. 153-160).

46 After Lucifer asks for approbation, *primus angelus malus* answers in three lines, balanced by *primus angelus bonus* in three lines; *secundus bonus angelus* offers four lines, *secundus malus angelus* replies with eight. Lucifer asks another question, and gets contrasted, one-line answers from the first good and first bad angel.

47 By placing Lucifer's fall so late in the sequence of creation, the Wakefield dramatist brings it closer to man's fall, just as putting both falls in the same play assimilates them more closely. Pollard and England (p. 5, n. 1) believe that either a speech by God or exclamations by the falling devils have been omitted after Lucifer announces that he will "take a flyght" (1. 131), but their argument from the analogy of the other "Fall of Lucifer" plays overlooks the individuality of treatment in each play which this examination has discovered.

48 See 11. 9-16; the Monk is concerned that Lucifer doesn't entirely fit his definition of fortune-tragedy (11. 11-12). Cf. the use of the image of Lucifer's leap of pride in the *Ancrene Wisse* (ed. J. R. R. Tolkien [Oxford, 1962], part II, p. 31: "Lucifer þurh þ he seh / biheold on him seolf his ahne feiernesse leop in to prude / bicom of angel eatelich deouel."

49 I cite H. Deimling, ed., *The Chester Plays* (Oxford, 1892), I, 9-20. The device of creating a relationship between mortals paralleling that between man and God is used frequently by the Wakefield Master, e.g., Cain and Garcio in the *"Mactacio Abel,"* Noah and his wife in the *"Processus Noe cum filiis."*

50 Of course, the existence of Lightborne as a proto-tempter spoils Augustine's point that there was no exterior motivation for Lucifer's primal sin—or rather, it externalizes the debate within Lucifer by means of symbolic personages and voices. See below.

51 This type of verse is not used in the play after 1. 52. God does not return to this style in his speeches after Lucifer's fall. The dramatist thus seems to be attempting to establish a "pre-dramatic" world through style; by the end of the play, drama has been born and even God must change his voice accordingly. Cf. Craig's brief remark on this feature of the play, *English Religious Drama*, p. 183.

52 God leaves, "to be revisible in short space" (1. 103). Cf. 11. 49, 89-90. Such an action by the omnipresent Deity is, of course, logically impossible, but dramatically necessary; see above.

53 Lightborne says that Lucifer is a thousand times brighter than God (11. 137-44), and wishes to sit next to Lucifer to share in his newly-seized power (11. 173-80). This grosser parody of Lucifer's own opinion and desire is the means by which Lightborne (and the playwright) introduces a comic element into the rebellion simultaneously with Lucifer's introduction of drama into the universe.

54 The numerical balance is exact between Part I (11. 1-104) and Part II 11. 105-208).

55 I am here adapting for my purposes the well-known definition of suspense used by the film director Alfred Hitchcock to distinguish between a mystery and a suspense film.

56 See especially 11. 169-72:

> All Angelles turne to me, I redd,
> and to your Soveraigne knele on your knee!

I am your Comfort, both Lord and head,
the myrth and might of the maiesty.

57 See ex-Lightborne's accusation and angry abuse (11. 213-16), and Satan's reply (11. 217-20). The rest of this part is taken up with serious laments for what the fallen angels have lost, as in the Wakefield version.

58 One thinks, almost, of the famous *Wahnmonolog* of Hans Sachs at the beginning of Act III of Wagner's *Meistersinger,* where the sadness of a wise spectator of scenes of human folly is also represented. See 11. 253-58 (God addressing Lucifer):

Ah! wicked pryde aye work thee wo!
my myrth hast thou made amisse.
I may well suffer: my will is not soe
that they shold part thus from my bliss.
Ah! pryde, whi hast thou not burst in 2?
Why did they that? Why did they this?

59 See the extremes to which this vein could be exploited, in the Brome *Play of Abraham and Isaac.* An unpublished Columbia University dissertation by Hope P. Weissman, "Chaucer's Bad Tales" (1973), explores the uses of the pathetic style in Chaucer and elsewhere in late medieval literature and art.

60 I use the text printed in A. W. Pollard, ed., *English Miracle Plays Moralities and Interludes* (Oxford, 1927), pp. 1-7.

61 Lucifer speaks of "beeldand" a place for himself in the highest part of heaven (11. 87-88) in the future tense. This tense continues to be used until 1. 92, in the first part of which Lucifer exclaims, in the present tense, that he is "derworth and defte." The "look at me!" tone of this exclamation might best be interpreted as resulting from Lucifer's slipping into God's chair, even as he talks of how he will eventually place himself higher than the Deity. Such a staging is, needless to say, completely conjectural on my part.

62 Cf. 1. 113 and the complaint of the third shepherd in the Wakefield "Second Shepherd's Play," 11. 118-19: "Crystys crosse me spede and sant nycholas!/ Ther of had I nede it is wars then it was." I cannot help wondering if there is an echoing, perhaps unconscious, on the part of the Wakefield Master, of the York line, suggesting that the bad weather on the Yorkshire moors is to be understood as a symbolic representation of the world which has been created by the alienation of creature from creator—an alienation about to be remedied by the birth of Christ in the course of the Shepherds' play. On the relationship between the York and Wakefield cycles generally, see Craig, pp. 199-238.

63 I assume that the last line of this quotation is accompanied by the outbreak of a scuffle, in which all dignity and chance for discourse are destroyed.

64 On the parallel between this passage and that of the Chester version, see note 45, above. Once again, there is the echo of the Augustinian allegorical interpretation of the separation of light from darkness as the banishment of the fallen angels, in, however, a rationalized form: God tells the faithful angels to "gyf lyghte/ To the erthe, for it faded when the fendes fell" (11. 147-48), and then goes on to name the darkness "night" and the light "day" (11. 150-51).

Why Do the Shepherds Prophesy?

Thomas P. Campbell

The Wakefield *Secunda Pastorum*, by all means the best-known pageant in the Middle English Mystery Cycles, has drawn much commentary, the majority of it directed toward the contrast between the humorous mock-nativity staged by Mak and Gill to conceal their stolen sheep and the pious conclusion of the play in which the shepherds reverently worship the Christ-child at Bethlehem.[1] Yet, much of this commentary has led us away from the connections between this superbly comic piece and the many other depictions of the shepherds in the history of medieval drama. If we are to understand the traditions under which the Wakefield Master is writing, we must examine more carefully a moment in this play which as yet has received little attention: the point at which the shepherds prophesy the birth of Christ. Typically, the Wakefield Master is able simultaneously to communicate both humor and reverence. The three shepherds have caught Mak red-handed. Realizing that they could by right hang this criminal for his robbery, they charitably "cast hym in canvas." They fall asleep from their exertions, and are awakened by the song of the angel announcing Christ's birth. They begin to imitate it haltingly, but are interrupted by the second shepherd, Gyb, who suddenly begins to cite Old Testament prophecies:

> We fynde by the prophecy—let be youre dyn!—
> Of Dauid and Isay and mo then I myn—
> Thay prophecyed by clergy—that in a vyrgyn
> Shuld he lyght and ly, to slokyn oure syn,
> And slake it,
> Oure kynde, from wo;
> For Isay sayd so:
> *Ecce virgo*
> *Concipiet* a chylde that is nakyd.[2]

Why should he interrupt the action of the play at this point? The transition from the mock-nativity to the real one has already been accomplished both by a demonstration of the shepherds' charity and by the announcement of the angel. The prophecies seem to be an intrusion into the form of the play. In fact, however, the shepherds' recognition of Old Testament prophecies of the Savior is one of the few elements which the *Secunda Pastorum* shares in common with all medieval English shepherds' plays; and, as I shall argue, it may be traced back to the very roots of the Christmas drama itself.

Yet, why should the shepherds prophesy? They do not in the scriptural source. Nor does there seem to be a firm tradition in the exegetical literature linking the shepherds with the recitation of Old Testament prophecies.3 Scholarly opinion on this topic is divided. The standard view, which held that the mystery cycles were the linear outgrowths of liturgical drama, maintained that prophecy in the shepherd plays was attributable to its presence in liturgical plays; that it was a logical and evolutionary expansion of an established tradition.4 This view is now on the wane, and few modern scholars would assume a direct, linear relationship between liturgical and secular drama. In its place, more recent theorists have argued that the shepherds prophesy because they are antetypes of the clergy; or because they function to tie the Old Testament and New Testament together; or because the playwrights are drawing upon conventional folk wisdom.5 It is not enough to maintain, as the evolutionary critics held, that prophecy occurs in these plays simply because it appears in liturgical drama; nor can we synthesize the varying theories of the modern organicists. What is needed is a new attempt, drawing upon the insights of both schools.

It is my purpose in the following paper to trace the function and meaning of prophecy in the medieval shepherds' plays. We will begin with a brief literary analysis of the English cycle plays; but our study will take us back to the liturgical drama, and from there into the medieval liturgy itself. At that point I shall examine the reasons for the association of shepherds and prophecy from the earliest history of medieval drama. For it is my contention that this association is an important key to understanding the origin and meaning of the Christmas plays.

The medieval English playwrights seem to have felt an obligation to fit prophetic testimony into the dramatic shape of each shepherd pageant. In the York Cycle, the testimony defines the very structure of the play: the shepherds prophesy at the very beginning of the pageant, establishing a sense of expectation. Their prophecy centers specifically upon the star of Bethlehem, which has appeared to Joseph and Mary in the pageant immediately preceding,6 and its appearance at the end of the play signals the fulfillment of the shepherds' prophecies and their expectations:

> An aungell brought vs tythandes newe,
> A babe in Bedlem shulde be borne,
> Of whom þan spake oure prophicie trewe. . . .
>   (*York Plays*, p. 120, 11. 72-74)

In fact, an emphasis on *fulfillment* is the common factor in all of the shepherd pageants. In the Towneley *Prima Pastorum,* Daw's learned recitation of Virgil's Fourth Eclogue is ridiculed by the others. But its fulfillment in the person of the infant Christ is handled seriously and reverently:

> *1 Pastor.* Wold God that we myght this yong bab see!
> *2 Pastor.* Many prophetys that syght desyryd veralee,
>   To haue seen that bright.
> *3 Pastor.*   And God so hee
>   Would shew vs that wyght, we myght say, perdé,
>   We had sene
>   That many sant desyryd,
>   With prophetys inspyryd;
>   If thay hym requyryd,
>   Yit closyd ar thare eene.
>   (*Wakefield Pageants*, p. 41, 11. 440-48)

In *Ludus Coventrie* and the Coventry "Pageant of the Shearmen and Taylors," prophecy occurs as merely a stimulus-response reaction to the angel's song; yet both plays emphasize that it is now fulfilled by Christ's birth.7 In Chester, the shepherds laboriously unravel the meaning of the angel's song, testifying in their devotions to Christ:

> Hayle, kynge, borne in a maydens bowre.
> Profettes did tell thow should be our succour;
> this clarkes do saye.
>   (*Chester Mystery Cycle*, p. 150, 11. 556-58)

Another, equally important element in the shepherds' prophecies, one which we also find uniformly throughout the cycles, is its close association with an anachronistic Christian community surrounding the manger in Bethlehem. Consider, for

instance, the reaction of the first shepherd to the angel's song
in the *Secunda Pastorum:*

> Patryarkes that has bene, and prophetys beforne,
> Thay desyryd to haue sene this chylde that is borne.
> They ar gone full clene; that haue thay lorne.
> We shall se hym, I weyn, or it be morne,
> To tokyn.
> When I se hym and fele,
> Then wote I full weyll
> It is true as steyll
> That prophetys haue spokyn:
>
> To so poore as we ar that he wold appere,
> Fyrst fynd, and declare by his messyngere.
>   (*Wakefield Pageants,* pp. 61-62, 11. 692-702)

Here, and in all the cycles, the shepherds testify to their own
participation in the Nativity: what the Old Testament patriarchs
and prophets have longed for, they themselves have witnessed.[8]
Their recognition is more than simple testimony, however. The
shepherds actually pledge themselves to become members of a
Christian community. In their prayers and offerings to the
Christ-child, they show an awareness that they are participating
in a Christian service of worship.[9] They offer Him the best they
have, and pray for His grace. Their prayers are often answered
by Mary, as mediatrix, who vows to intercede for their salvation.
In Chester, this sense is even more clearly denoted by the
shepherds' vow to become preachers and to spread the gospel.[10]
    The Christian community is not established merely for the
shepherds' sake. Rather, the shepherds' devotions are a focus for
the participation of all Christians in the birth of Christ as both
an historical and a spiritual event. The medieval audience was
simultaneously aware of the shepherds as both historical participants in the Nativity drama and as contemporary people,
caught up in the trials and complaints of the late Middle Ages.
Devices such as action, costuming, Christian expletive, and geographical reference serve to extend the shepherds' activities into
the audience, to sweep them out of the narrow historical moment of Christ's birth, directly into the present time and place
of the dramatization.[11] Perhaps, as Kolve asserts, this would
identify the shepherds as types of the contemporary clergy,[12]
but I do not think the audience would necessarily have noticed
it. What they would have noticed, though, was the similarity
between the Christian community established around the man-

ger, and their own community of Christian worshippers in the medieval church.

From a literary point of view, the English shepherds' pageants depict two consistent themes associated with the recitation of prophecy: its fulfillment in the historical birth of Christ, and its role in the establishment of an anachronistic Christian community surrounding the manger. Yet surely these observations would be of more interest if it could be shown that they are not simply limited to an analysis of shepherd plays in the English cycles, but in fact tell us something about dramatic treatments of the Nativity throughout the Middle Ages; that they reveal information about the *traditions* in which the English playwrights are working. Although it has been established that the mystery cycles did not evolve directly from liturgical drama, nevertheless liturgical shepherd plays remain close analogues to the English versions, whatever different techniques they represent. And an examination of the liturgical *Ordines Pastorum* reveals that the same two themes are of fundamental importance to the form and meaning of the Church's Christmas drama.

As an example, let us examine one of the simpler *Pastores,* a fourteenth-century *ordo* from the Cathedral of Clermont-Ferrand:13

> Quo dicto, duo pueri cantent iuxta altare versum:
> > *Quem queritis in presepe, pastores, dicite?*
> Pastores versum:
> > *Saluatorem <Christum> Dominum, infantem pannis*
> > *inuolutum, secundum sermonem angelicum.*
> Pueri versum:
> > *Adest hic paruulus cum Maria matre sua, de qua*
> > *dudum vaticinando Ysaias dixerat propheta: Ecce uirgo*
> > *concipiet et pariet filium; et nunc euntes dicite*
> > *quia natus est.*
> Pastores:
> > *Alleluia, alleluia! Iam uere scimus Christum natum*
> > *in terris, <de quo> canite omnes cum propheta dicentes.*
> Quo finito, chori prouisores incipiant ad Missam in Gallicantu.
> [Officium:
> > *Dominus dixit ad me.*]

The *ordo* begins on Christmas Day, at the end of the *Te Deum,* the closing hymn of Matins. Two boys stand before the altar and address those playing the shepherds in the familiar phrases of the Easter trope, *"Quem queritis . . . ?"* The shepherds respond, indicating their debt to the angelic announcement. The two boys then presumably point to a representation of the Virgin and child, singing "Here is the little one with Mary his Mother, of whom formerly in prophesying the prophet Isaiah had said: Behold a virgin shall conceive and bear a son; now as you go announce that he is born." "Alleluia! Alleluia!" reply the shepherds, "for we now know truly that Christ is born upon earth, of whom let us all sing with the prophet, saying: The Lord said to me: you are my son, today I beget you."

A number of elements in this brief dramatization deserve our attention. First, prophecy is referred to twice, specifically within the context of its fulfillment. The specific attribution of "Ecce virgo" to Isaiah appears in all *ordines;* in most, the final antiphon is not *Dominus dixit,* as in our example, but more appropriately, the introit chant for the third Christmas mass, a prophecy from *Isaiah* 9.6: *"Natus est nobis"*—"Unto us this day a child is born, and his name shall be called Almighty God." Second, the *ordo* is an integral part of the worship service, since it directly follows the finale of Matins, the *Te Deum,* and leads directly into the introit for the first morning mass of Christmas Day, *"Dominus dixit ad me."* Finally, the piece exists in two times simultaneously: the historical time of the birth, and the present time of the commemorative service. In this *ordo,* the historical shepherds respond to the contemporary choir, testifying to their recognition of the Savior's birth, and request that all sing His praises *cum propheta.* Yet, participation is by no means confined to a close relationship between worship service and dramatization. In other *ordines,* it is given overtly dramatic forms. Karl Young observed: "The impersonated characters of no other play so freely extend their activities outside the strict limits of the representation itself, and take a ceremonial, and sometimes a dramatic, part in the official liturgy."14 In an especially striking thirteenth-century dramatization from Rouen, the shepherds take part in the entire service. They enter just before the first Christmas mass begins, enact their adoration of the Christ-child, and during the mass "rule the choir" taking major responsibility for singing liturgical prayers and chants. They also seem to take part in the next canonical service, Lauds.15 Many other *ordines* allow similar activities.16 Such an extension of the drama outside the play itself is not limited solely to those impersonating the shepherds. All *ordines pas-*

torum seem to take place before either the altar or, more often, a representation of the *praesepe,* the Christmas crib. In fact, Mary and Joseph have no speaking parts in any of the liturgical shepherd plays; rather, they, like the Christ-child, are simply represented by statues.17 Throughout the Middle Ages the Christmas crib was an important center of communal devotion, and its importance is not a result of liturgical drama alone.18 Thus, it is not hard to speculate that the *praesepe* which is the focus of the shepherds' devotion—or the altar, which was often treated as a crib in artistic and homiletic renderings—is also a center for the congregation's devotion. Both actors and audience then participate in worship and oblation before the Christ-child—acts which unify them into a spiritual community of belief, as they together affirm the miracle of Christ's birth.

The liturgical dramatizations, then, are structured around the same two themes we have seen present in the secular cycles— that is, prophetic fulfillment and spiritual community. These themes are united by the recitation of prophecy, which provides a verbal and historical link between the testimony of the shepherds and the affirmations of the congregation. Yet, are these themes in themselves the innovations of liturgical drama? The fact that they occur so uniformly in the *ordines pastorum* leads one to suspect that they are not, that perhaps they are incorporations of elements to be found within the medieval liturgy. The liturgy itself has been undervalued as an important contributor to the shape and function of medieval religious drama, for it alone gave form and meaning to liturgical dramatizations.19 What, then, are the characteristics of the liturgy which defined the shape and function of the shepherd plays occurring within it?20

The Christmas liturgy is inextricably bound to Advent, the season which precedes it. Advent is a season of preparation, and its liturgy is a strange combination of both penance and joy. This combination can be most easily explained by noting the central importance of prophecy in Advent chants, prayers, and readings. Much of the Advent liturgy concerns the testimonies of the Old Testament prophets, and looks forward to the coming of the Savior with both joy (His coming as a child on Christmas) and dread (His coming as a judge on the Last Days).21 The Old Testament readings for all services are taken from Isaiah, the chief prophet of the Incarnation. This prophetic

anticipation culminates in the celebrations of Christmas. On
Christmas Day, the first service, that of Matins, represents the
birth of Christ within the context of prophetic expectations. The
first readings, or *lectiones,* are taken from the book of Isaiah,
and recapitulate three important passages which prophesy the
Incarnation: *Is.* 9.1-8 (including the prophecy, *"Natus est
nobis"*); *Is.* 40.1-11 (containing prophecies of John the Baptist); and *Is.* 52.1-10 (concerning the redemption of Israel).
Matins ends with the solemn singing of the generations of
Christ, according to *Matthew* 1.1-16. The birth of Christ as fulfillment of prophecy also pervades the three masses of Christmas, particularly the second, or morning mass. All three masses
contain readings from *Isaiah* which predict various aspects of
the Savior's advent (*Is.* 2.6-7; *Is.* 61.1-3; *Is.* 62.11-22, and *Is.*
52.6-10). Further, the introit chants for the second and third
masses are also derived from the prophecies of Isaiah. The introit of the third mass, *"Natus est nobis,"* is particularly important, for it contributed the finale to most liturgical shepherds'
plays.

Perhaps more striking than its emphasis upon prophecy is
another aspect of the Christmas liturgy—its awareness of the
spiritual community established by the birth of the Savior. This
awareness is most often signalled in many liturgical chants by
the adverb, *"hodie,"* tying prophetic anticipation of the birth to
its fulfillment during the time of the commemorative service:

> R.1.   Hodie nobis caelorum rex de virgine nasci dignatus
>   est: ut hominem perditum ad caelestia regna revocaret:
>   gaudet exercitus angelorum. Quia salus aeterna humano
>   generi apparuit.
>   V. Gloria in excelsis Deo: et in terra pax hominibus
>   bonae voluntatibus. Quia. . . .
>   (*Brev. Sar.,* I, clxxiv; *Liber,* col. 734)
>
> R.2.   Hodie nobis de caelo pax vera descendit. Hodie
>   per totum mundum melliflui facti sunt caeli.
>   V.   Hodie illuxit dies redemptionis novae reparationis
>   antiquae: felicitatis aeternae. Hodie. . . .
>   (*Brev Sar.,* I, clxxv; *Liber,* col. 734)

Almost all prayers in the Christmas services are devoted specifically to explicating the birth in terms of man's present hope
of redemption, for it is the liberation of mankind at the moment
of the "new birth" of Christ which frees him from the yoke of
sins (Collect and Secret, third mass; Postcommunion, second

mass) and delivers him into salvation (Secret, first mass; Post-communion, first and third masses.)

The theme finds its most striking manifestation, however, in several antiphons and responds which address the shepherds as simultaneously participants in the historical Nativity, and anachronistic members of the present congregation. In these chants, the shepherds are called upon to testify to their recognition of the Savior's birth:

> Quem vidistis pastores, dicite? annunciate nobis in
> terris quis apparuit. Natum vidimus in choro angelorum
> Salvatorem Dominum.
> V. Natus est nobis hodie Salvator, qui est Christus
> Dominus in civitate David. Natum. . . .22
> Pastores, dicite, quidnam vidistis, et annuniate
> Xpisti nativitatem.
> V. Infantem vidimus involutum et choros angelorum
> laudentes Salvatorem.
> V. Dominus dixit.23

These chants in the medieval Christmas liturgy provide a specific focus for the congregation's understanding of the Nativity. Furthermore, they express in dialogue form the two basic themes we have been considering throughout this paper—that is, the birth of Christ as fulfillment of prophecy (seen in the verses which follow the responds) and the anachronistic treatment of the shepherds as members of the present congregation. Significantly, all of these chants may be found in liturgies which precede by two hundred years the first examples of the *officium pastorum*.24

This suggests that the association between the shepherds and prophecy arose from within elements particular to the Christmas liturgy. Yet, why did such an association come about? Especially, why are the shepherds treated so uniformly as anachronistic members of the worshipping community? The answer lies in the nature of the ritual in which this association is contained. According to modern thinking, ritual is primarily the communication of religious, or perhaps more accurately, sacred, behavior. Within the context of ritual the events of the mythic past became present and available to the worshipping community. In contrast to other rituals, Christian ritual has as its core a series of historical acts which have gained theological interpretation in the light of the Christian experience. Thus, the historical baptism of Christ or the events of the Last Supper have been interpreted as recreating the "fellowship with the Sacred Spirit or Power that the early disciples had experienced in the life and after the death of the man Jesus."25 The Christian ritual, then, seeks to integrate secular man into a community which recognizes the historical events in Christ's life as sanctified history, and which re-presents those events within the context of the ritual act.26

We can now understand why the early medieval liturgy treated the shepherds as centrally important to the meaning of the Christmas celebrations. In the cyclical re-creation of divine history, the birth of Christ is the gateway between two times—the Old Law and the New. In both of these times, according to scriptural testimony, God has intervened. He has given the word of His actions to His prophets and makes His grace continually present to the Faithful through the intervention of the Holy Spirit. As our analysis of the Christmas liturgy has shown, this period is a celebration of fulfillment *par excellence*—the fulfillment of the Old Testament prophets in the coming of Christ; the fulfillment of the longings of the congregation for renewal in spiritual rebirth. These two communities are united in the ritual act, and form a larger community outside of historical time. Yet, it is an essential aspect of Christianity, in contrast to other religions, that this fulfillment took place at a definite historical point of time. Hence, the shepherds, as participants in the historical Christmas, become united with the Old Testament prophets and the congregation of believers. But why should the shepherds prophesy? In contrast to the community of prophets, who awaited the coming of the Messiah, and the community of Christians, who have been given salvation by His coming, the shepherds stand at the precise historical moment of that change. They are, in a very real sense, the signals of that change. As creatures of the Old Testament world, they hear God's word as did the prophets through the revelations of the angel; as participants in the New, they join the congregation in worshipping the Savior. Thus, they become intermediaries between the expectation and its fulfillment, and simultaneously a part of the historical moment itself. The medieval liturgy made this ritual significance manifest in its treatment of the shepherds, addressing them as a way of breaching the gap between the expectation of the Savior in the prophecies of the Old Testament patriarchs and the renewal of His birth in the spiritual regeneration of the congregation. This ritual tradition long antedates the first appearance of the shepherds' plays. And through it, Christmas drama makes its appearance, uniting the longings of the prophets with those of the present congregation.

What began as an observation of a literary phenomenon has involved, ultimately, an investigation of the ritual origins of Christmas drama. My main concern has been to account for the uniform association of three aspects of the Christmas story in the Middle Ages: prophecy, spiritual community, and the shepherds. It can be seen that in all of their manifestations, liturgical and dramatic, these three aspects are inseparable; and their combination can be best explained by understanding the ritual function of the Christmas liturgy itself. Before concluding, however, I would like to return from the eighth-century liturgy to the fifteenth-century English shepherds' plays. What was at the beginning of this paper merely a literary concern can now be seen to be much more. In fact, these late medieval plays are permeated with the ritual form of the Christmas event, as it was communicated through the liturgy of the Catholic church. For despite the many other influences which have poured into these plays—as the studies of Kolve and Woolf, among others, have shown—nevertheless the English shepherds' plays remain excellent illustrations of the pervasive influence of ritual form on the composition of secular religious drama. It seems entirely possible that other elements in these plays which we are apt to attribute to other sources—the meal eaten by the shepherds in the Chester play and the Wakefield *Prima Pastorum;* the eschatological undertones in the shepherds' speeches in the Coventry "Pageant of the Shearmen and Tailors" and the *Secunda Pastorum;* the forms of the adorations before the creche; and even the humorous inversions of order in the wrestling and sheep-stealing scenes in the Chester and Wakefield cycles—are at their heart ritual acts which were drawn upon because of a ritual understanding of the birth of Christ.[27] Whatever their ultimate sources, it is at least clear that the medieval English dramatists were writing within a tradition in which the shepherds, standing at the gateway between expectation and fulfillment, united the prophets and audience in a moment of sacred time. The shepherds' play became the finest example of medieval comedy in the hands of the Wakefield Master; yet even he had to let them prophesy.

NOTES

1 For a convenient summary of critical approaches, see Lawrence J. Ross, "Symbol and Structure in the *Secunda Pastorum*," *Comparative Drama*, 1 (1967-68), 122-43; reprinted in *Medieval English Drama: Essays Critical and Contextual*, ed. Jerome Taylor and Alan H. Nelson (Chicago: Univ. of Chicago Press, 1972), pp. 177-211.

2 *The Wakefield Pageants in the Towneley Cycle*, ed. A. C. Cawley (Manchester: Manchester Univ. Press, 1958), p. 61. Four complete cycles are nearly all that remain of what seems to have been a great body of English cyclic drama. Although new editions of all of them are planned, only one, that of the Chester cycle, has appeared; my references therefore will be to the present authoritative editions: *The Chester Mystery Cycle*, ed. R. M. Lumiansky and David Mills, EETS, s.s. 3 (London, 1974); *Ludus Coventriae*, ed. K. S. Block, EETS, e.s. CXX (London, 1922); *York Plays*, ed. Lucy T. Smith (1885; rpt. New York: Russell and Russell, 1963). All subsequent references to these editions will be indicated in parentheses by page and line.

3 In Luke 2.7-20, the shepherds hear the announcement of the angel (9-14) informing them of Christ's birth and, seeing the child in the manger, *cognoverunt de verbo, quod dictum erat illis de puero hoc* (17). Traditional exegesis stressed the shepherds' willingness to believe the announcement, despite their low station and relative ignorance; in this they are often contrasted with the Jews who chose not to believe, or with the Magi who did not receive specific revelation. Although prophecy is naturally of importance in establishing the significance of the event, it does not seem to have been applied to the shepherds' reception of the angelic announcement. See, for instance, *Glossa Ordinaria, Patrologia Latina*, 114, col. 249-50; Ambrose, *Expositionis in Lucam*, Lib. ii, *PL* 15, 1651-55; Bede, *In Lucae Evangelium Expositio*, Lib. i, *PL* 92, 331-39; Leo, *Sermo XXV (in Nativitate Domini, V), PL* 64, 208-12. Ambrose, in particular, points out the verbal parallels between the angel's announcement in Luke 2.11 *(Natus est vobis hodie Salvator)* and the prophecy of Isaiah 9.6: *Puer natus est nobis, Filius datus est nobis (PL* 15, 1655); however, he does not make an explicit connection with the shepherds.

4 See, for instance, the studies of E. K. Chambers, *The Mediaeval Stage*, 2 vols. (Oxford: Oxford Univ. Press, 1902); Hardin Craig, *English Religious Drama of the Middle Ages* (Oxford: Clarendon Press, 1955); Samuel B. Hemingway, *English Nativity Plays* (1909; rpt. New York: Russell and Russell, 1964).

5 For discussion, see: V. A. Kolve, *The Play Called Corpus Christi* (Stanford: Stanford Univ. Press, 1966), pp. 152-55, 206; Rosemary Woolf, *The English Mystery Plays* (Berkeley: Univ. of California Press, 1972), pp. 183-85.

6 In the York pageant XIV, which depicts the birth of Jesus, Joseph complains of the cold and lack of light; as soon as Christ is born, however, Joseph perceives a light "þat comes shynyng þus sodenly" (p. 114, 1. 79). Mary herself explains that it is the star which "Balam tolde ful longe be-forne." Thus, when the York shepherds also refer to Balaam's prophecy, they obviously play upon the audience's recognition of its significance. Perhaps the discontinuous staging of the separate York pageants (on wagons and by different guilds) led the playwright to attempt such verbal parallels for the sake of continuity.

7 *Ludus Coventriae*, pp. 146-48, 11. 21-62; *Two Coventry Corpus Christi Plays*, 2nd ed., ed. Hardin Craig, EETS, e.s. 87 (London, 1957), p. 9, 11. 247-50.

8 *Ludus Coventriae*, pp. 146-48, 11. 21-62; *Two Coventry . . . Plays*, 11. 268-71; *The Shrewsbury Fragments*, in *Non-Cycle Plays and Fragments*, ed. Norman Davis, EETS, s.s. 1 (London, 1970), pp. 1-2, 11. 18-23. In the "Pageant of the Shearmen and Tailors," this sense of fulfillment is emphasized by the inclusion of a scene following the shepherds' adoration in which two prophets debate the meaning of the birth, concluding that
>   now ys the tyme cum
> And the date there-of run
> Off his Natevete. *(Two Coventry . . . Plays*, 11. 428-30)

9 See Woolf, pp. 184ff.; E. B. Cantelupe and R. Griffith, "The Gifts of the Shepherds in the Wakefield *Secunda Pastorum;* An Iconographical Interpretation," *Mediaeval Studies*, 28 (1966), 328-35.

10 *Chester Mystery Cycle*, pp. 154-55, 11. 656-76.

11 Kolve, p. 113: "The Corpus Christi drama, then, establishes by costumes, settings, and verbal reference a time and place that are roughly contemporary, and more or less English." These views have been refined by Woolf, pp. 184-93. See also the comments by William M. Manly, "Shepherds and Prophets: Religious Unity in the Towneley *Secunda Pastorum,*" *PMLA*, 78 (1963), 151-55.

12 Kolve, pp. 152-55.

13 Karl Young, *The Drama of the Medieval Church* (Oxford: Clarendon Press, 1933), II, 12. The complete context of this particular representation of the *pastores,* including texts of both Matins and Lauds, may be found in Karl Young, "Officium Pastorum: A Study of the Dramatic Developments within the Liturgy of Christmas," *Transactions of the Wisconsin Academy of Sciences, Arts, and Letters*, 17 (1912), 369-78.

14 Young, *Drama*, II, 20.

15 Young, *Drama*, II, 14-16.

16 Other examples of the shepherds' participation in the Christmas services may be found in the following texts edited by Young: Padua (thirteenth century; Young, *Drama*, II, 10); Rouen (fourteenth century; Young, *Drama*, II, 16-19); Senlis (fourteenth century; Young, *Drama*, II, 21); Rome (?) (fifteenth century; Young, "Officium Pastorum," p. 356); and an especially early version from Rouen (twelfth century; Young, "Officium Pastorum," p. 391).

17 Young, "Officium Pastorum," pp. 309-11. For equivalent treatments in medieval art, see Émile Mâle, *L'Art Religieux du XIIIe Siècle en France*, 6th ed. (Paris: Libraire Armand Colin, 1925), pp. 179-88.

18 Young, *Drama*, II, 24-28, discusses the importance of the *praesepe* as a center of communal devotion in the Middle Ages. In his somewhat fuller discussion in "Officium Pastorum," he offers the suggestion that the traditional use of relics of the historic crib on the altar at St. Mary Major in Rome from the eighth century on may have influenced the dramatists (p. 340). See also Francis X. Weiser, *A Handbook of Christian Feasts and Customs* (New York: Harcourt, Brace, 1952), pp. 94-95.

19 The two most important studies of this relationship are: O. B. Hardison, Jr., *Christian Rite and Christian Drama in the Middle Ages* (Baltimore: Johns Hopkins Press, 1965); and Helmut de Boor, *Die Textgeschichte der lateinischen Osterfeiern* (Tübingen: Max Niemeyer, 1967).

20 There is a bewildering variety of liturgies in the Middle Ages; yet chant texts, for the most part, remain consistent. For the sake of convenience, I will refer to the English liturgical usage of Salisbury Cathedral, since it is roughly contemporaneous with the Middle English mystery cycles. The available editions are: *Breviarum ad usum insignis ecclesiae Sarum*, ed. Francis Proctor and Christopher Wordsworth, 3 vols. (Cambridge: Cambridge Univ. Press, 1879-86)—henceforth cited in parentheses as *Brev. Sar.; The Sarum Missal*, ed. J. Wickham Legg (Oxford: Clarendon Press, 1916)—henceforth cited in parentheses as *Sar. Miss.* Since I am arguing that the liturgical dramatizations are dependent upon the liturgy in which they occurred, I will also cite references to chant texts in the eleventh-century Gregorian *Liber Responsalis*, in *PL* 78, indicated in parentheses as *Liber.*

21 This two-fold meaning of "advent" has long been recognized. For instance, the thirteenth-century writer Guijelmus Durandus, *Rationale Divinorum Officiorum* (Lyons: Antonii Cellier, 1672), VI, ii, 3: "Verumtamen Ecclesiae non celebrat nisi duos aduentus, scilicet in carnem & ad iudicium." According to recent historical studies, the eschatological content of Advent was an innovation of the Gallican

church; originally, Advent was a season of joyous preparation for Christmas. See Walter Croce, "Die Adventsliturgie im Licht ihrer geschichtlichen Entwicklung," *Zeitschrift für katholische Theologie*, 76 (1954), 258-96.

22 *Liber Responsalis, PL* 78, col. 734,; see also the citation in the important edition of early medieval antiphons, *Corpus Antiphonalium Officii*, ed. R. J. Hesbert (Rome: Herder, 1970), IV, 365.

23 Young, "Officium Pastorum," p. 351. It is worth noting that here the antiphon has been adopted as a trope of the introit to the first Christmas mass, hence the second versicle, *Dominus dixit*.

24 According to Willi Apel, *Gregorian Chant* (Bloomington: Indiana Univ. Press, 1958), p. 96, the respond *Quem vidistis* may be dated as early as the fourth or fifth century. The obvious influence of this respond on the text of the trope *Quem queritis in praesepe* was pointed out by Young, *Drama*, II, 5n.

25 Larry D. Shinn, *Two Sacred Worlds* (Nashville: Abingdon, 1977), p. 110. And see the important studies by Mircea Eliade, *The Sacred and the Profane: The Nature of Religion*, trans. Willard R. Trask (New York: Harcourt, Brace, 1959), esp. pp. 68-113; and Louis Bouyer, *Rite and Man: Natural Sacredness and Christian Liturgy*, trans. M. Joseph Costelloe (Notre Dame Press, 1963).

26 "Every ritual has the character of happening *now*, at this very moment. The time of the event that the ritual commemorates or re-enacts it made *present*, 're-presented' so to speak, however far back it may have been in ordinary reckoning. Christ's passion, death and resurrection are not simply remembered during the services of Holy Week; they really happen *then* before the eyes of the faithful. And a convinced Christian must feel that he is *contemporary* with these transhistoric events, for, by being re-enacted, the time of the theophany becomes actual" (Mircea Eliade, *Patterns in Comparative Religion*, trans. Rosemary Sheed [Cleveland: World, 1963], pp. 392-93). For the nature of ritual, see also, Arnold van Gennep, *The Rites of Passage*, trans. Monika B. Vizedom and Gabrielle L. Caffee (Chicago: Univ. of Chicago Press, 1960); and Clyde Kluckhohn, "Myths and Rituals: A General Theory," *Harvard Theological Review*, 35 (1942), 45-79.

27 The meal eaten by the shepherds reflects the mythic "sacred meal" which is of great importance in the history of religions (Bouyer, *Rite and Man*, 78-94) and, of course, echoes the central sacrifice of the mass. Eschatology plays an important role in the liturgy of Advent and Christmas, since both seasons look forward to the second coming of the Savior. The adorations obviously echo the liturgical offertory; the shepherds pray for salvation; and Mary as mediatrix offers to intercede for them before God. The humorous inversions of order in the Chester and Wakefield plays seem to echo the ritual mockings in which societal taboos are permitted and even encouraged during the moment of the ritual act. Chambers devoted much space to the Feast of Fools and its parallels with Saturnalian rituals; and A. P. Rossiter, *English Drama from Early Times to the Elizabethans* (1950; rpr. New York: Barnes and Noble, 1967) mentioned its importance in understanding the "nearly exact parallelism in . . . 'opposite senses' " in the *Secunda Pastorum* (p. 78). Although Kolve (134-44) and others have more recently abjured this source for the comedy in the shepherds' plays, it is worthwhile noting that anthropologists have long recognized the association between role-reversal ceremonies and regeneration of sacred time in ceremonies of ritual renewal. In this regard, see particularly Eliade, *The Sacred and the Profane*, pp. 77-85; and Edmund R. Leach, "Ritual," in *International Encyclopedia of the Social Sciences* (New York: Macmillan, 1968), XIII, 520-26.

Audience and Meaning in Two Medieval Dramatic Realisms

William F. Munson

Although it has been more common recently to stress religious doctrine than realism in English mystery plays, J. M. Manly's judgment in 1897 has probably not been superseded: "The Towneley *Secunda Pastorum* has so long been recognized as the best extant example of individualization of typical characters and of rapid transition from the farcical to the sublime that it is expected in every book of selections."[1] There is a modern bias here in the interest in a realism involving individualization of dramatic character, an interest which searches out a play which is justly celebrated though hardly characteristic of medieval drama in this respect. Most moderns, on the other hand, have regarded with less ease the "rapid transition from the farcical to the sublime" which is common in medieval drama, often minimizing it and treating it as needing justification in a religious play. Low comedy involves a "realism" usually of a different sort from a psychological character realism: it is the realism of "English shepherds" making references to contemporary life and also making low jest of high things. This is the kind of realism the Wakefield shepherds' plays share with other mystery plays; it is what makes them most traditional, least extraordinary. I should like here to elaborate the interpretive implications of two realisms—a less traditional one involving some individualization of character and some stage illusion, the other more traditional and involving character stereotypes and a nonillusionistic topicality—primarily by example of some English adoration plays.

Criticism of English mystery plays has had difficulty appreciating a comic drama which habitually ignores dramatic illusion, employs stereotypes, and seems casually indifferent to realistic

probabilities in character and plot—characteristics obtaining also
for Greek Old Comedy. The Wakefield *First Shepherds' Play*
and the Chester *Adoration of the Shepherds* have apparently random quarrels and feasts in common with Aristophanic comedy
and seem more similar to it than to the later, more plotted farces
of New Comedy and the Roman imitations. Modern theorists of
drama often attempt to locate the nature of comedy by contrasting a drama of types to a drama of individuals. S. H. Butcher's
interpretation and elaboration of Aristotle's *Poetics,* for example,
sees broad alternatives in comedy and tragedy: "Whereas comedy
tends to merge the individual in the type, tragedy manifests the
type through the individual."[2] A distinction which is difficult to
sustain solely in terms of content may be easier to make in terms
of function for an audience, specifically the social nature of much
comic art and the dynamics of audience participation as opposed
to the more individualistic and disinterested nature of tragedy.
Henri Bergson's essay on laughter is a key statement locating
comic experience as distinctively social in contrast to the experience of the other arts, including tragedy. Tragedy gives the hero
"an individuality unique of its kind," while comedy looks "out-
wards" to surface resemblances of character to construct an
"average" by a process of "abstraction and generalization."[3]
The type-character of comedy, it is implied, serves a "social gesture" (p. 20) which is a form of pressure for a social end:

> The pleasure caused by laughter, even on the stage, is not an
> unadulterated enjoyment; it is not a pleasure that is exclusively
> esthetic or altogether disinterested. It always implies a secret or
> unconscious intent, if not of each one of us, at all events of
> society as a whole. In laughter we always find an unavowed in-
> tention to humiliate, and consequently to correct our neigh-
> bour, if not in his will, at least in his deed. (pp. 135-36)

The immediate, semi-utilitarian function is what makes comedy
for Bergson both close to "life" and at the same time the alternative to seeing a profounder inner reality of unique individual
experience, of natural feelings as opposed to social law. This
fuller truth is what art proper pursues:

> Art . . . has no other object than to brush aside the utilitarian
> symbols, the conventional and socially accepted generalities, in
> short, everything that veils reality from us, in order to bring
> us face to face with reality itself. (p. 157)

> Comedy lies midway between art and life. It is not disinterested

as genuine art is. By organising laughter, comedy accepts social
life as a natural environment, it even obeys an impulse of social
life. And in this respect it turns its back upon art, which is a
breaking away from society and a return to pure nature.
(pp. 170-71)

The art of the mystery plays, like the art of much classical
comedy, is emphatically not a disinterested art. It belongs, instead, to "life," specifically the holiday life of the community.
The context of the Corpus Christi cycle plays was the festivity
of civic holiday, usually Corpus Christi, in which there was
procession, liturgy, and feast organized under the supervision of
the town authorities.4 The general similarity to the emergence of
drama in classical Athens in the context of cult and civic ceremony is striking. In Greek town life, cult became the concern of
the state. Although old rituals were kept, especially in the sixth
century the tyrants had large temples built and made much
pomp of a procession, sacrifice, and meal.5 Tragedy's first appearance was in Athens at the new civic festival, the City
Dionysia, instituted by Pisistratus, for which he built a theater
orchestra of stone and a stone temple beside it.6 In the festival
procession the statue of the god was carried in a chariot.7 The
medieval English festival of Corpus Christi has a general parallel
in the honorific procession with host, and in the mystery plays
performed for the same occasion. The Greek practice of
choregia, in which the main expenses of dithyramb, tragedy, and
comedy at the Dionysiac festival at Athens were assigned a
wealthy citizen, was begun about 500 for tragedy and 486 for
comedy. Such duties of the *choregos* as supplying chorus, rehearsal rooms, and costumes were, in England, similar to those
filled by the craft guilds. The *choregia* was in Greece just one of
a number of civic services called *leitourgia,* just as in England
the craft guilds had various ceremonial obligations among which
the Corpus Christi play was one.8 Plays in both cases thus belonged to a context of civic "liturgy" by which a community
identity was affirmed. The civic records of a medieval town such
as York are testimony to effort parallel to Athens' on the part
of the civic authorities to enhance civic prestige through their
Corpus Christi procession, feasts, and play. The York City
Council through the fifteenth and sixteenth centuries continuously enjoined and regulated craft guild participation in the
ceremonies much as Athenians required of colonies and allies

the tribute of sacrificial animals for the festivals. What has been said for the Greek festivals might be said of the medieval, that they were "for a great part an expression of the political aspirations of the cities."9

The connection of drama with communal holiday activity has important literary implications for both classical and medieval comedy. It is thought that the origin of the word "comedy" is *komos,* which meant a festival practice (particularly honoring Dionysus) involving a procession of revelers. F. M. Cornford, in tracing the structure of Old Comedy to archaic ritual and festival, saw a survival of the festive *komos* in the procession of chorus and hero leaving the orchestra at the end of a comedy.10 George E. Duckworth sees influence of a *komos* in the choral *parabasis* of Old Comedy:

> The nature of early comedy is best explained by an origin in a procession of revelers, often masquerading as animals, who danced and sang and uttered impromptu lampoons against bystanders or important public characters. Such a revel doubtless concluded with a song, in part satirical and jesting, addressed to those standing by. These performances were essentially choral, and after a time were no longer improvised; poets wrote more elaborate songs and touched upon serious themes of literature and politics in the final address to the audience, or *parabasis,* which became a regular feature of Old Comedy.11

Regardless of whether or not the comic chorus was a direct consequence of some festive phallic procession or animal masquerade, comedy does compel and structure direct audience participation in the same way community holiday activity does. In medieval mystery plays the chorus may not be present as formal *personae,* but its method of partly maintaining a dramatic role and partly breaking illusion to speak directly to the audience is also the method of the figures of medieval drama. Also, a final *Te Deum* or other song of praise, like the choral *exodos* of Greek comedy, often concludes a mystery play. In both dramas choral-like involvement of audience goes with a characteristic indifference to illusionistic time and place. There is, instead, a "realism" of a different sort: frequent references to audience, theater, and occasion of performance. Instead of making a realistic illusion of natural space and time, both Old Comedy and medieval drama are more concerned with creating a festive reality for the audience which is present. In Old Comedy, interest in naturalistic plot sequence is submerged in the noise of song and dance, reminding us, the audience, "that we are gathered together in the theater to amuse ourselves and Dionysus by a gay show."12 A consequence of this audience-involved topicality and jest is the comic method of characterization by stereotype, of generalized figures, as opposed to the character individuality of a more disinterested art.13

The mystery plays may not have had as many grotesque masks as Old Comedy did, but at least devils and tyrants did have them; there was not the phallus and padding but there was a good deal of body humor. There are some external references which support the internal evidence of the mystery plays—the prominence of humorous type-characters such as tyrants, devils and shrews—that a decorum of festive involvement obtained at a Corpus Christi play done in a station-to-station procession through, for example, the streets of York. A reference in the York Memorandum Book to a play in which Fergus tries to desecrate the body of Mary (in a play no longer extant) suggests audience behavior which must have paralleled that of a Greek *komos* or other festal procession: the beating of Fergus, we are told, "caused more laughter and clamor than devotion, and sometimes quarrels, contentions, and fights arose thereupon among the people."14 In 1426 a preacher complains of the same York plays that although they are laudable, they are accompanied by "feastings, drunkenness, shouts, songs, and other insolences."15

A. S. Cook comments on the address by the figures of comedy:

> In tragedy the players on the stage are as objective to the spectators as if they were in a book. But comedy always violates this convention; the actor reaches out of the frame of objectivity and addresses the audience second-personally.16

Trowle, in the Chester *Adoration,* is such a player when he jestingly rejects the festive hospitality of the other shepherds and then tells the audience exactly what he is doing: "No hap to your hoote meat have I,/ but flyte with my fellowes in feare" (217-19).17 His performance is thus a game, a semi-ceremonial holiday activity, in which players and audience are cooperating. The purpose of such jest in a religious play is to enable the audience to experience religious affirmation as the final issue of an unfolding experience of pleasure, vitality, and unity with others. Comedy, Cook says, effects social unity through a contrast between the buffoonish clown who is the central figure and the norms he implies by violating them:

> Part of the clown's meaning is, "those who indulge to excess their normal appetites for sex, eating, beating their friends, saying what they please, will be expelled from the normal society for their nonconformity to manners." We laugh, and society draws together into the conformity of its norm, expelling the abnormal individualist. (p. 39)

In the Chester *Adoration* Trowle is the clown. He is mock lazy, and he jests at kings, dukes, and popes:

> if any man come me by,
> and wold wit which way best were,
> my leg I lift up, where I lie,
> and wish him the way by east-and west-where.
>
> and I rose when I lay,
> me wold thinke that traveyle lost were:
> for King nor Duke, by this daye,
> rise I will not but take my rest here.
>
> now will I set me adowne
> and pipe at this pot like a pope. (189-98)

But such an "abnormal individualist" in comedy is often not expelled, especially when the emphasis, as here, is on incorporating indulgence instead of expelling evil. Since the "drawing together into conformity with the norm" is accomplished through the audience indulging first in the pleasure of the violation, a clown like Trowle suddenly changes his behavior (implausibly by psychological standards) and remains in the drama.[18] Trowle leaves, after he defeats the shepherds at wrestling and curses them, taking with him the jesting impulse in order to reappear later in changed aspect as chief spokesman for the religious norm.

The social and psychological effect is accomplished through a character typology and plot pattern such as have been outlined by Northrop Frye. Various "blocking characters"—such as the braggart soldier, the shrew, the pedant—serve as unsympathetic impostor *(alazon);* the impostor is opposed by a sympathetic ironic hero (the *eiron,* or self-deprecator)—including tricky servants and benevolent old men—who emerges triumphant, bringing back the good society of a former golden age. Frye then lo-

cates another pair of characters, buffoon and churl, who embody
the poles of the comic mood: the buffoon (often cook or host)
speaks for festive license, the churl is a refuser of festivity.[19]
The ironical hero is often also buffoon, as F. M. Cornford
earlier pointed out,[20] and if impostor and churl are also combined there is a possible comic pattern of ironical buffoon opposing an impostor churl. In the *Second Shepherds' Play* the
buffoon is Daw, the impudent servant; he is the chief instrument
of God (the "benevolent old man" of secular comedy) triumph-
ing over the impostor Mak, who pretends, at first, to be a petty
official (one of the many professional types of impostor) and
who, like a churl, finally refuses hospitality to the shepherds.
The other English adoration plays emphasize the assimilation of
the buffoon and do not have humorous butts who are finally excluded from the community. The nearest is Slawpase in the
quarreling episode of the *First Shepherds' Play,* who refuses the
festive spirit of play, who also has some features of the pedant
type, and over whom the first two jesting shepherds triumph in
their debate. Slawpase, however, does join the feast which follows. In both the *First Shepherds' Play* and the Chester *Adoration* drinking and feasting help set the mood for the comic action.
(Just as discussion of food was conspicuous in Greek Middle
Comedy, the *First Shepherds' Play* has an entire feasting scene
with details excerpted from a book on banquets.)[21] In the
Chester play Trowle, the sympathetic impudent boy, playfully
refuses the feast and defeats the other shepherds at wrestling
before eating, and then joins them to form the new society which
sees the Christ child. The prototypical mystery play of humorous
conflict and victory is the Harrowing of Hell play, even though
here the pleasurable amusement is displaced from the figure of
Christ, the hero, to the devils: Christ, the unlikely victor "hid-
den" in his humanity and having gone to death, binds the boasting impostors in the pit of hell and departs with the saved. The
feeling structured by the harrowing episode is echoed in Trowle's
victory as he throws to the ground all his opponents, commits
them to the devil (as Christ binds Satan in hell), then seizes
his food (as Christ takes the saved):

> Lye there, lydder, in the lake,
> my liueray nowe I will lach,
> this cup, this clowt, and this cake,
> for ye be cast, now will I cach.

> to the devill I all you betake,
> and, traytors, taynt of your tach.
> on this would [with] this will I wake;
> all the world wonder on the wach! (291-98)22

The special position which Trowle has assumed at this point
as a voice for jest is made continuous with his special position as
a voice for serious truth. Since figures in such comic plays are not
personae with their own psychology but stereotypes serving the
audience's sense of vitality and affirmation, Trowle can suddenly
retire (as a rubric after line 298 indicates) after the wrestling
only to reappear, for no internal reason, to discuss seriously with
the other shepherds. Such "contradictory" juxtapositions of behavior belong to the general comic characteristic of "arbitrary
plot over consistency of character."23 To the audience of comedy
properly attuned to the spirit of holiday celebration, delight in
the game of jesting contentiousness can be continuous with—and
almost experienced as—a sense of joy at God's grace. When the
star appears, there is a shift in the order of speeches so that
Trowle speaks first instead of last.24 He is standing apart from
the others when he first sees the star, and the rubric calls attention to his beginning a new series of speeches:

> (*Tunc respiciens firmamentum dicat*)
> *Gartius.* A! Gods might is,
>   in yonder star light is,
>   of the sonne this sight is,
>   as it now semes. (335-38)

Trowle is given emphasis because he is the first to give the religious significance of the star. From the time the normal order
of speeches is resumed (as soon as the Angel sings the *Gloria*),
Trowle's speeches have the special function of climaxing the
others' naive curiosity and wonderment with a reaction suggesting theological meaning. First he furnishes a proper translation
of "gloria," correcting the nonsensical renderings of the others.
In the next round of speeches the third shepherd ventures the
theory that the angel is "some spie our sheepe for to steale"
(405-06), but *Gartius* again makes a pregnant correction: "Nay,
he come by night—all things lafte—/ our tuppes with tar to
tayle" (409-10). With this speech *Gartius* begins a series of three
in which he makes almost explicit the theological symbolism of
the play's opening discussion among the shepherds regarding
sheep tending and sheep healing. He comments on the "tar" (a

sheep salve) he hears in the angel's song (423) and then mentions a God who heals:

> Yet and yet he sang more too,
> from my mynde it may not start,
> he sang also of a 'Deo'
> me thought that healed my hart. (439-42)

Thus in the star section of the play, Trowle supplies a normative judgment whereas in the preceding wrestling section he controlled the jest. The experience for the audience is a progressive unfolding of thought as well as of feeling. Trowle's first suggestion about the star—"Gods might is/ in yonder star light is" (335-36)—is vindicated and made authoritative by both the angel ("be you not afright,/ for this is godes might" [476-77]) and Mary ("Shepheards, sothlie I see,/ that my sonne you hither sent/ through Gods might in maiesty" [519-21]). Implicit theological meaning has become explicit.

The play is constructed to make audience delight in jest and issue in decorous joy as well as in theological affirmation. The shepherds' procession with song to the Christ child combines the pleasure with religious affirmation. Trowle climaxes the discussion of the angel's Gloria with an invitation to an indefinite audience to join in a "mery song us to solace":

> Nowe sing on! let us see!
> some songe I will assaie,
> All men singes after me,
> for musique of me learne you may. (455-58)

The rubric, "cum aliis adiuvantibus," shows that the shepherds are joined by other singers, whose effect is to give a voice to audience presence and unity. "As the final society reached by comedy is the one that the audience has recognized all along to be the proper and desirable state of affairs," Northrop Frye remarks, "an act of communion with the audience is in order" (p. 164). Trowle now once more initiates the sequence of speeches by starting the procession to Bethlehem:

> Now wend we forth to Bethlem,
> that is best our song to be,
> for to se the starre gleame,
> the frute also of that mayden free. (459-62)

This is a procession of actors, but the feeling and intention is that the audience participates through the actors. This form of

participation would be as thoroughly natural for a medieval
spectator accustomed to processional ceremony as it would be
for a Greek audience accustomed to festal procession or to a pro-
cessing chorus in comedy. The rubric specifies that the song be
sung cheerfully ("hilare"); on the other hand the procession to
the child is done decorously, so that shared religious obedience
and affirmation accompanied by delight becomes the play's final
"meaning," emerging from the experience of the drama. The joy
is founded on the pleasure in jest and contention. The drama's
progressing action, therefore, accomplishes a sleight-of-hand for
the audience: affirmation issues from play, and grace is perceived as delight. Having been its spokesman throughout, it is
fitting that Trowle finally gives the blessing to the audience:

> well for to fare, each frend,
> god of his might graunt you!
> for here nowe we make an Ende.
> fare well! for we from you goe nowe. (659-62)

The Wakefield *First Shepherds' Play* has plot episodes similar to those in the Chester *Adoration of the Shepherds*: a contention, a feast, a discussion of the star both humorous and serious,
and an adoration. It could not exist without traditional expectations about audience participation in jest and devotion. Nevertheless, its jesting episodes, especially, are distinctive among the
mystery plays. The holiday participation which accounts for features of the characterization and action in a play like the Chester
Adoration of the Shepherds also provides a means of seeing the
distinctive qualities of the Wakefield play in perspective. What
C. L. Barber understands to be occurring on a large scale in the
late sixteenth century when Shakespeare's art was transforming
holiday ceremony into "festive comedy" is already occurring a
century earlier in the extraordinary work of the Wakefield
Master. This transformation turns the unselfconscious rhythms
of holiday participation into a form which can be used by a self-
conscious culture: a "ceremonial, ritualistic conception" of human life was yielding to an "historical, psychological conception."[25] Drama, Barber contends, was agent and vehicle of the
transformation, providing a "place apart" where new relations
between language and action could be understood as personality.
The difference between the Chester shepherds' play and the
Wakefield *First Shepherds' Play* is the difference between a tradi-

tional, holiday art and a more self-conscious art. In the former, the social gesture, in Bergson's terms, gives way in the latter to a greater disinterestedness, to reflection on individual experience. This involves differences in the mode of characterization and in uses of language and setting. These structure a new relationship of spectator and play which changes the sense of dramatic reality: the drama becomes more a "thing apart" where the self can be observed than a ceremonial occasion where the unity of the community is affirmed.

The traditional comic dynamics of the quarrel between Gyb and Iohn, on the one hand, and Slawpase, on the other, have not been generally understood fully. Having come from the mill with a sack of grain, Slawpase interrupts Iohn's and Gyb's fun by berating the two for quarreling over imaginary sheep. Slawpase tries to demonstrate the folly of the others by emptying his sack of grain on the ground in order to compare their empty-headedness and scattered wits to the empty sack and scattered grain. His reprimand has uniformly been taken to be normative because the contention of the shepherds can be seen as moral disorder, based on illusion—even though a certain Iak Garcio enters the play to pronounce all three of the shepherds fools. To call the two quarreling shepherds fools, following the example of Slawpase, is a distortion, for they are not fools in any sense except that in which Trowle is a fool—that is, they are sympathetic fools with a necessary function in a comic play.26 To consider Coll and Gyb to exhibit intellectual or moral disorder is not appropriate, even though the humor certainly depends on acknowledging the norms of order. Sympathy in comedy, temporarily at least, favors the one who inverts decorum and embodies license. Conversely, Slawpase is the churl who brings a sour everyday discipline and is consequently the target of dislike.27 To interrupt, and then to depreciate fooling or "flyting," as Slawpase does (148-49), is to take the wrong side at this moment of the play. The events establishing Slawpase's foolishness confirm and inform audience sympathy, and the normative voice in this episode is not Slawpase but Iohn. Slawpase's grain is irretrievably scattered on the ground. No sooner has he made his triumphant demonstration,

> So gose youre wyttys owte, evyn as it com in.
> Geder vp
> And seke it agane! (173-75)

than Iohn gibes at the stupidity of wasting real food for an intellectual truth:

> May we not be fane?
> He has told vs full plane
> Wysdom to sup. (176-78)

One must confront this hard point of the lost grain, and see that
Slawpase's words "so gose youre wyttys owte, even as it com
in" (173), as A. C. Cawley observes, "are ambiguous, and may
refer either to the meal that is lying on the ground or to the scattered wits of the First and Second Shepherds."28 Iohn's rebuke
which humorously takes food as the touchstone of wisdom is one
instance of the deflation central to comedy whereby spiritual
values are reduced to the materialistic ones of food, sex, and
money. This kind of wit prevails in the mock feast which follows
the quarreling scene, and is reflected in the parodic deflation of
religious salvation to drink: "This is boyte of oure bayll,/ Good
holsom ayll" (247-48). The method is not different from that
of Aristophanes' critic from the market (Agoracritus), the
Sausage Seller, who in the *Knights* brings out his political oracles treating

> Of Athens, pottage,
> Of Lacedaemon, mackerel freshly caught,
> Of swindling barley-measurers in the mart.29

Such comic deflation is also achieved by verbal parody of
a high style, in Aristophanes' case, especially of tragic lines from
Euripides, and therefore it creates an awareness of language itself. But in the *First Shepherds' Play* there is an interest in the
relation of language, wisdom, and physical reality which goes
beyond Aristophanes' purposes in the *Knights,* and beyond anything comparable in the Chester play or in any other mystery
play except the *Second Shepherds' Play.* The ambiguous "it"
which Slawpase indiscriminately applies to both grain and wisdom is the key to his error: he equates things which should be
distinguished. The theme of words and reality has already been
introduced by Gyb and Iohn, who deliberately create a fictional
reality, something not physically present, by means of their
words.30 Gyb pretends to be driving sheep which have not yet
been purchased, and Iohn pretends to obstruct them. As they slip
into this playing, Iohn uses the very language—"dreme," "slepe,"

"here"—which implies the distinctions of reality and fiction which he soon gleefully pretends to ignore:

1 Pastor. I go to by shepe.
2 Pastor.   Nay, not so!
       What, dreme ye or slepe? Where shuld thay go?
       Here shall thou none kepe. (101-03)

At this point the pretense is not full-fledged: the argument is still whether Iohn *will* allow Gyb to pass when he will in fact have the sheep. But a moment later the language slips from future to present:

1 Pastor. I shall bryng, no fayll, a hundreth togedyr.
2 Pastor. What, art thou in ayll? Longys thou oght-whedir?
1 Pastor. Thay shall go, saunce fayll. Go now, bell-weder!
2 Pastor. I say, tyr!
1 Pastor. I say, tyr, now agane! (110-14)

Slawpase comes from the mill-wheel, with a logic as stolid as his name implies with which to oppose their playful disjunction of words and reality. His program is an exact correspondence of word and reality, in which words are to subserve present reality. He purports to show the folly of Gyb's and Iohn's playful interest in things beyond the physical present:

Ye fysh before the nett,
And stryfe on this flett;
Sich folys neuer I mett
Evyn or at morow. (139-42)

The similar lesson of counting unhatched eggs then leads to the example of Moll, whose counting cannot change realities: "Ye brayde of Mowll that went by the way—/ Many shepe can she poll, bot oone had she ay" (153-54). If reality should not be exaggerated optimistically (as imagined sheep), neither should it be exaggerated pessimistically, he claims, by the kind of complaint which preceded the playing. For just as Moll's counting does not produce sheep, neither does her complaint about her broken pitcher affect the sheep she does have: "'Ho, God!' she sayde;/ Bot oone shepe yit she hade" (157-58).

The over-simplicity of Slawpase's view, however, is betrayed partly by an irony which Slawpase himself invites. He accuses the others of a folly to be measured by practical consequences:

It is wonder to wyt where wytt shuld be fownde.
Here ar old knafys yit standys on this grownde:
These wold by thare wytt make a shyp be drownde. (143-45)

By his own standard of physical reality (the ship), he ironically
is deficient in wit himself when he proceeds to his culminating
argument and uses—not a verbal example—but a real sack of
grain. Letting himself in for ironic disclosure, "Take hede how
I fare and lere at my lawe" (162), he empties his sack of meal.
The lesson is exact, he boasts in accordance with his principle
of the exact correspondence of reality and verbal wisdom: "So
is youre wyttys thyn,/ And ye look well abowte, nawther more
nor myn" (171-72).

Slawpase's wisdom, therefore, is a specious wisdom of mere
words, revealed through an irony involving motive interacting
with its setting of people and things. Speech style is implicated in
a way entirely uncharacteristic in the mystery plays. Slawpase in
fact identifies his own style in his ironic boast "Ye nede not to
care, if ye folow my sawe" (163), for his advice is a continuous
tissue of saws, of sententious sayings:

> Ye fysh before the nett. (139)
>
> These wold by thare wytt make a shyp be drownde. (145)
>
> It is far to byd 'hyte'/ To an eg or it go. (150-51)

These are followed by a proverbial anecdote of Moll. But proverbial or doctrinaire speech is fatal in its setting; it has consequences in a concrete world of grain and of hunger. When Slawpase draws out exemplary speech to its ultimate assumptions,
and makes an actual bag of grain an exemplum, there is uncharacteristic complexity of speech in relation to setting—a new kind
of characterization and ultimately of audience relationship to
dramatic fiction. Irony is not unusual in the mystery plays, but
a dramatic irony based on character and setting is.

The Wakefield shepherd plays have been justly singled out
for an unusual kind of realization of physical setting at the crucial moment in which Slawpase loses his grain; he asks one of
the others to hold his mare so that he has a free hand to loosen
the tie on the grain sack.[31] But concrete details, such as the
brutalities of the crucifixion or the Chester shepherds' account
of sheep diseases, do not necessarily serve the delineation of
character and motive in a setting. This latter realism, Hans
Diller has usefully distinguished, involves relations between
"speech and action, between cause and effect, and between
people";

the reflection in the dramatic medium of these relations demands
an awareness which is rare among Middle English playwrights
and which, let it be admitted at once, is not called for by the
religious conception of the earlier authors: an awareness that
no two people are exactly the same, that the relation between
them changes with the mood they are in, that they do not
normally describe what they are feeling or doing, that one mood
generates a corresponding but not necessarily identical mood in
the other person. A scene does not become realistic in our sense
of the word simply for a few allusions to contemporary events
and customs.32

The difference between the two realisms is, for purposes here,
not in the content but, instead, in the relation of viewer to content. The difference is between a fiction conceived to be independent of the spectator and "play" in which he directly engages.
When we must be aware that Slawpase inhabits a physical space
which includes mill, mare, sack of grain, and other people, then
this fictional space is discontinuous with the physical space of the
audience. It is its own "world," and within it characters interact
and move with an independence we begin to perceive as "individuality."33 Their relationship with each other and with the
setting becomes as important as their interaction with the audience, so that an audience realism begins to yield to a representational realism. Speech takes on a radically expanded function: it
is no longer simply audience speech, or speech addressed to the
audience, but, in addition, speech which is a function of the
characters.

For a mystery play, Slawpase, Gyb, and Iohn are unusual
because they do acquire dramatic motives which propel the plot
as they interact with each other and with their setting. The ironic
boasts and flat proverbs of Slawpase go beyond what is required
of a comic *alazon* who is a simple vehicle of audience mirth.
Slawpase's speech gives the impression of individual personality
and makes him more than a butt of humor: it tells of a pedes-
trian conventionality, repetitive, inured to work, unimagina-
tively righteous. It is thus possible to speak of motive while, on
the other hand, it is not useful to ascribe motive to the ironic
boast of the Chester First Shepherd, "Falce lad, fie on thy face!/
on this ground thou shalt haue a fall!" (261-62). The difference
is between an irony based partly on characterization and an irony
based only on audience expectation. The joke on the Chester
shepherd is exclusively an audience joke: the audience knows he

is, for the moment, the boaster who will have a fall at the hands of the underdog. And he will fall because that is the comic expectation, not because of any individuality the figure is invested with. Like Slawpase's failure, the success of Gyb and Iohn not only serves the audience pleasure but, in addition, gives the audience the sense of telling something about character; the audience's social response to a type recedes in favor of its seeing psychological traits in an "individual." Gyb and Iohn have an imaginativeness and flexibility which contrast with Slawpase's single direction. First they gradually slide—in a psychologically realistic way—into a game of pretending. Then, at the interruption, Iohn shows a similarly realistic disposition to slide out of it again once Slawpase asks the question which shows him incapable of such playful pretense:

> *Slawpase.* Yey, bot tell me, good, where ar youre shepe, lo?
> *Iohn.*   Now, syr, by my hode, yit se I no mo,
>   Not syn I here stode. (135-37)

Iohn's remark is a fine put-down of Slawpase; it extricates him from the game while continuing to insist, playfully, on its validity by maintaining the "reality" of the sheep they were quarreling over. Trowle, fulfilling in the Chester play the same function as Gyb and Iohn, has no comparable "character": his insults are straight abuse, voicing the audience's vicarious assertion in behalf of the underdog:

> Have done! begin we this game,
> but ware lest your Golians glente!
> that were lyttle dole to your dame
> though in the myddest of Dee ye were drent. (257-60)

Trowle's topical invective, in what is the rough equivalent of "Go drown yourself in the Dee," is the invective of a local Chester audience. This is traditional topical realism of a kind to be expected in mystery plays, since the fundamental assumption is audience participation in a present reality, not representation of an independent reality. The difference, in terms of setting, between this kind of audience "realism" and a representational comic realism is seen by comparing the shepherds' feasts in the Chester play and the *First Shepherds' Play*. The effect of the mock feast of the Wakefield shepherds depends on the same dramatic assumption which operated in the quarreling scene: there must be a firm sense of what is physically actual in the space and time of the shepherds' fictional world in order to appreciate the spirited pretense they indulge in. This pretense, like the pretensc of the one hundred sheep, grandly and playfully imagines a great abundance of food which, in fact, contrasts with the austere actuality.34 A. C. Cawley has given a detailed dcmonstration of how the imaginary meal humorously mixes aristocratic and common dishes.35 One of the purposes of this mixture is to establish the sense of what is playful and imaginary—elaborate banquet fare—in the fictional situation of poor shepherds on the heath. When the shepherds gather up scraps as alms for friars, the joke is partly that in the fictional world of shepherds there are few, if any, scraps, and in that world one does not observe banquet decorum.

In the Chester play only common dishes, those appropriate to shepherds, are mentioned. The gap betwccn what is pretended and what is actual is not simply blunted: the fictional reality of the meal in space and time is not even a consideration. There is no objective physical reality being represented, no play of motive in a dramatic setting, no irony of character. Instead, the meal has a symbolic reality for the audience and the abundance has immediate festive and religious meaning. The Third Shepherd apparently even invites the audience to share: "come, eate with us, God on heaven hy,/ and take no heed, though here be no housing" (147-48).36 If the performance context was anything like that of the York Corpus Christi plays, for example, this offer reinforccd the actual social feasting known to accompany play performance. The remark regarding housing is developed by the Second Shepherd, who explicates the religious meaning which audience and actors are cooperatively affirming under the spirit of play:

> Howsing enough have we here,
> while we have heaven ouer our heades;
> Now to weete our mouthes tyme it were:
> this flaggen will I tame, if thou red us. (149-52)

What the audience is affirming through the mood of social play is man's universal condition in a world under God's heaven; more specifically, it is affirming the combined promise and fact of a savior born on earth among lowly shepherds. The scene thus has more the character of an entertaining pageant tableau, even of a religious icon, than of a dramatic setting.

The Wakefield play is based on traditional forms but it complicates and deepens the way religious meaning is affirmed in the traditional plays. By conceiving shepherds who have a measure of independence in their own world, religious truth is not merely a function of audience participation in present grace but a function also of a character's choice in his own setting. This means that conventional wisdom may be misapplied, so that we can have the pious fool like Slawpase who evades the energetic initiative and imagination of Gyb and Iohn. When holiday audience experience becomes dramatic, holiday play is transformed into a conception of individual imagination, and holy day affirmation is changed into a conception of individual will or initiative.37 Such individual responsibility for choosing truth is what Iak Garcio, who comes in briefly to bring miraculous news of the sheep, suggests in his concluding remark: "If ye will ye may se; youre bestes ye ken" (190).

The basis of the desirable initiative of Gyb and Iohn is a clear-sighted appreciation of the limitation of the world and of themselves. They have no illusions that old proverbs can eliminate worldly grief, as Slawpase foolishly claims ("ye nede not to care, if ye folow my sawe" [163]). They are then able to pretend abundance without being deceived, to engage in abusive play without being disobedient or uncharitable. As the ale goes around, convivial abuse prevails:

> *1 Pastor.* And it were for a sogh
> Ther is drynk enogh.
> *3 Pastor.* I shrew the handys it drogh!
> Ye be both knafys. (274-77)

Gyb then picks up the abusive word "knaves," turns it into the meaning of "lowly men" and implies the humility of sharing the common human condition: "Nay, we knaues all; thus thynk me best,/ So, syr, shuld ye call" (278-79). The commonplaces about the evils of the world or about Fortune in the unstable world—"after oure play com sorows vnryde" (11)—they transform, as individuals, into awareness of personal limitation, ultimately into personal humility and charitable restraint. Such awareness is the basis of the decision of Iohn to call the jesting to a stop: "Furth let it rest;/ We will not brall" (279-80). The same awareness of limitation which gave piquancy to jesting pretense now gives reason for charitable restraint. Gyb and Iohn *are* thus fools,

along with Slawpase, as Iak Garcio had called them, very enig-
matically, earlier (1. 179)—but in a very special sense. In this
ultimate perspective which sees the limitations of each human,
folly itself is levelled out and Gyb and Iohn join Slawpase without distinction. Slawpase's special foolishness is only one instance
of every single man's foolishness. The charity here enacted thus
becomes a dramatic choice, a function of a character, rather than
a symbolic fact communally affirmed.

The *First Shepherds' Play* suggests throughout that language
styles are conditioned by character and setting and that truth has
to do with imagination and choice. This applies no less to religious truth than to truth about sheep, grain, or feasts. The shepherds continue to make us aware of religious formulation as
verbal artifact, as a function of a high style: the angel's song is
"wonder curiose, with small noytys emang" (306), and it says
something confirmed by "the wordys of Isae" (335). Virgil's
prophecy occasions explicit reminder of stylistic level:

> *1 Pastor.* Virgill in his poetré sayde in his verse,
> Euen thus by grameré, as I shall reherse:
> *Iam noua progenies celo demittitur alto;*
> *Iam rediet Virgo, redeunt Saturnia regna.*
> *2 Pastor.* Weme! tord! what speke ye here in myn eeres?
> Tell vs no clergé! I hold you of the freres;
> Ye preche.
> It semys by youre Laton
> Ye haue lerd youre Caton. (386-92)

Learned style in the service of truth here is merely an extension
of high style used jestingly in connection with the feast. There
the first shepherd mocked the third's high diction and reduced
grammar to the touchstone of drink:

> Cowth ye by youre gramery reche vs a drynk,
> I shuld be more mery—ye wote what I thynk. (242-43)

The shepherds' prophecies conclude with the "fygure" of the
fiery furnace as a "good lesson" prefiguring Christ (357). In
Slawpase we have already seen one other good lesson go wrong.
How are we to understand this one?

The prophetic assertion has infinitely more tension than those
in the Chester or other adoration plays by the continuing insistence not only on language as a function of choice but on a
physical setting for the "artificial" symbolic fact. Gyb develops
the traditional interpretation of the burning bush as a figure of

the virgin birth, casually concluding, in an honorific throwaway
tag, that she "shuld haue a chyld *sich was neuer sene*" (368).
But Iohn's following remark blocks simple audience affirmation
of a traditional symbolism put in conventional phraseology:

> Pese, man, thou art begyld! Thou shall se hym with eene—
> Of a madyn myld greatt meruell I mene. (369-70)

The insistence here is on the physicality and on the newly specific
linguistic responsibility which have been dramatically created in
character and action. Traditional, purely symbolic reading does
not worry about the physical context of the symbol which this
play encourages, just as the fooling of the Chester shepherds'
meal does not involve the issue of its physical reality.

For this reason, the three gifts which climax the play—spruce
coffer, ball, and bottle for drink—are a culminating challenge to
interpretation. Are they audience symbols of grace or dramatic
expressions of choice? The playwright rises to the occasion demanded by his rich play by directing attention not only to traditional religious symbolisms but to the themes of physical world,
imaginative play, and language.38 The spruce coffer suggests not
only Christ's redeeming death but also the limitations of the
physical world in which, for individual man, imagination and
charity are exercised. The ball may well suggest the traditional
orb as emblem of Christ's kingship, but it is also a ball which
alludes to play and thus to the meaning of play worked out in
the quarreling and feasting episodes: "This wyll I vowchesaue,/
To play the withall" (474-75). (The coffer is also offered as
plaything: "With this may thou lake" [465].) Slawpase, finally,
offers a bottle for festive drinking and, with it, one last proverb:

> It is an old byworde,
> 'It is a good bowrde
> For to drynk of a gowrde'. (481-83)

We are again made conscious that language, though the vehicle
of religious truth, is spoken by fallible humans and that in the
last analysis all language, even Slawpase's language, is, like Slawpase's folly, an index of man's condition.

Slawpase's proverb, with the other offerings, is also given up
to God. What makes the meaning of this offering different from
the audience offering through the shepherds in a traditional play
or devotional procession is that offering becomes more self-
conscious. We take on our corporate nature out of a more vivid

sense of separate selfhood. The play concludes with words of traditional belief and praise, but they are words of dramatic characters as well as our own words. The characters now speak as beings *like* ourselves, not as mere extensions *of* ourselves. Normative reality becomes something partly "outside" the play in addition to inside the holiday reality present to the audience. Being reflectively aware of character and setting independent of ourselves, we must make the traditional affirmation with more sense of individual choice and responsibility than was traditional: it takes a deliberate instead of an implicit choice to affirm participation in the festive and solemn truth. This consciousness of choice is not applicable to the Chester play or other traditional plays. It makes the religious affirmation of the *First Shepherds' Play* profounder, in a modern sense, than that of those plays. This play has closer affinities with the tragic than traditional religious drama does since it finds selfhood to be relatively more individual and relatively less social.

NOTES

1 *Specimens of the Pre-Shakesperean Drama* (Boston: Ginn, 1897), I, vii.

2 *Aristotle's Theory of Poetry and Fine Art,* 4th edn. (1907; rpt. New York: Dover, 1951), p. 388.

3 *Laughter: An Essay on the Meaning of the Comic,* trans. C. Brereton and F. Rothwell (New York: Macmillan, 1911), pp. 164, 168-69.

4 I have discussed the civic holiday context and its consequences for audience involvement in "Holiday, Audience Participation, and Characterization in the Shepherds' Plays," *Research Opportunities in Renaissance Drama,* 15-16 (1972-73), 97-115.

5 *The Oxford Classical Dictionary,* ed. N. G. L. Hammond and H. H. Scullard, 2nd. edn. (Oxford: Clarendon Press, 1970), p. 435 (hereafter *OCD*).

6 Jane E. Harrison, *Ancient Art and Ritual* (New York: Holt, 1913), p. 152; *OCD*, p. 1062.

7 *The Oxford Companion to Classical Literature,* ed. Sir Paul Harvey (Oxford: Clarendon Press, 1937), p. 177.

8 *OCD*, pp. 230, 613; E. K. Chambers, *The Mediaeval Stage* (Oxford: Oxford Univ. Press, 1903), II, 115.

9 *OCD*, p. 435. Many of the major documents for York are in the *York Memorandum Book,* ed. Maud Sellers, 2 vols., Surtees Soc., 120 (1912), 125 (1915). They are discussed in *York Memorandum Book,* II, xli-li.

10 Francis M. Cornford, *The Origin of Attic Comedy,* ed. Theodor H. Gaster (Garden City: Doubleday, 1961), p. 56.

11 *The Nature of Roman Comedy: A Study in Popular Entertainment* (Princeton: Princeton Univ. Press, 1952), p. 20.

12 *OCD*, p. 269.

13 Philip W. Harsh, in *A Handbook of Classical Drama* (Stanford: Stanford Univ. Press, 1944), p. 267, observes, "the characters of Aristophanes are generalized, and the situations are topical and specific."

14 "... magis risum et clamorem causabat quam devocionem, et quandoque lites, contenciones et pugne inde proveniebant in populo" (*York Memorandum Book*, II, 124).

15 "... comessacionibus, ebrietatibus, clamoribus, cantilenis, et aliis insolenciis" (*York Memorandum Book*, II, 156).

16 *The Dark Voyage and the Golden Mean: A Philosophy of Comedy* (Cambridge, Mass.: Harvard Univ. Press, 1949), p. 44. Duckworth, pp. 132-37, discusses direct address in Roman comedy.

17 Quotations from the Chester *Adoration of the Shepherds* are from *The Chester Plays*, Part I, ed. Hermann Deimling, EETS, e.s. 62 (1892), pp. 132-60. Quotations from the Wakefield *First Shepherds' Play* are from *The Wakefield Pageants in the Towneley Cycle*, ed. A. C. Cawley (Manchester: Manchester Univ. Press, 1958).

18 Freud's statement on humour (as opposed to wit), in *Collected Papers*, V, ed. James Strachey (New York: Basic Books, 1959), pp. 215-21, probes this more kindly variety of the comic, which indulges rebelliousness and accommodates pleasure. Northrop Frye, *Anatomy of Criticism: Four Essays* (Princeton: Princeton Univ. Press, 1957), pp. 165-66, remarks on the general tendency of comedy to include the blocking characters in the new society.

19 *Anatomy of Criticism*, pp. 172-76. Frye's "total *mythos* of comedy" applies particularly closely to a medieval Christian nativity play: "the hero's society is a Saturnalia, a reversal of social standards which recalls a golden age in the past before the main action of the play begins"(p. 171).

20 *The Origin of Attic Comedy*, p. 120.

21 For example see the fragment quoted by Allardyce Nicoll, in *Masks Mimes and Miracles: Studies in the Popular Theatre* (1931; repr. New York: Cooper Square, 1963), p. 53. Regarding Wakefield see A. C. Cawley, "The 'Grotesque' Feast in the *Prima Pastorum*," *Speculum*, 30 (1955), 213-17. Rosemary Woolf, in *The English Mystery Plays* (London: Routledge & Kegan Paul, 1972), pp. 186, 387, notices the prevalence of food in shepherds' plays and nativity poetry generally.

22 Compare, for example, the Wakefield *Harrowing of Hell*, in *The Towneley Plays*, ed. George England and Alfred W. Pollard, EETS, e.s. 71 (1897), p. 304, 11. 357-66. V. A. Kolve, in *The Play Called Corpus Christi* (Stanford: Stanford Univ. Press, 1966), pp. 156-58, discusses the theological idea (the humble exalted and the mighty put down of the *Magnificat*) which invites comparison of Daw's to Christ's triumphs, especially the harrowing of hell, and rightly insists it is a comic parallel to "create festival mirth," not serious allegory.

23 Frye, p. 170. An analagous case for Old Comedy is Aristophanes' Sausage Seller who suddenly becomes morally worthy and "cooks" Demos back to health, one instance of "Aristophanic comedy's disregard of plausibility and its contempt for realistic psychology" mentioned by Harsh (*Handbook*, pp. 267-68). Woolf, p. 190, mentions the lack of "psychological continuity" in the Chester shepherds, including Trowle, between the parts before and after the angel's announcement. She understands Trowle, however, to be also morally distinctive, one who, "though impudent, is conscientious in his care for the sheep and satisfied with his lot"; his abuse of the others is "well-founded in their lazy self-indulgence" (p. 187). Such an account of

Trowle, I am arguing, is based on an incorrect understanding of the function of jest—both in discounting its presence in Trowle, and in making it morally undesirable for the others.

24 A point made by Woolf, p. 187, who also remarks that "each step forward in religious understanding is taken first by the boy."

25 *Shakespeare's Festive Comedy* (1959; Cleveland: Meridian Books, 1963), p. 15.

26 A. C. Cawley, in "Iak Garcio of the *Prima Pastorum*," *MLN*, 68 (1953), 171, says of Slawpase,

> He is master of the situation, as befits a man who can make such apt use of the age-old tale of Moll and her pitcher of milk (11. 153-60).
> The Third Shepherd, unlike his companions, is no simpleton, nor does he deserve or need to be called a fool by Iak Garcio.

Woolf, p. 189, however, understands Slawpase also to be foolish even though his rebukes are justified. The most misleading form of a moral thematic reading occurs in David L. Jeffrey, "Pastoral Care in the Wakefield Shepherd Plays," *American Benedictine Review*, 22 (1971), 211: "Consumed in their growing despair, the shepherds become inactive (slothful), cannot view their troubles in a proper perspective, and are imperceptive of their proper duty." Slawpase is initially "much more perceptive" than the others, and his fish proverb (1. 139) is an "apostolic image" signalling Gyb's and Iohn's failure in duty. Kolve's formulation is more tactful: the episode is there "simply in order that contention and discord may be established as a dramatic fact, as mood, so that a dramatic progress from it can be made" (p. 158). Kolve is finely appreciative of the appropriateness of the playful element: the strife is "simply a mock-quarrel among friends amusing themselves" (p. 302n). Appreciation of the function of jest is an important contribution of the "pagan ritual" reading adumbrated by Chambers' treatment of folk customs in *The Mediaeval Stage* and formulated as "ceremonial joking" in the presence of death by John Speirs, "The *Towneley Shepherds' Plays*," in *The Age of Chaucer*, ed. Boris Ford (Baltimore: Penguin Books, 1954), p. 168. The communal, ritualistic function of jest informs throughout the treatment by Robert Weiman, "Realismus and Simultankonvention im Misteriendrama: Mimesis, Parodie und Utopie in den Towneley-Hirtenszenen," *Shakespeare-Jahrbuch* (Weimar), 103 (1967), 108-35. Since this essay was completed, traditions of mimicry and "folk" festivity have been discussed and sensitively interpreted by Richard Axton in *European Drama of the Early Middle Ages* (London: Hutchinson, 1974). He treats Trowle as the "profane boy-fool" or the "fool-king" who engages in the activities of a folk ale (pp. 189-90), and also discusses the game playing in the *First Shepherds' Play* but does not distinguish Slawpase's role: "The late (and apparently unauthentic) introduction of Garcio into this scene is again for the purpose of 'showing up' the foolery of the other three" (p. 191).

27 Cornford observes that "the Impostor's standing role is to disturb the scenes of sacrifice, cooking, or feasting" (p. 119). In Frye's formula, the Saturnalian inversion is associated with the hero's society and the golden age which is recovered (see n. 19 above).

28 "Iak Garcio of the *Prima Pastorum*," p. 171n.

29 *Aristophanes*, I, trans. Benjamin B. Rogers, Loeb Classical Library (Cambridge, Mass.: Harvard Univ. Press, 1924), p. 223, 11. 1001-03.

30 Woolf, pp. 180-90, identifies the theme of "make-believe" for both the shepherds and Moll but associates it with moral folly.

31 Weiman, p. 134.

32 "The Craftsmanship of the 'Wakefield Master'," *Anglia*, 83 (1965), 272-73.

33 Weiman raises the issue of audience relation to the representation by drawing on an interesting analysis distinguishing between a speech convention in the *platea*

where characters directly address the audience ("simultankonvention") and speech on a *locus* where they interact realistically. Though the latter "realismus" suggests Diller's realism in some ways, it turns out in Weiman's application to serve traditional ritualistic jest. Likewise I find other principal categories, "parody" and "utopia," to be aligned ambiguously with, on the one hand, implications of audience distance and realistic illusion-making, and, on the other, mythic or cult participation. This is reflected in the levelling of the distinction between the *First Shepherds' Play* and the Chester *Adoration* on which my analysis turns.

34 There is probably only ale, as A. C. Cawley says in "The Wakefield First Shepherds' Play," *Proceedings of the Leeds Philosophical and Literary Society,* 7 (1953), 116. Over-emphasis on the ritualistic function of jest misleads both Weiman (128-31) and Speirs (169) into thinking that there is a magical abundance of food. The matter is made more difficult by the momentary dropping of a realistic convention for the sudden appearance of sheep announced by Iak Garcio.

35 "The 'Grotesque' Feast in the *Prima Pastorum*," pp. 213-17.

36 Weiman, pp. 128-31, thinks that actual food is shared with the audience both in this play and in the *First Shepherds' Play*. Frye, p. 164, remarks that Old Comedy and modern Christmas pantomimes sometimes threw food to the audience. At Chester such a device would be appropriate; for the Wakefield play it would not.

37 C. L. Barber says of Shakespeare, "his comedy presents holiday magic as imagination, games as expressive gestures" (p. 15).

38 The several readings agree that in the *Second Shepherds' Play* the shepherds' gifts, like the gifts of the Magi, symbolize aspects of the three-person God: mortal humanity, sovereignty, divinity. John P. Cutts, in "The Shepherds' Gifts in *The Second Shepherds' Play* and Bosch's 'Adoration of the Magi'," *Comparative Drama,* 4 (1970-71), 122, applies the system to the *First Shepherds' Play* by retaining the ball as the symbolic orb of sovereignty, then making the gourd the fruits of Christ's sacrifice, which leaves the coffer for the "evergreen nature of man's spirit which aspires toward heaven." But the latter two surely should be reversed: the coffer fits Christ's mortality (entombment), the wine gourd the "drunkenness" in the Holy Spirit. Eugene B. Cantelupe and Richard Griffith, in "The Gifts of the Shepherds in the Wakefield *Secunda Pastorum*: An Iconographical Interpretation," *Mediaeval Studies,* 28 (1966), 331, find only literal appropriateness to the birth and impending journey in the gifts of the *First Shepherds' Play* (so that the Trinitarian symbolism in the *Second Shepherds' Play* becomes an artistic advance). Robert J. Blanch, in "The Gifts of the Shepherds in *Prima Pastorum*: A Symbolic Interpretation," *Cithara,* 13 (1974), 69-75, and in "The Symbolic Gifts of the Shepherds in the *Secunda Pastorum*," *Tennessee Studies in Literature,* 17 (1972), 25-36, arrives at the same alignment of symbols as Cutts.

To Out-Herod Herod:
The Development of a Dramatic Character

David Staines

Hamlet condemns Herod to an important but one-dimensional position in the development of English drama when he commands the touring players:

> O, it offends me to the soul to hear a robustious periwig-pated fellow tear a passion to totters, to very rags, to spleet the ears of the groundlings, who for the most part are capable of nothing but inexplicable dumb shows and noise. I would have such a fellow whipt for o'erdoing Termagant, it out-Herods Herod, pray you avoid it.   (III.ii)

Though Hamlet refers to the presentation of Herod as a raging braggart in the English mystery cycles, he is selecting only one of the two divergent strains which form medieval drama's continual fascination with the depiction of Herod. Hamlet's admonishment to the players, his objection to overacting, is based on the ranting tyrant who appears in some of the cycles.

Within the figure of Herod, however, medieval drama finds much more than merely a bragging buffoon. Some cycles portray Herod as a tragic figure, the fatal victim of overreaching pride. More than any other single character in medieval drama, Herod becomes a variety of persons under one name. From the wretched villain of biblical and apocryphal accounts, Herod grows in liturgical drama to a figure of potential comedy, potential tragedy, and increasingly less villainy. In the mystery cycles he reaches the apex of his dramatic career as he becomes at times the comic braggart, at times the tragic ruler, at times a combination of comic and tragic hero.

Through a brief study of Herod's growth, first in the apocryphal works and biblical commentaries and then in the liturgical drama, we can begin to see the formation of two separate strains,

the comic and the tragic, which will be developed fully only in
the vernacular drama of medieval England. And the diversity of
the presentations of Herod in the mystery cycles gives him a host
of contrasting descendants in the Elizabethan theater.1

I

The historical Herod bears little resemblance to the complex
figure of Herod in medieval drama. In the New Testament, there
are three not distinctly differentiated rulers named Herod; each
of these men contributes in his own way to the growth of Herod
as a dramatic character. Herod the Great, the figure of primary
importance in medieval drama and the focus of our study, makes
his sole biblical appearance in Matthew's Gospel. Appointed
King of the Jews by the Romans, he reigned at the time of
Christ's nativity. When he learned of the Magi's mission, he
asked his scribes to ascertain the region where the child was born.
Then he summoned the Magi and sent them to Bethlehem to
worship the infant; he demanded only that they return to him so
that he might also adore the new king. When they failed to return, he decreed the slaughter of all male children two years of
age and under. Shortly after the slaughter, Herod died and his
son Archelaus became ruler in his father's place. This brief narrative is the foundation of the elaboration and confusion found
in the apocryphal accounts of Herod's life.2

Matthew's presentation of Herod the Great stands in contrast
to Josephus' lengthy account of his exploits in the first book of
The Jewish War and three books (XV-XVII) of *Jewish An-
tiquities.* Though Josephus makes no reference to the slaughter
of the children, he does delineate quite vividly Herod's death:
"He had fever, though not a raging fever, an intolerable
itching of the whole skin, continuous pains in the intestines,
tumors in the feet as in dropsy, inflammation of the abdomen
and gangrene of the privy parts, engendering worms, in addition
to asthma, with great difficulty in breathing, and convulsion in
all his limbs."3 The description will complement the biblical account as the source for the apocryphal presentations of Herod
the Great.

Another son of Herod the Great, Herod Antipas, appears in
the Gospels of Matthew, Mark, and Luke, where he is responsible for the beheading of John the Baptist. In addition, as
Tetrarch of Galilee at the time when Pilate was Governor of

Judea, he received Christ for trial; though he treated Christ with contempt, he found no fault with him and returned him to Pilate for sentence. The third Herod, Herod Agrippa, grandson of Herod the Great, appears in the *Acts of the Apostles*. He beheaded James and sent Peter to prison; shortly thereafter, he "was eaten by worms and died" (*Acts* 12.20-23).4

Though these New Testament accounts of the three Herods do not contradict each other, their simple and undetailed references do lead to some confusion. The apocryphal gospels follow Matthew's presentation of Herod the Great as the agent of the slaughter of the children. The *History of Joseph the Carpenter,* however, adds a depiction of Herod's death from Josephus' account:

> But Satan went and told this to Herod the Great, the father of Archelaus. And it was this same Herod who ordered my friend and relative John to be beheaded. . . . Having therefore set out from home, [Joseph] returned into Egypt, and remained there the space of one whole year, until the hatred of Herod passed away.
>
> Now Herod dies by the worst form of death, atoning for the shedding of the blood of the children whom he wickedly cut off, though there was no sin in them. And that impious tyrant Herod being dead, they returned into the land of Israel.5

By assigning the beheading of John the Baptist to Herod the Great, the anonymous author confuses the son with his more famous father. This confusion will grow in subsequent writings.6

The apocryphal tradition created a figure of Herod which would be the ideal subject of a morality lesson. It was natural, therefore, that later commentators and historians turn to Herod as an exemplum of the horror of vice and a frank warning to mankind to avoid evil. In his *Historia Ecclesiastica,* Eusebius extends the moralizing denunciation of Herod in apocryphal tradition by emphasizing the propriety of the retribution: "It is also worth while to observe the reward which Herod received for his criminal audacity against Christ and the infants; how, without the least delay, the Divine justice immediately overtook him . . . the successive calamities of his family, the slaughter of his wife and children, and the rest of his kindred allied to him by the closest and most tender relations. . . . The chastisement of Heaven scourged him onwards to the period of death."7 In the following century Saint John Chrysostom describes Herod as the personification of vice, "Attempting to slay that which was born—an act of extreme idiocy, not of madness only. . . . A soul taken captive by any wickedness becomes more utterly senseless than anything."8 Herod is a man immersed in evil; stupidity, born of wickedness and madness, is his motivating force. The distance between this foolish but evil tyrant and the buffoon who will elicit laughter instead of fear is not great, yet only in the medieval vernacular drama will Herod's folly become the basis for his comic delineation.

Later biblical commentaries follow Eusebius and Chrysostom in their depictions of Herod the Great.9 When Herod appears in the *Legenda Aurea,* a compilation not completed until about 1275, he is the product of an accumulation of stories found in earlier accounts. The compiler emphasizes Herod's alien status as King of Judea; his fear at the news of the birth grows out of his understanding of his own precarious position. Following the pattern established by Peter Comestor's *Historia Scholastica,* he includes the story of Herod's suspicions about his children's loyalty to him and his subsequent execution of two of them. After the execution, Herod becomes grievously sick: "In gravissimam aegritudinem cecidit, nam fabre valida, prerigine corporis, continuis tormentis, pedum inflammatione vermescentibus testiculis, intolerabili foetore, crebre anhelitre et interruptis suspiriis torquebatur."10 For our study the most important passage in the compilation is the brief account of the unexpected murder of one of Herod's sons in the slaughter: "Ipse autem Herodes statim ibi punitus est, nam (sicut dixit Macrobius et in quandam Chronica legitur) unus parvulus filius Herodes ibidem ad nutriendum fuerat datus, qui cum aliis a carnificibus est occisus."11 The incident introduces a possible element of tragedy, a moment when Herod is confronted with his dead son, the powerful condemnation of his evil life; the scene will be employed by some medieval dramatists to create a tragic conclusion to the portrait of Herod.

By the thirteenth century the name of Herod represents the epitome of human wickedness. A man without a conscience, Herod is the consummate villain without any potentially redeeming character trait.

II

The development of Herod within the liturgical Latin drama presents a figure seemingly unrelated to any of the developments in the apocryphal and later prose writings. The Herod of the liturgical drama shares many of the same traits and actions which the commentators emphasized, yet he remains a character not fully realized within the confines of the Church and its drama.

In the earliest extant Latin play which includes Herod, an eleventh-century *Officium Stellae* from the cathedral of Nevers,[12] Herod makes an unimpressive entrance upon the medieval stage; he asks the Magi their mission and requests that they return so that he may also worship the infant king. Matthew's brief portrait of Herod is reproduced faithfully and simply in the dramatized liturgy. In an eleventh-century *Officium Stellae* from Compiègne (Young, II, 53-56), a scene between Herod and his scribes is added in which Herod learns that the new ruler shall be born in Bethlehem. When a military attendant advises the slaughter of the children, Herod readily assents.[13] Though the Compiègne version increases only slightly the number of lines assigned to Herod, the dramatist furnishes him with a retinue of servants, soldiers, messengers, and armed knights. The external trappings give the role a dramatic dimension which the texture of the role will eventually come to merit. Karl Young praises the anonymous author: "The play is no longer a compilation of liturgical and Biblical passages, but an independent literary composition. Through this freedom and inventiveness, moreover, is achieved a highly acceptable gain in characterization. Herod himself begins to disclose those traits of pomposity, impetuousness and violence which promise well both for dramatic conflict and for comedy" (Young, II, 58). In the text itself, however, Herod's character does not disclose the early traces of such traits. Young correctly praises the author for his freedom and inventiveness, but the author's true dramatic achievement lies primarily in the court setting and the atmosphere he creates within which the figure of Herod will come to assume a distinct and full dramatic shape. Only when the liturgical drama frees itself from a strict representation of the biblical scene can Herod begin to develop as an independent character.

In a twelfth-century *Officium Stellae* from Sicily (Young, II, 59-62), the formality of Herod's court is accentuated. The Magi receive a summons from the messenger; they greet Herod with a new degree of regal reverence. Though the representation does not develop the figure of Herod, it does present an enlargement of the court; the play's dramatic center is no longer the manger, but the court, a locale emphasized by the manuscript heading "Versus ad Herodem Faciendum." A twelfth-century version of the same play from Strassburg (Young II, 64-66) continues to expand verbally the activities at Herod's court; once again, however, Herod's role is not increased, though his messengers and his knights do receive some new dialogue.

In a twelfth-century *Officium Trium Regum* from Rouen (Young, II, 68-72), Herod has no new dialogue, but his kingly character is delineated by the grandiose epithets with which other characters address him. The messenger refers to his monarch as "Rex Iudeorum," "Dominus Rex," and "Rex inclite." The first of the three kings opens his questioning with the exclamation, "Salve, rex populi fortis, dominator et orbis." Herod's role is further strengthened by a new rubric, placed after the scribes recount the prophecy, "Quo audito, Herodes prospiciens in libro prophitie iratus proiciat." Such an action exposes Herod's irascibility, the only character trait explicitly mentioned in the New Testament. When the military attendant presents the plan for the slaughter, Herod's response is physical, not verbal: "Herodes acceptum gladium librans hac et illac reddat a quo sumpsit." The rubric stresses the possibility that a characterization of Herod may be created through actions which emphasize the violence of his nature. The audience can feel fear at this character.

With a further augmentation of the pomposity and imbecility of this potentially dangerous ruler, however, a dramatist can change an audience's reaction from fear to amusement. Such a possible direction is evident in a twelfth-century *Ordo Stelle* from Bilsen which attempts to enliven Herod's character (Young, II, 75-80). The convention of addressing the king in exalted language now receives a final thrust which may produce a comic effect. When the Magi inquire about the new-born king, they are threatened with violence. Informed, however, that they are being summoned by the king of the whole world, they express a desire to make the acquaintance of such a powerful monarch. Meanwhile, a second messenger arrives at the court. The rubric which describes his arrival, "occurrens alter," emphasizes the comedy inherent in the delivery of his speech: "Rex, Rex, Rex!/ Rex, regem natum constat per carmina uatum." When the Magi announce their purpose, Herod's anger surmounts his self-composure: "Ira tumens gladios sternens Rex ista redundat."

When they show him their gifts for the child, he promptly sends them to prison. At the scribes' enunciation of the prophecies, Herod's action reflects his frame of mind: "Inspiciat libros ac illos reddat amare." Finally, he summons the Magi from prison in order to question them, "fuste minando," as to their place of origin.

In the Bilsen play the presentation of Herod moves more closely to the dimensions of a fully realized character. The author makes the court a scene of frenzied activity. Since Herod retains a comparatively small vocal role, he becomes less regal, less threatening, more suitable for comic development. Any kingly qualities which he may display are continually undercut. The Magi's eager desire to meet the king of the whole world removes any respect which may have been established by the exaggerated phrases of the messengers. Herod's horror at the Magi's mission does not lead him to vocal comments. His anger shows itself in such rash actions as the brandishing of a sword, the imprisonment of the kings, and the confiscation of their books. His impotence as a monarch is emphasized not only by his childish displays of bad temper, but also by his inability to speak. What might be a strong king's consultation with his nobility is only a weak king's desperate need for any form of guidance. The author perceives the potential comedy that was innate in the earlier versions and brings his work closer to the comic portrait of Herod which will dominate many of the cycles. Yet the comedy remains potential rather than realized; liturgical drama prepares the way for comedy, but does not create a comic figure.

In a thirteenth-century *Ordo Rachelis* from the Fleury playbook (Young, II, 110-13), Herod attempts suicide when he learns of the Magi's description: "Tunc Herodes, quasi corruptus, arrepto gladio, paret seipsum occidere; sed prohibeatur tandem a suis et pacificetur." He is removed later from his throne in a dumb show: "Dum hec fiunt, tollatur Herodes et substituatur in loco eius Filius eius, Archelaus, et exaltetur in regem." The Benediktbeuern Christmas Play (Young, II, 172-90) expands the death scene. Herod is now a stupid tyrant. For consultation regarding the new-born child, he summons Archisynagogus, who has already appeared in the play as an ignorant and ridiculous halfwit whose hilarious arguments against the possibility of a virgin birth were solemnly demolished by Augustine and the

prophets. Herod's stupidity is evident in his appellation of Archisynagogus as his "magister." In his indignation at the Magi's
statements, he accepts his teacher's advice to control his anger
and receive the kings with an appearance of goodwill; when the
Magi fail to return, he seeks further advice from his mentor. The
play ends with his death: "Postea Herodes corrodatur a vermi-
nibus, et excedens de sede sua mortuus accipiatur a Diabolis
multum congaudentibus. Et Herodis corona inponatur Archelao
filio suo." The Benediktbeuern Herod is liturgical drama's final
attempt to present a humorous Herod; no extant liturgical play
creates a more potentially comic tyrant, yet this Herod remains
a minor figure in a carefully delineated setting.

Though the Latin drama of the church shows the growth
of Herod as a character of increasing importance in the plays,
this brief chronological study prevents the assertion that his role
evolves progressively into a fully developed major figure; a more
accurate conclusion is that his character lends itself to the kind
of enrichment that occurs in varying degrees of quality and
quantity throughout the extant versions of the *Officium Stellae*.
As Grace Frank notes,

> As soon as Herod himself appeared in the plays further op-
> portunities for dramatic development became obvious and litur-
> gical authors soon made effective use of his presence. They
> could introduce not only a more complicated plot, with an ele-
> ment of suspense, but also portray a villain whose speech and
> actions, costume and accessories might be used to suggest his
> vicious character. The Three Kings had been slightly individ-
> ualized in dress, perhaps in deportment, but Herod's was the
> first role capable of giving us a real person and not a type.[14]

Herod's court allows the liturgical dramatist to array his play
with servants and messengers, knights and counsellors. Herod
himself begins as the wicked ruler of the New Testament, the
villain whose sole aim is to kill the child who threatens his
security. Though he becomes "a real person and not a type," his
emergence as a character stems mainly from the external circumstances around him.

Though Herod succeeds in murdering countless children, he
fails in his ultimate purpose, which is to slay Christ. The success and the simultaneous failure of his major undertaking
prompt the liturgical dramatists to depict Herod as an ineffectual
tyrant to be scorned rather than a vicious ruler to be feared.

Herein lies the primary distinction between the Herod of apocryphal and later prose writings and the Herod of liturgical drama. As the king who tries to kill Christ, Herod of the church drama is the Herod of apocryphal tradition, a symbol of evil. Yet in the liturgical drama Herod never becomes a malicious and fearful agent of evil because the audience, like the dramatist, is aware of his ultimate failure. The dramatist can exaggerate his pomposity without undermining his potentially dangerous nature and his one evil action, the slaughter of the children. To the medieval audience, evil, confronted by good, becomes powerless; within the setting of the church Herod's evil cannot be a fatal challenge. Like Chrysostom, the dramatists note Herod's combination of wickedness and folly, though they choose to emphasize folly. In this emphasis lies the later development of Herod as a purely comic figure.

Finally, Herod does not emerge as a full character in his own right because the liturgical authors do not give him ample speech through which he can express himself. With only one or two major additions and a few relatively minor alterations, Herod's verbal role remains constant through the Latin plays. Though the rubrics suggest the increasing amount of action with which his role is invested, there is a definite lack of speech which might express verbally what the actions express physically. Here is the central area in which the English cycles enrich Herod's character.

III

The authors of medieval vernacular drama are confronted with a wealth of dramatic choices in their presentations of Herod. From the apocryphal tradition comes a tyrant who personifies vice, a murderer who symbolizes this world's wickedness, and a sinner who meets his retribution in eternal damnation and also, at times, in the present life. Yet this serious and powerful presentation of Herod stands in partial contrast to the portrait of Herod slowly emerging in the Latin drama. Often denied the opportunity for much speech in the church plays, Herod becomes a man of violent action. In the church milieu, however, his brandishing a sword and throwing books appear childish, the pitiable actions of a man incapable of reasonable thought or action. Rather than develop his character, the plays develop the setting until the court is a world of flattery, pomposity, and pretense in

direct contrast to the simplicity, solemnity, and divinity of the
manger setting. As his court develops, Herod becomes the essence of the vanity of his setting. Though some plays do present Herod's death, its tragic implications as retribution remain
implicit and undeveloped. The vernacular dramatists, therefore,
have a choice in their depictions of Herod: the evil monarch
committed to the realm of sin and immortal damnation or the
foolish tyrant dedicated to the vanity of his extravagant court.

The vernacular drama of medieval France seems content to
leave Herod the basically undeveloped figure of the church
drama; little attempt is made to expand his role.[15] In English
drama, however, Herod becomes a major character. Each mystery cycle chooses one approach to his presentation—the dangerous villain or the foolish and vain ruler—and creates a unique
and full depiction of Herod to such a degree that medieval
English drama boasts an astonishing variety of different figures
under the name of Herod. From the serious and tragic portrait
of Herod in the N-Town cycle to the light-hearted and bombastic
buffoon of the Coventry *Pageant of the Shearmen and Taylors,*
each of the Herods of vernacular English drama reveals a dramatist's conscious decision to depict either a tragic or a comic
figure from a man who was once the personification of vice.

The most serious presentation of Herod appears in the
N-Town cycle, though even this cycle, so solemn and didactic in
its purpose, cannot restrain some of the comedy which has become an essential part of his character. The prologue to the cycle
describes Herod as an heroic figure ruined by pride:

> Than kyng herownde with-owtyn wene
> is sett to mete at his lykyng
> in his most pride xal come gret tene
> As ye xal se at oure pleyng
> his sorwe xal a-wake
> whan he is sett at hese most pryde
> Sodeyn deth xal thrylle his syde
> and kylle his knyttys that with hym byde
> the devyl ther soulys xal take.   (234-42)[16]

Pride is the dominant theme of the N-Town presentation of
Herod. In contrast to the other cycles, the N-Town *Adoration of
the Magi* does not open with the meeting of the Magi, but pre-
fixes a comical soliloquy in which Herod lists his many
perfections:

As a lord in ryalte in non Regyon so ryche
and rulere of all remys I ryde in ryal a-ray
Ther is no lord of lond in lordchep to me lyche
non lofflyere non lofsummere evyr lastyng is my lay.

Of bewte and of boldnes I bere ever-more the belle
Of mayn and of myght I master every man
I dynge with my dowtynes the devyl down to helle
Ffor bothe of hevyn and of herth I am kyng sertayn. (1-8)

In Herod's second speech, however, the emphasis shifts from pride to the fear behind the pride; his self-laudatory strains reveal his anxiety, "Boys now blaberyn hostynge of a baron bad/ In bedde is born be bestys suche bost is blowe/ I xal prune that paphawk and prevyn hym as a pad."

The play's action consists mainly in the confrontation of Herod and the Magi. There is a noticeable absence of learned scribes and messengers, the accoutrements which tend, in the church drama, to diminish the seriousness of the scene. Though Herod speaks calmly with the Magi, his tone changes immediately after their departure. During their visit jovial kindness covers his true ambitions; he dispatches his visitors with deceptive friendliness. Then he reveals himself to the audience, "How xulde a barn wax so bolde/ be bestys yf he born be/ he is yong and I am old/ An hardy kyng of hye degre/ This daye the kynggys xal be kold/ If they cum ageyne be me." His fear comes from his wounded pride. He leaves the stage with the vow to kill the Magi upon their return.

In a series of two monologues and six short speeches, Herod shows himself to be a powerful and effectual tyrant. Though his opening boasts are conventionally comic in their extravagance, the playwright makes them an exterior manifestation of the strength Herod would like to find in himself. By the end of the second soliloquy Herod admits the fears which threaten his throne. The remaining speeches are short and forceful. Here is a ruler who needs no advice; he can and does act on his own thoughts. Herod, therefore, is not slow to action; he displays an impetuous forcefulness which leads him to immediate decisions. Lastly, this Herod is surfeited with pride, a pride which is humorous in its early extravagance, but which turns him into a dreaded tyrant when his position is threatened. By the end of the play the audience can perceive a vein of cruelty in his character which becomes the center of his actions in his next appearance in the cycle.

Herod's opening speech in the N-Town *Slaughter of the Innocents* juxtaposes his two main traits in the cycle: his excessive boasting and his violent cruelty. Though he begins in a manner almost verbally identical to his boasting in the earlier play, there is a complete absence of humor here. His cruel nature asserts itself in the graphic brutality of his description of the slaughter; the carnage is delineated with no degree of bombast which might undercut the violence of his thoughts. There is a fury in his language which befits a bloodthirsty tyrant. Moreover, this kind of tyrant surrounds himself with the knights who appear in the play. Both soldiers delight in their new undertaking; they exhibit a forthright and demonic brutality which parallels the kind of delight Satan will exhibit when he comes to claim his prey.

As Herod boasts of the successful slaughter, Mors enters with his own boasting: "Ow I herde a page make preysyng of pride/ all prynces he passyth he wenyth of powste/ he wenyth to be the wurthyest of all this werde wyde/ kynge ovyr All kyngys that page wenyth to be." Just as Herod sent his soldiers to murder the children in order to uphold his throne, Mors arrives from him who "ouer all lordys he is kynge" to manifest divine justice. Mors imitates Herod, not only in the content of his speeches, but also in the phrases he employs: "All thynge that is on grownd I welde at my wylle/ both man and beste and byrdys wylde and tame/ Whan that I come them to · with deth I do them kylle." Mors takes a delight in his killing, just as Herod took an excessive joy in delineating the impending slaughter of the children. At the end, Mors points out the play's moral: "Off kynge herowde all men beware/ That hath rejoyced in pompe and pryde/ Ffor all his boste of blysse ful bare/ he lyth now ded here on his syde."

Although the primary subject of the play would seem to be the slaughter, Herod and his death dominate the action and the theme. The final speech of Mors moves away from the character of Herod to the inevitability of death: "All men dwellyng upon the grownde/ Be-ware of me be myn councel/ Ffor feynt felachep in me is fownde/ I kan no curtesy as I yow tel." His sentiment echoes the final lines of the cycle's prologue: "Who so to god · hath be vnkende/ Ffrendchep ther xal he non ffynde/ ne ther get he no grace."

In the N-Town cycle Herod is a boastful, proud tyrant whose pride is the source of his selfish cruelty and whose cruelty is the direct cause of his own death. The *Slaughter of the Innocents* does not allow Herod an opportunity to speak at the time of his death, but chooses to introduce a lengthy moral exposition spoken by Mors. The emphasis on overt didacticism limits the humorous dimension of Herod's character; indeed, the humor here is more curtailed than it will be in any of the other cycles. Herod is a bloodthirsty tyrant whose savage instruction and actions are more to be feared than to be ridiculed.

Like the N-Town cycle, the Chester cycle includes an account of Herod's death; moreover, the Chester version moves closer to a tragic denouement in that Herod displays some awareness of the evil of his actions and the justice of his death and damnation. At the same time, however, that it heightens the tragic implications of Herod's life, the Chester account also develops the comic dimension of Herod's character.

The eighth play of the Chester cycle, *The Three Kings,* assigned to the vintners, centers on the figure of Herod. When the three kings announce their mission to Herod's messenger, his response suggests his master's uncontrolled irascibility: "Hould your peace, syrs, I you praye!/ For if kinge Herode here you soe saye,/ he would goe wood, by my faye,/ and flye out of his skynne."[17] He warns them to be extremely careful of their speech in Herod's presence: "But maye hee wott withowten were/ that anye is borne of more powere,/ you bringe yourselves in greate dangere/ such tidinges for to tell." The third king does announce their purpose, to seek the king of heaven and earth; this direct insult to Herod's majesty launches the tyrant into a fifty-two-line declamation on his regal position. His speech is a litany of self-praise which becomes humorous merely because of the extravagant titles he assigns himself. The frantic boasting quickly reveals the reason why he feels obliged to discuss his authority: "What the devell should this bee?/ A boye, a growme of lowe degree,/ should raygne above my ryalltee/ and make me but a goose." Herod's speech fails to achieve its intended effect. Far from acknowledging his omnipotence, the Magi reiterate their description of Christ. Herod's further exclamation—"This realme moves all of mee;/ other kinges non shall be here" —proves equally ineffectual.

The comic dimension of this Herod is not constant. He may be humorous in his extravagant ranting, but he is a determined tyrant. There is no suggestion that he is a weak ruler whose

kingdom is governed by his advisors. After the Magi depart, he
reveals his plan to the audience:

> By cockes sowle, come they agayne
> all three traytors shall bee slayne,
> and that ylke swedlynge swayne—
> I shall choppe of his head.
> Godes grace shall them not gayne,
> nor noe prophecye save them from payne.
> That rocked rybauld, and I may rayne,
> rufully shalbe his reade.   (398-405)

In the tenth play of the Chester cycle, *The Slaughter of the
Innocents,* Herod's decision to kill the innocent children reflects
his moral awareness of the wickedness of his behavior: "Therfore that boye, by God almight,/ shall be slayne soone in your
sight,/ and—though it be agaynst the right—/ a thousand for
his sake." In his address to his knights, he stresses his moral consciousness: "For wee knowe not that child well,/ though wee
therfore should goe to hell,/ all the children of Israell/ wee
deeme them to be slayne." Employing the royal "we" throughout
his address, Herod is an imposing monarch; his boasting is less
inflated than in the vintners' play; the humor is restrained. Only
in the knights' reply to his command is there any display of
comedy. Both knights object to the plan; the killing of a few
children is beneath their dignity. When Herod reports that they
may kill "a thousand and yett moo," they consent.

After a conventional representation of the slaughter, a woman appears before the king with the body of his dead son who
was killed in the massacre. Herod immediately responds, "But
yt is vengeance, as drinke I wyne,/ and that is now well seene."
Though he berates her for failing to inform the soldiers of the
child's parentage, he soon understands the dire situation; his personal fate is the consequence of his brutal decision:

> Alas, what the divell is this to meane?
> Alas, my dayes binne now donne!
> I wott I must dye soone.
> Booteles is me to make mone,
> for dampned I must bee.
> My legges roten and my armes;
> that nowe I see of feindes swarmes—
> I have donne so many harmes—
> from hell comminge after mee.
>
> I have done so much woo
> and never good syth I might goo;

> therfore I se nowe comminge my foe
> to fetch me to hell.
> I bequeath here in this place
> my soule to be with Sathanas.
> I dye now; alas, alas!
> I may no longer dwell. (417-33)

The Devil appears to reiterate the horrid afterlife that awaits Herod; his closing statement is a candid address to the audience to avoid Herod's ruin.

Though Herod's initial boasting is comic, the dramatist undercuts the potential comedy by emphasizing Herod's power. The king receives no bickerings from his messengers; the knights' grumbling turns to submissive obedience when Herod explains his command. The king himself makes all the decisions in both plays. Finally, there are a few moments when Herod reveals a clear understanding of the impropriety of his actions. The death of his son leads him to a realization of the justice of his own damnation. This final scene comes in the tradition that will produce the great tragic heroes of Marlowe and Shakespeare. When the Chester Herod reaches some awareness of the ruin he has brought upon himself, his perception anticipates the more developed moments of awareness wherein the heroes of Elizabethan tragedy come to understand the nature and the value of their lives. Thus the Chester Herod may be regarded as a direct if distant ancestor of Faustus, Macbeth, and Lear, his more fully matured tragic descendants.

The vernacular medieval drama of England, however, finds the comic Herod more interesting than the tragic Herod. The comic potential overrides the final serious moment to the degree that the one remaining play which also depicts Herod's death is essentially a comic play. In the Digby *Herod's Killing of the Children,* the presence of the death scene does not prompt the dramatist to retain any of the serious intensity of the Chester and N-Town versions. The Digby play is unusual in its introduction of a new element into the conventional framework with the appearance of a sharply individualized messenger. After the knights depart in obedience to Herod's plan for the slaughter, Watkyn, the king's messenger, detains his master to ask that he be knighted. Like Herod, Watkyn is a braggart, "though I sey it my-self · I am a man of myght."[18] He undercuts his boasting by disclosing one failing: "but yitt I drede no thyng more than a woman with a Rokke,/ for if I se ony suche,

be my feith I come a-geyn." As he continues to praise his
prowess, he continues to reveal his fears: "And therfor my
lord · ye may trust vnto me,/ for all the children of Israell
your knyghtes and I shall kylle,/ I wyll not spare on, but
dede thei shalbe/ If the ffader and moder will lete me haue
my wille." The scene is an hilarious confrontation between
two ineffectual braggarts. Herod issues his cruel plans and
Watkyn agrees to execute them provided that all parents stay
away. The seemingly absolute tyrant cannot control his boastful
and ludicrously weak messenger, and the audience must wonder
at the boasting with which Herod opens the play.

The actual massacre is a farce. The Digby dramatist makes
the mothers a physically and vocally strong opposition. The first
mother dubs Watkyn knight: "ffye upon the, coward, of the I will
not faile/ to dubbe the knyght · with my rokke rounde!" Watkyn
vows to "bete you bak and side tyll it were blewe," and the stage
directions emphasize the impotence of his boast: "Here thei
shall bete watkyn · and the knyghtes shall come to rescue hym,
and than thei go to Herowd." Herod does not rejoice at the news
of the murders; his reaction is bitter sorrow and fear—sorrow for
his own actions and fear that Christ may not be dead. His final
lament becomes a graphic representation of his death: "What
out, out, allas! · I wene I shall dey this day;/ my hert tremelith
and quakith for ffeer,/ my Robys I rende a to · for I am in a
fray/ that my hert will brest a-sunder evyn heer."

The Digby play offers a less powerful combination of the
comic and the serious Herod of the Chester cycle. In the opening
scene, Herod the braggart is moderately humorous because his
ranting is unrestrained. In his death scene, he fails to reach the
limited degree of self-awareness which his Chester counterpart
obtains. Yet even the inclusion of the death scene cannot alter
the avenue of comedy which this dramatist chooses. The long
scene between Watkyn and Herod undercuts the ferocity of the
slaughter and changes potential horror into farce. The proud
tyrant cannot command his messenger, and his bragging messenger, following his master's example, turns his own pompous
self-praise into folly by exposing glimpses of his own fears. Thus
the Digby Herod ultimately follows the comic dimension which
will reach its fullest employment in the remaining cyclic
accounts.[19]

In the York and Towneley cycles and in the Coventry

Pageant of the Shearmen and Taylors, comedy becomes the determining, indeed sole, factor in the depiction of Herod. The potential tragedy of his career is eliminated by the exclusion of the death scene. In these plays, Herod is only the cause of laughter.

In the York cycle, the comic potential of Herod is developed with freedom. In the *Adoration of the Magi,* Herod does not see his power confined to the earth; he proclaims that all the planets dutifully obey him; the sun and the moon pay homage to him; he rides on the clouds. His court is the home of vain simpletons and dumb sycophants. In the *Massacre of the Innocents,* Herod identifies himself with Mahomet in power; his counsellors are worshipful idolators who pamper his whims: "Lord, what you likis to do/ All folke will be full fayne,/ To take entente ther-to,/ And none grucche ther-agayne."20 Herod gleefully adopts the suggestion to kill the young child. The final scene shows that the York Herod is a deeply suspicious human being. He becomes uncontrollably angry when his soldiers admit that, though they have killed all the chidren in Bethlehem, they had no means of identifying Christ. Herod's final speech is humorously ironic in that his greatest fear has been realized in the preceding play, *The Flight into Egypt*: "So may that boy be fledde,/ For in waste haue ye wroght/ Or that same ladde be sought,/ Schalle I neure byde in bedde." The counsellors end the play by promising to serve Herod and to allay his fears through their deeds.

The Towneley Herod, even more than the York Herod, completely dominates the plays in which he appears.21 The *Oblacio Magorum* opens with a fifty-two-line address by Herod to the audience. Once again he swears to kill disobedient subjects; he proclaims that his kingdom encompasses the entire physical universe; he boasts extravagantly about his striking appearance. As in the York cycle, he identifies himself as a faithful servant of Mahomet "that weldys water and wynde"; his devotion becomes an identification of himself with the pagan deity: "Man and wyfe, that warne I you,/ That in this warld is lyfand now,/ To mahowne & me all shall bow,/ Both old and ying."

A further source of comedy in the Towneley depiction of Herod is the tyrant's direct contrast with the Magi. Whereas he invokes Mahomet, they invoke God. His kingdom embraces the entire world, while each of the three kings outlines the limited geographical region under his rule. Moreover, the Magi employ the same phrases Herod uses, though in different contexts. He craves supreme obedience to himself, they swear obedience to Christ: "All folk shalbe to hym obeyng/ That berys the lyfe." The Magi bring gifts "in tokyn that he kyng shalbe/ Of alkyn thyng," which is the power Herod claims for himself. The first king asks his fellow-travellers the location of Christ in phrases identical to Herod's earlier boast: "Where is that kyng of Iues land,/ That shalbe lord of se and sand,/ And folk shall bow unto his hand/ Both more and myn?" Even Herod's messenger contributes to this echoing technique when he relates that the Magi proclaim Christ to be "kyng of towne and towre."

Like his York counterpart, the Towneley Herod falls into a childish rage and despair at the news of the Magi's mission. The scribes' account of the prophecies only increases his anxiety. After cursing the scribes, Herod begins a self-pitying soliloquy indicative of the extravagant overacting which must dominate any presentation of the Towneley Herod: "Alas, wherto were I a crowne?/ Or is cald of greatt renowne?/ I am the fowlest borne downe/ That euer was man."

As Herod dominates this fourteenth play of the Towneley cycle, so he controls the entire action of the sixteenth play, which is appropriately titled not *Slaughter of the Innocents*, but *Magnus Herodes*. Though Herod's messenger prepares the stage for his master by praising the tyrant and describing the punishments he inflicts on disloyal subjects, the potentially fearful and solemn portrait of a cruel tyrant is quickly turned to farce when Herod learns that his messenger is unable to quell the rumors spreading through the city. He determines to stifle these stories; accordingly he describes his power in a series of august declarations. The scene presents the perfect delineation of the impotent tyrant terrified at the prospect of a boy usurper.

In the scene with his scribes, the Towneley Herod stands in direct contrast with the Chester Herod. The latter displayed great erudition when he listed the many works from the Old Testament which his counsellors should read. The Towneley Herod offers a catalogue of books which will have no relevance to the subject of investigation. Unresourceful in thought and deed, he has no dramatic stature except as the source of humor. The second counsellor advises the slaughter and even adds the direction that it include all male children two years of age and under; without any questioning Herod adopts the plan.

After the futile slaughter, Herod closes the play with a long address to the audience in which he takes demonic delight in the carnage. Since the audience knows the ineffectiveness of his scheme, the dramatist intensified the scene's humor through dramatic irony. Herod boasts of his successful slaughter; his actions serve as an example to those who attempt to usurp his position. He continually emphasizes his cruelty and violence, as he did in his opening address, but the terror of such a potential fiend is undercut by the knowledge of the failure of his violence.

Both the York and the Towneley Herods show remarkable similarities. Both cycles emphasize Herod's allegiance to Mahomet; both reveal his extravagant boasting about his personal appearance; in both cycles, the obedience of the court is flattery to a ridiculous excess. Both Herods are impotent tyrants incapable of forming their own plans.

Many of the speeches of the Towneley Herod are expansions of the speeches of the York Herod.22 The Towneley Herod pushes ideas expressed by his York counterpart to a complete and therefore ludicrous end. Whereas the York Herod stresses his allegiance to Mahomet, the Towneley Herod imposes the worship of the pagan deity on all his subjects. In a similar manner, not content with the York Herod's assertion that he rules every land, the Towneley Herod enumerates all the lands which he rules. More significant, however, is a final difference between the two tyrants. The ending of the York play leaves Herod in a state of perplexity as to the efficacy of the slaughter; he believes it may have failed. The Towneley Herod, on the other hand, acknowledging only momentarily the remote possibility of failure, rejoices exuberantly in the brilliance of his completed scheme. The ending of the Towneley play is more ironic and humorous; it leaves Herod a boastful and stupid fool unaware of the failure of his enterprise.

The Herods of the York and Towneley cycles stand in contrast to the Herods of the N-Town and Chester cycles and, to a smaller degree, to the Herod of the Digby play. In the York and Towneley plays, Herod's pride is boastful and ludicrous arrogance. His consultation of the scribes is the desperate search by an unthinking tyrant for any possible guidance. The reports of the Magi no longer prompt Herod to preventative measures; quite to the contrary, he throws himself into a lament of self-pitying despair. Most important, the York and Towneley Herods do not die. By ignoring the subject of death and divine retribution, the York and Towneley dramatists ignore the tragic potential and commit themselves completely to the realm of farce; Herod is such a caricature that the audience can only laugh at his threats. Laughter becomes the aim of these entertaining plays, whereas seriousness is more dominant in the plays of a more didactic nature.

The fullest development of Herod as a figure for laughter appears in the Coventry *Pageant of the Shearmen and Taylors.* Herod's extravagant boasting, his uncontrollable irascibility, his ranting behavior, all these traits receive complete depiction with no degree of subtlety in the presentation. The first half of the play recounts the adoration of the Magi and the slaughter of the children. Herod's opening speech exceeds the opening address of the Towneley Herod in the extravagance of his claims. Not only did he make heaven and hell, but his power sustains the whole world. He causes the lightning and the thunder; indeed, "To reycownt vnto you myn innevmerabull substance,—/ Thatt were to muche for any tong to tell."23 When the messenger reports the homeward departure of the Magi, Herod rages in grand style:

> A-nothur wey? owt! owt! owtt!
>   Hath those fawls traytvrs done me this ded?
> I stampe! I stare! I loke all abowtt!
>   Myght I them take, I schuld them bren at a glede!
> I rent! I rawe! and now run I wode!
> A! thatt these velen trayturs hath mard this my mode!
>   The schalbe hangid yf I ma cum them to! (777-83)
> *Here Erode ragis in the pagond and in the strete also.*

The rubric emphasizes the dramatist's ability to create a more extravagantly ranting tyrant than in any of the other plays.

When the Coventry Herod decides to kill the children, he turns to his knights, not for their advice, but with an eager desire for their consent. The knights vehemently object to his plan, and though they ultimately swear obedience under his forceful insistence, they continue to stress the difference between their desires and their actions. Furthermore, during the slaughter both soldiers maintain that they act against their own wills in order to fulfill Herod's decree. The instinctively moral soldiers prophesy that Herod's actions will not end well: "For thys grett wreyche that here ys done/ I feyre moche wengance ther-off woll cum." Before Herod can rejoice over the slaughter, a messenger announces the flight into Egypt. The play ends with Herod riding off to Egypt: "Now all men hy fast/ In-to Egyipte in hast!/ All thatt cuntrey woll I tast,/ Tyll I ma cum them to."

Though the Coventry Herod's brutality and his knights' constant protestations prepare for a possibly tragic delineation of Herod, there is no attempt to give him any dramatic dimension beyond caricature. The final development of the comic Herod, the Coventry tyrant is essentially the bragging fool, the ineffectual weakling, the raving buffoon. His role is pure farce. His raging even into the street only increases the foolish behavior which is his way of life. He is evil in his actions; even his knights emphasize his immoral decree. Yet his impotence makes him a figure of farce rather than the awesome tyrant of a potential tragedy. Herod is the court's fool rather than its ruler.

In the records of the trading companies of Coventry that refer to the Corpus Christi plays,[24] there is a long list of expenses for the extravagant physical trappings used by the actor who plays Herod. His costume reflects his magnificence; it is remarkably rich and spectacular, so ostentatious that it must have appeared ludicrous to the audience. His vain physical appearance reflects his vain nature, and his bombast is now complemented by the extravagance of his attire. Herod, the figure who became an almost tragic character in the N-Town and Chester cycles, is now the fully realized hero of farce.

IV

Following the growth of Herod as he assumes increasingly greater prominence in the medieval English drama, we see that the development often becomes a matter of out-Heroding a former Herod. To out-Herod Herod is an adequate description of the method of many medieval English dramatists in their treatment of his character. Often his role grows through the accentuation of his anger, through the expansion of his bombast, and through the addition of more curses and swearing. One Herod outdoes his predecessor by being a more accomplished and boisterous braggart.

The comic Herod does not die with the demise of the mystery cycles. He survives and re-appears in a variety of new guises. He merges with his close relative, the *miles gloriosus* of the Roman comedies. Ralph Roister Doister may find his origin in the comedies of Plautus and Terence, but his character already appeared on the English stage in the figure of Herod. And this pattern of the braggart, the ineffectual boaster, leads to such major Elizabethan figures as Pistol and Bobadill. Even Sir John Falstaff, Shakespeare's immense comic figure with such a wide literary ancestry, is a distant member of the Herod family, as Mistress Page realizes in reading his extravagant profession of love: "What a Herod of Jewry is this!" (*The Merry Wives of Windsor,* II.i).

In the history of English drama Herod is a central character because he stands in two traditions, the tradition of the comic braggart and the tradition of the tragic hero. The slaughter of the children, his lasting claim to fame, is the fact that prevents him from remaining solely a figure of farce. Though dramatists make his boasting an occasion for laughter, the murder of so many children leads some dramatists in another direction. The moral didacticism of the N-town cycle creates a Herod who is an exemplum of man's ruinous fall through pride. The Chester Herod becomes an early Faustus, a potentially tragic figure who sees too late that his wickedness brings about his eternal damnation. Yet this tragic dimension remains basically undeveloped because Herod cannot emerge as a true tragic hero. As a figure of evil, he remains the product of the apocryphal tradition, the personification of vice rather than a human being choosing evil and denying good. Consequently he never receives any good qualities; he lacks nobility of character, personal integrity, and profound powers of judgment. The first of the English stage villains after Cain, he is too one-dimensionally evil to become a valid and interesting tragic hero.

The liturgical drama, on the other hand, develops a presentation of Herod which prepares the way for his role as the great figure of farce. The Herod of the Latin drama, as we have seen, is a figure of evil whose anger expresses itself mainly through his actions; his language remains close to the limiting phrases of scripture. As the Latin drama develops his court as the home of flattery, vanity may become a part of Herod's character. When the vernacular drama of England allows Herod to express his anger vocally as well as physically, his character seems to demand a farcical treatment. His anger, when expressed vocally, becomes bombast, and his bombast, aided by insistence on his dignity and power, produces laughter.

As Herod becomes the great creation of farce in medieval

English drama, it is clearly evident that many dramatists are heeding the pressure of the final force shaping the figure of Herod, namely the audience. His expanded role reflects the delight he gave to his audience and the dramatists' ability to cater to this delight. Certain complexities, as I have shown, do exist in the figure of Herod and are occasionally evident in some dramatic presentations. The serious dimension of his character, however, will await further development in the tragedies of the Elizabethan theater. More often than not, medieval dramatists do not heed the kind of advice Hamlet gives to the touring players and prefer to create the kind of buffoon who will delight their audiences as well as the common audiences of the touring players. The potentially tragic tyrant becomes the raving braggart of farce, and his delineation becomes so extravagant that the stage is no longer large enough to contain his personality; he "ragis in the pagond and in the strete also." Certainly the grateful medieval audience is likely to espouse the shouts of approval which Bottom holds as the ultimate measure of dramatic success: "Let him roar again: let him roar again" (*A Midsummer Night's Dream*, I.ii).

NOTES

1 Though criticism of medieval drama often refers to Herod, there are few studies of this figure. Isaak Sondheimer, *Die Herodes-Partien* (Halle: Max Niemeyer, 1912), offers a detailed contrast of Herod's role in Latin drama and the vernacular drama of medieval France. Warren E. Tomlinson, *Der Herodes-Charakter im Englischen Drama* (Leipzig: Mayer and Müller, 1934), surveys all of Herod's appearances in English drama from the earliest church drama until the twentieth century. Roscoe E. Parker, "The Reputation of Herod in Early English Literature," *Speculum*, 8 (1933), 59-67, confines himself to the raging element of Herod's character and sees a clear evolution from the apocrypha until the mystery cycles. S. S. Hussey, "How Many Herods in the Middle English Drama?" *Neophilologus*, 48 (1964), 252-59, speculates on the degree to which medieval English drama differentiated the three Herods. Penelope Doob, *Nebuchadnezzar's Children: Conventions of Madness in Middle English Literature* (New Haven: Yale University Press, 1974), has a fine study of Herod as a mad sinner.

2 The contrast between the paucity of historical details about Herod the Great and the abundance of material for his medieval stage appearances recalls the similar contrast between the historical Crucifixion and its elaborate depictions in medieval art. For an important study of the historical Crucifixon and its evolution as subject-matter in medieval art, see F. P. Pickering, *Literature and Art in the Middle Ages* (Coral Gables, Florida: University of Miami Press, 1970), pp. 223ff.

3 Josephus, *The Jewish War*, edited and translated by H. St. John Thackeray (London: William Heinemann, 1956-57), Book I, Chapter 656.

4 Josephus offers a different version of the death, *The Jewish War*, II, 219.

5 *The Ante-Nicene Fathers*, ed. Alexander Roberts and James Donaldson (New York, 1896), VIII, 389.

6 See, for example, *The Apocryphal New Testament*, trans. M. R. James (Oxford: Clarendon Press, 1945), pp. 155-56.

7 *The Ecclesiastical History of Eusebius Pamphilus*, edited and translated by C. F. Cruse (London, 1870), Book I, Chapter 8.

8 Philip Schaff, ed., *The Nicene and Post-Nicene Fathers of the Christian Church* (New York, 1888), X, 45.

9 Bede, in his commentaries on the Gospels, "Expositio in Evangelium S. Matthaei," "Expositio in Evangelium S. Marci," and "Expositio in Evangelium S. Lucae," and in his study of the *Acts of the Apostles*, "Expositio in Actus Apostolorum," all of which are found in *Patrologiae Cursus Completus: Patrologia Latina*, ed. J. P. Migne (Paris, 1844-64), 92, often mentions the three Herods and refers to Josephus in order to distinguish among the trio. Remigius, in his sixth and seventh homilies, *Patrologia Latina*, 131, 895-907, takes great care to differentiate among the three Herods. In his "Historia Scholastica," *Patrologia Latina*, 198, Peter Comestor continues the expansion of the presentation of the Herods by developing Herod the Great as a monarch of increasing impotence and madness; in his discussion he quotes directly from Josephus and Chrysostom.

10 Jacobus de Voragine, *Legenda Aurea*, ed. T. Graesse (Leipzig, 1850), p. 66.

11 *Legenda Aurea*, p. 65. Later writers record the incident as evidence of divine justice. In translating the passage, Caxton adds the phrase "by right vengeance of God."

12 Karl Young, *The Drama of the Medieval Church* (Oxford: Clarendon Press, 1933), II, 50-51. Henceforth in this discussion the name "Herod" will refer only to Herod the Great, the subject of the study, though traits of the other Herods now form part of the composite creation of Herod. The two later Herods do not appear in the Latin liturgical drama; Herod Antipas has a small role in the Passion plays of the Chester, York, and N-Town cycles and in the Digby *Mary Magdalene*.

13 The acceptance of the military attendant's suggestion is a prelude to possible dramatic representations of the slaughter. An eleventh-century *Ordo Rachelis* from the cathedral of Freising (Young, II, 117-20) does depict the murder. After a brief presentation of the adoration of the shepherds and the flight into Egypt, the setting of the play is Herod's court. Herod does not accept the messenger's advice to apprehend the Magi; instead, he immediately orders the death of the new-born child. An armed knight offers to accomplish the massacre. By making Herod the instigator of the slaughter, the author also develops the king's dramatic importance.

14 Grace Frank, *Medieval French Drama* (Oxford: Clarendon Press, 1954), p. 34.

15 For a survey of Herod's few appearances in the vernacular drama of medieval France and his relative unimportance, see Isaak Sondheimer, *Die Herodes-Partien*.

16 All quotations are from K. S. Block, ed., *Ludus Coventriae*, EETS, e.s. 120 (1922).

17 All quotations are from R. M. Lumiansky and David Mills, eds., *The Chester Mystery Cycle*, EETS, s.s. 3 (1974).

18 All quotations are from F. J. Furnivall, ed., *The Digby Plays*, EETS, e.s. 70 (1896).

19 In the Digby *Mary Magdalene*, Part I, Scene 4, Herod makes an appearance which is wholly comic; after a twenty-seven-line monologue about his personal glory, he becomes enraged when philosophers tell him of the new-born king; his knights comfort him and promise to defend his kingship. This Herod is a pompous fool, closely akin to the York and Towneley Herods.

20 All quotations are from Lucy Toulmin Smith, ed., *The York Mystery Plays* (Oxford, 1885).

21 In "The Later Miracle Plays of England," *International Quarterly*, 12 (1905), 67-88, C. M. Gayley claims that there are two distinct Herods in the Towneley cycle; he confuses the power of the dramatist's characterization with the character he is depicting. There is no doubt that the Herod of the *Magnus Herodes* is a richer character than the Herod of the *Oblacio Magorum*; he is, however, primarily a detailed and clever elaboration of the same basic figure. "But though the Herod rant is more developed in this play than in the Magi, he is essentially the same Herod in both and a character type that had not needed to be specially invented for them" (John Speirs, "The Mystery Cycle: Some Towneley Cycle Plays," *Scrutiny*, 18 [1951-52], 246). Hence I refer to one basic Herod of the Towneley cycle. All quotations from the cycle are from George England and Alfred Pollard, eds., *The Towneley Plays*, EETS, e.s. 71 (1897).

22 M. C. Lyle, *The Original Identity of the York and Towneley Cycles* (Minneapolis: University of Minnesota Press, 1919) posits the possibility of an original identity between the two cycles. Later criticism and clarification of her thesis are summarized by Hardin Craig, *English Religious Drama of the Middle Ages* (Oxford: Clarendon Press, 1955), pp. 214ff.

23 All quotations are from Hardin Craig, ed., *Two Coventry Corpus Christi Plays*, EETS, e.s. 87, second edition (1957).

24 *Two Coventry Corpus Christi Plays*, pp. 86ff.

Time, Eternity, and Dramatic form in *Ludus Coventriae* "Passion Play I"

Daniel P. Poteet II

Few students of the English mystery cycles would contest the truism that, in general, the dramatic conventions of *Ludus Coventriae* "Passion Play I" and all other medieval plays are intended to interpret a Christian world and universe.[1] Yet even the most perceptive critics appear reluctant to construe "conventions" as more comprehensive than staging and theme, or to consider the fundamental likelihood that such touchstones of analysis as character, conflict, and development possess a low priority in the interpretation of a medieval Christian universe. These concerns, which are inseparable from the post-medieval appeal of world, individual, and time, however, bear only minimal relation to the primary medieval interest in the timeless structure of eternity and reality. The liturgy and sacramental system, philosophical interest in being rather than becoming, and the iconographic and typological system of correspondences between earth and heaven—all relevant in some degree to "Passion I"—demonstrate the seminal position of timelessness in medieval thought. Time itself, with its attributes of causality, sequence, and change, was thought to be of secondary and deceptive importance.[2] In "Passion I," which dramatizes the intersection of history and eternity in the displacement of the Paschal Feast by the Eucharist, the distinction between time and timelessness is crucial not only to theme, but to the action and total structure of the play. The ways in which the play gives substance and shape to this distinction challenge the reliability of time oriented interpretive criteria and indicate that medieval belief and aesthetic imagination and medieval dramatic decorum are sometimes indivisible.

Critical investigation of the play has established many of its distinguishing characteristics—e.g., a high level of dramatic irony, rigid adherence to theme, startling moral contrasts among situations and characters—but usually in studies that stress isolated insights rather than wider generic qualities. Eleanor Prosser's description of "Passion Play I," for instance, as "a carefully unified sermon on repentance: a sermon with exhortations, *exempla,* and meditations," pinpoints an important theme, but blurs the basic aesthetic differences between expository forms of theology and moral philosophy and imaginative drama.3 Rosemary Woolf recognizes the theme of God's redemptive love and the eucharistic and liturgical emphasis of the play, but attempts no comprehensive interpretation.4 Of greater value, in terms of aesthetics, are analyses of multiple staging, simultaneous scenes, and telescoping action by Stanley Kahrl and Kenneth Cameron and by Glynne Wickham, but even these studies do little to demonstrate the formative impact of theological milieu on dramatic form.5 No study to date, in other words, has attempted to interpret these attractive elements of the play in the context of its remarkable time suppressing characteristics—the rearrangement of historical order, the total lack of moral development among characters, common sacramental imagery, the ironically futile temporal sequence attending the denigration and capture of Jesus —which collectively suggest the influence of a non-naturalistic informing milieu and objectify a spiritual alternative to the worldly significance of sequential time. Together with other plays in the *Ludus Coventriae,* "Passion I" may well represent a kind of drama that, in its purest form, is highly symbolic, free from meaningful overt conflict, and theoretically timeless among its exemplars of virtue—a kind of drama whose theologically based principles of organization and their aesthetic consequences distinguish it from drama that is Christian only in theme.

Indications of the influence and nature of these principles occur with provocative frequency. Sacramental representation and imagery, the prologues by Demon and John the Baptist, and the healing of two blind paupers, for instance, all imply the association of illusion with time and truth with eternity. They encourage the search for evidence of this distinction in more basic qualities of the play, and they remind us, more importantly, that the distinction is a matter of Christian metaphysics as well as of simple definition. Sacramentalism is obvious in a central episode, the Last Supper, and in the detailed institution of the Lord's

Supper; the later appearance of an angel bearing *"A chalys with An host þer in"* sustains eucharistic imagery.6 Although the importance of other sacraments is less certain, the initial presence of John the Baptist and the later washing of the disciples' feet by Jesus are conventional reminders of baptism.7 Mary Magdalene's quest for forgiveness suggests the sacrament of penance. Representation of these three sacraments together is common in other medieval art, and at least in some earlier cases their eschatological and mystical significance and context are reinforced by the added presence of a *Majestas Domini*.8 "Passion I" is of course hardly a perfect and static analogue for such a visual concept, but sacramental overtone calls to mind the intersection of eternity with world as well as the ultimate reality of the eternal reference. The conjunction here of three sacraments commonly associated elsewhere can only reinforce audience awareness of this eternal dimension, whether or not the play successfully objectifies it. This mystical presence of God, superior to earthly enactment of the sacraments is, in fact, explicitly stated and a worldless eternal eschatology theorized in connection with their visible representation. In the words of the play Jesus, one drinks His blood, "To ben partabyl with [Him] in [His] reyn above" (1. 804).

Although the two prologues have no explicit concern with time and eternity, the association of Demon, lacking any clear scriptural relation to subsequent events, with John the Baptist, who historically had died years earlier, does occur as a static, non-narrative juxtaposition existing outside the logic of time. Their absolute lack of acknowledgement or recognition emphasizes this disjunction, while the content of their speeches similarly indicates extreme contrast rather than potential interaction and conflict developing within the passage of time. Demon, whose commitment to the things of this world (such as cordovan shoes and costly crimson hose, 11. 69-70) is unmistakable, explains his role in the three temptations of Christ, and his much earlier contributions to the sins of the fallen angels and Adam. He is something of a historian, although his confidence—despite recent setbacks by Christ—that past successes and patterns of destruction can be repeated undermines both his own reliability and that of argument based on precedent: "I xal Arere new Engynes · of malycious conspiracy/ Plente of reprevys · I xal provide · to his confusyon" (11. 50-51). The prologue of John the Baptist, as abstract and principled as Demon's is concrete and detailed, advocates a spiritual course between the extremes of presumption and despair; it is a model of comparative simplicity and liberty. His prophesied "kyngdham of hevyn" (1. 8) is quite the opposite of Demon's "þis werd" (1. 2); his preferred "patthe of hope and drede" (1. 24) leading to that kingdom is distinct from Demon's worldly particularity and pattern. Taken together, these prologues—in a faintly sacramental fashion—thus juxtapose the concerns of time with those of eternity and establish the eschatological futility of one and the efficacy of the other; they show, in addition, that even scriptural chronology can be subordinated to the compiler's interpretive needs.

In corroborative ways, the healing of two blind paupers at the gates of Jerusalem also implies a spiritual alternative to worldly process and a readiness to alter scriptural temporal order. The cure, as Jesus says, is a result of belief—the proper frame of mind, in other words—rather than of some morally developmental sequence: "ȝowre be-leve hath mad ȝou for to se/ And delyveryd ȝou fro All mortal peyn" (11. 314-15). Worldly condition again is secondary and without inevitability. With no concession whatsoever to naturalistic probability, the change in physical state occurs instantaneously and reflects no gradual, time consuming process. Furthermore, in the manner of John the Baptist's surprising attachment to the beginning of the play, this action has been moved from its customary placing on the outskirts of Jericho. Once more, even in this brief incident, the alteration of chronology, possibly according to thematic requirement, the precedence of moral condition over moral change, and the lack of spiritual concern with the necessity of qualities that normally mark human time, all seem to imply more than passing interest in the conventional medieval distinction between time and eternity.

This difficult contrastive relationship between existing time and theoretical eternity, in a comprehensive sense, is the subject of "Passion Play I," placing great concern for the sanctity of Jewish law, precedent, and history against the far simpler timeless morality of Jesus. His dramatic celebration of the Paschal Feast, consistent with Old Testament instructions but interpreted in patristic fashion, makes it clear that although the lessons of time are genuine, history nevertheless is fully understandable only in a spiritual way. Jesus is concerned that the meal be eaten "as þe eld lawe doth specyfye" (1. 715), but is equally insistent on providing for this form the "gostly interpretacyon" (1. 716). Prescribed details of dress and position, and consumption of the entire lamb along with sweet breads and bitter herbs, according to Jesus, evoke His own charity, godhead, and humanity, and thus figure the mystery of His flesh and blood; the feast in effect is a figure of both Passion and Eucharist, even though Jewish practitioners had no idea of this truth:

> Brederyn þis lambe þat was set us beforn
> Þat we Alle haue eten in þis nyth
> it was comawndyd be my fadyr to moyses and Aaron
> Whan þei weryn with þe chylderyn of israel in egythp.

> And as we with swete bredys haue it ete
> And Also with þe byttyr sokelyng
> And as we take þe hed with þe fete
> So dede þei in all maner thyng

> And as we stodyn so dede þei stond
> and here reynes þei gyrdyn veryly
> With schon on here fete and stavys in here hond
> And as we ete it so dede þei hastyly
> þis fygure xal sesse A-nothyr xal folwe þer-by
> Weche xal be of my body þat am ȝour hed
> weche xal be shewyd to ȝow be A mystery
> Of my ffIesch and blood in forme of bred.   (11. 670-85)

This interpretation, while stressing the importance of historical precedent, nevertheless implies a permanence of effect significantly different from the Law's insistence on repetition, and de-emphasizes the significance of time in its own right. Time's meaning lies instead in a moral and spiritual interpretation. Jesus's words are of course perfectly consistent with New Testament explanation (which in turn roughly characterizes the delusions of the conspirators regarding the inviolability of the Law) and the wisdom of the virtuous in "Passion I." In *I Corinthians* 5.7, Paul describes the Passover as a type of the Passion: "even Christ our passover is sacrificed for us." A more generally descriptive gloss in his letter to the *Hebrews* 10.1 suggests that customs under the Law are merely shadows of things to come; they constitute instructive but inadequate repetition, which is to be replaced by a permanent offering of perfection: "The law, having a shadow of good things to come, and not the very image of the things, can never with these sacrifices which they offered year by year continually make those who come to it perfect."

In addition, in *Hebrews* 10.10, he points out that "by the will of God we are sanctified through the offering of the body of Jesus Christ once for all."9 The time of mercy, therefore, is seen in scripture as in play to be an alternative to letter, justice, and repetition. The combined sense here of ancestry and departure from its inherent value coincides with the general pattern proposed as basic to "Passion I," and again indicates that the play is fundamentally concerned with a particular Christian interpretation of the universe that exalts timelessness and ignores or criticizes time itself.

The most formidable and influential of medieval theologians, Augustine and St. Thomas, elaborate on this distinction and agree that the real meaning of the two does not reside merely in the comfort of permanence and the insecurity of successiveness. In asserting both a practical and moral difference between time and eternity, they continue a tradition at least as old as the *Timaeus,* which placed truth apart from time and considered the visible world "a moving likeness of eternity."10 St. Thomas believes that all aspects of reality are above time. "We can," he writes in *de Causis,* "mark three general levels of reality: first, above eternity . . . second, with eternity . . . third, under eternity but above time." He also argues in the *Summa Theologica* 10a. 10,1 that constancy and completeness are characteristic of eternity, while change and fragment are indicative of time: "So two things characterize eternity. First, anything existing in eternity is *unending,* that is to say, lacks both beginning and end. . . . Secondly, eternity itself exists as an *instantaneous whole* lacking successiveness." In *Summa Theologica* 1a. 10,4 he adds "that eternity is an instantaneous whole whilst time is not, eternity measuring abiding existence and time measuring change."11 As Augustine views it, furthermore, time in its association with world and change is an artifact—an aspect of creation quite different from the eternal stability of the creator, and at best only a shadow of the reality inherent in that stability: "For if eternity and time are rightly distinguished in that time does not exist without some movement and change, while there is no change in eternity, who could not see that time would not have existed unless something had been created to cause change by some movement? . . . Now the universe was created along with time if in the course of its framing a changing motion was created."12 The cumulative impact of such theory is, within broad limits, general medieval agreement that time—identified with motion, change, and world—is merely an aspect of creation; in its motion it is qualitatively distinct from eternal reality; it is an incomplete, imperfect, moving image of that reality. Eternity, by contrast, is constant, whole, and especially, real.

I

Time and the Conflation of History. The frequent recurrence, noted earlier, of varying aspects of this interpretation—by direct statement and implication—suggests that in areas as fundamental to "Passion I" as its organization of events an informing medieval attitude toward time may well be objectified. In this time oriented context, the rearrangement of historical sequence is not easily to be taken simply as an artistic convenience. The dramatic dislocation of scriptural sequence can also be interpreted as evidence that history, in the mind of the compiler, provides the unassimilated data necessary for constructing a visible representation of the spiritual. In general, his method was to conflate traditionally discrete events in the life of Jesus, and to embellish and expand the activities of the conspirators, although the Gospel of John and the *Northern Passion* apparently have some influence on this reordering. The synoptic gospels are hardly in perfect agreement concerning the events of Holy Week, but a rough harmony is possible: on His way to Jerusalem, Jesus cures one (or two) blind men at Jericho; after entering Jerusalem, He spends several days challenging Jewish authority, but retreats in the evenings to the home of Simon the Leper in nearby Bethany. There He is anointed one evening by Mary of Bethany, whose generous action motivates the subsequent treachery of Judas. The disciples, the next day, are to prepare for the Passover feast at the home of an anonymous water carrier, whom they will encounter inside the city. At the feast itself, Jesus initiates the Lord's Supper. Unhappiness over His immediate future, comfort from an angel, and betrayal and capture, all occur reasonably quickly. In the meantime, of course, the plot to destroy Jesus has been organized at the palace of Caiaphas, the chief priest; it is mentioned only briefly, however, with little attention to identity or individuality among various of the conspirators.

The comparative compression of the play sequence, especially with respect to the affairs of Jesus, is readily apparent. The healing of the blind occurs at the gates of Jerusalem as Jesus makes His one and only entry. There are no evening retreats to Bethany nor any indication that several days are passing. Instead, the events normally associated with Bethany are made part of the Last Supper: the water carrier turns out to be Simon the Leper; the anointing woman, identified now according to patristic tradition as Mary Magdalene, appears prior to the beginning of the meal. Excepting the final laments by Mary Magdalene and the Virgin Mary, the remainder is approximately as expected: Judas leaves the feast to arrange the sale of Jesus, returns and attends the institution of the Lord's Supper, and then goes again to the conspirators. The capture occurs shortly after the footwashing, visit from the angel (bearing eucharistic symbols), and prayers in Gethsemane. In the meantime, the conspiratorial machinations of the priests and judges, which actually begin the play, have been periodically exposed, repeatedly in invidious juxtaposition with the love and calmness of Jesus.

This particular conflation of events may well impose dramatic unity on potentially amorphous material and achieve the dramatically satisfying "structural economy" noted by Rosemary Woolf (p. 233), but it also undermines the importance of historical sequence and accuracy and represents the coalescence—even the theoretical elimination—of passing time. The historically discrete pardon of Mary Magdalene, cure of the blind, refreshment at the home of Simon, anointment by Mary of Bethany, and the Last Supper itself have been made virtually into one event. Because these figures all evoke the healing and liberating efficacy of Jesus, the play emphasizes that the importance of a segment of Jesus's life lies more properly in a thematically justifiable unit, presented outside the logic of time, than in some kind of developing causal sequence. The passing of time is hardly relevant to the nature of Jesus, who is in no way developing or maturing—or being revealed through gradual exposition.

It is only a slight digression to propose that the common anachronism of "Passion I" functions analogously to identify, in moral and spiritual terms, past with present, and to obliterate for the English audience 1400 years of sequential history beginning at the Last Supper. V. A. Kolve is not alone in supposing that the anachronism of medieval English literature results in part from the belief that the past was both a reflection of the eternal unchanging plan of God and an image of the present.13 The anachronism within this play seems hardly accidental. Jewish leaders are bishops; Judas is paid in pence; Demon's promises include Holland linen, flax and wool, and other goods prized by fifteenth-century Englishmen. It would be difficult to dispute Kolve's belief that such anglicanization imposes an image of the present on biblical history and thus emphasizes the constancy of God's eternal plan, but there are additional theoretical consequences. To imply that the actual past being re-enacted and the English present at the moment of re-enactment are identifiable with one another is to stress again the primacy of constant idea, and to eliminate the concept of several hundred years of progressive, causal development resulting somehow in late medieval England. Thus, important consequences of both the sequential conflation within the play, and the anachronistic identification of first-century Jerusalem with fifteenth-century England, are emphasis on the permanence of moral hierarchy and human condition and the denial of any special inherent significance of passing time.

II

Time and Sacramental Efficacy. The historical conflation is, however, only the most obvious way in which "Passion I" alters traditional conceptions of time and process, and only one way in which it stresses condition rather than change. These same historically dislocated figures manifest and represent spiritual achievements to which passing time is irrelevant. Although the two blind men and Mary Magdalene do request aid from Jesus, their subsequent change occurs not in personal moral state but in degree of acceptance by God. They aspire to blessedness and grace—that is, to Christian fulfillment or actuality, a condition dependent on faith already present. The paupers and Mary Magdalene after all are never sinful within the play; they speak of their faith and sorrow, not of current wickedness. This desire for closeness to God, based on belief, is made absolutely clear by one of the paupers: "As we must stedfast be-levyn in þe/ þi goodnesse lord lete us be nye" (11. 307-08). Mary Magdalene's faith and sorrow are equally apparent in her first words: "Alas Alas I xal for fare/ ffor þo grete synnys þat I haue do/ lesse than my lord god sum-del spare/ and his grett mercy receyve me to . . . ffor he is lord of all vertu" (11. 466-74). Only the proper attitude, "sorwefful hert," Jesus points out, "may synne Amende" (1. 491). As a result of existing faith and sorrow, what He in fact offers is blessedness to the blind—"blyssyd be All þo þat beleve on me" (1. 316)—and grace to Mary Magdalene—"In my grace she xal evyr fflowre" (1. 499).

In each instance, formerly alienated humans have instantaneously achieved acceptance by God or, more generally, have attained spiritual fulfillment for a human condition that had already become moral, virtuous, and faithful. Such a moral and static response to these figures is consistent not only with their dramatic behavior, but also with external tropological stress on personal virtue, apparent in patristic interpretation. The cured blind men represent belief in redemption and the gift of divine illumination; Mary Magdalene and the anointing woman suggest faith, devotion, and piety; Simon typifies obedience.[14] Collectively, in both drama and commentary, they symbolize desirable states of being rather than gradual and processional changes toward those states, which, as the drama shows, are the basis for the reality of God's perfecting acceptance. This emphasis on condition and the non-temporal nature of approach to God—with dramatic consequences not readily adaptable to conventional notions of plot and development—is consistent with the attitude of medieval man toward time and change as that attitude is usually understood by modern scholars. Medieval man apparently felt that being rather than succeeding was his mode of existence, and that real change was from potentiality to actuality— to divine acceptance—with nothing of the change, as Georges Poulet points out, necessarily related to time, succession, or process. If in fact, genuinely to be is to be close to God, then the virtuous figures in "Passion I"—those accepted by God—do reflect and symbolize medieval confidence, again described by Poulet, that to exist was to feel oneself to be, neither changing nor becoming, nor in any way succeeding oneself.[15]

"Passion Play I" thus goes well beyond the simple but provocative dramatization of sacramental action and symbol noted earlier. It presents a conjoining of symbolic humans who may dimly recall past sinfulness but who now stress constancy and faith, and who show a sense of liberty that stems from divine acceptance. Their fundamental faith and resultant liberating interaction with Jesus correspond to what we understand, even today, of sacraments. Sacraments are not merely "spiritual machines" for earning God's grace; they are signs of the Passion, grace, and glory, and especially of faith. Sacraments and faith are inseparable means of union with God. The effect of this union and rite is the gift of grace, or the attainment of ultimate human reality.16 For the two blind men and Mary Magdalene, their spiritual achievement—founded on an obvious manifestation of faith rather than on gradual change and maturation—is clearly analogous to successful participation in a sacrament. These faithful figures, without processional or successive development, receive internally, as well as representationally, the grace-giving attention of Jesus.

The generally sacramental nature of their relationship with Jesus becomes clear as He explicates the one complete sacrament in the play—the Lord's Supper, or first Eucharist—which is efficacious just as His actions have been. According to His interpretation, effective participation allows one to share with God in the reign above and provides defense from Satan and fortification for the soul: "With no byttyr bred þis bred [the oble, now] ete xal be/ þat is to say with no byttyrnesse of hate and envye/ But with þe suete bred of loue and charyte/ Weche ffortefyet þe soule gretlye" (11. 718-21). "As oftyn as ȝe do þis [drink the wine] with trewe intent," He later adds, "It xal defende ȝow fro the ffende" (11. 809-10). The emphasis in these passages on sacraments as endorsements of belief rather than as cures is obvious, but it is also clear that the being to be shared in a sacramental experience—"þe fadyr of hefne þat art eternall . . . To whom be þe godhed I am eqwall" (11.694-96)—is eternal. Furthermore, these words of Jesus show that He is likewise to be considered eternal and that He may be taken to represent the eternal presence in an earthly context. And in a sense, sacrament transcends mere reference to the eternal; it necessarily for an instant arrests the passage of time. The receiving of the bread and wine commemorates the Passion—one participates "in þe memory of my passyon" (1. 803)—which occurred centuries ago, although in the play the response is especially complex because the Passion to be remembered has not yet occurred. The medieval audience, therefore, would recognize the prescience of Jesus, and more important, the staged coalescence of an ancient Jewish custom with the revision of that custom by Jesus, and the representation of that coalescence in contemporary England, together with inevitable overtones of the actual Eucharist. The result would be not only a truncation of history similar to that effected by the play's rearrangement of scripture, but a union of widely separated events—Paschal Feast, Last Supper, Eucharist, Passion, symbolically identified in a way that must imitate the timeless nature of eternity.

"Passion Play I" obviously is not genuine sacrament, but its imitation of the Eucharist should also imitate this conjunction of eternity and time and the theoretical escape from time implicit in any sacrament. In addition to having the multiple signification noted earlier, the sacraments link their spiritual effect with its cause, the mystery of Christ's Passion, and with its final end, the life of glory in heaven. In the Mass, in other words, the world beyond reaches into the earthly world and offers a glimpse of the future without time. This phenomenon occurs partly because a sacrament must unite in itself past, present, and future, as it makes present the whole mystery of Christ (Merton, p. 202). Such theoretical freedom from time, if not the occurrence itself, is implicit, and to a degree even objectified, in "Passion I," within the limits of dramatic process and possibility. This freedom, together with an emphasis on the stability and being of virtuous figures, once again undermines the priority of narrative and development.

III

Time and Plot. While Jesus and His associates evoke themes of release and eternity and operate in a milieu that strives to be free from time, the conspirators are burdened by precedent and fears of change. The attitude assumed in "Passion Play I" toward so-called real time—toward such phenomena as cause and effect, sequence, and chronological development, often considered inherent in both human condition and dramatic plot—is most apparent in the progress of the conspiracy. While the actions of Jesus are concentrated, those of the conspirators are expanded far beyond the limits of their concise scriptural basis. Only these actions compose a genuine, on-going plan, complete with beginning, middle, and end: Caiaphas and Annas, the temporal judges Rewfyn and Leyon, and various other counsellors express concern at the beginning of the play that Jesus will destroy their law and misdirect the loyalty of the people. Specifically, Annas

fears the violation of both civil authority and historical precedent: "Ffor yf we let hym þus go . . ./ Ageyn sesare and oure
lawe we do trespace" (11. 19-20). The plan is to spy on Jesus
and gather evidence for formal charges. When this proves frustrating because so many people are attracted to Jesus, the decision is made to capture Him as soon as possible. All that is
needed, according to Rewfyn, is a subtle means to find Jesus
without hordes of followers and to distinguish Him from His
disciples. Judas, of course, solves this minor complication by his
timely arrival at the conspiratorial council and his agreement to
sell Jesus. This event can be considered the climax of both plan
and play (from a conventional viewpoint) because all that remains is to fulfill the terms of the capture established by Judas.

The significance of this sequential action is totally misunderstood by its perpetrators; its real importance—known ironically
by the audience—lies not in the temporal and physical defeat of
Jesus, but in its contribution to the ultimate defeat of law, precedent, and world. Its seriousness is also undermined by repeated
juxtaposition with the calmness of Jesus and His followers at the
Last Supper, and by resemblance to the futile plans of Demon
outlined in the first prologue. Relishing both the earthly and
eschatological time of mercy, the virtuous figures in the play
further reduce the stature of the conspiracy by refusing to resist
it. Conflict exists here as something meaningful only in the
minds of the conspirators, even though Jesus well knows that
His betrayal and capture are imminent. Because the real meaning of the conspiracy is spiritual and lies in the eternity and
worldlessness it inadvertently helps to promote, and because the
main occurrences in the play of qualities that humans associate
with time—e.g., urgency, succession, development—are seen to
be ironically irrelevant in their own terms, time itself as defined
by its innate qualities is rendered as an illusion, or at best as a
mask of truth. It is surely important as an aspect of God's creation, but its importance lies in the means of prophecy it offers,
in its memory of the future, and in its moral and spiritual (invisible) significance, as Jesus has shown in His allegorization of
the Paschal Feast and in His moral interpretation of its various
components.

It could be argued that the crucial distinction in this play is
between spirit and nature rather than between eternity and time,
and in the broadest sense, such an observation is true. But the

spiritual here is overtly teleological, reminding always of the kingdom of heaven and providing means through the efficacy of Jesus and Eucharist for sharing immediately in that end. Although the spiritual-eternal obviously is not dramatically representable, its special conception of timelessness can be both enunciated and visually approximated, so that certain aspects of the play come to stand for the eternal and real. The rhetoric of Jesus, indicative of constancy and ideal rather than change, supplements the worldless, timeless orientation apparent in His actions and effectiveness. He speaks repeatedly of souls, bliss, comfort, mercy, joy, and charity—concepts and states—and thus dramatizes a most reasonable nature, quite in contrast to the erratic passion of the conspirators. Their interest in witchcraft, torture, and treason betrays only too clearly the moody insecurity and aggressiveness of natural, time-oriented man. The futility and emptiness of this mode compared to that of Jesus is rendered thematically and visually obvious by the movement of Judas—the quintessential worldly man, ally of the conspirators, "Derlyng" of Demon—between the two groups and by his uneasy incongruity among the calmer disciples. Men such as the conspirators may well have been able to live without clocks, but it is apparent that their natural world is marked by change and insecurity and by memory rather than vision, and is thus distinguishable by major aspects of man's consciousness of time— "the number of motion"—held throughout the middle ages to be merely an image of the reality existing above time.

IV

Time and the Imitation of Reality. The nature and arrangement of events, as well as theme—virtually all significant aspects of "Passion Play I"—function harmoniously to establish and interpret concepts of time and reality that are generally consistent, in other words, with medieval theory. The manipulation of sequence according to moral signification and the consequent historical conflation, similar conflation together with escape from time implicit in sacrament, the scrupulous avoidance of character change, and the ironic subversion of the qualities and assumed values of time itself, all tend to imitate the supposed view of this world from the world above. No play, of course, can achieve much more than a theoretical presentation of such a mystery, but "Passion I" offers additional formal and architectural approximation of timelessness. The multiple staging possibilities and requirements of the play, including the likelihood of stage, scaffold, platea, and *loci* (and probably a heaven), have been frequently described. Within this physical arrangement, the council of the conspirators and the Last Supper, and earlier the entry, are occurring simultaneously. By appropriate use of curtains, it is possible for the audience to be switched abruptly from one to the other, or to see both good and evil at once, and in either case to respond to visual and moral contrast rather than to interaction and development.

Eleanor Prosser has shown that stage directions provide evidence for simultaneous action "carefully plotted to build a specific effect" (pp. 124-25), but she apparently does not consider the effect to be meaningful in itself. Although the events are at times simultaneous, there is no contact between the opposing groups until the very end of the play, nor is there any mutual recognition. Thus, even though the audience obviously cannot perceive the entire play at a glance, on certain occasions the scene does seem to comprise a spatial collage of discrete symbols arranged according to moral hierarchy rather than narrative temporal sequence. This "talking picture" or "tableau" effect has also been observed by critics but again never as an intentional imitation of timelessness. In fact, the total effect of this play, deriving from abrupt shifts, startling contrasts and juxtapositions of morally antipodal figures, and telescoping dramatic action, is a reasonable facsimile of timeless eternity—of the real existence that at once gives spiritual meaning to temporal sequence and lessens its earthly significance.

Too often critics overlook the probability that, for medieval man, time and eternity, and image and truth—aspects of belief clearly fundamental to aesthetic conventions intended to imitate reality—are radically different from modern conceptions and that the play world interpreting these early conceptions is also radically different. In *Peri Hermenias,* St. Thomas suggests that God's view of earthly time is analogous to the experience of a man, stationed in a high place, watching a procession of humans pass below him. "He would at once see all who were on the road —not under the formality of preceding and subsequent . . . but all at the same time and how one precedes another. Now, our cognition falls under the order of time . . .," he continues. "Consequently, things are subject to our cognition under the aspect of present, past, and future. . . . God, however, is wholly outside the order of time, stationed as it were at the summit of eternity, which is wholly simultaneous, and to Him the whole course of time is subjected in one simple intuition."[17] Although the audience does not exactly become divine as it watches medieval English mystery plays, it does see them from above the order of time, approximately as the God of medieval theology saw human life. When the themes of such a play also pertain to release from time, and when form and stage conventions seem to elicit a static rather than narrative response, the audience may well be experiencing a specific kind of drama which is alien and frustrating to traditional critical practices.

In many cases, particularly in the *Ludus Coventriae,* the very qualities that are often condemned—lack of character interaction and change, lack of causal sequence, lack of plot development—are in fact iconographic in their tendency to objectify a particular medieval attitude toward time and timelessness, shadow and reality, and the barely crossable gulf between such opposites. In the largest sense, these qualities urge the audience to view history and humanity as the church assumed God did. Acceptance of these qualities as conventional and iconographic is thus fundamental to our understanding of the non-naturalistic cycle episodes. For "Passion Play I" in particular, theology, theme, and aesthetic become inseparable. The reality of Jesus and heaven, the illusion inherent in earth and time, the calmness and stability of one, the insecurity and emotionalism of the other, the spiritual significance of time, and the timelessness of divine perspective, are all imitated by the events of the play, and particularly by its form and structure. The play world of "Passion I" is a clear representation of the world of medieval theology—a representation that, in the absence of a specific set of dramatic rules, is surely to be expected.

NOTES

1 An early version of this paper was presented at the annual conference of the Medieval Institute, Western Michigan University, in the spring of 1973.

2 For more detailed summary of these commonplaces, see F. W. Dillistone, *Christianity and Symbolism* (Philadelphia: Westminster Press, 1955) and William G. Madsen, *From Shadowy Types to Truth* (New Haven: Yale Univ. Press, 1958), pp. 85-86.

3 Eleanor Prosser, *Drama and Religion in the English Mystery Plays* (1961; rpt. Stanford: Stanford Univ. Press, 1966), p. 121.

4 Rosemary Woolf, *The English Mystery Plays* (Berkeley: Univ. California Press, 1972), pp. 234-36.

5 Cameron and Kahrl, *Theatre Notebook*, 21 (1967), 158-65; Wickham, *Early English Stages* (London: Routledge and Kegan Paul, 1959), I, 154-56.

6 "Passion Play I," *Ludus Coventriae or the Plaie Called Corpus Christi*, ed. K. S. Block (1922; rpt. Bungay, Suffolk: Richard Hall, 1960), p. 263. Subsequent references to the play, all from this edition, appear by line number in text of paper.

7 Jesus's words to Peter, "No part with me haue þou xal" [if you forsake this service that I offer you], are interpreted in the *Glossa Ordinaria*, in fact, as a reference to both baptism and penance: Qui non lavatur per baptismum et confessionem poenitentiae, non habet partem cum Jesu" (*Patrologia Latina*, ed. J.-P. Migne [Paris, 1844ff], CXIV, col. 405). *Patrologia Latina* is hereafter referred to as *PL*.

8 *The New Catholic Encyclopedia* (Washington: Catholic Univ. of America, 1967), XII, 802-03, notes that a *Majestas Domini* is set in the tympanum of several doorways whose lintels are carved with figures of Eucharist, Baptism, and Penance: Saint-Julien at Jonzy, Vandeins, Bellenaves, Savigny, Saint-Pons at Thomières, and Saint-Gilles-du-Gard.

9 *I Corinthians* 5.7: Etenim Pascha nostrum immolatus est Christus. Hebrews 10.1. Umbram enim habens lex futurorum bonorum, non ipsam imaginem rerum: per singulos annos eisdem ipsis hostiis, quas offerunt indesinenter, numquam potest accedentes perfectos facere. *Hebrews* 10.10: In qua voluntate sanctificati sumus per oblationem corporis Jesu Christi semel. *Biblia Sacra Vulgatae Editionis*, ed. P. Michael Hetzenauer (Ratisbon: Pustet, 1922).

10 Plato, *Timaeus*, 37d, trans. Francis M. Cornford (New York: Bobbs-Merrill, 1959), p. 29.

11 St. Thomas Aquinas, "de Causis lect. 6," *St. Thomas Aquinas: Philosophical Texts*, trans. Thomas Gilby (London: Oxford Univ. Press, 1951), p. 83; *Summa Theologica*, 1a. 10,1 and 1a. 10,4, trans. Timothy McDermott O. P. (New York: McGraw-Hill, 1964), II, 137, 145.

12 St. Augustine *City of God*, XI, vi, trans. David S. Wiesen (Cambridge: Harvard Univ. Press, 1968), III, 447-49.

13 V. A. Kolve, "Medieval Time and English Place," *The Play Called Corpus Christi* (Stanford: Stanford Univ. Press, 1966), pp. 101-23.

14 Regarding the blind men: sed si jam in Redemptorem credit, juxta viam sedet. Si autem iam credit, sed ut aeternam lucem recipiat (Bede, *PL*, XCII, col. 558). Regarding Mary Magdalene: Mystice autem devotio haec Mariae Domino ministrantis, fidem ac pietatem designat Ecclesiae sanctae (Rabanus Maurus, *PL*, CVII, col. 1101). Regarding Simon: *Simon*, id est obediens (*Glossa Ordinaria, PL*, CXIV, col. 167). Simon leprosus mundum infidelem primo, postea fidelem significat (*Glossa Ordinaria, PL*, CXIV, col. 229).

15 Georges Poulet, *Studies in Human Time*, trans. Elliott Coleman (Baltimore: Johns Hopkins Univ. Press, 1956), pp. 3-7.

16 This and subsequent discussion of the sacraments presents primarily commonplaces, but it relies heavily on *The New Catholic Encyclopedia; O. B. Hardison, Christian Rite and Christian Drama in the Middle Ages* (Baltimore: Johns Hopkins Univ. Press, 1965); Thomas Merton, *The New Man* (New York: Farrar, Straus, and Cudahy, 1961), pp. 199-202.

17 St. Thomas Aquinas, *Peri Hermenias*, Lesson 14, in *Aristotle: On Interpretation: Commentary by St. Thomas and Cajetan*, trans. Jean T. Oesterle (Milwaukee: Marquette Univ. Press, 1962), pp. 117-18.

Devotional Iconography in the N-Town Marian Plays

Theresa Coletti

The Middle English N-Town cycle evinces an extraordinary consciousness of the motifs and interpretations that characterized late medieval devotion to the Virgin. Of the four Middle English Corpus Christi plays, only the N-Town cycle includes a group of plays, extending from *The Conception of Mary* to *The Trial of Joseph and Mary,* specifically concerned with the life of the Virgin before the birth of Christ.[1] The scope of Marian attention in the cycle also embraces plays such as the *Nativity* and *The Adoration of the Magi,* and the N-Town manuscript shares a *Death and Assumption* play only with the York cycle. Many scholars have noted the unique Marian preoccupation of the cycle,[2] but the iconographic and devotional richness of this group of plays remains largely unexamined. The cycle's manifest awareness of Marian concerns thus invites an exploration of the relationship of devotional iconography to dramatic import. This study explores the N-Town Marian plays as a form of devotional art. It proposes ways in which stage iconography could have embodied the spiritual concerns of the dramatic audience.

Since the publication of Émile Mâle's *L'art religieux de la fin du moyen âge,* few students of the medieval religious drama have disputed the significant relationship of late medieval art forms to the affective spirituality that characterized Christian devotion in the fourteenth and fifteenth centuries. Among the dominant forms of pictorial art in the late Middle Ages, the illuminated Book of Hours is particularly relevant to a consideration of devotional iconography in the N-Town Marian plays. For like that cycle, this most popular of late medieval prayerbooks emphasized the Virgin; the Book of Hours always con-

tained the Little Office of the Virgin, which was frequently
illustrated by a pictorial narrative sequence of scenes from her
life. The typological meanings of the Virgin, her role in the
miraculous nativity of Christ, and her capacity as intercessor
are only some of the subjects of the N-Town Marian plays represented in the illuminated Book of Hours. Because the miniatures
of Books of Hours suggestively illustrate how the late Middle
Ages visualized the relationship of the Virgin to redemptive
history, they offer persuasive evidence for an imaginative reconstruction of devotional iconography in the Marian plays.[3]

I

Recent students of the N-Town cycle agree that the entire
play is amenable to *platea* and *loca* staging, with a variety of
stations situated around or inside a rather large playing space.[4]
The Marian plays call for an elevated Heaven, a Temple, several *loca* (variously designated as the homes of Anna and
Joachim, Mary and Joseph, and Elizabeth and Zechariah) and
a playing area for numerous journeys.[5] We can suppose Heaven
to be a raised scaffold centrally located toward the edge of the
platea. The repeated requirement for a Temple in the early
Marian plays and the frequent juxtaposition of activities in the
Temple with God's presence in Heaven suggest that the Temple
would have been placed near Heaven. The proliferation of
divine messengers in these plays (angels visit Anna, Joachim,
Mary, Joseph, the shepherds, and the Magi) suggests that other
principal *loca,* and especially the place of the Annunciation,
would have been arranged relatively close to the Heaven scaffold. Such a stage plan would confer a visual as well as a dramatic unity upon the events in the life of the Virgin and the
early life of Christ.

The Conception of Mary, the first of the Marian plays,
presents a microcosm of universal history after the Fall. The
play dramatizes the movement from *tristitia* to *gaudium* by
showing the transformation of Anna's barrenness to blessedness
through the birth of Mary. The *Conception* thus provides a
spiritually resonant opening for the series of plays elaborating
the Virgin's crucial role in God's redemption of mankind. The
text of the N-Town cycle shows an awareness of the interpretive
tradition which found Christological meanings in the activities

of the Virgin before the birth of Christ, meanings which are
also apparent in Marian iconography of Books of Hours.

In the play *Mary in the Temple* the Virgin receives these
instructions from Episcopus as she enters the Temple:

> ȝe must serve · and wurchep god here dayly
> Ffor with prayȝer · with grace and mercy
> Se the haue · A resonable tyme to fede
> Thanne to haue a labour bodyly
> Þat þer in be gostly and bodely mede.   (78.171-75)

Though Episcopus does not designate the nature of Mary's
"labour bodyly," the ultimate source for his directive is the
apocryphal *Protevangelium* 10.2, which states that the Virgin
and the women in the Temple engaged in cloth-making.[6] The
motif of the Virgin's spinning and weaving in the Temple was
a popular one in the later Middle Ages. For example, *The
Golden Legend* notes that work and prayer wcre Mary's principal activities in the Temple. The *Meditations on the Life of
Christ* specifically observes that the Virgin worked daily at her
spinning from the third to the ninth canonical hour; after that
she prayed until an angel brought her food.[7] Also the presence
of the cloth-making motif in the Middle English *Evangelie* and
in the Towneley cycle assurcs that it would have been well
known to the English dramatic audience.[8]

The "Presentation" miniature in the *Hours of Catherine of
Cleves* (fig. 6) shows two women spinning at the Bishop's feet
as the Virgin enters the Temple.[9] This pictorial motif also
occurs in a number of miniatures executed by the Boucicaut
Master and his shop (fig. 51, 129, 263). One "Annunciation"
miniature from the Boucicaut workshop (fig. 128) shows in the
marginal illustration an imposing portrait of the Virgin weaving
as an angel brings food to her. The Boucicaut Master frequently
juxtaposed images of the cloth-making Virgin with representations of the Annunciation, thereby suggesting a theological and
historical relationship through the spatial proximity of the two
themes.

In the N-Town play of *Mary in the Temple* we find a clear
analogue to the Boucicaut miniature. Shortly after the Virgin
enters the Temple, the bishop, his ministers, and Anna and
Joachim depart, and Mary remains alone with her maidens
(79.208ff). She kneels before "þis holy awtere" and prays until
an angel "bryngyth manna in A cowpe of gold" (80). The angel

praises Mary, alluding to her role in the coming redemption
(80.244-51) and to the Annunciation: "Ffor ȝe xal here aftere
haue A salutacion/þat xal þis excede" (254-55). The stage
directions then call for a lengthy spectacle: "here xal comyn
Allwey An Aungel with dyvers presentys goynge and comyng
and in þe tyme þei xal synge in hefne þis hympne · Jhesu corona
virginum · And After þer comyth A minister" (81). The most
likely activity for the Virgin during her discourse with the angel,
the presentation of the heavenly gifts, and the singing of the
hymn is surely spinning or weaving. The Bishop's advice about
the necessity of a "labour bodyly" and the presence of the cloth-
making motif in late medieval miniatures and spiritual texts
support the iconographic presence of the Virgin's handiwork.
Moreover, the meaning of this activity in its pre-Annunciation
context further corroborates its dramatic presence on stage. The
Annunciate Virgin is important because she is the agent through
whom Christ assumes His human nature. St. Anthony of Padua,
a principal Franciscan exegete, in fact describes the Incarnation
in terms of a cloth-making metaphor: "Out of the sackcloth of
our nature Jesus Christ made a tunic for Himself which He made
with the needle of the subtle work of the Holy Spirit and the
thread of the Blessed Virgin's faith . . . ."[10]

The Virgin's cloth-making could thus serve as a visual
allusion to the approaching Incarnation; furthermore, it evokes
the Passion because it suggests the *tunica inconsutilis* which appears regularly in Passion narratives as a garment that the Virgin made for Christ.[11] The *Stanzaic Life of Christ* describes
Christ's seamless robe as "that wede . . . that wroght our lady
swete Mary" and as that "wiche Mary hys moder hym made."[12]
Rosemary Woolf observes that in the popular medieval allegorical tradition of Christ as the knight of the Crucifixion, his
aketoun was understood as "the human flesh which the Virgin
gave him in her womb" (*English Mystery Plays,* p. 267). Significant too is a speech by Filius in the N-Town *Parliament of
Heaven* play in which He refers to the Incarnation as the taking
on of a garment: "lete me se how I may were þat wede" (103.
178). The Towneley cycle devotes an entire play, *The Play of
the Talents,* to Christ's seamless garment; and in the Towneley
Crucifixion the Virgin conflates the idea of the woven garment
and the garment of flesh in her speech at the Cross:

To deth my dere is dryffen,
his robe is all to-ryffen
That of me was hym gyffen
  And shapen with my sydys.   (270.386-89)

Showing the Virgin involved in her cloth making activity in the Temple scene would thus provide an unusually resonant piece of stage iconography, suggesting both the birth and death of Christ.

The apocryphal tradition that named spinning as the Virgin's activity in the Temple is even richer in associations. Though Scripture provided no specific warrant for it (Gen. 3.16-19), spinning was also designated as Eve's immediate occupation after the Fall. In the N-Town cycle Eve laments her punishment to Adam: "ȝe must delve and I xal spynne/in care to ledyn oure lyff" (29.415-16). A curious miniature in the *Rohan Hours* (fig. 18) shows Adam and Eve at work; it also conflates this image with what the legend calls "la nativité de Caym et d'Abel," and thus the picture combines three different Eves in a single image. Dressed in blue, Eve, the mother of Abel (himself a type of Christ), holds a child. The image is virtually indistinguishable from countless representations of the Virgin and child, and it assaults visual expectation because it depicts a Virgin-like Eve in a scene that illustrates the punishment of man's first parents. What the Rohan miniature calls to mind, however, is the common medieval juxtaposition of Eve, the mother of sin, and Mary, the mother of grace. If Eve spins as a labor of restitution for her sin, then the Virgin's handiwork, because it is associated with the Incarnation, subtly alludes to the event which brings ultimate restitution to Adam, Eve, and all mankind. In view of the N-Town cycle's deliberate reference to Eve's post-lapsarian labor, the likelihood of its presenting the Virgin's spinning in a pre-Annunciation context appears all the more strong.

In the N-Town cycle the Annunciation occurs in the play that begins with the *Parliament of Heaven* (No. 11). Following the *Betrothal* play, the *Parliament of Heaven* takes place after Joseph finds Mary "a lytyl praty hous" and then departs, leaving her in her "conclaue." The modulation of scenes is extremely dramatic at this point, for the action moves from earth to heaven, then back to earth again as Gabriel descends to the Virgin. In this rapid change of dramatic focus the audience would see a strikingly unified stage image, for the action requires that the Virgin remain in view while the Trinity holds the Parliament in Heaven. Gabriel in fact moves from Heaven to earth and makes his Salutation in only two lines: "I take my fflyth and byde nowth/Ave Maria gratia plena Dominus tecum" (104.216-17). The scenic juxtaposition of Heaven and earth would furnish opportunities for meaningful stage action; e.g., God the Father might gesture toward the Virgin when he says: "The name of þe mayd ffre/Is Mary þat xal Al Restore" (103.195-96). Furthermore this juxtaposition would assert the solution of the heavenly Parliament—the Incarnation—even while the dispute in Heaven takes place and thus confirm the redemptive promise.

Given the visible theological significance inherent in the cycle's placement of the *Salutation and Conception* immediately after the *Parliament of Heaven,* we might consider how stage iconography for the Annunciation could have expressed devotional concerns. Each of the "Annunciation" miniatures in the Books of Hours under consideration shows the Virgin either seated or kneeling, a consummate symbol of her humility.13 Medieval emphasis on this virtue derived from interpretations of the Virgin's reply to Gabriel in Luke 1.38: "Ecce ancilla domini." A twelfth century treatise on the virtues attributed to Hugh of St. Victor, *De fructibus carnis et spiritus,* defined humility as the *radix virtutum;* because of her humility the Virgin became the mother of Christ.14 The N-Town Marian plays repeatedly evince an awareness of the Virgin's humility. When angels visit Mary in the Temple, she expresses her unworthiness: "Mercy my makere · how may þis be ment/I am þe sympelest creature · þat is levynge here" (80.242-43). Similarly, at the Annunciation she speaks of her "grett shamfastness" (105.236) and humbly receives Gabriel's message:

> With All mekenes I clyne to þis A-corde
> Bowynge down my face with All benyngnyte
> Se here þe hand-mayden of oure lorde
> Aftyr þi worde · be it don to me.   (106-07.285-88).

The angel responds with praise for her "grett humylyte" (107.291). In the N-Town Annunciation, then, the audience would surely see a seated or kneeling Virgin.

The presentation of individual scriptural events in relation to the teleological design of Christian history was, of course, a fundamental structural and dramatic principle of the Corpus Christi play. Late medieval pictorial art also reveals this consciousness of redemptive history, as the Boucicaut workshop's "Annunciation" with the marginal illustration of the Virgin weaving has shown. In several instances the N-Town Annunciation calls attention to the meaning of the Incarnation in the plan of universal history; and we can, I believe, assume that this awareness undoubtedly informed and vitalized stage iconography.

When Gabriel addresses the Virgin, he urges her to assent to the Incarnation in order to win "All man-kende savacion" (106.282). Two Annunciation miniatures supply iconographic details which illustrate the import of Gabriel's words. Both the Boucicaut and Chevalier "Annunciation" miniatures show altars on which burning candles rest. Millard Meiss notes that miniatures of the Boucicaut workshop frequently place the Annunciate Virgin at an altar instead of the usual *prie-dieu,* though the two motifs often exist side by side.15 The *Speculum humanae salvationis* glosses the candle as Christ, the candlestick as the Virgin: "Ipsa enim est candelabrum et ipsa est lucerna . . . Christus, Mariae filius, est candela accensa."16 The altar is still more evocative, for by its very lack of any detail except the candle, it alludes to both the coming of the Savior and His sacrifice, which is reenacted at the altar in the Eucharist.17 Though the text provides no specific warrant for it, the transposition of a motif such as this into the dramatic setting would serve as a visible referent to Gabriel's words to Mary. It would also confirm through stage iconography the promise of salvation which Gabriel announces in his final speech:

> qwen of hefne · lady of erth · and empres of helle be ӡe
> socour to All synful · þat wole to ӡow sew
> Thour ӡour body berythe þe babe · oure blysse xal renew.
>
> (108.335-37)

At the moment of the Incarnation in the N-Town Marian plays, there occurs an interesting and detailed stage direction: "here þe holy gost discendit with iij bemys to our lady · the sone of the þe godhed nest with iij bemys · to þe holy gost · the fadyr godly with iij bemys to þe sone · And so entre All thre to here bosom . . ." (107). The direction undoubtedly describes stage iconography at this highly dramatic moment. Though the significance of the action is not immediately appar-

ent, it seems to refer to an explicit theological meaning which
would not have been lost on the dramatic audience. Most in-
triguing in the stage direction for the Incarnation is the emphasis
on light, the "iij bemys" that descend from the Father to the
Son to the Holy Ghost, to rest finally in Mary's bosom.

From the beginnings of Christian theology light had supplied a metaphor for religious mysteries, and the Incarnation
was frequently compared to sunlight passing through glass:
"Just as the brilliance of the sun fills and penetrates a glass
window without damaging it . . . neither hurting it when entering nor destroying it when emerging: thus the word of God, the
Splendor of the Father, entered the Virgin chamber and then
came forth from the closed womb. . . ."18 The metaphor became
extremely popular among late medieval painters, who frequently
employed it to illustrate the Incarnation. The Chevalier "Annunciation" shows a golden light focusing on the Virgin from a
great Gothic window; the Rohan and Boucicaut miniatures
draw deliberate attention to beams of light which suggest the
splendor Patris, for their source is an image of God the Father.
In each miniature the Holy Ghost appears as a dove.

The presence of this motif in many late medieval paintings
of the Annunciation, Meiss notes, is explained by its wide dif-
fusion in theological treatises, hymns, and Latin and vernacular
poems ("Light as Form and Symbol," pp. 176-77). Undoubtedly instrumental in spreading its popularity was *The Revelations
of St. Bridget,* in which Christ likens his Incarnation to the
passage of sunlight through glass.19 Possibly Bridget's *Revelations* provided the source for the metaphor in the N-Town
cycle, where it occurs in the play of *Christ with the Doctors*
(181.97-100) and in *The Resurrection* (328.18).

The N-Town stage direction for the Incarnation suggests an
awareness of the popular metaphor that compared the event to
sunlight passing through glass; the explicit reference to this
metaphor in other parts of the N-Town cycle supports this reading. At the moment of the Incarnation the stage requirement
for "iij bemys" calls to mind the Incarnational light which
pierced the Virgin while still preserving her purity; the Holy
Ghost probably appears in the form of a dove, just as in the
miniatures described above. The expressive power of this stage
image is suggested by its counterpart in the *Rohan Hours* (Pl.
1), where an imposing God the Father, displaying the symbol

of His power, points to the Incarnational light directed toward the Virgin's breast. His Word becomes flesh at that moment through the Holy Ghost, and Mary confirms the Trinitarian participation in the event when she states: "Now blyssyd be þe hyȝ trynyte" (107.312).20

II

Like the early Marian plays, The N-Town *Nativity* employs theological motifs appearing in late medieval spiritual texts and miniature illustrations. The play seems to have been influenced by *The Revelations of St. Bridget*. We have already noted the presence of one Brigittine motif in three places in the cycle, a motif which also occurred in the iconography of Books of Hours. Bridget's text was in fact a major source for Nativity iconography in the late Middle Ages, and thus it may prove useful in proposing devotional stage iconography for the N-Town *Nativity* play.

Henrik Cornell attributes the appearance of a new iconographic type of the Nativity in the late Middle Ages to *The Revelations of St. Bridget*.21 While earlier representations show the Virgin lying in bed and the Christ child nearby in the manger, later Nativity scenes present her kneeling, as she adores the child on the ground before her. A reverent Joseph is often present as well. According to St. Bridget, the Virgin, Joseph, the ox, and the ass enter the place of the Nativity; Joseph brings Mary a burning candle and goes outside so that he will not witness the birth. The Virgin makes herself ready for the birth, removing her shoes, mantle, and veil and turning her back to the manger. She kneels in prayer and the Christ child is miraculously born. Bridget tells how she saw radiating from Christ "such an ineffable light and splendour, that the sun was not comparable to it, nor did the candle, that Joseph put there, give any light at all." After the birth Mary worships the child; and when Joseph returns, he joins in the adoration (Cornell, p. 12).

The important characteristics of the Brigittine Nativity are all present in the "Nativity" miniature in the *Hours of Catherine of Cleves* (Pl. 2), which shows the Virgin with her back to the manger. Mary and Joseph kneel on the ground, the naked Christ child before them. Joseph holds his useless burning candle in a scene bathed in light. The N-Town *Nativity* play also contains evidence of a Brigittine version of this event, thereby suggesting its iconographic resemblance with the Cleves miniature.

In the N-Town play Joseph and the Virgin seek their lodging in a poor "chawmere." The place is probably dark and barren, for Joseph mentions "An hous þat is desolat with-owty Any wall/Ffyer nor wood non here is" (138.101-02).22 Perhaps at this moment Joseph lights a candle. Further evidence for a Brigittine version of the play, however, is supplied by the Virgin's speech immediately before the birth of Christ:

> Therfore husbond of ȝour honeste
> A-voyd ȝow hens out of þis place
> And I a-lone with humylite
> here xal abyde goddys hyȝ grace.   (139.113-16)

The Virgin describes a stage image that accords with two of the primary features of the Brigittine Nativity: Mary asks Joseph to go out of the place, and she calls attention to her "humylite," a detail which iconographically could only mean that she is sitting or kneeling. Joseph then departs, seeking "sum mydwyuys ȝow for to ese" (139.119), and the stage direction indicates: "hic dum joseph est Absens parit Maria filium unigenitum."

The influence of Bridget's *Revelations* on the N-Town *Nativity* also appears in the response of the midwives who return with Joseph. Though Bridget does not include the midwives in her *Revelations,* in the N-Town play they call attention to an important iconographic motif of her version of the Nativity. They marvel at the "gret bryghtness" which illuminates the scene: "mone be nyght nor sunne be day/Shone nevyr so clere in þer lyghtness" (140.163-64). Their comment on the "woundyrfful lyght" in fact strengthens the possibility of Joseph's earlier appearance with a candle, for Bridget contrasts the divine light emanating from Christ with Joseph's mundane attempt to brighten the darkness. When Mary cheerfully reproves his doubt, Joseph asks forgiveness: "I Aske ȝow grace for I dyde raue/O gracyous childe I aske mercy" (141.193-94). At the moment of his plea, Joseph might kneel alongside the Virgin in worship of the child before them.

Still other iconographic motifs can be suggested for the cycle's *Nativity* play. From early Christian times the Incarnation had been given Eucharistic interpretations, and patristic writers such as Ambrose, John Chrysostom, and Gregory the Great developed and expanded the sacramental associations of the

Nativity. The Eucharistic meanings of the Nativity were strengthened by the etymological interpretation of Bethlehem as the *domus panis*—house of bread—and hence by the analogy between the birth of Christ and the Bread of Life.[23] By the late Middle Ages this analogy was extremely widespread, appearing in a variety of spiritual texts. The Middle English *Meditations on the Supper of Our Lord,* for example, equates the Christ child with the Eucharist: "Þat sacrament þat þou seest þe before/Wundyrfully of a mayden was bore."[24]

The N-Town *Nativity* and the scenes that follow it surely were intended to evoke sacramental meanings, and undoubtedly these meanings would have been translated into stage iconography. The speeches of the shepherds point to the salvific promise inherent in the Nativity, for they allude to the benefits that will be won from the sacrifice on the Cross (147.34-37, 42-43; 149.93). The angel who proclaims the Nativity to the shepherds also says that "Sacramentys þer xul be vij/Wonnyn þurowe þat childys wounde" (146.5-6). Perhaps the best evidence, however, for the appropriateness of Eucharistic iconography in the N-Town *Nativity* play is supplied by the Towneley cycle, which includes two entire plays elaborating the meanings of food and the Eucharist, Christ and the lamb—the *First* and *Second Shepherds' Plays.* That the Wakefield Master saw fit to give extensive play to Eucharistic meanings at the dramatic moment of the Nativity certainly indicates that the dramatic audience would have been familiar with these meanings and further that they would have expected them.

Eucharistic interpretations are also apparent in pictorial representations of the Nativity, which supply suggestive possibilities for stage iconography. An "Adoration" miniature in the *Boucicaut Hours* (fig. 31) shows the Christ child lying on a white cloth that is spread on an elaborately decorated bed. To the left of Christ, the Virgin kneels before an open book that also rests on the bed.[25] The miniature displays a ritualistic quality which glosses the scene it presents. The white cloth suggests that the bed, which here replaces the manger, is a symbol of the altar, where the Eucharist becomes the body of Christ. The association of the manger and the altar was well known, appearing in various places in the writings of the Church Fathers (Nilgen, pp. 311, 315). The iconographically rich Cleves "Nativity" also may allude to Eucharistic meanings. It

Plate 1. Annunciation. *Rohan Hours*. Courtesy of Bibliothèque Nationale.

Plate 2. Nativity. *Hours of Catherine of Cleves.* Courtesy of Pierpont Morgan Library.

Plate 3. Crucifixion with Duchess Catherine, Virgin Mary, and Patron
    Saint. *Hours of Catherine of Cleves.* Courtesy of Pierpont
    Morgan Library.

Plate 4. Funeral of the Virgin. *Hours of Etienne Chevalier.* Courtesy of Bibliothèque Nationale.

too shows the Christ child resting on a white cloth and displays a curious basket hanging on the wall above the Virgin's head. Ursula Nilgen mentions an Epiphany panel painting that shows a bread basket hanging by a hook from the roof directly over the Christ child.[26] Given the clear sacramental references in the N-Town *Nativity,* we can imagine that iconographic details such as these easily could have been translated into stage iconography. Indeed the absence of visible reference to the Eucharist at this dramatic moment would be the more surprising eventuality.

In the N-Town *Magi* play the first king to address the Christ child states: "Heyle be þou kyng Cold clade/heyll with maydynnys mylk fade" (159.235-36). The king's speech calls attention to a motif extremely popular in the late Middle Ages—the *Maria lactans,* or the Virgin nursing the Christ child. The precedent for linking the Magi's visit with the *Maria lactans* image may be in St. Bernard's Epiphany sermons: "Adorant Magi, et offrunt munera adhuc sugenti matris ubera."[27]

The abundance of pictorial representations of the Virgin nursing in medieval painting suggests that the image had a marked spiritual significance. Millard Meiss states that the image of *Maria lactans* "set forth that character and power which arose from her motherhood, i.e. her role as *Maria mediatrix,* compassionate intercessor for humanity before the impartial justice of Christ or God the Father. . . . In the Middle Ages the Virgin was believed to be the mother and nurse not only of Christ but of all mankind" (*Painting in Florence and Siena,* pp. 151-52). One popular fifteenth century version of the *Maria lactans* image shows the Virgin exposing her breast to her son. Speaking of this type, Yrjö Hirn points out that Christ "could not . . . refuse His assent to any of her prayers, if only she reminded Him of the time when He lay as a child at her bosom."[28] The conjunction of the Virgin's functions as *nutrix* and *mediatrix* is well illustrated by a fourteenth century sequence which associates Christ's nursing at the Virgin's breast with the nourishment mankind derives from the blood of his wounds.[29] The Virgin's milk serves as an analogue to the salvific nourishment of Christ's blood, and consequently images of *Maria lactans* inevitably evoke associations with the redemptive promise.

Pictorial representations of *Maria lactans* in the Louvre fragment of the *Belles Heures de Notre Dame,* known as the *Turin*

Hours, and in a psalter illuminated for Henry VI of England show the Virgin exposing her breast to her Son, while Christ shows His wounds to the Father.[30] A comparable configuration occurs in the *Hours of Catherine of Cleves* (Pl. 3), where a saint and Duchess Catherine pray before a crucifix. The Virgin kneels, exposing a breast that spurts milk, and she looks up to her Son on the Cross, who in turn casts an appealing glance to God the Father. The miniature illustrates a passage from St. Bernard quoted in the *Stanzaic Life of Christ:* "Securum accessum habes, o homo, ad Deum vbi mater ante filium, filius ante patrem, mater ostendit filio pectus & vbera, filius ostendit patri latus & vulnera: Nulla ergo poterit esse repulsa, vbi tot concurrent caritatis insignia" (p. 318). The *Turin Hours,* the illuminated psalter, the *Stanzaic Life,* and the *Cleves Hours* all present a chain of intercession. In the Cleves miniature Catherine appeals to the Virgin, the Virgin to Christ, and Christ to the Father. The image, "caritatis insignia," is a visual assurance of the capacity of the Virgin and Christ to intercede for sinful man. The Virgin makes her plea to Christ in terms of her capacity as *nutrix.* In the Cleves miniature Catherine's banderole reads: "Ora pro me sancta dei genetrix"; the Virgin in turn appeals "propter ubera."

The rich spiritual content of the Cleves miniature helps to explain how fitting an image of *Maria lactans,* signalled by the first king's speech, would be at the dramatic moment of the N-Town Epiphany. When the Magi depart, one of the kings asserts: "we haue fownde our lord and lech" (160.270). The *Maria lactans* image would lend visual corroboration to the play's primary theological action. Christ became the sinner's "lech" when he became man to die for man's sins. And the promise that Christ the physician extends to mankind finds an echo in the iconography of the Virgin nursing, for the milk that nourished the redeemer is at the same time the milk of salvation.

III

If the N-Town *Magi* play provides the opportunity for the dramatic representation of the Virgin's capacity as intercessor, the *Death and Assumption* play celebrates that capacity with lavish grandeur. The Assumption is the honor bestowed on the Virgin for her role in man's redemption and for her potential to participate continuously in the redemptive action through her prayers. The liturgy for the Vigil of the Assumption emphasizes this attribute of the Virgin, and the N-Town play asserts it as well. Paul praises the Virgin with "heyl incomparabil quen · goddis holy tron/of you spreng salvacyon · and all oure glorye/ heyl mene for mankynde · and mendere of mys" (364.250-52). At the moment of her death, the Virgin assumes her role as intercessor: "A swete sone Jhesu now mercy I cry/ouer alle synful thy mercy let sprede" (365.282-83). Textual evidence suggests that the *Death and Assumption* play presented an elaborate spetcacle, with the mysterious apparition of the Apostles, the solemn procession, the comings and goings of *Dominus* and angels, and the actual ascent of Mary. The play also evinces an awareness of its sources and a consciousness of both theological and iconographic tradition.

The N-Town *Death and Assumption* closely follows the account of the event presented in *The Golden Legend,* from which it adopts its description of the Virgin's funeral procession. In the *Golden Legend* the apostle John asks Peter to lead the procession. Peter declines, insisting on John's greater worthiness, and says that instead he will bear the body. Then Paul offers to assist Peter in carrying the bier (IV.239). The same dialogue occurs in the N-Town play (367.328-40). *The Golden Legend* also seems to have been the source for Fouquet's miniature of the "Funeral of the Virgin" (Pl. 4). Fouquet meticulously maintains his manner of representing the apostles throughout the Chevalier miniatures, and there can be no doubt that here he shows John leading the funeral procession as Peter and Paul take up the bier. The display of tall lit candles corresponds to the N-Town stage direction: "hic portabunt corpus versus sepulturam cum eorum luminibus" (367).

The *Cleves Hours* also suggests possible stage iconography for the N-Town *Assumption.* One of its miniatures (fig. 39) shows a Trinity after the Crucifixion. Christ appears as conqueror, His feet on the globe of the earth, and He displays His wounds. Such a dramatic image at the Virgin's Assumption would add an historical dimension to the event and visually reinforce the means by which the Virgin became the intercessor for mankind—she is the mother of the One who was crucified. The N-Town *Assumption* text does not describe the *Dominus* who comes to take the Virgin to Heaven; but a regallooking Christ, still bearing the mark of His wounds, could descend to the *platea,* while the Father and Holy Ghost remain on the Heaven scaffold. Peter remarks that *Dominus* appears in his "manhed clere" (372.470); because Christ suffered His wounds as man, stage iconography along these lines seems all the more appropriate.

Iconographic motifs and interpretive tradition may also help us to imagine stage iconography for the actual ascent of the Virgin into Heaven. The Virgin at her Assumption was frequently associated with the Woman of the Apocalypse of Rev. 12.1. The biblical passage furnished the Introit for the Feast of the Assumption, and the image of the Woman of the Apocalypse was extremely popular in Assumption iconography, occurring in works such as the *Speculum humanae salvationis*.31 The Assumption miniature in the *Cleves Hours* (fig. 15) shows the Virgin as the Woman of the Apocalypse, clothed in the Sun, the moon at her feet. It is wholly credible that the N-Town Assumption could have been managed on a platform appropriately adorned after the manner depicted in the Cleves miniature. The ability of late medieval dramatic craftsmen to execute vertical spatial movement with remarkable ingenuity has been noted by Orville Larson.32

A stronger justification for such an iconographic presentation, however, arises from the forms of late medieval spirituality. The image of *Maria in Sole* was very popular in the late Middle Ages; indulgences were granted for saying a prayer before an image of the Virgin in the Sun.33 A miniature in the *Boucicaut Hours* (fig. 12), which shows the Maréchal and his wife kneeling in prayer before an image of the Virgin as the Woman of the Apocalypse, provides a particularly good illustration of the devotional efficacy that the late Middle Ages attributed to such images. Depicting the Virgin as both mother and queen, the miniature illustrates the tribute that *Dominus* gives to her in the N-Town *Assumption* play: "thus schul ye clepyd be/qwen of hefne and moder of mercy" (373.497-98). To conclude the play with an iconographic motif sanctioned by pictorial tradition and informed by the late medieval understanding of the Virgin's role as merciful mother and intercessory queen would be a profound visual testimony to the devotional meanings inherent in the treatment of the Virgin throughout the cycle.

Sarah Appleton Weber notes that through her Assumption Mary becomes the means for reuniting man and God: "As Queen of Heaven she becomes intercessor for man. Her role is the full fruit of the pain she suffered at the crucifixion which made her the mother of man, and it provides the basis of the title . . . Mother of Mercy." Moreover, the Virgin's Assumption is "both the pledge and type of man's own future resurrection and glory."[34] In the iconography of the Virgin's Assumption and in the words with which *Dominus* receives her—"ye schal have the blysse wyth me moder · that hath non ende" (372. 484)—the dramatic audience would see and hear the fulfillment of the salvific promise which was in fact the central theme of the Middle English cycle play. Stage iconography thus embodies the play's deepest religious meaning. Drama and devotion are one.[35]

NOTES

[1] The plays are numbered 8-14 consecutively in K. S. Block's edition, *Ludus Coventriae, or The Plaie Called Corpus Christi*, EETS, e.s. 120 (London: Oxford Univ. Press, 1922). All quotations, cited by page and line numbers, refer to this edition.

[2] See Sister M. Patricia Forrest, "Apocryphal Sources of the St. Anne's Day Plays in the Hegge Cycle," *Medievalia et Humanistica*, 17 (1966), 38-50, and "The Role of the Expositor Contemplacio in the St. Anne's Day Plays of the Hegge Cycle," *Medieval Studies*, 28 (1966), 60-67; Timothy Fry, "The Unity of the *Ludus Coventriae*," *Studies in Philology*, 48 (1951), 544-51; Esther Swenson, *An Inquiry into the Composition and Structure of the Ludus Coventriae*, University of Minnesota Studies in Language and Literature, No. 1 (1914), p. 17; J. Vriend, *The Blessed Virgin Mary in the Medieval Drama of England* (Purmerend, Holland: J. Muusses, 1928), *passim*; Rosemary Woolf, *The English Mystery Plays* (Berkeley and Los Angeles: Univ. of California Press, 1972), pp. 160-61.

[3] The affinities of late medieval pictorial and dramatic art extend far beyond their shared participation in an affective spiritual tradition that assigned a crucial role to religious art. There are striking social as well as spiritual correspondences between the producers and audiences of drama and devotional painting in the late Middle Ages. For a fuller discussion of this subject, see my doctoral dissertation, "Spirituality and Devotional Images: The Staging of the Hegge Cycle," University of Rochester (1975), especially chapters 1-3.

[4] Anne Gay, "The 'Stage' and the Staging of the N-Town Plays," *Research Opportunities in Renaissance Drama*, 10 (1967), 135-40; Alan Nelson, "Some Configurations of Staging in Medieval English Drama," *Medieval Drama*, ed. Jerome Taylor and Alan Nelson (Chicago: Univ. of Chicago Press, 1972), pp. 131-47; Martial Rose, "The Staging of the Hegge Plays," *Medieval Drama*, ed. Neville Denny, Stratford-upon-Avon Studies, 16 (London: Edward Arnold, 1973), pp. 196-221. Though Stanley Kahrl and Kenneth Cameron see no unified manner of staging in the N-Town cycle, they note that the Marian plays were probably produced on a fixed stage; "Staging the N-Town Cycle," *Theatre Notebook*, 21 (1967), 155-56.

[5] This stage plan is corrobrated by Rose, pp. 204-08, and Nelson, pp. 135-37.

[6] *New Testament Apocrypha*, ed. Edgar Hennecke *et al.* (Philadelphia: Westminster Press, 1963), I, 380.

7 *The Golden Legend or Lives of the Saints as Englished by William Caxton,* ed. F. S. Ellis (London: Dent, 1900), V, 102; *The Meditations on the Life of Christ,* trans. and ed. Isa Ragusa and Rosalie Green (Princeton: Princeton Univ. Press, 1961), p. 12. Fig. 6 in Ragusa and Green's text illustrates this passage.

8 Gertrude II. Campbell, "The Middle English *Evangelie*," *PMLA*, 30 (1915), 581, lines 528-531; *The Towneley Plays,* ed. George England and Alfred W. Pollard, EETS, e.s. 171 (1897, rpt. London: Oxford Univ. Press, 1925), 94.269-274.

9 The illustrations used in this study are from the following Books of Hours, all available in facsimile: *The Hours of Catherine of Cleves,* John Plummer (New York: Braziller, 1966); *The Boucicaut Hours,* in Millard Meiss, *French Painting in the Time of Jean de Berry: The Boucicaut Master,* 2 vols. (London: Phaidon Press, 1968); *The Rohan Master: A Book of Hours,* Millard Meiss and Marcel Thomas (New York: Braziller, 1973); Jean Fouquet, *The Hours of Etienne Chevalier,* Charles Sterling and Claude Schaefer (New York: Braziller, 1971). Except for the illustrations reproduced in this study, citations in the text refer to figure numbers in the printed editions.

10 Quoted by Louis F. Rohr, *The Use of Sacred Scripture in the Sermons of St. Anthony of Padua* (Washington: Catholic Univ. of America Press, 1948), p. 72.

11 F. P. Pickering, *Literature and Art in the Middle Ages* (Coral Gables: Univ. of Miami Press, 1970), pp. 314-18.

12 *A Stanzaic Life of Christ,* ed. Frances A. Foster, EETS, o.s. 166 (London: Oxford Univ. Press, 1926), lines 6729-6730, 6699.

13 *Rohan Hours,* fig. 43; *Boucicaut Hours,* fig. 29; *Chevalier Hours,* fig. 6; *Cleves Hours,* fig. 10.

14 Millard Meiss, *Painting in Florence and Siena after the Black Death* (New York: Harper and Row, 1964), pp. 149, n. 72; 153-54. Meiss notes the "polar thinking" which characterized medieval conceptions of the Virgin as the Madonna of Humility and the sublime Woman of the Apocalypse. The paradox of humility and sublimity, he states, is present everywhere in medieval writings. Thus, the Virgin is *"Regina coeli* as well as *Nostra domina de humilitate,* and thus *'Regina humilitatis'."*

15 *The Boucicaut Master,* I, 28; see figs. 120-22, 124-25, 128-31.

16 Quoted by Erwin Panofsky, *Early Netherlandish Painting* (New York: Harper and Row, 1971), I, 143. See also Margaret B. Freeman, "The Iconography of the Merode Altarpiece," *Metropolitan Museum of Art Bulletin,* n.s. 16 (1957-58), 134. For a discussion of the general characteristics of Annunciation symbolism, see Panofsky, I, 131ff.

17 Panofsky suggests the symbolic value of significantly empty spaces; ibid., I, 134.

18 From A. Salzer's *Die Sinnbilder und Beiworte Mariens in der deutschen Literatur und lateinischen Hymnenpoesie des Mittelalters* (Linz, 1893), p. 74; quoted by Millard Meiss, "Light as Form and Symbol in Some Fifteenth-Century Paintings," *Art Bulletin,* 27 (1945), 176.

19 *The Revelations of Saint Birgitta,* ed. William Patterson Cumming, EETS, o.s. 178 (London: Oxford Univ. Press, 1929), p. 36, fol. 12a. On the popularity of the Brigittine cult in England, see pp. xxix-xxxix. The image was also a favorite of the fifteenth century Franciscan James Ryman, who used it in at least a dozen of his carols; see *The Early English Carols,* ed. Richard L. Green (Oxford: Clarendon Press, 1935), nos. 56, 63, 66, 67, 84, 174, 194, 200, 207-08, 246, 281.

20 The association of the Trinity with the "light passing through glass" metaphor in the N-Town cycle may have still other implications. Douglas Gray notes the stage direction in conjunction with the popular late medieval idea of the Virgin as the "chambre of the trynyte"; *Themes* and *Images in the Medieval English Religious*

Lyric (London: Routledge and Kegan Paul, 1972), pp. 36, 237, n. 20. Significantly, the N-Town stage direction requires that "All thre" enter Mary's bosom. Furthermore, Gabriel addresses Mary as "goddys chawmere and his boure" (107.316) and as the "trone of þe trinyte" (108.333). Statues of the Virgin appeared which had small doors that, when opened, revealed the Trinity. For example the "Lady of Boulton" in Durham was opened every day so that all "might se pictured within her, the father, the sonne, and the holy ghost, most curiouslye and fynely gilted"; *Rites of Durham*, ed. J. T. Fowler, Surtees Society, 107 (Durham: Andrews, 1903), p. 30.

21 *The Iconography of the Nativity of Christ*, Uppsala Universitets Arsskrift (Uppsala, 1924), pp. 1-44.

22 The absence of light and fuel is a characteristic of the Brigittine Nativity which J. W. Robinson points out in the York *Nativity* play; see his article "A Commentary on the York Play of the Birth of Christ," *Journal of English and Germanic Philology*, 70 (1971), 241-54. Robinson's essay discusses the York *Nativity*'s consistent adherence to details of the Brigittine narrative.

23 Ursula Nilgen, "The Epiphany and the Eucharist: On the Interpretation of Eucharistic Motifs in Medieval Epiphany Scenes," *Art Bulletin*, 49 (1967), 311. For a wealth of information on Eucharistic meanings of the Nativity which corrobrate the discussion that follows see Leah Sinanoglou, "The Christ Child as Sacrifice: A Medieval Tradition and the Corpus Christi Plays," *Speculum*, 48 (1973), 491-509.

24 Robert Mannyng, *Meditations on the Supper of our Lord*, ed. J. Meadows Cooper, EETS, o.s. 60 (London: Trübner, 1875), lines 205-06.

25 An English Passion meditation attributed to Richard Rolle supplies various conceits for the wounds in the body of Christ, among them one that compares His body to a book; quoted by Gray, *Themes and Images*, p. 70.

26 "The Epiphany and the Eucharist," p. 315; see fig. 13, *The Ortenberg Altarpiece*. James Ryman in one of his carols refers to Christ as the bread baked in the Virgin's womb; *Early English Carols*, no. 318. In late medieval pictorial representations of the Nativity, other iconographic details, such as the sheaf of wheat, also suggest the extent to which the scene was regularly endowed with Eucharistic meaning. See M. B. McNamee, "Further Symbolism in the Portinari Altarpiece," *Art Bulletin*, 45 (1963), 142-43.

27 *In Epiphania Domini*, sermo 2, *PL* 183.147; cf. *PL* 183.145, 151. The Middle English *Meditations on the Life and Passion of Christ* also associates the Adoration of the Magi with the Virgin nursing; ed. Charlotte d'Evelyn, EETS, o.s. 158 (London: Oxford Univ. Press, 1921), lines 143-54.

28 *The Sacred Shrine* (London: MacMillan, 1912), p. 360.

29 Quoted by Maurice Vloberg, *La vierge et l'enfant dans l'art francais*, 3rd ed. (Grenoble: B. Arthaud, 1939), p. 84; see also pp. 92-96. The *Meditations on the Life and Passion of Christ* (lines 37-42) suggests that the Virgin's breast is the source of the milk of salvation.

30 For other examples, see Vloberg, pp. 96-97.

31 Louis Réau, *Iconographié de l'art chrétien* (Paris: Presses Universitaires de France, 1955-59), II, 2, 617. A Middle English sermon for the feast takes its text from Rev. 12.1, interpreting the sign that appeared in the heavens as a "token of hasty saluacion"; see *Middle English Sermons*, ed. Woodburn O. Ross, EETS, o.s. 209 (London: Oxford Univ. Press, 1940), p. 246.

32 "Ascension Images in Art and Theatre," *Gazette des Beaux-Arts*, 6th ser., 54 (1959), 161-76.

33 Sixten Ringbom, *"Maria in Sole* and the Virgin in the Rosary," *Journal of the Warburg and Courtauld Institutes*, 25 (1962), 328.

34 *Theology and Poetry in the Middle English Lyric* (Columbus: Ohio State Univ. Press, 1969), p. 151.

35 The author wishes to thank the General Research Board of the University of Maryland for a grant which supported this project and the Division of Arts and Humanities at Maryland for providing funds which made possible the reproduction of the illustrations.

Law and Disorder in *Ludus Coventriae*

Lynn Squires

My purpose is to provide a new context for the late medieval cycle of plays traditionally referred to as *Ludus Coventriae* by investigating the fifteenth-century legal conditions reflected in these plays. Critics of medieval drama have not recognized the importance of laws as a religious ideal and so have not noticed its significance in late medieval and early Renaissance religious drama. Because we no longer link law with religion, we must remind ourselves that law, for the medieval Englishman, was the formal expression of divine will; it was the common belief that the common as well as the ecclesiastical law originated in the mind of God. This did not prevent Englishmen from criticizing their legal institutions, however; law was, in fact, an extremely controversial topic in the fifteenth century, no less so than in the sixteenth.

Law stood for the principle of virtue itself; it stood for the ordering forces in society[1] and, more importantly for our purposes, in drama. When fifteenth-century lawyers, politicians and dramatists argued for legal reform, like John Wyclif before them, they were arguing for reform of their entire society. Although it was an age of reverence for law, in theory, and an age of prosperity and relatively good repute for the legal profession,[2] it was also an age critical of its degenerate common law system and of its litigious citizens who overtaxed that system. The plays in *Ludus Coventriae* speak out against the people responsible for vexatious prosecutions in court and against the many legal abuses practiced in and out of court as well as against the inadequacy of the old legal system to curb lawlessness. In the words of the legal historian William Holdsworth, the law itself had become a "sword for the unscrupulous": "The forms of law and physical violence had come to be merely alternative instruments to be used as seemed most expedient."[3] The forms of law are used, for example, in the *Ludus Coventriae* passion sequence as a means of destroying Jesus. The plays in that sequence show how the crucifixion of Christ, far from being a travesty of justice, accurately reflects justice as Englishmen then knew it; in that sequence, the trial and punishment of Christ is carried out specifically within the jurisdiction and following the procedures of the fifteenth-century court of common law. In other words, Englishmen watched themselves try, condemn, and crucify Christ, and in this way they took responsibility *themselves* for his death. Not only did Christ die *for* them but also *because* of them—as a victim of their own courts of law. Thus the passion sequence—which I will discuss in some detail—leads its audience to a re-evaluation of the existing court system and of their own principles of justice.

It can be argued that parallels between English and Judaic legal matters are due simply to the habit of anachronism or that, for example, contemporary clothing had to be used for costuming because no one knew how a Jewish bishop or judge would have dressed during Jesus' lifetime. The plays go so far beyond scriptural requirements, however, that it becomes necessary to attribute special meaning to contemporary characters, costumes, and incidents which serve non-scriptural purposes. For example, the *Ludus Coventriae* playwright uses the capture of Jesus to demonstrate the most familiar evil of the age: maintenance, and its attendant evils perjury, champerty, and conspiracy to defraud.[4] The retrogression to feudal disorder in the fifteenth century is a historical commonplace; the cause of disorder is said most usually to be the indentured retinue or band of retainers serving the often violent purposes of their sworn lords.[5] In *The Taking of Jesus,* the adherents of the Old Law have gathered a fellowship and armed themselves with "Cressetys lanternys and torchys lyth/ And þis nyth to be þer redy/ With exys gleyvis and swerdys bryth" (27.663-65)[6] in order to capture Christ. This represents a considerable embellishment and particularization of the capture as set forth in the Gospels: "Therfor whanne Judas hadde takun a cumpany of knyȝtis, and mynystris of the bischopis and of the Fariseis, he cam thidur with lanternys, and brondis, and armeris" (*John* 18.3-4), and *Luke* 22.66-67 tells us only that the "eldre men of the puple, and the princis of prestis, and the scribis camen togidir, and ledden hym in to her councel" [Wycliffe *New Testament*]. Taking scripture as a point of departure for criticizing the practice of retaining, the *Ludus Coventriae* playwright shows each of the judges going to stand with his "meny" (company). The stage directions for the taking of Jesus indicate ten persons *"weyl be-seen in white Arneys and breganderys and some dysgysed in odyr garmentys with swerdys gleyvys and other straunge wepone as cressettys with feyr and lanternys and torchis lyth"* (28. 972*sd*). This must have evoked a common enough scene, the liveried band with torches and weapons at the ready. This is just one example of the way in which the *Ludus Coventriae* playwright embellishes the biblical story to make political and legal commentary.

The parallels that I draw between the plays and the problems of law and order in the period in which they were written are necessarily conjectural. Still, there is strong evidence, in the stage directions and elsewhere, to support a direct connection. For example, the striped robes of the doctors described in the stage directions for *The Council of the Jews I* correspond exactly to the dress for sergeants-at-law as described by Sir John Fortescue.7 And Herod, in *Herod and the Three Kings,* oversteps the biblical requirements of his role and sends out spies to gather evidence (18.94-110), an offense commonly complained of during this time.8 Whatever the playwright's intentions were, the audience could hardly have been blind to the persistent and accurate paralleling of the old Judaic law to their present-day law, and of the practices of Jewish rulers to those of their present-day kings. Nor could they have failed to notice that the New Law of Christ—which the plays promote—bears resemblance to the new wave of equitable law practiced in Chancery and in mercantile courts during their own day.9 The contrast between mercy and the old law which Stanley Kahrl notices in the council scenes and *Maundy III*10 operates throughout these plays to create dramatic tension and to emphasize the need for legal reform.

Since it is not possible here to discuss the entire cycle of 43 plays, I will focus on the Passion I segment and broadly outline the plays which lead up to it. In so doing, I necessarily leave out much that is interesting from a legal and political point of view, especially in the trial of Jesus in Passion II where the English courts and their exact procedures are satirized.11

The cycle begins with four plays which teach obedience to the law: *Creation and Fall, Cain and Abel, Noah,* and *Abraham*

and Isaac. They each (1) state a law, (2) show someone breaking or keeping it, and (3) show the immediate punishments or
rewards. By demonstrating the perils of breaking and the profits
of keeping the law, these four plays set the tone and introduce
a major theme of the cycle. In case the audience misses the
point, the fifth play, *Moses,* restates it in the form of a lengthy
sermon intended to teach God's law to man: "ʒour soulys may
þei [laws] saue at þe last Asyse" (6.58). The threats and promises of the first plays prepare the audience for the more detailed
explanation in *Moses* of what these laws in fact are. With the
sense of urgency established, the lesson follows. The lesson is
actually a descriptive sermon on the ten commandments. God
gives Moses the stone tables, saying, "with my ffynger in hem
is wrete/ all my lawys þou vndyrstonde" (6.39-40) and then
commands Moses to teach them to the people. Moses interprets
the commandments in terms of the commonplace sins of his
fifteenth-century audience: he interprets "non habebis deos
alienos" (6.67) as a prohibition against the worship of worldly
riches—a problem especially acute in this prosperous age;
"memento vt sabbatum sanctificets" (6.99) as a prohibition
against wearing showy garments on Holy days (there were
fifteenth-century laws to control over-elegant or extravagant
dress);[12] and "non occides" (6.131) as a prohibition against
wicked language, for "wyckyd spech many on doth spyll"
(6.137)—a contemporary problem to be taken up below with
The Trial of Joseph and Mary. In a significant variation from
his treatment of other laws, Moses delivers the eighth commandment strictly as it stands, without any homely embellishment:

> The viij[te] precept þus doth þe bydde
> Ffals wyttnes loke non þou bere
> þe trowth nevyr more loke þat þou hyde
> with ffals wyttnes no man þou dere
> Nowther ffor love ne dred ne fere
> Sey non other than trowth is
> Ffals wytnes yf þat þou rere
> Aʒens god þou dost grettly amys.   (6.155-62)

False witness was, in fact, one of the chief sources of injustice
at the time that these plays were performed (Ogilvie, p. 36).

    Strictly speaking, *Moses* is not a play at all; it is a lecture
illustrating the ten commandments in light of contemporary
problems. It is easy to understand why a playwright might de-

viate from dramatic action to include a lecture on obeying the law if we keep in mind that the law was so seldom obeyed at this time: royal orders were regularly ignored and writ-bearers are known to have been forced to eat their writs by disgruntled citizens.13

After the five plays which teach obedience to the law, the next group, designated by R. T. Davies as the *Mother of Mercy* sequence, takes up a more theoretical legal subject. The plays contain a crucial debate between the advocates of the Old and of the New Law—the Old Testament law of an eye for an eye and the New Testament law of mercy. The debate takes the form of a trial, wherein Jesus is "sentenced" to atone for man's sins. Jesus is to be reminded of this "supreme court" decision later in *Agony at Olivet* before he is taken by the Jews for his earthly trial, and he admits "It is nowth to say A-ȝens þe case" (28.958). The Old Law (defended by Righteousness and Truth) and the New Law (defended by Mercy and Peace) are formally tried in conjunction with Jesus in *Parliament of Heaven.* The arguments put forth by Truth, the rebuttals of Mercy, the counter-arguments of Righteousness, and finally the concluding statements by Peace together constitute an able and informed theological review of man's position as suppliant vis-à-vis God as his divine judge. In both format and subject matter, this debate is strikingly similar to the *Somnium Vigilantis,* a 1459 tract dealing with the defeat of the Yorkists, in which several orators debate the wisdom of giving clemency to the exiled lords who had opposed the king. In this pamphlet, perhaps the oldest political pamphlet in English prose, the king's orator argues for punishment according to the letter of the law and the orator for the exiled lords argues, like Peace and Mercy in the *Parliament of Heaven,* for clemency.14 Political necessity was no doubt responsible for the summing up in *Somnium Vigilantis* in the king's favor; the opposite conclusion is arrived at in the *Parliament of Heaven* where the ideal view, rather than the politically realistic one, could prevail. The four advocates in *Parliament of Heaven* accept the suggestion of Peace: "putt bothe ȝour sentens in oure lorde/ And in his hyȝ wysdam lete hym deme" (11.123-24). The arguments made, they turn to the judge for a verdict. Righteousness attributes "very equyte" to God's judgment, thereby indicating the nature of the divine court. It is a court of "conscience," according to the nomenclature of the fifteenth century ("equity" was the rarer synonym[15]). The Son as Judge pursues a complex reasoning to arrive at his decision: "þat helle may holde hym [man] be no lawe" (11.147). The "sentence" is determined out of court, as it were, by a "counsel of þe trinite." The three voices of God briefly decide "Whiche of vs xal man restore" (11.172), and Mercy joyfully announces the "loveday" to follow (11.185), that is, the occasion of settling a legal dispute out of court (Davies, p. 129, note 4).[16] The device of the Parliament of Heaven is used here, as in the *Castle of Perseverence*, to justify man's salvation and to describe the nature of God's mercy. Although the Old Law/New Law conflict was as old as Christianity itself, here it is used as a formal rationalization for the triumph of the New Law over the Old Law which is a major theme of the cycle—and a major issue at the time: the New Testament was in circulation for the first time in English; several hundred copies are known to have circulated among the increasingly literate population[17] and the transition from a stern view of justice to a gentle one was proving understandably difficult.

The superiority of the New Law over the Old is actually demonstrated in the eleventh play, *The Trial of Joseph and Mary*. In this play the ecclesiastical court, which is clearly an English rather than an ancient Judaic institution, is shown to adhere to the Old Law which prescribes revenge against moral offenders. Mary and Joseph, on the other hand, adhere to the New Law of mercy which prohibits taking earthly revenge against wrong-doers. The play, like others in the cycle, warns against taking personal vengeance, particularly in the form of an unnecessary law suit. The law suit in this case is between Mary and the so-called "detractors" (and the bishop's court which supports them); it arises from some gossip about Mary's "unseemly" pregnancy which is overheard by the bishop. In fact, numerous fifteenth-century lawsuits were based on rumor, gossip, and imagined wrongs, often severely damaging an innocent defendant (Holdsworth, II, 382-84). This occurred in the fifteenth century (and before) because remedies were readily available under English law to each citizen, male or female, free or villein, lettered or unlearned (Holdsworth, II, 377-78). Naturally in a society where for centuries each man has been responsible for apprehending criminals (once the hue and cry is raised), where each legal division of the population is responsible to some degree for crimes committed within its boundaries, and where each person is empowered to bring suit against a neighbor in the king's name, there will be the problem of over-use or of too-ready application to legal process. Sir William Plumpton, for example, who figures in an important set of private correspondence of the fifteenth-century, was said to be so fond of litigation that he was suing "every true man in the Forest of Knaresborough, where he lived" (Abram, 89-90, note 1).

The Trial of Joseph and Mary provides an example of a too-hasty condemnation. The Bishop overhears the two detractors, Raise-Slander and Back-Biter, slandering Mary; as was common with moral offences, the Bishop, after hearing the detractors' charges, then conducts the suit himself.18 As early as Edward I's time, the common law had provided for the punishment of defamation of magnates (though not of commoners) primarily to safeguard the peace of the kingdom: "This was no vain fear at a time when the offended great one was only too ready to resort to arms to redress a fancied injury" (Holdworth, III, 409). The audience knows that there indeed are offended great ones, that God himself could destroy their enemies, but lacking this insight, the detractors and judges act with the assurance that Joseph and Mary would have no legal recourse for the slander-ing of their names. Local courts freely entertained cases of defamation (Holdsworth, III, 409-11) as did ecclesiastical courts, but the worst that would happen in real life to the de-tractors would be the fine of a few pence. Thus the second de-tractor in the Trial of Joseph and Mary can taunt the bishop and his lawyers by saying of Mary: "a fayr wench/ And feetly with help sche can consent/ to set A cokewolde on þe hye benche" (14.94-96).19 As might be expected under such con-ditions, the plays argue for forgiveness and argue against bring-ing suit against one's neighbor. At the end of the cycle, in the Doomsday play, the devils point accusingly at the damned souls whose sins are written on their foreheads:

> In wratth þi neybore to bakbyte
> them for to hangere was þi delyte
> þou were evyr redy them to endyte. . . .
>   (42.101-03)

Looking ahead to the first Passion sequence, we find the focus narrowing from a general concern with obedience to God's elaborates on the brief biblical description of the council ("alle the prestis and scribis and eldere men"21) in order to describe contemporary figures of authority. He dresses Annas like a fifteenth-century ecclesiastical judge: *"in a skarlet gowne and ouer þat a blew tabbard furryd with whyte and a mytere on his hed after þe hoold lawe"* (26.40sd). R. T. Davies explains that Annas is described as a bishop of the Old Law as contrasted with the New Law of Christ and that Jewish High Priests were commonly represented as mitred bishops. Obviously, the association was a damaging one for contemporary English bishops. To the common people, Annas and Caiaphas presented a realistic picture of English bishops—who were hardly known, even to their clergy, except in their judicial capacity22—as well as an imaginary picture of Jewish judges. Their entourage is also realistic in fifteenth-century terms. The two doctors accompanying Annas wear furred hoods and furred caps, the traditional dress of fifteenth-century lay and ecclesiastical judges. Caiaphas, also accompanied by two lawyers, is arrayed like Annas. Rewfyn and Lyon, two more furred judges, represent the common law; more specifically, their striped robes identify them as sergeants-at-law. This makes six realistically costumed lawyers. The council scene as a whole is carefully constructed so as to impress the audience with a show of contemporary power: the costumes and characters represent the range of authority in a late medieval town.

These lawyers and judges meet in a council strikingly similar to the so-called king's "Council Learned in the Law," a part of Henry VII's council especially concerned with judiciary matters.23 This body was composed of two bishops and ten other justices and lawyers. Since the council appears to have functioned mainly as a debt-collecting agency for the king, it seems unlikely that it served as a model for the council of the Jews. However, the king's council at large, whether under Henry VII or any of his predecessors, might well have served as such a model. As a court of law,24 the king's council acted like a presenting jury, that is, it investigated charges, examined witnesses, and drew up indictments. Its jurisdiction did not extend to treason, so it would have referred a case like that of Jesus to a common law court, which is precisely what happens in *Ludus Coventriae*. The fifteenth-century council's indictment procedure was supposedly an unbiased attempt to find the facts before elaborates on the brief biblical description of the council ("alle the prestis and scribis and eldere men"21) in order to describe contemporary figures of authority. He dresses Annas like a fifteenth-century ecclesiastical judge: *"in a skarlet gowne and ouer þat a blew tabbard furryd with whyte and a mytere on his hed after þe hoold lawe"* (26.40*sd*). R. T. Davies explains that Annas is described as a bishop of the Old Law as contrasted with the New Law of Christ and that Jewish High Priests were commonly represented as mitred bishops. Obviously, the association was a damaging one for contemporary English bishops. To the common people, Annas and Caiaphas presented a realistic picture of English bishops—who were hardly known, even to their clergy, except in their judicial capacity22—as well as an imaginary picture of Jewish judges. Their entourage is also realistic in fifteenth-century terms. The two doctors accompanying Annas wear furred hoods and furred caps, the traditional dress of fifteenth-century lay and ecclesiastical judges. Caiaphas, also accompanied by two lawyers, is arrayed like Annas. Rewfyn and Lyon, two more furred judges, represent the common law; more specifically, their striped robes identify them as sergeants-at-law. This makes six realistically costumed lawyers. The council scene as a whole is carefully constructed so as to impress the audience with a show of contemporary power: the costumes and characters represent the range of authority in a late medieval town.

These lawyers and judges meet in a council strikingly similar to the so-called king's "Council Learned in the Law," a part of Henry VII's council especially concerned with judiciary matters.23 This body was composed of two bishops and ten other justices and lawyers. Since the council appears to have functioned mainly as a debt-collecting agency for the king, it seems unlikely that it served as a model for the council of the Jews. However, the king's council at large, whether under Henry VII or any of his predecessors, might well have served as such a model. As a court of law,24 the king's council acted like a presenting jury, that is, it investigated charges, examined witnesses, and drew up indictments. Its jurisdiction did not extend to treason, so it would have referred a case like that of Jesus to a common law court, which is precisely what happens in *Ludus Coventriae*. The fifteenth-century council's indictment procedure was supposedly an unbiased attempt to find the facts before arresting a subject. In reality, the council rarely went to the trouble to indict unless its objective was to get an offender before the courts.25 In this respect, the Council of the Jews is realistic; it is biased from the start. It sends out for evidence which will support its views. The judges follow due process, as they must—"We may not do hym to meche myscheve/ þe worschep of oure lawe to save" (27.448-49)—but they have already decided to prosecute Jesus.

In the fifteenth century such an injustice could only be carried out by careful attention to procedural details. At the beginning of the *Passion I* sequence, in *Council of Jews I,* the second doctor of laws reminds Annas:

> Sere remembre þe gret charge þat on ȝow is leyd
> þe lawe to ke[ep] which may not ffayle
> Yf any defawth prevyd of ȝow be seyd
> þe jewys with trewth wyl ȝow a-sayl
> Tak hed whath cownsayl may best provayl.
>
> (26.25-29)

He goes on to suggest that Annas call two "temperal jewgys, þat knowyth þe parayl,"26 a procedure unique to this cycle. When Caiaphas appears, he agrees that they must "seke A mene on to hym reprevable" (26.55) which I understand to mean "seek a means of proving something against him" or, in practical terms, find an accusation which will ensure a conviction. He admits that they have nothing with which to convict him at the moment: "for yf he procede be prossesse oure lawys he wyl felle" (26.60), and again, "I cannot dem hym with-outh trespace" (26.140). The members of the council make their feelings clear to the audience, even while they mouth the appropriate legal formulas. Rewfin calls him "An eretyk and a tretour bolde . . . worthy to dey with mekyl peyn" (26.145-48), and the first lawyer with Annas informs the "rewelerys of þe lawe" that they must give judgment that "Let hym fyrst ben hangyn and drawe/ and þanne his body in fyre be brent" (26.153-56). Annas reasserts the "rule of law" with which they all agree, saying:

> These ix days let us A-byde
> We may not gyf so hasty jugement
> but eche man inqwere on his syde
> Send spyes A-bouth þe countre wyde
> to se and recorde and testymonye

And þan hese werkys he xal not hyde
nor haue no power hem to denye.

(26.170-76)

In the next play in *Passion I, Jesus' Entry into Jerusalem,*
Jesus' free and simple mercy contrasts markedly with the intricate manipulations of the law in the council play. His four-line
refrain beginning, "Ffrendys be-holde þe tyme of mercy/ þe
wich is come now with-owtyn dowth" is repeated again at the
end of the play. In contrast to the complexity of the Old Law,
or of the common law which is analogous to it, are Jesus' simple
laws, to love God above all else and to love thy neighbor as
thyself.

The second Council of the Jews play follows Jesus' entry
into Jerusalem; while he is preaching mercy, the judges and
lawyers are plotting. The dialogue in the second council play—
like that of the first—alternates between conscientious legalities
and brutality until finally the identification of one with the other
is inescapable.

This play, in its turn, is followed by two plays about mercy:
Maundy II in which Maria Magdalen appeals to Jesus for
mercy and is forgiven and *Maundy III* which, as Stanley Kahrl
suggests (p. 64), contrasts even more skillfully with the council
scenes. Jesus eats his paschal lamb "in the same form as the old
law does specify," and "as in the old law it was commanded."
Here as elsewhere he is careful to abide by the old precepts. As
he does so, the Jews in their council plot to kill him for supposedly disobeying those strictures. The irony works effectively
to stress the inhumanity of the Mosaic law and to promote the
New Law of mercy.

What can we say, in summary, are the legal abuses complained of in the *Passion I* sequence and the legal reforms pro-
moted by these nine plays? The crimes described by Lucifer—
conspiracy, use of false evidence, and false witness—are committed by the bishops, Annas and Caiaphas, who are costumed
so as to implicate present-day bishops in their actions, and by
the council as a whole, whose costumes, as Eleanor Prosser
explains,27 were basically contemporary. The councilmen con-
spire to convict Jesus, they send out spies to gather evidence
against him, and they pay Judas to be their false witness. These
pretrial proceedings against Jesus are described in extra-scrip-
tural detail (the council scenes in *Ludus Coventriae* number a

total of 242 lines as compared to the biblical 2) because these formed the weakest link in common law procedure at that time (Bellamy, pp. 213-14). Those in power, particularly the king, tampered with legal process only where no proper rules existed, that is, most especially with the machinery for indictment. Thus, in the fifteenth century, we find the king's legal advisers increasingly framing indictments and conducting extensive interrogations in order to get a confession before putting a defendant on trial (Bellamy, p. 213) which is precisely the situation presented in *Passion I*. This covert form of pressure is protested most strongly in the council scenes. These scenes, reflecting as they do the range of authority in a late medieval town, contain severe criticism of the fifteenth-century legal establishment as a whole—an establishment which is shown to be prone to bias, to perversion of procedures, to hypocrisy, and to brutality. Annas and Caiaphas clearly state their rejection of the supremacy of law—that is, of the rule of law—and they state this twice for emphasis. The plays, using Jesus as an exemplar, promote instead acceptance of the rule of law (Jesus is shown carefully obeying the law in both spirit and letter) and reformation of the Old Law into the New Law. Jesus stands as a living symbol of the New Law: he is the sacrifice which will redeem all men. He enters Jerusalem, holding open his arms, saying "Ffrendys be-holde þe tyme of mercy," offering the audience his simple all-embracing law. Coming as it does after the backroom scheming and conscientious but hypocritical legalities of the council scenes, Jesus' entrance dramatizes the desired legal reform: the audience is invited to turn away from the complexity and corruption of the common law and accept instead Jesus' two simple laws: to love God above all else and to love thy neighbor as thyself.

NOTES

1 Fritz Kern, *Kingship and Law in the Middle Ages,* trans. S. B. Chrimes (Oxford: Blackwell, 1939), p. 153.

2 Alan Harding, *The Law Courts of Medieval England* (New York: Barnes and Noble, 1973), p. 113.

3 W. S. Holdsworth, *A History of English Law* (London: Methuen, 1923), II, 416.

4 Sir Charles Ogilvie, *The King's Government and the Common Law 1471-1641* (Oxford: Blackwell, 1958), p. 36. See also Holdsworth, II, 416.

5 See, for example, G. M. Trevelyan, *A Shortened History of England* (Baltimore: Penguin, 1974), pp. 194-95.

6 *Ludus Coventriae*, ed. K. S. Block, EETS, e.s. 120 (1922); subsequent references to *Ludus Coventriae* are also to this edition. See also R. T. Davies, ed., *The Corpus Christi Play of the English Middle Ages* (Totowa, N. J.: Rowman and Littlefield, 1972).

7 Sir John Fortescue, *De Laudibus Legum Anglie,* ed. S. B. Chrimes (Cambridge: Cambridge Univ. Press, 1942), p. 129.

8 The fear of civil espionage is discussed at length in G. R. Elton's *Policy and Police, The Enforcement of the Reformation in the Age of Thomas Cromwell* (Cambridge: Cambridge Univ. Press, 1972). He considers both its prevalence and the lack of substantiation for it under Cromwell.

9 Theodore F. T. Plucknett, *A Concise History of the Common Law,* 3rd ed. (London: Butterworth, 1940), pp. 145, 160, 168, 614-15. See also DeLloyd J. Guth, "Notes on the Early Tudor Exchequer of Pleas," *Tudor Men and Institutions. Studies in Law and Government,* ed. Arthur J. Slavin (Baton Rouge: Louisiana State Univ. Press, 1972), p. 120, and *Select Cases Concerning the Law Merchant, A. D. 1270-1638, Vol. I: Local Courts,* ed. Charles Gross (London: Selden Society, 1908), pp. 23, xvii.

10 Stanley J. Kahrl, *Traditions of Medieval English Drama* (Pittsburgh: Univ. of Pittsburgh Press, 1975), p. 64.

11 The two passion segments are believed to have been used on alternate years although they contain different material.

12 In *Social England in the 15th Century: A Study of the Effects of Economic Conditions* (London: George Routledge and Sons, 1909), A. Abram tells us that there were many complaints in Commons in Parliament of men using "inordinate array" in spite of statutes and ordinances against it; all classes of the community were condemned so all must have shared in the rising standards of dress. Sleeves were so capacious, Abram continues, that a prison escapee, taking refuge in Canterbury Cathedral, was beaten with sticks by a mob who had concealed the sticks in their sleeves (pp. 150-51).

13 Charles Ross, *Edward IV* (Berkeley: Univ. of California Press, 1974), p. 389.

14 Charles L. Kingsford, *English Historical Literature in the Fifteenth Century* (Oxford: Clarendon Press, 1913), p. 145.

15 *Select Cases in Chancery (A. D. 1364-1471),* ed. William Paley Baildon, Selden Society, 10 (London: Bernard Quaritch, 1869), pp. xxix-xxx.

16 Ross describes a so-called Loveday of 24 March 1458 which offers a wonderful contradiction in terms: the opposing sides which were to make peace with one another consisted of thousands of armed retainers quartered inside and outside the gates of London (p. 19).

17 Conrad Lindberg, in "The Manuscripts and Versions of the Wycliffite Bible," *Studia Neophilologica,* 42 (1970), 333-47, lists 230 surviving manuscripts. See the *Cambridge History of the Bible, Vol. II: The West from the Fathers to the Reformation,* ed. G. W. H. Lampe (Cambridge Univ. Press, 1969), pp. 387-415, for further information on the translation and circulation of the Wycliffe Bible.

18 E. F. Jacob, *The Fifteenth Century, 1399-1485* (Oxford: Clarendon Press, 1961), p. 275.

19 Davies is uncertain of the meaning of this. Since there is an ecclesiastical

"bench" of judges just as there is a King's Bench, for example, I interpret it as an insult to the bishop, who sits on the judge's bench and is Mary's kinsman—if he were her husband, she could have made a cuckold of him as easily as she has (apparently) of Joseph.

[20] Assize and quarter sessions.

[21] Mark 14.53-54 in the *Wycliffe New Testament.*

[22] Hamilton A. Thompson, *The English Clergy and their Organization in the Later Middle Ages* (Oxford: Clarendon Press, 1947), pp. 6-7. See also Jacob, pp. 272-75.

[23] S. B. Chrimes, *Henry VII* (London: Eyre Methuen, 1972), pp. 99-100.

[24] The council then and always was seen by the commons primarily as a court of law. *Select Cases in the Council of Henry VII,* ed. C. G. Bayne, Selden Society, 75 (London, 1958), p. xxxiv.

[25] J. G. Bellamy, *The Law of Treason in England in the Later Middle Ages,* Cambridge Studies in English Legal History (Cambridge: Cambridge Univ. Press, 1970), 213-14.

[26] Ways and means.

[27] Eleanor Prosser makes this observation in *Drama and Religion in the English Mystery Plays* (Palo Alto: Stanford Univ. Press, 1961), p. 124.

The Community of Morality Plays

Merle Fifield

I

Plays variously labelled *moralities, moralités, histoires, zin-nespelen,* and *abele spelen* were written and performed in medieval and renaissance England, France, and the Lowlands. When these plays have been considered sufficiently important for critical analysis, they have been studied, with one exception, in restricted groups based upon identities of language or provenance. The extrinsic evidence of an international tradition is minimal, but it buttresses the intrinsic evidence of repeated forms to be found in a single type of moralizing drama.

There is some proof of a communality of source materials for moralizing drama or of imitation without regard for cultural boundaries. According to majority opinion, the English *Everyman* was nearly translated from the Flemish *Elckerlijc.* The question of priority of the moralized Dutch verse miracle, *Marieken von Niemegen,* and the English non-dramatic prose *Mary of Nimmegen* has yet to be resolved. The Pyramus and Thisbe legend was dramatized with moral intent in Haarlem (after 1525), in France (c. 1535), and in Antwerp (before 1548). Chaucer's non-dramatic *Clerk's Tale* has the same subject as the contemporary *Histoire de Griseledis.* England, France, and the Lowlands unquestionably shared at least the same sources for moralizing literature, which could be and indeed was dramatized.

A common selection of materials for dramatized moralizing is revealed by even a cursory survey of the types of plays which fall under the term *moralities* and equivalent terms in other languages. Biblical plays, including characterizations based upon personifications of moral behavior, were written in England, in France, and in the Lowlands, though British critics do not classify their examples as moralities. Plays which present the lives of secular historical or pseudo-historical personages for a stated moral purpose were composed in France and in the Lowlands. The moralizing speech, not truly a play, occurs in France and the Lowlands. Finally, a type of play to which this essay shall henceforth restrict the term *morality* remains in all three national literatures under consideration. These plays, as the only dramatic expression of a moral intent in all three cultures, provide the best evidence for the thesis that the composition of morality plays was an international movement. They meet a single definition of the genre and develop their morals by identifiable and parallel techniques, one of which is a strictly artificial complication of the content.

II

Neither the critics in their expositions nor the bibliographers in their practice have presented a definition of the morality which is both precise enough to be operable and inclusive enough to be applicable inter-culturally. The medieval English moralities have been identified primarily by criticial *fiat* and by contrasts with the mystery or cycle plays. Such simple listings may be adequate for medieval English literature, but prove impossible for the more numerous and varied examples extant in renaissance British literature and in continental moral drama.

French literary historians tend to ignore their moralities, and the bibliographers are too inclusive.[1] The leading Dutch bibliographer, W. M. H. Hummelen, places all types of moral drama in the category of *zinnespelen,* sin plays.[2] The present state of English, French, and Dutch scholarship does not admit comparison of similar expressions of the morality tradition, and a definition must be prepared to meet this need.

It is already apparent that there were plays specifically designed to present a *moralitas,* and such is the first prerequisite of a morality. This definition is not, however, sufficiently exclusive. For the purposes of this study, the *morality* is a moral play developed essentially through the interactions of characterizations designed to realize a generalization rather than a fictional or historical individuation. In other words, a *morality* is a play which enacts a *moralitas* by means of characterizations which are based on allegory or typification. Plays meeting this definition were written in England, in France, and in the Lowlands.

More importantly, a comparison of plays selected by this definition reveals that the interaction of the characterizations is developed by three internationally known techniques.

III

The most elementary technique for developing the interaction of characterizations is dialogue. There are plays which
have no narrative, but which consist entirely of exchanges of
speeches. These speeches, which sometimes approximate ora-
tions, need not clash; they may merely state the ideological
position of the character speaking. Many examples of plays
based exclusively on characterization and dialogue exist in
French literature: *L' Eglise et le Commun*3 is representative of
this form. L' Eglise identifies herself and states her desire to be
unified with Le Commun. After L' Eglise has made some inquiries of Le Commun, she declares herself oppressed by Le
Commun. The two characters recite their disbelief of each
other's statements. Le Commun finally describes the state of the
world, and the play closes in a kind of paean of agreement between the two. The political *moralitas* of the play is enacted
through allegorical impersonations exchanging opinions. L'
Eglise establishes a problem, Le Commun disagrees, and the
concluding unity results from argument. There is no narrative
action, and dialogue not only characterizes, but also is the sole
carrier of the *moralitas*.

Dutch literature also includes moralities based upon the
dialogue of allegorized impersonations. *A Present of Love,
Friendship, and Loyalty* by Cassiers (21 January 1560) differs
from the French examples in that the dialogue is directed to
the audience rather than to either members of the cast. The
interaction of the characters is limited to their unity on stage.4
First, Love, Friendship, and Loyalty conjointly describe their
natures for the audience. Then they give various historical and
Biblical examples of the virtues impersonated. Finally, they
explain their New Year's gifts, which are emblematic of the
definitions of love, friendship, and loyalty. The drama lacks
conflict, and again there is no narrative. Dialogue and characterization represent the *moralitas*.

No pure examples of this form of morality survive from
medieval England, but the pageants of the Seven Deadly Sins
and Vicious in the Beverley Pater Noster play of 1469 suggest

the form was known in England before 1500. Furthermore, the Continental practice of the form may explain the often criticized verbiage of *Wisdom Who is Christ*.5 Though the narrative events of this play are structured according to a rhetorical organization which assigns the play to the most complex form of moralities, all meaningful narrative events result from expository dialogue and visual effects. Usually only the conclusion of the narrative event is enacted on stage. In contrast to the other English moralities of the medieval period, the enactment of the narrative events of *Wisdom Who is Christ* is restricted to dialogue and pageantry. To be sure, the narrative so represented is structured in accordance with the rhetorical pattern of the most complex moralities, but the expression of that narrative on stage employs exclusively the techniques of moralities which develop the *moralitas* through characterization and dialogue.

The English renaissance produced several pure examples of this morality form. The dialogue often approximates the general outline of a debate. The argument of *Gentleness and Nobility* (1529?), for example, describes the drama as a statement of opinion by a Merchant, a Knight, and a Plowman on the question of who is a true gentleman and nobleman.6 The Merchant gives his definition, but the Knight disagrees on the grounds of land tenure. The Plowman speaks his alternative views. Part I consists of conflicting definitions delivered within character. In Part II, the Plowman continues his statement of his case, and ultimately the Philosopher decides the issue by defining nobility in term of virtue. Like the examples from France and the Lowlands, *Gentleness and Nobility* lacks a plot; it resembles a debate with a final judgment. A form of morality, the characterization and theme of which were entirely dependent upon costumes and dialogue, was written in England, in France, and in the Lowlands. Not only do these plays meet a single definition of the *morality,* but they also indicate the presence of a commonly practiced technique of representing the interactions of the characterizations.

IV

In other moralities, narrative events augment characterization and dialogue in the presentation of the *moralitas*. The individual narrative events are allegorical in significance, but the organization of those events is only rhetorical. The moralities

which develop narratives can be further classified according to
the rhetorical structure of this narrative. One type of rhetorical
structure may be termed simple. It need not have a dramatic
conflict. Its events are ordered in fairly elementary patterns.
They may be merely juxtaposed in a chronological sequence.
They may prepare for, represent, and resolve a climax. On occasion, these patterns may be incomplete, combined or repeated.
When there are more than one climax, the climaxes are not interrelated as are a catastrophe and a *dénouement*. The complex
rhetorical structure, on the other hand, presents a dramatic conflict in five interrelated actions primarily based on intrigue.
Moralities with simple rhetorical structure survive from France,
from the Lowlands, and from renaissance England.

Since *L'Eglise, Noblesse et Pouerte* is on the same broad
subject as *L'Eglise et le Commun,* it well exemplifies the formal
difference between the morality based on characterization and
dialogue and the morality based as well on narrative events in a
simple rhetorical structure.7 The drama opens with L'Eglise
singing a *reverdi,* which reveals the true state of the church.
Next, La Noblesse vaunts, and La Pouerte follows with a description of her condition. The play initially resembles the morality
of dialogue only, but L'Eglise begins a sequence of narrative
events by suggesting that the three characters do the laundry
together. La Pouerte volunteers to dry the wash, the final and
perhaps easiest of tasks; but La Noblesse insists La Pouerte lay
it out, the heaviest of tasks. La Pouerte pleads her arms are
broken. La Noblesse and L'Eglise abandon the wash to beat
La Pouerte. After the beating, La Noblesse returns to the narrative of the laundry and discovers the dirty clothes harbored
by L'Eglise. The narrative then shifts with a request by La
Pouerte to L'Eglise for a change of clothes. L'Eglise refuses,
unless La Pouerte has friends or money. La Pouerte ends the
play with a summary of the state of the church. Certainly the
actual events—the preparations for doing the laundry, the beating of La Pouerte, and the finding of new clothes independently
from L'Eglise—allegorize the conditions of the three estates and
the need for social reform, but the rhetorical relationship of the
events in the conflict is a chronological sequence of two plots
connected only by the obvious need for clean clothes. One of the
plots is never completed. The laundry plot is prepared, but it
never reaches a climax or a resolution. The finding-of-clean-

clothes plot is prepared, reaches a climax which avoids the problem stated in the preparation, and is resolved. The narrative
structure of both plots is simple. The play is complicated by the
presence of two plots, but the plots are related only by content
and not by structure.

Because *La Moralité à quatre personnages,* which dramatizes
the figures of Chascun, Plusieurs, Le Temps qui Court, and Le
Monde, has been briefly alluded to as the French *Everyman,* it
deserves some notice here.8 Unlike the Lowland *Elckerlijc* and
the English *Everyman, La Moralité à quatre personnages* employs a simple rhetorical structure. Plusieurs informs Chascun
of an important event at court, but the two are more concerned
over their poverty. After a lyrical interchange on the four ages
of Man, Chascun and Plusieurs glimpse Le Temps qui Court.
They are surprised and puzzled, but Chascun recognizes Le
Temps qui Court on his second appearance. The two plan the
capture of Le Temps qui Court and succeed when he passes a
third time. Le Temps qui Court explains society without offering
a remedy. Le Monde enters to state his point of view. Chascun
and Plusieurs declare their allegiance to Le Monde. This French
Everyman has no dramatic conflict. After an extraneous introduction, the play presents a problem, the capture of Le Temps
qui Court, which is developed in repetitive episodes. The
climactic capture of Le Tempe qui Court does not resolve the
moral problem. The concluding scene with Le Monde which does
resolve the problem has no rhetorical relationship to the preceding intrigue.

The Lowland morality, *Brother William,* neatly utilizes cause
and effect in a three-part narrative.9 Though the morality is
named for the pseudo-historical Brother William, a good monk,
his role is not expanded, and the protagonist is Half-Crazed.
Half-Crazed abandons the monastery to see the world. After this
first decision, Half-Crazed is pursued by Fear of Sin, who attempts to serve as guide. In his wanderings, Half-Crazed comes
upon three ladders. Fear of Sin explains the ladders as three
walks of life—i.e., the clergy, "the farmers of the world," and
the common man. After Fear of Sin has explained the virtues
of the three ladders, Half-Crazed discovers a fourth, a crooked
one, the path of sin. Fear of Sin clearly explains the dangers of
the fourth ladder, but Half-Crazed chooses to climb it. While
Half-Crazed is on the ladder of sin, a demonic Catyvigue de-

scribes to him the dangers of the world and Fear of Sin expands upon them. Half-Crazed resolves the problem he has precipitated by deciding to return to the monastery.

The choice of ladders obviously allegorizes human selections of sin or virtue. Leaving the monastery exposes Half-Crazed to choice. The scene with the ladders, having as its climax the encounter with sin, defines the choices. Half-Crazed's decision to return to the monastery results from his encounter with the fourth ladder of sin and resolves the choice. *Brother William* enacts the *Moralitas* in a narrative having three interrelated parts, an exposition, a climax, and a resolution. Though the play represents an ethical dichotomy, there is no dramatic conflict, for Fear of Sin cannot be cast as an antagonist.

The narratives of all extant medieval English moralities contain examples of the allegorical event. As previously noted, the rhetorical structure which orders these events within the whole play is always complex, but a series of incidents may be arranged in a single action in a simple narrative pattern. At the end of the first action of *Mankind* the protagonist plans to fight his antagonist through labor.[10] Tityvillus, the leading antagonist, states, on the other hand, an encompassing intention to pervert Mankind by defeating his labor. Tityvillus hopes to achieve his goal through two incidents, placing a board in Mankind's soil and spoiling his corn, but four incidents are required. Each of the incidents allegorizes another step in gradual fall of Mankind, but together they form a single action initiated by the protagonist's and antagonist's original plans and concluded by Mankind's change of plan. The incidents within the action are arranged in a chronological sequence of causes and effects, in which each effect becomes a new cause. Mankind reacts to his situation; Tityvillus counters Mankind's reaction. There follows a series of stimuli-responses, in which every response motivates a new stimulus until the conclusion desired by Tityvillus is obtained.

The greater variety of forms in the English renaissance provides several examples of the morality based upon narrative events in a simple rhetorical organization. Ulpian Fulwell's *Like Will to Like* is composed of three sections.[11] The first section illustrates the title in a series of events connected just by chronology. Nicol Newfangle, a vice, describes his life as Lucifer's apprentice. Lucifer then admonishes Newfangle to join like to like.

Newfangle fulfills the directive by marrying Collier and Lucifer; by deciding that Tom Tosspot and he are equally knaves; and by celebrating a friendship with Philip Fleming. Virtuous Living introduces a brief dramatic conflict by confronting Newfangle, but the conflict is never developed. The second section has no dramatic conflict and is bound to the first section as a contrastive demonstration of the *moralitas*. Good Fame, God's Promises, and Honor crown Virtuous Living. The third section is united to the first as a continuation of Newfangle's successes, but prepares a climax which is unsuccessfully resolved. Newfangle returns to implement his program further, but he fails. His thieves are caught; Newfangle, however, escapes scot free to Lucifer.

Though a three-part structure—the rise, defeat, and escape of Newfangle, as interrupted by the coronation of Virtuous Living—might be forced upon the whole, the *moralitas* is actually demonstrated by the juxtaposition of isolated narrative events. The *moralitas,* as indicated by the title, by Lucifer's directive, and by the concluding explanations recited by Virtuous Living, Good Fame, and Honor, is like will to like, not the defeat of vice by virtue. This *moralitas* is proved by the effectiveness of Newfangle in the first section and by the coronation of Virtuous Living in the second section.

The use of allegorical events in a simple rhetorical structure to develop a *moralitas* was common to renaissance England, to France, and to the Lowlands. The extant medieval English plays all have a complex rhetorical structure, but individual actions of that structure might be developed by incidents ordered according to a simple rhetoric. The play which presents a *moralitas* through characterization, dialogue, and allegorical events in a simple rhetorical structure is a second international form of the morality. The last form of the morality, in which allegorical events are arranged in a complex rhetorical structure, also appears in England, in France, and in the Lowlands.

V

In complex rhetorical structure, a dramatic conflict is evolved in five actions. Each action, except the first and last, begins with the enactment of an intrigue and ends with an explanation of a new intrigue. This new intrigue is motivated by the conclusion of the intrigue which had been presented in the action. The first action or exposition introduces the characters and the dramatic conflict. The final scenes of the exposition are marked by the explanation of an intrigue. The fifth action enacts an intrigue which precipitates the second and final climax of the play. The resolution of this climax is the *dénouement* of the dramatic conflict. Each action affects the balance of the dramatic conflict in a regular, definable direction. At the end of the exposition, the opposed forces of the dramatic conflict are usually in equilibrium. In the second action, the protagonist and antagonist test each other, and the protagonist may be partially defeated. The third-action intrigue reaches a climax which defeats the protagonist. This catastrophe is often represented in the protagonist's changing his moral intention or in his death. During the fourth action the protagonist begins to rise in the balance of the dramatic conflict. The protagonist either returns to his original moral intention, or he is provided with a powerful guide who effects this return. The climax of the fifth action tests the protagonist's renewed intention. Its confirmation is the resolution of the drama. Though the third and fifth actions both contain climaxes, these climaxes are related as catastrophe and *dénouement*. Admittedly individual plays vary in single actions from this rigid model, but there is no consistent distribution of the variations. The pattern may, therefore, serve as a definitive rhetorical structure.12

All extant moralities from medieval England follow this rhetorical structure, which decays only in the Renaissance. Furthermore, a tragic five-action structure began to be explored in the English Renaissance, but it never reached perfection. The tragic five-action structure differs from the comic in that the protagonist repulses his aide and refuses to change his intention in the fourth action. The fifth action confirms the protagonist's moral collapse.

The five-action structure of the morality play was known in England as early as the fragmentary *Pride of Life* (1400-1450).13 Since analysis of the full structure of this play depends on the accuracy of the Prologue in summarizing the narrative, the other early medieval morality, *The Castle of Perseverance* (c. 1425) will be used to demonstrate the perfection of the form at the beginning of the fifteenth century in Engand.14 *The Castle of Perseverance* deviates from the model of five-action structure in that the exposition develops intrigues, which, in contrast to the sequential events of the second action of *Mankind*, are also arranged according to the model of five-action structure. This variation, the only extant one of its kind, illustrates the pervasiveness of the five-action structure in England.

The play opens with the vaunts of Mundus, Belyal, and Caro. Humanum Genus enters accompanied by Malus and Bonus Angelus, whom he introduces. After the debate of the angels, Humanum Genus decides to go to the World. He proceeds to the scaffold of Mundus and is welcomed. His change of clothes reveals his disgrace, but his fall is not yet complete. Mundus proposes another intrigue, a visit to Coveytyse. Humanum Genus enacts this visit and accepts the Deadly Sins as the completion of his fall. The lamentations of Bonus Angelus after the catastrophe motivate Confession, who challenges Humanum Genus. The correction is at first rebuffed, but Penitencia succeeds. After confession, a proof of the reversal of the intentions of Humanum Genus, the protagonist institutes the final intrigue —where may he dwell in safety. Humanum Genus is housed in the Castle of Perseverance.

The exposition of *The Castle of Perseverance* is a miniature morality play in five actions. The characters and conflict are introduced and an intrigue, the visit to Mundus, is explained. The catastrophe is prepared by two intrigues, proposals of alliance with Mundus and of alliance with Coveytyse. The protagonist's intention is reversed by powerful guides; the reversal is confirmed in the housing in the castle. The play, however, is not over. Malus Angelus explains a plan to storm the castle and orders Detraccio to call up the armies of the antagonists. Though the balance of the dramatic conflict has been deflected and restored in the opening scenes, it is now at a stationary point and an intrigue has been announced. *The Castle of Perseverance* has an exposition, which itself is based on five-action structure.

In the second action the armies collect, storm the castle, and face defeat. The intrigue of Malus Angelus has been enacted and the forces of the dramatic conflict have tested each other. Mundus concludes the second action with his plan to call out Coveytyse. Coveytyse succeeds in enticing Humanum Genus from the castle—the catastrophe. The helpless Virtues can offer no counter intrigue. It is Mors who forces the fourth-action intrigue. Abandoned by Mundus, Humanum Genus dies, but Anima expresses the protagonist's reversal. She calls upon Mercy, who responds. The ensuing Debate of the Four Daughters of

God results in the concluding intrigue, the presentation of the case to God. Pater resolves this intrigue and the play by accepting Anima, who is rescued from Hell and installed in Heaven.

The Castle of Perseverance has an exposition, a second action in which the protagonist and antagonist explore each other's defenses, a third action in which the protagonist reverses his intention, and a fifth action in which not only the protagonist's original case is confirmed, but the protagonist is also in a position in the balance of the conflict above his initial state. The earliest complete extant English morality is developed in five actions including an exposition based on five-action structure. Plays such as *Lusty Juventus* (c. 1547-53) evidence the survival of the five-action comic morality structure in renaissance England, though the form gradually decayed. Thomas Ingland's *The Disobedient Child* (printed edition, c. 1560) is the first extant attempt at a tragic morality in five actions in England. Better versions of this form were written, but it too had decayed by the time of Robert Wilson's *The Three Ladies of London* (printed edition, 1584).

The five-action structure did not have great popularity in France, but a morality play of this type was so integrated in the Mons *mystère* of 1501 that the events of the *mystère* become the fourth and fifth actions of the morality. The first scenes of the *mystère* may even be considered part of the exposition of the morality.15 The inclusion of the Mons *mystère* in this study may appear a violation of the definition of *morality* on which the selections for comparison have been used. The second and third actions of the morality sequence in the Mons *mystère*, however, exactly meet the definition of *morality*. It must further be remembered that the existence of the morality as an exclusively separate genre is the invention of the critic and not necessarily reflective of contemporary practice, as witnessed by the English miracle Digby *Mary Magdalene*.

The Mons play opens with the traditional Biblical scenes: the Fall of the Angels, Creation, Temptation and Expulsion, the Cain and Abel narrative, and the Death of Adam followed by the jubilation of the devils. Humain Lignaige, the protagonist of the morality, interrupts the devils to lament the fact that he too must die and go to Hell. The words of Humain Lignaige universalize the earlier Biblical history, which may be considered a prelude to the morality or a part of its exposition as a presentation of causes for the morality conflict. After a second celebration by the devils, Prologeur announces that the story of Adam is finished and asks the audience to consider its implications. Though Humain Lignaige has spoken during the Biblical scenes, the words of Prologeur mark the opening of the unmixed morality actions.

The grieving Humain Lignaige places his faith in God's justice, but the devils plan his fall. The pure morality exposition is most brief. The second and third actions are a series of temptations by the devils, divided into two actions by the severity of the test, by the reactions of Humain Lignaige, and by a procession. Sathan leads the attack in offering pity, but Humain Lignaige trusts in God's mercy. Sathan presses his argument and introduces Humain Lignaige to Orgoeul and Ire. After meeting all the vices, Humain Lignaige joins in a procession during which he tells Orgoeul of his continuing doubts. Humain Lignaige has yet to meet his chief adversary, and his fall is complete. This series of intrigue, related by cause and effect, constitute a second action in which the protagonist is partially defeated.

After the procession, La Char shows Humain Lignaige Convoitise, and Humain Lignaige completes his fall. This catastrophe is enacted in the reception of Humain Lignaige at the mansion of Le Monde, where he is given new clothes and set to a feast. The devils celebrate. If the Mons morality is considered to begin after the speech of Prologeur, the morality has an exposition, a second action, and a third action, the materials of which are restricted to those of the definition. If the morality begins with the first words of Humain Lignaige, the scenes from Genesis may be linked to the morality exposition, but again the second and third actions employ morality materials exclusively.

In the remaining scenes of the *mystère,* the Biblical events directly affect the balance of the morality conflict, through the reactions of Humain Lignaige to the tropological and analogical significance of those events. The responses of Humain Lignaige are identical to the reactions of the protagonist in the fourth and fifth actions of an unmixed morality. The Flood sequence, which immediately follows the catastrophe of Humain Lignaige, reverses his fall. When the waters fall, Orgoeul hurries away. The Deadly sins, who have been soaked, flee. The Flood has defeated the antagonists of the morality. The Flood sequence

continues in usual fashion, but Humain Lignaige has apparently
withstood the deluge and is able to watch. At the end of the
Flood sequence, Humain Lignaige prays to God and thanks Him
for the lesson he has learned. The Flood has routed the antagonists and has reversed the moral conviction of the protagonist;
it has fulfilled the rhetorical purpose of a fourth action in a five-
action morality.

Humain Lignaige seeks restitution in the following scenes
of the *mystère* and finds it in the Entombment. His continued
search and his eventual satisfaction confirms his reversal in the
Flood sequence, but the entombment absolves him. Humain
Lignaige expects the sacrifice of Isaac to be his absolution, and
he laments the rescue of Isaac. After the Prologeur has announced the end of Araham and Isaac sequence, Humain Lignaige again prays for comfort. His prayer motivates the prophet
sequence, which is a dialogue between David and Isaiah and
Humain Lignaige. The hope suggested in this sequence is affirmed when Gabriel, in a kind of pre-Annunciation, reassures
Humain Lignaige. The following Debate of the Four Daughters
of God, who recommend the sacrifice of Christ, has immediate
bearing on the *dénouement* of the morality. Dieu agrees to the
Crucifixion "Pour le salut d'Humain Lignaige" (I. 1097). The
absolution in the fifth-action climax is approaching, but Humain
Lignaige is ignorant.

Humain Ligaige is puzzled by the marriage of the Blessed
Mother, and, despite the earlier warning by Gabriel, he is confused by the Annunciation. He hopes at the birth of John the
Baptist, and he finally has a glimmer of understanding at the
accouchement of the Blessed Mother. He perseveres at the Presentation at the Temple, but laments his damnation when
Raphael alerts John the Baptist to expect Christ. Though still
depressed, Humain Lignaige chats with the Apostles before the
Transfiguration. The Raising of Lazarus leaves him expectant,
but he is troubled by the plans for the Crucifixion and miserable
at the Washing of the Feet. He celebrates Christ the King at
the entry to Jerusalem, but doubts his redemption during the
Trial. To Humain Lignaige the Crucifixion is a mere fact, but
the Entombment proves to him the sacrifice of the Crucifixion.
He praises God humbly in the awareness of his having survived
the final climax, the Crucifixion. Humain Lignaige demonstrates

his restoration when he harangues the doubting Thomas and the worried Apostles who are fishing.

After the Flood sequence, Humain Lignaige is the only morality character who remains on stage during the *mystère*. He reacts constantly, however, and occasionally participates in the *mystère* scenes; he views his case as incomplete until the Entombment. The Biblical scenes can be grouped as phases of an intrigue, one might say by God, to redeem Humain Lignaige from the consequences of his fall in the morality catastrophe. Certainly Humain Lignaige initiated this redemption in his reversal during the Flood sequence, but he is not cleansed until the Entombment, the proof of Christ's actual death on the Cross. The *mystère* scenes after the Flood sequence affect the balance of conflict established in the morality as does a fifth action. Though the morality elements of the Mons *mystère* are inextricably interwoven with Biblical history and even emphasize the tropological and anagogical meanings of that history, they are sufficiently developed independently to permit consideration of a morality embedded within the Mons *mystère*.

The complete corpus of Lowland moralities is not yet available in English, but there are at least two examples of the morality having five-action structure. The Flemish *Elckerlijc,* like its successor the English *Everyman,* has the most perfect five-action structure known to date. The protagonist's intention in the usual morality of five actions is to maintain either a virtuous life or to triumph in an immoral existence. The catastrophe, therefore, must be enacted in the alliance of the protagonist with the antagonist or, as in the case of the fragmentary *Pride of Life,* in the death of the protagonist. Such techniques for representing the catastrophe temporarily remove the protagonist from the dramatic conflict in the opening scenes of the fourth action. Elckerlijc and Everyman have different resolutions: to find a companion in the grave and to cleanse the Book of Life. The intentions may be apparently defeated, as they are by Goods, without the protagonists necessarily changing their intentions. In *Elckerlijc* and *Everyman* the protagonists continue their roles in the dramatic conflict into the fourth action. The resultant beauty of form creates the dramatic intensity of the plays so strongly felt by audiences of later centuries.

The Sensuous Man, not yet known to the English-speaking audience, follows the more typical five-action model in which

the protagonist changes his intention at the catastrophe.16
Sensuous Man enters accompanied by Grace of God and sings
of his prudent stewardship of worldly goods. Bad Faith and
Carnal Sin overhear Sensuous Man and decide to pervert him.
They accost Sensuous Man and introduce the idea of Worldly
Consolation, a role played as an innkeeper's wife. Sensuous Man
orders the inn readied. Bad Faith and Carnal Sin chat jovially
on their way to the inn. When they reach the inn, Worldly Consolation agrees to provide Sensuous Man with a woman. Whether
or not the playwright had a sense of acts as well as of actions,
this section of the play is divided from the ensuing scenes by a
pausa. Though the formal definition of an exposition includes
the lines immediately after the *pausa,* the *pausa* may be used to
demarcate the end of an exposition which presents the major
characters, the conflict, and, in this case, the complete controlling
intrigue.

After the *pausa,* Sensuous Man laments his unavoidable
death. Bad Faith and Carnal Sin return from the inn to invite
Sensuous Man to join them. The ringing of the sermon bell
during their dialogue institutes the first intrigue to be enacted.
The antagonists and the protagonist will attend the sermon.
During the sermon, Sensuous Man thinks only of his worldly
goods and becomes upset about the possible loss of his affluence.
Bad Faith and Carnal Sin console him and Sensuous Man agrees
to go to the inn. The failure of Daily Sermon to preserve Sensuous Man's intention constitutes the second action.

The effect of the second action on the balance of the dramatic conflict is enacted literally in the opening scenes of the
third action. Sensuous Man trips and almost has a very bad fall
while he is walking to the inn. His enjoyment of the inn comprises the third action. He meets the matchmaker, Lust of the
Eyes, who brings him together with the whore, Pompous Ambition. Another prostitute, Luxury, with her maid Excess arrives,
and Sensuous Man decides to bed her. Two guildsmen, both
Like the World, join this party. Brief Luxury comes to sing and
drink. The enjoyment of the inn life signals the fall of Sensuous
Man in a third-action catastrophe.

The fourth-action reversal is seemingly begun by Sensuous
Man, who laments his condition, but it is actually effected by
new forces. God orders Anger to descend on Sensuous Man.
Anger and Day of Vengeance challenge the protagonist; the

antagonists flee. Anger wants to tie up Sensuous Man and haul him up before God. Grace of God intervenes, and Anger and Grace of God argue in a manner reminiscent of Mercy and Justice in debates of the Four Daughters of God. The fourth action ends with the decision for Grace of God, Anger, and Sensuous Man to appear before God. The fifth action employs two familiar motifs. Grace of God and Anger argue their cases before God. Grace of God then lectures Sensuous Man, who confesses to God. God absolves him and assigns him Tribulation to keep him in order.

Sensuous Man has five actions—an exposition, an initial intrigue, an intrigue resulting in a catastrophe, a reversal, and a climax which demonstrates the validity of the reversal. It differs from the formal outline of five-action structure in that the initial intrigue is not planned in the exposition, but interrupts the enactment of the catastrophe intrigue. The five-action structure in which the protagonist changes his intention in the third action was utilized in the Lowlands. A Lowland writer, furthermore, was capable of improving upon this form in *Elcklijc* by constructing a third-action catastrophe in which the protagonist is temporarily defeated, but maintains his intention.

Despite the paucity of the extrinsic evidence, the material surveyed in this paper suggests that a complex international tradition of moralizing drama existed in England, in France, and in the Lowlands. The identical subjects of dramatic and nondramatic works demonstrates the presence of a body of commonly known moralizing literature which, depending upon the preference of the artist, could be and was dramatized.

The various genres of moralizing drama appeared in at least two of the three language areas considered. The genre termed *morality* in this study—that is, a drama which presents a *moralitas* through the interaction of characterizations based on allegory or typification—was written in all three languages during the late Middle Ages and early Renaissance. Furthermore, the techniques for developing the interaction of the characterizations in these moralities recur in the three cultures. Characters may present the *moralitas* exclusively in dialogue, or the dialogue may be supplemented by a narrative. This narrative is either organized in a variety of simple patterns or in the complex structure of five specifically defined actions.

Certainly, with the presence of a well-known tradition of

moralizing allegorical literature, the international appearance of the morality might be attributed to spontaneous, contemporary, independent, national inspirations. The international creation of moralities based upon dialogue or upon dialogue in a simple narrative might be assumed the result of the playwrights' obvious means of development. The five-action structure, however, is an artificial expansion of content, which is in no way dictated by the content. The content requires only three actions: exposition, catastrophe, and resolution. It is difficult to explain isolated inventions of this contrived structure which could not be based upon either subject matter or any other known form of medieval drama. A particular morality play, therefore, should not be analyzed as only a discreet literary artifact; it is the consequence of and a potential contributor to a larger dramaturgic context.

NOTES

1 Gustav Cohen, *Le Théâtre en France au Moyen Age* (Paris, 1928) and Grace Frank, *The Medieval French Drama* (Oxford, 1954, 1960) give little if any attention to moralizing drama. Though Louis Petit de Julleville seems to exclude *farce* and *mystère* in his definition, he cites a miracle of St. Martin in his listings (*Histoire de Théâtre en France*, Répertoire du Théâtre Comique [1887; rpt. Geneva, 1967], p. 36).

2 *Repertorium van het Rederijkersdrama*, 155—ca. 1620 (Assen, 1968).

3 *Recueil de farces, moralités et sermons joyeux publié d'apres le manuscrit de le bibliotheque royale*, ed. Le Roux de Lincy et Francisque Michel, I (Paris, 1837), 1-16.

4 *Het raadsel der vier Cassieres (ca. 1555-ca. 1585)*, Verslagen en Medelingen van Koninklijke Vlaamse Academie voor Teal-en Letterkunde, ed. W. van Eeghem (1938), pp. 126-44. This and all other Dutch dramas have been translated by Nicholas Roozen.

5 *Wisdom Who Is Christ*, in *The Marco Plays*, ed. Mark Eccles, EETS, o.s. 262 (1969), pp. 113-52.

6 *Gentleness and Nobility*, Malone Soc. Reprints (1950 [for 1949]).

7 Le Roux de Lincy, I, 1-16.

8 Ibid., II, 1-26.

9 O. van den Daele and F. van Veerdeghem, *De Roode Roos, Zinnespelen en andere Toonoolstukken der Zestiende eeuw* (Bergen [Mons], 1889), pp. 251-70.

10 *Mankind*, in *Macro Plays*, pp. 153-84

11 Ulpian Fulwell, *Like Will to Like*, Tudor Facsimile Texts (1908).

12 For a full analysis of the five-action structure as it applies to English morali-

ties, see Merle Fifield, *The Rhetoric of Free Will; The Five-Action Structure of the English Moralities,* University of Leeds Texts and Monographs Ser., 5 (Leeds, 1974).

13 *Non-Cycle Plays and Fragments,* ed. Norman Davis, EETS, suppl. ser. 1 (1970), pp. 90-105.

14 *Macro Plays,* pp. 1-112.

15 *Le Livre de Conduite du régisseur et le Compte des Depenses pour le mystère de la Passion jouè à Mons en 1501,* ed. Gustav Cohen (Paris, 1925).

16 C. Kruyskamp, *Dichten en spelen van Jan van den Berghe* ('s-Gravenhage, 1950), pp. 91-144.

The Idea of a Person in Medieval Morality Plays

Natalie Crohn Schmitt

In 1914, W. Roy Mackenzie explained that *"A Morality is a play, allegorical in structure, which has for its main object the teaching of some lesson for the guidance of life, and in which the principal characters are personified abstractions or highly universalized types."*[1] By and large critics of medieval morality plays have continued to work within the limitations of Mackenzie's description, refining our understanding of the object of the lesson, and of the concepts "allegory," "personified abstraction," and "universalized type." There has been no substantial change in our understanding of these plays.

In this paper I argue that while the object of the plays is didactic, their effect is mimetic; that, more literally than the analyses have allowed, the plays provide a phenomenological account of existence, and that the concepts "allegory," "personified abstraction," and "universalized type" do not account for the whole of the medieval experience of the plays, nor for the whole of our experience of them either.

My starting point is Geoffrey Bullough's observation that "it has not yet been adequately realized how continuously English literature has been affected, both in matter and in form, by changes in men's notions of the human mind and of its relation to the body and the world about it."[2] This paper is an attempt to begin to recover the psychology inherent in the medieval morality plays. It shows that a number of things which have heretofore been dismissed as literary weaknesses can be understood as representation of the human experience. The paper has four parts: 1. Mimesis, in which I explain, in general, the view of man in the world which the plays express, and 2. Allegory, 3. Personified Abstractions, and 4. Universalized Type, in which

I explore the difficulties these concepts present in our understanding of these plays.

I

Mimesis: Mind, Body, and World. The war between Good and Evil was the profoundest reality of life, since upon the issue hung the eternal destiny of the soul. The salvation of the hard-pressed soul was the supreme prize of existence, and mortal life became subject to a single evaluation—the soul's progress toward God or its defection away from Him. The adventure of life was, in our sense, inward and spiritual. God created the earth and the heavens and all things therein so that man might work out his life and destiny. Man was at the center of the universe and everything possessed significance not in itself but for man's pilgrimage. The Devil and his demons indeed were very real and very close, and the powers of God and his angels needed constantly to be drawn upon to combat them. What we call external reality was subordinate to the central conflict. The observer was himself in the picture at the center, and the world was more like a garment man wore about him than a stage on which he moved. The internal and external world were identified in a state of fusion and wholeness.3

Robert Potter believes the events which occur in the course of a morality play to be not mimetic representations of life, but analogical demonstrations of what life is about.4 The distinction, however, does not seem medieval. The world itself was a great analogy making manifest the otherwise invisible and only reality of God. The medieval artists were Realists;5 they believed that the world was to be understood not in terms of operations and causes, but in terms of its meaning.

The part of man which is the nearest image of God is his mind. Those activities which seem to belong to man as an organic creature but do not proceed from his will are reckoned as outside his "self." The automatic functions of the body are grouped together as "lower functions"; they become dissociated from the self, which is increasingly thought of as limited to activities of the mind. Self-expression, then, becomes associated with what we would think of as self-repression.6

This picture of mind, body, and world and their relationship, which we are told is the one generally to have prevailed, is just the picture we are provided with in *The Castle of Perseverance.*

The castle of man's soul is set at the center of the playing area which represents at once the universe and the self; the boundaries between the internal and the external are not clear. Ideally, man resides within the castle watched over by the powers of good and protected from the realms of the world, the flesh, and the devil beyond. Outside the castle man is in exile and wilderness. All is shown from the perspective in which the war for man's salvation is the central reality, a very inward view in which that which acts upon the embattled self—world, flesh, and devil—are things of equal reality.

II

Allegory. Definitions of allegory and explanations of the distinction between it and symbolism are readily found. The most influential for the reading of medieval morality plays is probably that of C. S. Lewis. According to him allegory starts from the immaterial, usually passions or thoughts, and materializes them. Symbolism starts from the material and puts an immaterial meaning into it.7 But, as Robert Frank has observed, the medieval person did not distinguish between allegory and symbol and confounded our categories by employing both modes in the same work. Moreover, our categories assume a clear distinction between allegory and symbol on the one hand and the literal on the other. Such an assumption lies behind the commonplace comment that the medieval person was not given to thinking in abstractions and so personified them. Our presupposition is that what is literally there is sensibly, materially there and that every medieval person really knew this, and knew that what we call abstractions are in the mind only, but that for convenience and ease he thought of the abstract in terms of the concrete. But, the predominant medieval view was that the Real was unseen and immaterial. And, as Owen Barfield has argued at length, the idea of objectivity, of the existence of things the identity of which can be known quite apart from ourselves, is a product of a scientific rationalist age; it is not a medieval idea. Medieval people consciously participated in what they perceived. The distinction between passions and thought on the one hand and the material world on the other is not medieval. Barfield tells us that

> exceptional men did sometimes distinguish between the literal
> and the symbolical use of words and images before the scientific

revolution. On the question of hell, for instance, John Scotus Erigena distinguished in the seventh century between the symbol and the symbolized or the representation and the represented, emphasizing that the sufferings of hell are purely spiritual, and that they are described physically for the benefit of simple understandings. The point I am making is that, precisely to those simple understandings, the 'physical' and 'literal' themselves were not what 'physical' and 'literal' are to us. Rather, the phenomena themselves carried the sort of multiple significance which we to-day find in symbols. Accordingly, the issue, in a given case, between a literal and a symbolical interpretation, though it could be raised, had not the same sharpness as of contradictories.9

The distinction between symbol and allegory was not a clear one for the medieval person and the distinction between both these modes and the literal was not as firm as our own. We must deny Lewis's dictum that allegory was but a mode of expression, not a mode of thought.10

III

Personified Abstractions. E. N. S. Thompson explained the idea of personified abstractions: "The motives and impulses of man's own heart were taken from him, and clothed in flesh and blood and given him again for companions."11 They appear in the plays along with real people. This mixing bothered C. S. Lewis. James Wimsatt is more tolerant; he argues that variety is obtained when personifications are "involved in stories with individuals who are not personifications. Thus, Satan deals with Sin and Death in Paradise Lost."12 Wimsatt accepts Satan as real—that is, as external to man—but not Sin and Death. He does not question that there is a clear demarcation between internal and external, but he places it for the medieval person elsewhere than where most of us today would place it for ourselves. Other critics go further in denying that the demarcation is like our own. Carolly Erickson tells us that for the medieval person there was a vast world of figures—ghosts, demons, and angels—more numerous than mankind and no less real though less corporeal.13 Morton Bloomfield tells us that "the Sins were from their earliest appearance in Christian thought considered concrete devils or demons, and throughout the Middle Ages they continued, at times, to be so visualized." This was "the popular, and often learned, attitude toward sin which prevailed in the Middle Ages, when demons, which were often regarded as spe-

cific sins or vices, were considered lieutenants of the devil."14
In *The Castle of Perseverance* we are told that Mankind shall
creep into Lechery's cunt and sow his seed. And Robert Potter
has pointed out that many of the so-called virtues in the morality
plays are, in fact, priests.15 Are all these figures, then, "motives
and impulses of man's own heart" or separate persons? The
concept "personified abstraction" seems a badly confused one:
the plays do not allow us to make a clear distinction between
that which exists independently as outside agent and that which
is internal motive. The homiletic progression David Bevington
sees in *Mundus et Infans* is at the same time a psychological
progression: "Worldly pomp and vanity naturally give rise to
frivolity and abandoned living, and thus Mundus gives way to
Folly. Similarly, Conscience is the first step in the reclamation
of a fallen soul; once Conscience has done his work and salvation is in progress, Perseverance must ensue."16 There is here a
conjunction of internal and external.

Experientially the distinction between the two is not easily
made and disagreement on it exists in our own society. Some of
us believe God and heaven and the Devil and hell have real
external validity; some do not. Some men would explain the
desire to rape to be as much as a result of the woman's provo-
cation as of their own lechery. Gregory Bateson says that the
alcoholic places his drinking habit outside himself, whereas
Alcoholics Anonymous forces him to redefine himself as an
alcoholic, his alcoholism as central to his being.17 The genuine
lack of clarity between what we do to ourselves and what is
done to us arises in any account we try to provide of our own
histories, and is obvious in the disparities between what we know
to do, on the one hand, and our sexual disfunction, lapses of
memory, and what we uncomprehendingly call "reflexes," and
"instinctual" and "unconscious" behavior on the other. C. S.
Lewis himself acknowledges the validity of the experiential
account provided by the plays. "It is idle," he says, to tell someone "that something with which he has been at death-grips for
the last twenty-four hours is an 'abstraction'."18

We can understand that the idea of self-expression as what
is, in our terms, self-repression would serve to intensify the
objectification of that which we regard as internal. David Cole,
writing about demonic possession, explains that an impulse
denied its rightful role in mental life and repressed eventually

returns with redoubled force and totally swamps the personality that had refused it even the limited role in mental life to which it was entitled. The person denying the inner drive projects it as other—another person or a god or spirit—precisely *because* he cannot acknowledge it as an aspect of himself. Its otherness is a metaphor for his mind's disavowal of it and for its intensity.19

The idea that these plays are largely peopled with what appear to readers to be personified abstractions has caused critics to deny the dramatic nature of these pieces, their existence as theatrical performance. Joanne Kantrowitz sees the morality play as "a didactic, allegorical drama whose character lies in the exposition of a thesis." The persona she thinks of as "simply a convenient means of representation."20 J. Leeds Barroll tells us that the human actor is "actually irrelevant to the process."21 Robert Potter, who has directed morality plays, argues otherwise: "The characters of the morality plays though fitted out with abstract names, are impersonated by human actors. This obvious fact (generally the major discovery in any modern production) adds a dimension of humanity to the most theological of moralities."22 In other words, in production the figures are experienced as far more real than a reading suggests. Production, the means by which the medieval audience knew the plays, challenges the interpretation in terms of personified abstraction, the only essential part of which is the abstraction.

It seems to me that the concept "personified abstraction" has made the account of the development of drama from medieval times to Elizabethan more difficult to comprehend than need be. If the abstraction is the only essential aspect and the character, merely a convenience in the exposition of a thesis, then we must understand that history brought about a complete reversal: the character, which had no importance at all, became the only thing of importance. If, rather, the persona was important all along but ceased to have allegorical significance because Realism ceased to be the predominant belief, the change is less radical and more comprehensible.

IV

The Universalized Type. According to the account of Bernard Spivack,

> into the morality drama from its beginning there intruded under his various names and aspects, the figure of mankind, who

strictly speaking, does not belong in the allegory at all. He is
not a personification but a universalized type; and he is placed
in the position absurd from the viewpoint of allegory, of frater-
nizing with his personified attributes. In Medwall's *Nature,* for
instance, Man stands by a mute listener while his Sensuality
and his Reason argue their separate claims to dominion over
him until finally he bursts out like a wonder-stricken and utterly
forlorn third party:

> "O blessyd lord what maner of stryf ys thys
> Atyxt my reason and sensualyte."[23]

Now the presence of this wonder-stricken and utterly forlorn
third party may not accord with Spivack's understanding of
allegory, but it does accord with human experience. The following common expressions record an "I" present separate from
the emotions: "I was overcome with anger," "I was blinded by
ambition," "I was plagued by self-doubt," "A wave of joy swept
over me," "Something came over me," "I'm getting ahead of
myself," "I've lost my mind," "I'll try to collect my wits."
Annette Kolodny, writing about recent novels by women writers,
observes that the central character in them is commonly self-
reflexive; she experiences a certain amputation of self from self;
she is beside herself[24]

The separation of self from body, which we nowadays work
so hard to overcome, still finds ready expression; we say, for
instance, "My leg is giving me a lot of trouble." And when
theater director Richard Schechner insists that "Your body is
not your 'instrument'; your body is you,"[26] he thereby acknowledges this disjunction. According to R. D. Laing the dissocia-
tion of self from body is quite common under stress—the
condition, of course, in which we see Mankind.

> It is well-known that temporary states of dissociation of the
> self from the body occur in normal people. In general, one can
> say that it is a response that appears to be available to most
> people who find themselves enclosed within a threatening
> experience from which there is no physical escape. . . . Despite
> the dream-nature or unreality of experience, and the automatic
> nature of action, the self is at the same time far from 'sleepy';
> indeed, it is excessively alert, and may be thinking and observ-
> ing with exceptional lucidity.

Instead of
           (self/body)   other
the situation is
           self   (body-other)[26]

In his history of psychology, Brett tells us that in medieval times, the prevailing notion was that of the Realists, namely that the soul or consciousness was an entity, an independent self-subsistent thing which, stripped of the senses and disconnected from the body, could "confront the Ideas or enter the presence of God."27 Among those who took the trouble to think about the question, there seems to have been disagreement about whether this soul was substanial or not, but as late as 1612 Charron argued emphatically that the soul, though invisible and impalpable, is corporeal.28

There are those who would argue that whether this self or consciousness exists as an independent entity, corporeal or incorporeal, it is not a three-dimensional character, and therefore can only be understood as a universalized type, and that the plays accordingly can only be understood as didactic because plays without characters are not moving. But as C. S. Lewis observes, "the gaze turned inward with a moral purpose does not discover *character*. No man is a 'character' to himself, and least of all while he thinks of good and evil."29 W .B. Yeats argues the power of the uncharacterized self to move us and, indeed, of the incapability of the three-dimensional character to do so. "One dogma of the printed criticism," he says, "is that if a play does not contain definite character, its constitution is not strong enough for the stage, and that the dramatic moment is always the contest of character with character." Instead, he argues, it is the case that character is only defined in comedy or in comic moments of tragi-comedy, and that the great tragic moments are moments of passion without characterization, for when we are moved it is always ourselves that we see upon the stage.30 To argue that because the central figure is not a three-dimensional character he must be an abstraction is to miss the power he has as consciousness, as pure self.

The central figure is also said to be a universalized type because he is, as his name makes clear, mankind—not merely one man. However, V. A. Kolve realized that he is both. In his analysis of *Everyman* he observes that Everyman is referred to both in the singular and in the plural. He argues that this ambiguity is intentional as if Everyman is saying, "*I* do not know when I will die; *we* do not know when as a race we will exceed the patience of God."31 Kolve's linguistic analysis supports Barfield's more general observation that while we, in our scientific rationalism, distinguish abruptly between "mankind in general" and "*a* man," this distinction was not central in medieval times when the person as perceiver was understood to interpenetrate with that which was perceived. "Therefore our predecessors were able, quite inwardly, to accept the sin of Adam as being *their* original sin also. And therefore we are not—because, for us, Adam (if he existed) was after all— somebody else!"32 Carolly Erickson makes the same point: "Medieval perception was characterized by an all-inclusive awareness of simultaneous realities"; "it was a cultural habit to endow individual things with multiple identities."33

An understanding of the concept of simultaneous realities informs our reading of *The Castle of Perseverance*. Paul Piehler believes that, following Augustine, the medieval person recognized not only a physical paradise as the place where man was first created, but also a spiritual paradise as every place where the soul is in a state of well-being or grace.34 As he associated Mankind with Adam, so the medieval person may have associated the Castle of Perseverance with paradise.35 More surely the Castle is also the castle of the blessed Virgin, for the text tells us this explicitly. And Owst notes that sermons often told how into the castle of the Virgin "the Savior entered at His incarnation, a feudal stronghold protecting Him from the Devil in an otherwise defenseless world."26 And so Mankind is identified with Christ and the Castle with a womb.

A final reason for understanding the central figure in a morality play as a universalized type has been put forward by Joanne Kantrowitz: "Allegoric character . . . is not verisimilar in the sense that the authors do not show us the slow development and shift of personality over an extended facsimile of time and space."37 This is not strictly true: Bevington's analysis of *Mundus et Infans* makes clear a developmental progression, and Everyman's progressive abandonment by money, friend, and kinsmen—and then by beauty, strength, discretion, and five wits—is a natural progression inward, a diminishing circle of life's light. Yet we must not assume that shifts in personality have to be developmental to be verisimilar. A familiar slogan of humanist psychology, "Today is the first day of the rest of your life," implies that change can be not only developmental but also transformational; this idea has deeply influenced acting technique in contemporary theatre. Traditionally such events as initiation, loss of virginity, parenthood, and moves from place to place have been understood as transformational, not developmental changes. Hardin Craig tells us that the Elizabethan account of personality change was not developmental: "the theory was that one emotion or passion drives out another, and that the substitution is immediately operative. The doctrine is enough to account for many sudden changes in character, changes without transitional stages, which appear frequently in Elizabethan drama."[38] It would seem that the theory can also help us to understand the character changes in medieval drama: in *Mundus et Infans* the changes may be progressive but they are not gradual. They may nonetheless be understood as more life-like than we have assumed. It has been observed that in the morality plays the character transformations have been marked by costume changes. The modern costume of mourning and others through which biography can be read are traditional in many cultures. And Kolodny observes that in the new women's fiction costume changes regularly mark character transformations.[39]

We have been told that we can only appreciate the central figure in a morality play as a universalized type. Analysis of the central figure as a universalized type is based on three assumptions: that to be dramatic the central figure in a drama must be perceived as a character, that personality is necessarily perceived as single and discrete at one time and through the passage of time. I have argued that these assumptions are inappropriate to an understanding of the morality plays. I have further argued that the distinction between that which is internal to ourselves and that which is in the external world has not remained constant through time and that it was anyway not a firm distinction for the medieval person—nor is it experientially for us. I have argued that for the medieval person the distinction between literal and allegorical was not what it is for us and had not the sharpness of a contradiction, and that these plays which we call allegories are to a far greater extent than we have realized representations of phenomenological reality. Our application of anachronistic concepts has confused our reading of the plays and has removed us from the psychology which they express.

NOTES

1 William Roy Mackenzie, *The English Moralities from the Point of View of Allegory*, Harvard Studies in English, 2 (Boston, 1914), p. 9.

2 Geoffrey Bullough, *Mirror of Minds* (Toronto, 1962), p. 1.

3 This description is derived from Bernard Spivack, *Shakespeare and the Allegory of Evil* (New York, 1958), p. 75; John Herman Randall, *The Making of the Modern Mind* (Cambridge, Mass., 1940), pp. 18, 29, 34-36; Owen Barfield, *Saving the Appearances* (New York, 1965), p. 94; Paul Piehler, *The Visionary Landscape* (London, 1971), p. 17.

4 Robert Potter, *The English Morality Play* (London, 1975), p. 33.

5 Arnold Williams, "The English Moral Play Before 1500," *Annuale Mediaevale*, 4 (1963), 12.

6 *Brett's History of Psychology*, edited and abridged by R. S. Peters (Cambridge, Mass., 1965), p. 233.

7 C. S. Lewis, *The Allegory of Love* (London, 1936), pp. 44ff.

8 Robert W. Frank, "The Art of Reading Medieval Personification Allegory," *ELH*, 20 (1953), 238.

9 Barfield, p. 74.

10 Lewis, p. 48.

11 Elbert N. S. Thompson, "The English Moral Play," *Transactions of the Connecticut Academy of Arts and Sciences*, 14 (1908-10), 315.

12 James I. Wimsatt, *Allegory and Mirror* (New York, 1970), p. 36.

13 Carolly Erickson, *The Medieval Vision* (Oxford, 1976), pp. 12-18.

14 Morton Bloomfield, *The Seven Deadly Sins* (East Lansing, Mich., 1967), pp. 34, 61.

15 Potter, p. 39.

16 David M. Bevington, *From Mankind to Marlowe* (Cambridge, Mass., 1962), p. 119.

17 Gregory Bateson, "The Cybernetics of 'Self': A Theory of Alcoholism," *Steps to an Ecology of Mind* (New York, 1972), pp. 309-38.

18 Lewis, p. 61.

19 David Cole, *The Theatrical Event* (Middletown, Conn., 1975), p. 44.

20 Joanne Spencer Kantrowitz, "Dramatic Allegory, or, Exploring the Moral Play," *Comparative Drama*, 7 (1973), 68, 72.

21 J. Leeds Barroll, *Artificial Persons* (Los Angeles, 1974), p. 252.

22 Potter, p. 34.

23 Spivack, p. 93.

24 Annette Kolodny, "Same Notes on Defining a 'Feminist Literary Criticism'," *Critical Inquiry*, 2 (1975), 79-80.

25 Richard Schechner, *Environmental Theatre* (New York, 1973), p. 145.

26 R. D. Laing, *The Divided Self* (Baltimore, 1965), pp. 78, 82. In *Wisdom* the self is most fragmented when most disturbed and most removed from goodness.

27 *Brett's History of Psychology*, pp. 264-65.

28 Hardin Craig, *The Enchanted Glass* (Oxford, 1950), p. 1. Brett tells us that in the eleventh century "spiritus" is "pneuma" and means the material basis of life (p. 258).

29 Lewis, p. 60.

30 W. B. Yeats, "The Tragic Theatre," *Essays and Introductions* (New York, 1968), pp. 239-41.

31 V. A. Kolve, "*Everyman* and the Parable of the Talents," *Medieval English Drama*, ed. Jerome Taylor and Alan H. Nelson (Chicago, 1972), pp. 328-29.

32 Barfield, p. 183.

33 Erickson, *The Medieval Vision*, pp. 8, 27.

34 Piehler, p. 79.

35 And, if the water referred to in the stage plan is a moat round the Castle and, at the same time, Mary's Well of Grace, as I have argued elsewhere, this would reinforce this interpretation because in various other works the Well of Grace is identified with the seven rivers surrounding the Garden of Paradise.

36 G. R. Owst, *Literature and Pulpit in Medieval England* (rpt. New York, 1966), p. 77.

37 Kantrowitz, p. 71.

38 Craig, p. 83.

39 Kolodny, p. 83.

The Morality Play:
Ancestor of Elizabethan Drama?

John Wasson

At least since A. P. Rossiter's edition of *Woodstock* in 1946 and Tillyard's *Shakespeare's History Plays* in 1947, critics have become accustomed to suppose that the Elizabethan history play had its "roots" in the medieval morality. Once that opinion was accepted as a settled fact, as it was by the time Ribner published *The English History Play in the Age of Shakespeare,* other scholars felt free to find morality roots for Elizabethan tragedy and comedy as well.[1] Thus in one view or another, virtually every Renaissance play was thought to exhibit direct and important influence by the moralities. The notion has not diminished much, and today the standard view seems to be that expressed by David Bevington:

> Shakespeare's acting company, too, was a direct descendant of those troupes that had acted morality plays all across Tudor England. The morality play thus became the chief dramatic link between the medieval stage and the Shakespearean.[2]

One would need courage, or perhaps more accurately something of Hotspur's rashness, to question an opinion so nearly unanimously held by respected scholars. One must certainly admit that their purposes are laudable: to challenge the old assumption that Renaissance drama derived from classical models, and to find instead native English prototypes for it. And where among medieval plays can one find any which more closely resemble Renaissance drama than the moralities? Only two considerations could have led me to suggest that it may be time to rethink this opinion: a desire to find among medieval plays more satisfactory ancestors for Renaissance drama, and an unavoidable recognition that morality plays were never part of the mainstream of medieval drama.

It was perhaps understandable that the first type of Renaissance plays to be connected with the moralities were the histories. These had no classical analogues and thus must have been of indigenous origin. And there were a few early Tudor plays such as Bale's *King Johan* and Skelton's *Magnificence* which seemed to represent a transitional stage between moralities and histories. The connection may, however, be more apparent than real. What we can safely do, I think, is see such plays as transitional between moralities and both court and school drama. Court drama was largely concerned with political ends, and the allegorical method of the moralities was suited to such ends, as well as a safer way of discussing them than the method of historical exampla chosen by the later history playwrights. And school drama, naturally concerned with instruction of youth, could profitably employ a didactic form which left no doubt about its message. But it is difficult to see clear morality characteristics in the professional history plays of the Renaissance. Although they may employ a bad counsellor and a good counsellor, not one of those plays follows the formula of moralities— a "mankind" figure being threatened or deserted by inimical forces and then saved by repentance and the intercession of the church. Even the history play which comes closest to such a formula, *The Famous Victories of Henry the Fifth*, seems to owe much more to *Robert the Devil* than it does to *Everyman*, emphasizing as it does the unexpected conversion and subsequent greatness of a hero who had shown little promise at the beginning of his career. More typical history plays, such as Lodge's *The Wounds of Civil War* or Heywood's *Edward IV*, have even less in common with moralities. But scholars have persisted in finding parallels which might indicate possible influence, and then assuming that the influence exists.[3] We seem to have come to the point, in short, at which a history play not showing morality roots is regarded as deficient, even if on other counts it may contain greatness. Tillyard was disappointed with Shakespeare's *Henry V* because it failed to fulfill his image of *respublica*.[4] In his brilliant book, *From Mankind to Marlowe*, Bevington gave only ten pages to *Edward II* because it did not exhibit morality characteristics, even though that play best exemplifies the traditions of alternation, doubling, and suppression.[5]

Despite the presence of a bad angel and a good angel in

Doctor Faustus, or of their counterparts the witches and Banquo in *Macbeth,* and other such superficial resemblances, the case for any appreciable influence by morality plays on Elizabethan tragedy seems still less convincing than for histories. The whole dramatic aims of the two genres are opposed. Most obviously, the morality protagonist, while he may backslide a bit, commits no *hamartia* which will lead inevitably to his downfall. In Elizabethan tragedy, of course, the tragic error and the subsequent fall are the chief concerns. Everyman dies, not because he has upset natural order, but simply because he is mortal. The imminence of death is emphasized only to show the pressing need for repentance on the part of Everyman. And all the moralities have a happy ending: man's physical fall being a given, the real subject of the moralities is the doctrine of repentance—how to be ready for the inevitable Death and thereby to win the eternal prize of salvation with the help of the church. (I shall return to this important distinction below.)

It should not be surprising, therefore, that the clearest influence of morality plays is to be seen in one type of comedy, that characteristic of school drama. Because most schoolmasters were required to have their boys perform at least one play a year, presumably before the parents, they understandably selected either Terence or plays in the morality tradition. If the boys did not learn to be diligent scholars from acting in *The Nice Wanton,* at least their parents could be satisfied that proper moral instruction was being given at school. Schoolmasters themselves seem to have been the chief writers of these plays, and certainly schoolchildren were the chief actors of them. As the later professional playwrights attended the schools which were producing such plays, it is reasonable to suppose that these moral comedies exerted some influence on professional comedies—at least those written for the children's companies. And we do find an occasional *Eastward Hoe!* to confirm that supposition. It may be, in fact, that the doctrine of repentance, so important to the morality plays, was a formative principle even in Shakespearean comedy.[6] But it is not clear that the morality plays were either needed or used as models in the construction of Shakespeare's comedies. The belief that they were, in any case, is not generally held by scholars.

I am not attempting to deny that parallels can be found between moralities and later drama; any number of ingenious scholarly publications have located such parallels. I wish to suggest merely that the morality plays were not really ideal models for any of the three major types of Elizabethan drama. If we could assume that there were no other more useful medieval models, and that morality plays were popular and widely known, we would be forced to conclude that the moralities, however unsatisfactory, must have been the medieval prototypes. Very likely the scholars who argue for "morality roots" operated under precisely those assumptions. I make it my task now to show that neither of those assumptions is essentially correct.

Part of the problem in our obtaining a clear perspective on the development of English drama is that we have, understandably, based our judgments on extant texts. David Bevington, in *From Mankind to Marlowe,* was led to base his conclusions upon plays "offered for acting" on the assumption that casting patterns published with them provided a "prima-facie inference" that they "were intended for the professional market."7 But those plays seem mostly to have been written by courtiers and schoolmasters, not the usual writers of plays for professional companies. In any case, one suspects that the plays were "offered for acting" by schoolboys; there would have been no profit in the few copies small professional troupes might purchase, but considerable profit if a hundred grammar schools decided to produce a particular play. Unlike the school plays, early professional plays, not being considered "art" and having no selling power by the names or prestige of their authors, were probably seldom printed. Later professional plays were printed for a new reading public, but not for the use of rival troupes. In short, the extant early Tudor interludes may not have been at all typical of the plays being acted by professionals, though they may still tell us much about principles of doubling, alternation, and suppression. Even more clearly, it now appears that of all the drama acted before 1500, it was the unusual, not the normal, which was preserved. For example, almost the only English mystery plays we have are those of the big cycles, even though the cycles represented a small percentage of mystery play productions. Of the rest of medieval drama, we have only five or six morality plays (three collected in one manuscript by the monks at Bury), a very few miracle plays, and half a dozen assorted fragments.

To what extent do these preserved texts reflect the kinds of drama actually performed in medieval England? And to what extent do their numbers indicate the relative frequency with which different types of plays were acted? Records of performance suggest that there is no close correlation on either score. For instance, we have about half of all the Corpus Christi cycles known to have been acted in England. But we have none of the many folk plays which can be certainly dated before 1500. And not only do the surviving manuscripts falsely suggest that Corpus Christi plays were the most common form of medieval drama, but they also suggest that the normal Corpus Christi play was a cycle play, which was not the case either. Only about one in three known Corpus Christi plays was a cycle, and possibly only one in six, depending on whether York, Chester, and Newcastle actually had cycle plays before 1500; the majority were single plays of uncertain or inconsistent subject matter. If we had all the pertinent records, the percentage of cycle plays would appear even smaller, for we are probably aware of all the cycle plays but of only a fraction of the single plays.

Combining the sparse information given in Chambers' *Mediaeval Stage* with the records collected for the Malone Society publications, we can arrive at a rough estimate of the percentages of different kinds of plays acted in medieval England. Before 1500, 16% of the plays with known subject or type were acted at Corpus Christi; 26% were non-cycle mysteries acted mostly at Christmas and Easter; 26% were saints' lives and other miracle plays; 31% were folk plays—almost double the Corpus Christi plays and far more in number of performances; of morality plays, there is not a single recorded performance in the middle ages. A more revealing set of statistics comes from three contiguous counties whose records have been systematically collected, Lincolnshire, Norfolk, and Suffolk. There, before 1500, we find six Corpus Christi plays, none of them cycles; six other non-cycle mysteries; thirteen saints' lives; eighteen folk plays; and of course no moralities (in the very counties where moralities were collected and supposedly acted).[8] *The Castle of Perseverance* seems to have been written with Lincoln in mind, but while we have clear reference to fifteen different plays acted at Lincoln, some of them many times, *The Castle of Perseverance* is not among them.[9]

Their total absence from the records does not necessarily mean that moralities were never acted, but it does suggest that they could not have represented a very popular or significant segment of medieval drama. In our laudable desire to find medieval roots for Renaissance drama we are, I suspect, looking in the wrong direction. Perhaps we ought to be looking at the kinds of plays we now know to have been most commonly acted in the middle ages—folk plays and miracle plays. The shortage of extant texts makes the task rather difficult, but we know enough about both types of drama that it should be possible to see some very clear areas of influence on Renaissance comedy, tragedy, and history play.

Professional comedy was in existence very much longer than was previously thought, at least as early as the fourteenth century. It is not likely to have been imitative of classical comedy, which seems not to have affected English drama before the sixteenth century. And it certainly was not influenced by the comic episodes of the much later Corpus Christi cycles, any influence being more likely in the other direction. Whatever it was like, early professional comedy had to be written for two and three man troupes, or four at the most. One would expect simple situation comedy, something on the order of the later *Johan the Husband.* The fragment dated about 1300 known as *Clerico et Puella,* for two or perhaps three actors, may be an early example.

Thematically, Renaissance comedy seems to be closely related to the medieval folk plays. The relationship has been noted before, but usually in a roundabout way. Most recently, Robert Potter has outlined the evidence supporting a strong influence of the mummers' plays on morality drama.[10] Potter then finds an influence of the moralities on subsequent playwrights, including Ben Jonson. But were the moralities not considered to be intermediaries, the influence of the mummers' plays on Elizabethan comedy would be much easier to see. The general pattern of a threat of disaster followed by redemption and rebirth is observable in most Renaissance comedies. In some, there is the magical "cure" effected by a counterpart of the doctor (the ghost of Jack in *The Old Wives' Tale,* for instance, or Oberon with his love-juice in *Midsummer Night's Dream*). In others, there is even an apparently miraculous resurrection from death (Sebastian in *Twelfth Night,* Claudio in *Measure for Measure,* Imogen and Posthumus in *Cymbeline,*

Hermione in *Winter's Tale*). It is not my business to develop such influences here, but only to suggest that they exist.

Perhaps the clearest medieval influence on Renaissance drama is that of the saints' lives on history plays. The miracles were the most numerous, popular, and widely varied of medieval religious dramas. They also had the longest tradition among the fully developed plays: the earliest performance of Christian drama on record in England is of a St. Catherine play before 1119 at Dunstable, and the last saints' lives were still being performed at the beginning of Elizabeth's reign.11 Almost none of the many British saints' lives plays are extant, but we know by numerous continental examples that they were structurally very like the Elizabethan history plays. The only surviving play about a British saint, the Cornish *Life of St. Meriasek* of about 1475, will demonstrate the structural similarity.12 This play dramatizes four periods in the life of Meriasek, including his connection with Cambourne, where the play was acted. Alternating with these four episodes are dramatizations of stories from the *Legenda Aurea* about St. Silvester and the Emperor Constantine, and the interlude of St. Mary and the Woman's Son. Thus we find a main plot alternating with a sub-plot which parallels and mirrors the main plot but is not closely related to it except by one anachronistic connection— much in the manner of *Edward III* or Shakespeare's *Henry IV* or almost any other Elizabethan history play.13 Like the authors who followed him, this playwright remains true to the spirit of history while feeling free to rearrange events, reassign action to different personages, telescope history and introduce anachronisms. He develops a variety of character types, from humble priest to raging tyrant. And he provides exciting action: two pitched battles and two fights with dragons, among other events, along with the threatened mass murder of 3140 innocent children to provide Constantine's famous bloodbath. There is not as much action, perhaps, as in Marlowe's *Massacre at Paris,* but it is considerably more exciting than *Mundus et Enfans.*

Even the Elizabethan history plays which seem most likely to be descended from the moralities would, I should think, have derived a good deal more that was useful in terms of character, structure, and thematic development from such miracle plays. Clearly, a play so important to later historical drama as *The Famous Victories of Henry the Fifth* owes more to the typical miracle play, with its emphasis on conversion and subsequent miracles wrought by the reformed hero, than it does to morality plays. And surely *Woodstock, Edward II,* and *Richard II* have more in common with *King Robert of Sicily* than with *The Castle of Perseverance.* Each of these histories deals with an English monarch who, like King Robert, is brought low by his own willfulness and lack of humility. One might add that the story of Robert of Sicily almost inevitably brings to mind Shakespeare's version of *King Lear,* where for the same reasons Lear is reduced to rags and the company of fools and madmen if not to being made into a fool himself. *King Lear,* of course, has many additional parallels with the mummers' plays, both in structure and in specific details of action, from an old man's legacies to his ungrateful children to the mock trial and the trial by combat and to the miraculous cure and "resurrection" of Lear and Gloucester.

But the two kinds of influence, saints' lives and mummers' plays, would seem ultimately to be a single source of inspiration. For the saints' lives may have been as popular as they were at least partly because they gave a specifically Christian sanction to the action of the mummers' plays. That is, the stories of miracles performed by saints following their martyrdoms provide firm evidence of a resurrection more significant (because eternal) than the standard physical resurrection of Pickle Herring and his like in the mummers' plays. Miracle plays perform the same ritual purpose, in short, but they also incorporate the Christian beliefs which turn the seasonal miracle into an everlasting one.

When one considers that the saints' lives continued until well into the sixteenth century and that the folk plays never did completely die out, one can see a continuous line of development from medieval to high Renaissance drama, even though most of the extant early Tudor plays are court or school plays. A drama such as Medwall's *Fulgens et Lucres,* while probably written for private performance and requiring more actors than a professional troupe could muster, seems to borrow ideas both from the professional drama with its alternating serious and comic episodes (compare even a late play such as *The Changeling*), and the folk drama with its mummers' dance, challenges, rivalry for the Bessie, mock combat, and apparent death and resurrection. What is harder to find is any clear medieval model for Renaissance tragedy. Nowhere in the records is there any reference to performance of a tragedy in the Middle Ages either by professionals or by amateurs. In fact, I am not aware of any specific evidence that tragedy was performed in Britain earlier than 1554, at Magdalen College, Oxford.[14] Are we therefore forced to conclude that Seneca was the chief influence on Renaissance tragedy? Or that the only medieval influences were the moralities, despite their virtual nonexistence and, with their aim of promulgating the sacrament of penance,[15] singularly inappropriate as models for tragedy of character employing the method of exempla rather than allegory?

I should like to suggest that we are not reduced to either expedient, and that there is abundant evidence, if I interpret it correctly, that tragedy was being acted in England from the twelfth right into the sixteenth century. Unfortunately, the texts which would prove the contention have all been destroyed, and the argument will have to be from antecedent probability. I am referring to the Thomas à Becket plays.

Although the records of medieval drama are disappointingly meager except in the case of the big Corpus Christi and Whitsun cycles and although the records of only a few counties have thus far been systematically collected, it is becoming clear that more plays on Thomas à Becket were performed than on any other subject except the traditional Christmas and Easter plays.[16] There was a play on St. Thomas in London as early as 1182, shortly after his death.[17] The earliest recorded drama in East Anglia was a Thomas à Becket play at Bishop's Lynn in 1385.[18] The earliest play with a known title in Kent was on St. Thomas, at Ham in 1453; Canterbury, as one might expect, presented St. Thomas plays yearly over a long period.[19] And there were others, as at Norwich, Bungay, and Mildenhall, at least as late as 1539.[20]

After Henry VIII personally and firmly demoted Becket from the ranks of saints, these plays understandably disappeared—along with virtually every other English miracle drama. But even without an extant text, it is possible to surmise with considerable confidence what the St. Thomas plays were like; that is, we can presuppose as accurately as we could about plays on Abraham and Isaac had we no extant mysteries on that subject. For it happens that, while we have numerous versions of the life of St. Thomas, from the *South English Legendary* to an

Icelandic version, they are all remarkably similar even when not dependent upon one another; and these lives would necessarily have been the sources for the plays.

The lives of St. Thomas differ from other medieval saints' lives in two important respects: they are specific and historical rather than fabulous and general, and they are not chiefly concerned either with a wondrous conversion or with miracles performed after that conversion or related to the saint's death. What these lives do present is the story of a man who was good, brilliant, and promising from early childhood and who rose to be second in temporal power and chief in spiritual power in the kingdom. From this position of eminence, he was forced to choose between church and state during the power struggle of Henry II's reign, and his choice resulted in his being murdered by supporters of the king. The materials presented in the sources are thus ready-made for tragedy: the protagonist falls, not because he is mortal like Everyman or because he is overwhelmed by external forces but because, after considerable soul-searching, he makes a crucial moral choice and abides by it. Like Antigone, his choice may be the right one (at least in the view of his biographers), but it still will cost him his life and he knows that it will do so. And also like Antigone, Becket wins his victory by sacrificing his life. The story is a tragedy in the finest and most uplifting tradition. It is difficult to imagine how a dramatist, working from such material, could have distorted it into any form other than tragedy. It is even harder to imagine that every playwright in the middle ages who worked with this story was equally determined to turn it from what it was into something different. One is almost forced to the conclusion that at least some of the Thomas à Becket plays were genuine tragedies— not mechanical *de casibus* dramas but tragedies of character hinging on a *hamartia* and culminating in victory through death.

One cannot, of course, go beyond the hypothesis until— and if—an authentic Thomas à Becket play is discovered. But if these plays were, as seems to me likely, true tragedies, we have a tradition of English tragedy extending over a period of 360 years and to within fifteen years of the first recorded tragedy in 1554. It is possible, then, that English tragedy was a continuously developing form from the twelfth century all the way through the Renaissance. At any rate, it no longer seems safe to echo earlier critics who contended that there was no medieval dramatic tragedy.

As it is more convenient to argue for dramatic influences if one has the texts before him, the few moralities we have seem more fruitful than the many miracles we do not have. And if both moralities and later drama happened to be influenced by now-extinct folk plays, the appearance will be that it was the extant moralities which influenced the later plays. We are not likely at this date to uncover dramatic manuscripts which will prove otherwise: the mummers' plays may never have been written down at all, and the Becket plays probably all suffered the fate of other "idolatrous" literature at the Reformation— Becket being more likely than any other saint to have plays about him destroyed. For he was not merely a latter-day saint but one who achieved martyrdom by refusing to recognize the temporal powers of an English monarch in spiritual matters. But we should keep in mind that both folk and miracle plays had a very long and widespread popular tradition, existing long before any morality plays were written and outlasting them as well. There is certainly no need to see moralities as links between medieval and Renaissance drama on chronological grounds— nor, so far as I can see, any need to do so on thematic or structural grounds.

NOTES

1 A. P. Rossiter, *Woodstock, a Moral History* (London: Chatto and Windus, 1946); E. M. W. Tillyard, *Shakespeare's History Plays* (New York: Macmillan, 1947); and Irving Ribner, *The English History Play in the Age of Shakespeare* (Princeton: Princeton Univ. Press, 1957).

2 David Bevington, *Medieval Drama* (Boston: Houghton Mifflin, 1975), p. 795.

3 See, for example, Robert Potter's list of "stock episodes" in Shakespeare's plays which may be derived from morality plays, in *The English Morality Play* (London: Routledge and Kegan Paul, 1975), p. 124.

4 Tillyard, pp. 306-10.

5 David Bevington, *From Mankind to Marlowe* (Cambridge: Harvard Univ. Press, 1962), pp. 234-44.

6 See Dolora G. Cunningham, "The Doctrine of Repentance as a Formal Principle in Some Elizabethan Plays," Diss. Stanford 1954.

7 Bevington, *From Mankind to Marlowe*, p. 62.

8 There was a Whitsun cycle at Norwich, but not certainly before 1534. I am indebted for this information to JoAnna Dutka, who is collecting the medieval Norwich records for *Records of Early English Drama.*

9 Stanley J. Kahrl, *Records of Plays and Players in Lincolnshire,* Malone Society Collections, VIII (Oxford: Oxford Univ. Press, 1974), pp. 21-69.

10 Potter, pp. 10-16.

11 E. K. Chambers, *The Mediaeval Stage* (Oxford: Oxford Univ. Press, 1903), II, 366, 394.

12 Markham Harris, trans., *The Life of St. Meriasek* (Washington: Catholic University of America, 1977).

13 For a brief description of elements common to Elizabethan history plays, see John Wasson, "In Defense of *King Henry VIII,*" *Research Studies,* 32 (1964), 261-76.

14 Chambers, II, 250.

15 Potter, pp. 16-20.

16 Because we have no assurance that there was a typical non-cycle Corpus Christi play, I am assuming that these plays could be on any convenient subject, as in the case of the Noah play at Boston in 1519. If the Corpus Christi plays were on a single subject, they would outnumber St. Thomas plays.

17 Chambers, II, 380.

18 John Wasson and David Galloway, *Records of Plays and Players in Norfolk and Suffolk,* Malone Society Collections, XI (Oxford: Oxford Univ. Press, 1979).

19 Giles Dawson, *Records of Plays and Players in Kent,* Malone Society Collections, VII (Oxford: Oxford Univ. Press, 1965), pp. 92, 191-200.

20 Wasson and Galloway, *passim.*

Anti-Semitism and the English Mystery Plays

Stephen Spector

The general tone of the medieval English mystery plays is affirmative. The early religious drama conveys a triumphant vision of temporal and cosmic symmetry that was designed to comfort and sustain the believing Christian. Yet there also exists within the plays a mood of unrelenting hostility, and this is directed in large part toward the disbeliever, the Jew. The mystery plays comprise, in fact, one of the most vehemently anti-Jewish genres in the history of English literature. I propose in this article to explore the character of this anti-Jewishness and to speculate about its function. I shall argue that the perspectives and dynamics of the drama parallel those of classic and clinical anti-Semitism: that the drama not only distorts and stereotypes the Jew, but more particularly that it assigns to the Jew the unwanted aspects of the Christian community and consequently execrates him.

I offer this analysis both in order to address an important issue that has been too often ignored, and also to attempt a more temperate and adequate assessment than those which now exist. This study is not an indictment of a single group, but rather a consideration of human failings. I describe here a mode of self-justification and self-defense that can operate in all men, Jews as well as Christians. Hannah Arendt, Jacob Katz, and others have demonstrated Jewish complicity in historical religious recriminations,[1] and this must be explored, as must Christian offenses, in the hope that both can be better understood and therefore avoided.

Most of the critics who discuss the anti-Semitism of the religious drama do so with an indignation that impedes accurate appraisal. Their work is neither systematic nor analytical, but only loosely descriptive and condemnatory. For example, Ed-

328

ward N. Calisch says in *The Jew in English Literature* that in the New Testament plays "there is no accusation [against the Jews] too horrible, no charge too monstrous to prevent its being given credence and repetition."2 M. J. Landa says in *The Jew in Drama* that "in every possible way the representation of the medieval drama vilified the Jew," and he adds that the Jews "were fair game for the merciless sport of the ignorant people whom the ecclesiastical writers of the Mysteries and the Miracle plays were anxious to impress. The convention of the Jew of the stage was thus born amidst fanaticism, intolerance and ignorance. . . ."3 These critics are right to condemn the anti-Semitism of the plays, but they are mistaken in their assessment of the insult and, in Landa's case, in the attribution of motive. The Jews in many of the plays are demeaned, but not in "every possible way." Rather, their vices are precisely and consistently delineated, and the nature of these vices reveals much about the plays themselves. To ascribe these stage-portraits to fanaticism, intolerance, and ignorance, as Landa does, is to ignore the significance of the Jew to the drama—and to the community that wrote, produced, and attended the plays.

That significance can be discovered by comparing the anti-Jewishness of the plays with the dominant psychoanalytic theory about real-life anti-Semitism. This conception of anti-Semitism was first tacitly suggested by Sigmund Freud, and has since been reiterated by historians, social commentators, and clinical psychologists. In essence, it portrays the anti-Semite as a person who condemns in the Jew those qualities, real or attributed, that he cannot tolerate in his experience or in himself.4 The anti-Semite attempts to externalize inner conflicts and to relieve anxieties by unconsciously scapegoating the Jew.5 He seizes on the Jew because the Jew is the available or culturally-defined target, the suspect, alien element in the community, and he projects onto the Jew dangers that the anti-Semite finds threatening. In this way, the anti-Semite's personal responsibility for his problems is reduced, and the problems themselves are readily located in an external and convenient repository: the Jew. The attributes perceived in the Jew are a function of the anti-Semitism, and will therefore reveal more about the anti-Semite than about the Jew.6

In *Anti-Semite and Jew,* Sartre arrives at many of these same insights by examining the motivations and perceptions of anti-Semites in twentieth-century France. Despite its narrow frame of reference, Sartre's analysis is widely applicable, and it serves as a convenient bridge to a discussion of the anti-Jewishness in the medieval English mystery plays. Sartre argues that the modern French anti-Semite simplifies the fearful complexities of his life by localizing all threats in the Jew. He can then extirpate his doubts and fears by execrating the Jew. Sartre's anti-Semite, fearing a rational encounter with the human condition, seeks to denigrate intellect and reason. He therefore seizes on the Jew's putative rationality and transforms it into a vice. He sees the Jew as unassimilable precisely because the Jew is no more than a reasoner, incapable of accepting truths on instinct, as a "real" Frenchman does. The anti-Semite believes that the Jew is incomplete in this way, that he is inherently different in kind from other men, and that this explains the Jew's evil.

A remarkably similar pattern occurs in the fifteenth-century mystery play cycles, which make the Jew represent precisely and only those evils that were most threatening to the goals of the plays. By rejecting the Jew, the auditor rejected the threats, which were the impediments to faith and salvation. Moreover, the particular form in which this happens in the drama closely parallels Sartre's analysis. Sartre's modern anti-Semite conceives of the Jew as unassimilable into the secular community because the Jew is a mere reasoner, incapable of accepting truth on *instinct*. The medieval playwrights also portrayed the Jew as unassimilable, in this case into the Christian community, because they too saw the Jew as entrapped in reason and thus as incapable of accepting Truth on *faith*. For the dramatist as for Sartre's anti-Semite, the Jew's inability to perceive higher truth makes him inherently different, deficient, and therefore dangerous. Both associate the Jew with the devil, and for both, Jewish-Christian differences are portrayed not in terms of a conflict of interest, but rather of the conflict between Evil and Good. I do not suggest that the dramatists and their audiences participated in the pathology and cowardice of Sartre's anti-Semite. To the contrary, I believe that the motivation for the anti-Jewishness of the plays, so far as it can be inferred, was pedantic and ideological. But I do propose that the similarity between these medieval and modern perceptions discloses a parallel function that the Jew is made to serve for both—though this is in one instance doctrinal and literary, and in the other unconscious and affective. Sartre says that if Jews did not exist the anti-Semite would have to invent them. In fifteenth-century England there were no Jews, or few at best, and the dramatists did invent them, so to speak, by consciously selecting specific models of the Jew, and then altering them to serve the didactic purposes of the plays.

Though most of the characters in the mystery plays are ethnically Jewish, comparatively few are referred to as Jews. "Jew," as the word is most often employed in the plays, is virtually a technical term, denoting spiritual rather than "racial," ethnic, or cultural identity.7 The Jew, as identified by dialogue, stage directions, and speaker headings, is a figure who utterly rejects Jesus' divinity and fervently opposes any alteration of the Old Law. Caiaphas and Annas, the high priests of the law, are frequently referred to as "the Jews," and the men who seize, torment, and crucify Jesus are specifically labelled *Iudeii* in the N-town and Chester cycles. Speaker headings call the correlative figures *Tortores* and *Milites* in the Towneley and York plays (though York has Iudeii accompany the soldiers who seize Jesus), but these characters are evidently Jews as well: they repeatedly defend "oure lawe" and "Oure Sabott day," and they accuse Jesus of boasts, lies, and heresy.8 In each of the cycles, the Jews are made to bear full responsibility for virtually every aspect of Jesus' death, even the part played by Pilate's soldiers according to the gospel accounts. In the Towneley plays, for example, Mary characterizes the Crucifixion as strife between the Jews and Jesus (23/390ff), and even the risen Jesus blames only "the Iues" (26/251, 271, 274).

The Jews in the plays are so eager to preserve the Old Law that they disallow any possibility of a divine intervention capable of altering the Law. They reject the idea of an intersection of the transcendent and the everyday: for them, such events are restricted to the past and captured in the Old Testament. In the present they insist on the inviolability of the customary and the traditional. To this end they rationalize the miraculous. Their zeal carries them to grotesque extremes, even to the point of dancing gleefully around the cross in the Crucifixion plays, and their brutality resembles the behavior of the demons, who, like the Jews, seek to defend the law. As Rybald says to Sathanas in the Towneley Harrowing of Hell play, "thou and the Iues

were at assent" (25/173).[9] In defending their law, the Jews
are implacable enemies of the plan of salvation, and they are
joined in this by Saracens[10] (with whom they are sometimes
confused), completing the theological panorama of the contest
for men's souls. The Jews are less human beings than demonic
forces of destruction, different in kind from men who are capable of faith. Their disbelief of miracle and divine truth reveals
them to be deficient, their sadistic energy shows them to be
dangerous. The Jew of the mystery plays is, in short, the same
dehumanized force of Evil, the same localized agency of threat
as the Jew perceived by Sartre's modern anti-Semite.

This shared perception spanning five hundred years reflects,
as I have said, a common function. The Jew in the mystery
plays is not a generalized bogeyman incarnating all conceivable
vices. Nor is he an extension of historical anti-Semitic stereotypy: he does not poison wells, spread plague, or murder children, as popular medieval superstition so often accused him of
doing. Rather, he is made to represent the specific evil that the
plays themselves portray as most threatening to the Christian
and to the purposes of the drama. Most importantly, the Jew
is made to embody an entrenched disbelief based on blind adherence to the reasonable and the natural. Good figures also
experience disbelief, and for them too doubt is founded on
reason (e.g., the reasonable conviction that God cannot be man,
or death life). Repeatedly and urgently the plays demonstrate
that this quality, reasoned doubt, is a profound threat to the
Christian, and that it must give way to faith when confronted
with the divine. This is, in fact, the paradigm of salvation and
the central structural dynamic of the New Testament plays.
The good figures invariably do move from doubt to faith—
most often through the agency of miracle—while the Jews,
consisting of doubt and defiance, do not and cannot. Quite the
contrary, the Jews take action to prevent the general transmission of faith, which, as they admit, would be inevitable except
for their intervention. By making the Jew embody the qualities
that most endanger the Christian, the plays isolate, externalize,
and repudiate the impediments to salvation. At the same time,
they portray the converted Christian as wholly purified of the
evil attributed to the Jew.

Both the structural movement from doubt to faith and the
question of anti-Semitism are absent in the Old Testament plays.

There, the structural dynamic involves a different contest, between obedience and disobedience to God's will. Lucifer establishes the pattern of disobedience, which is then repeated by Eve, Adam, Cain, and others. Internal struggle does occur, notably in the Abraham plays, but there too the crux is usually obedience rather than belief. Even Uxor Noah's refusal to board the ark is presented more in terms of scabrous disobedience to Noah than disbelief in God's power. There is no conflict between Jewish and Christian postures in these plays, and this is part and parcel of the drama's conception of Old Testament figures. Patriarchs, kings, and prophets are respectfully treated, and the virtue of their obedience to God's will is acknowledged. But this respect for the Hebrews is frequently mitigated by an implicit disrespect for Judaism, for the virtuous Old Testament figures are not Jewish; rather, they are explicitly made to avow Christianity. This results, in part, from the nature of dramatic presentation, in which the figural significance of the Old Testament characters and events has, in the absence of narrative commentary, to be conveyed by the *dramatis personae* themselves.[11] Old Testament scenes are often crafted so as to suggest Christian analogy, and Old Testament characters are made to speak of the Trinity, prefiguration, and Christian salvation—though they sometimes perceive these concepts only dimly. This process of disclosing the mystery thought to be inherent in the Old Testament reaches its climax in the Prophets plays, in which Old Testament figures, through Christian exposition of Old Testament texts, declare their faith in Christ. All accord "in on,"[12] as Amon Rex says at the close of the N-town *Jesse Root:* all are Christians. In this atmosphere of anticipation and affirmation there is no need to focus on doubt, and it is only after Jesus' birth that the movement from doubt to faith becomes central.

In the New Testament plays, doubt in both good men and bad is generally founded on reasoned observation of everyday experience. Joseph exemplifies this in the good man. He does not, for example, believe that a virgin can be pregnant. In Play 10 of the N-town Cycle, he warns against his January-May marriage to Mary, and her pregnancy two plays later seems to him to confirm his good sense. Mary's explanation of the Salutation and Conception only enrages him further: it is bad enough that she has cuckolded him, he says, must she blame an angel as well? "It was sum boy began þis game" (f. 68ʳ), he quite reasonably concludes, and only the miraculous appearance of an angel dissuades him. Joseph must suspend his disbelief, or more properly, his belief, and accept the selective transfiguration and abrogation of the old laws, physical and divine. He can then move from doubt to faith, with no harm done beyond the comedy.

In Joseph's experience as in the experience of the midwives and later the disciples, miracle allows the necessary spiritual movement toward faith and the New Law. In several of the early New Testament plays, this movement is facilitated by divine resolution of the apparently irreconcilable. As a result, good figures are not forced to choose between the Old Law and the New, but are instead allowed a transition between them. In the plays dealing with Mary's marriage, for example, the commandment to be fruitful and multiply, which is presented as an essential requirement under the Old Law, is challenged by Mary, who has vowed to be chaste. The bishop is perplexed, but the conundrum is resolved when Joseph, too old to "rage" with a woman, is selected by the miraculous flowering of his staff to wed Mary. The Virgin Birth then reconciles the demands of the Old Law to the requirements of the New by providing both childbirth and chastity, while fulfilling its primary function of bringing Jesus into the world. Similarly, the N-town Debate of the Four Daughters of God has Justice and Truth, who represent the Old Law, portray their disagreement with Peace and Mercy, representing the New Law, as mutually destructive. "Twey contraryes mow not togedyr dwelle," says Truth (f. 59^v), but "contraryes" are reconciled in this and many other plays, and the Daughters "acorde" when Filius offers to die for man's sake. The Old Law is allowed a dignified compromise so that it may give way peacefully to the New.

This mood of reconcilement through miracle is totally absent in the treatment of the Jews. The Jews will have no compromise, and so they are allowed no dignity. They are made to reject Jesus because of blind devotion to the Old Law, fierce self-interest, and an adherence to the natural and the reasonable that is so rigid as to be unnatural and irrational. "God lene you grace to knaw/ the sothe all way" (26/147), says the converted Centurion to the Jews in the Towneley Cycle, but they lack this grace and so discredit his account of the miracles that accompanied the Crucifixion, as they do all of Jesus' miracles. The blindness attributed to the Pharisees in *Matthew* and to Synagoga in art[13] is expressed in the drama as the Jews' blindness to visible proof of Jesus' divinity. When in Chester XIII Caecus tells the Pharisees that Jesus has healed him of blindness, they demonstrate their own inability to see by angrily disbelieving him. Secundus Phariseus says (205-09):

> O cursed caytyffe, yll moote thow thee!
> Would thou have us his disciples to bee?
> No, no! Moyses disciples binne wee,
> for God with him did speake.
> But whence this is, I never knewe.[14]

The Jews' faith is arrested in the Old Testament, to which they are so loyal that they blindly reject the basic tenet of the New— i.e., that God could become man. Jesus in the same play says to Primus and Secundus Iudeus:

> But you beleeve not as you seene,
> for of my sheepe yee ne beene. (243-44)

To put this in Sartre's terms, the Jews are deficient, for they cannot perceive higher truth; they are different in kind (of a different flock) from those who are capable of an understanding that transcends reason.[15]

The Jews are repeatedly made to hear of and witness miracle only to reject it. Later in Chester XIII, for example, Jesus miraculously vanishes from their midst. The Jews are confused but not impressed, and their response is to threaten violence. This contrasts sharply with a similar episode in the Peregrini plays, taken from *Luke*, in which Jesus vanishes suddenly from the presence of Cleophas and Luke. There, the miracle has the opposite effect: it dispels all doubt, and Cleophas and Luke accept Jesus' divinity. The Jews, however, find another explanation for Jesus' miracles: sorcery. Primus Tortor in the Towneley *Coliphizacio*, for example, says Jesus raised Lazarus through "wychcraft," and Cayphas in the York and Towneley Resurrection plays tells the Centurion that dead men rose during the Crucifixion through "socery." In the York Cycle the Jews repeatedly call Jesus a "warlow," which the *OED* defines not only as a wizard, but also as a devil and an oath-breaker. This evidences a curious reversal in which the Jews accuse Jesus of their own faults. They suggest that he is allied to the devil, and they frequently refer to him as a traitor. Moreover, they accuse him of being deficient: they tell him during his trials that he lacks, variously, sense, language, sanity, and the proper manners one should exhibit before a king! On a few occasions, the evil figures even call Jesus a Jew.

The Iudei who torture and crucify Jesus participate fully in the Pharisees' hatred of Jesus. They too decry Jesus' supposed boastfulness in claiming that he could destroy and raise the temple, and his heresy in violating "oure dere Sabott day" (York 34/23). V. A. Kolve, in his landmark study *The Play Called Corpus Christi,* speaks of these figures as "Natural Men," a term consistent with my contention that their perception is limited to the customary and the reasonable. But I must disagree with Kolve's theory that they are so concerned with the discharge of stored-up energy that they are indifferent to their victim. This analysis denies the Jews a motive, and what is more, it de-Judaizes them, thereby losing sight of the doctrinal conflict that runs through the plays. The Jews torment Jesus for religious reasons, and their actions are keyed to their perception of his crimes. They want to teach him the consequences of heresy, as Primus Miles says in York 34:

> I am sente fro sir Pilate with pride,
> To lede þis ladde oure lawes to abide. (6-7)

The Jews' mock "Hail" lyrics, for example, which in the gospels are spoken by Pilate's soldiers, are obviously meant to punish Jesus for what the Jews take to be his royal aspirations. Far from being indifferent, the Iudeii seek to cause Jesus pain, as their lowering the cross into the mortice in the York *Crucifixion* illustrates. Primus Miles says in that play:

> Nowe raise hym nemely for þe nonys,
> And sette hym be þis mortas heere.
> And latte hym falle in alle at ones,
> For certis þat payne schall haue no pere. (219-22)

The fact that they are able to torture Jesus is in itself their way of proving that he has no power to perform miracles.

"What! deuyll, whome schulde we drede?" declares Primus Miles in the York *Calvary* (286), and this ironically codifies the posture of the Jews: they dread no one, not even God. They defend God's laws but they abandon God himself, and in the end they deny truth as well. When the sepulchre guards tell Pilate that Jesus has risen, Cayphas and Annas arrange a cover-up, as in *Matthew.* Whether or not the York and Towneley

Cayphas accepts the Resurrection as miracle—and the matter seems to have little importance for him at this point—his response is a fear for the law that is not expressed in *Matthew:*

> Allas! þanne is our lawes lorne
> for euere-mare. (York 38/387-88)

The guards are then paid to keep silent in a last dishonest attempt to protect the law. As Pilate says at the end of the York play, "All is lesyng" (448).

The Judas of the mystery plays is sometimes said to have been the model for later stage depictions of the Jew, and one might expect him to be one of the "Jews" in the cycles, but he is not. He is not referred to as a Jew and he does not share the motives of the figures who are so designated. Judas' concern is with money, a feature in historical stereotypy, but not one of the concerns of the Jews in the cycles. He wants to make a good bargain, and in this he is similar to the guards of the sepulchre. Judas, like the guards, is not exercised by the defense of the Old Law, as the Jews are. And the Jews, for their part, are not concerned with money, only with destroying Jesus and safeguarding the law. Judas differs from the Jews also in that he is not, finally, fixed in disbelief. In the end he acknowledges Jesus' innocence and his own guilt, and in the York version he makes a statement made by no Jew: "I knawe my trespasse and my gilte" (32/211). In York, he refers to Cayphas and Annas as "þe Jues," as if to differentiate himself from them, and he even pleads with the Jews to free Jesus. This is an astonishing turnabout, for it makes Judas, the arch-traitor, ask men to release God from the vengeance imposed by law.

The treatment of time in the drama made the Jew a present reality, even in a nation from which he had been expelled centuries before. As the famous anachronisms of the plays attest, the past in the drama is invested with the accoutrements of the present. Moreover, the present is colored by its association with the past. The present invades the past in the Christianization of the Hebrews and the demystification of mystery. And the experience and significance of the past informs the present, ineluctably altering both. Cultural and racial distinctions are thereby effaced so that, for example, the shepherds in the splendid *Secunda Pastorum* are neither first-century Israelites nor fifteenth-century Englishmen, but rather they are both. The believing man exists anytime, anyplace, as does the disbeliever, the "Jew." The drama's Jew represents the spirit of disbelief, self-interest, and spiritual blindness, and this could exist in the fifteenth century as in the first, in the community and in the individual. The drama portrayed the Jew as despicable in order to compel the auditor to expel the Jew from himself.

The abasement of the Jew in the drama thus seems to have been essentially pedagogical, and one can say in addition that it was traditional and based on venerable *auctorité*. It was an expression through familiar literary devices of a long-sanctioned motif that derives ultimately from the New Testament. Jesus' allusions to the blindness of the Pharisees come primarily from *Matthew,* the use of the word "Jew" to designate Jesus' enemies is chiefly from *John,* and the Jews' supposed choice of law above faith is codified in *Romans.*16 Antagonistic aspects of the New Testament were selected and exaggerated so as to distort and reduce the Jew to the level of a one-dimensional figure. Projection operated here not necessarily as a defense mechanism, but as a literary technique, in order to create personification-allegory. The drama's Jew is, essentially and finally, a personification. Like many other medieval personifications, he is a literal type who embodies an imbalance of a particular quality, in this case reasoned doubt.17 He is depersonalized, not really a historical figure at all, nor even a member of an ethnic group, and this explains his occasional confusion with Saracens as well as Romans and medieval Englishmen. Historicity is far less important than doctrine in the plays, and the integrity of the historical Jew (like that of the Old Testament Hebrew) is sacrificed to the imperatives of doctrine.

Leo Spitzer tells us in "Classical and Christian Ideas of World Harmony" that the medieval mind "knew hatred only on dogmatic, not on racial, grounds."18 Centainly the drama's reverential treatment of the pious Old Testament Hebrews (though not of their Judaism) disallows the possibility of anti-Semitism in a racial sense. Instead, the hostility in the plays is doctrinally based. It is directed not so much toward a people as toward disbelief. The central locus of evil in the New Testament plays is the disbelief itself, and the Jew's grotesquery reflects the dramatists' perception of that disbelief.

Thus, the drama's portrait of the Jew is impersonal, and is more revealing of the world-view of the plays than of perceptions about actual Jews. This as we have seen, is equally true of the real-life pathological anti-Semite. In this regard the religious plays convey a lesson about one aspect of faith to which their authors were presumably themselves insensitive: the anti-Jewishness of the plays testifies that any faith, when predicated on absolute pre-emptive denial of challenge or alternatives, is a form of authoritarianism, and can culminate in intolerance. The drama's Jew may have been depicted for purposes of pious instruction, but it is the nature of intolerance to make victims of all parties involved, so that even intended piety can be made to mimic pathology. The modern scholar and teacher is morally obligated to confront this fact in the plays. Only then can he accept on their own merits the many aspects of the drama that delight, instruct, and confirm man's faith in forgiveness and providential design.[19]

NOTES

[1] Hannah Arendt, *The Origins of Totalitarianism* (1951; rpt. New York, 1973), pp. xi-xvi *et passim;* Jacob Katz, *Exclusiveness and Tolerance, Jewish-Gentile Relations in Modern Times* (New York, 1962).

[2] Edward N. Calisch, *The Jew in English Literature* (1909; rpt. Port Washington, New York, 1969), p. 20.

[3] M. J. Landa, *The Jew in Drama* (1926; rpt. Port Washington, New York, 1968), pp. 38, 10-11. Montagu Frank Modder in *The Jew in the Literature of England* (Philadelphia, 1944), p. 15, repeats Landa's sentiments and language without crediting him: "In every manner possible, the players vilified the Jewish characters. . . ." This illustrates the unusual degree of indebtedness in this area; contentions have often been echoed uncritically for several generations of scholarship.

[4] Freud, in a digression in *Moses and Monotheism,* trans. Katherine Jones (1939; rpt. New York, 1967), pp. 116-17, proposes that anti-Semitism is a projected anti-Christianity that the anti-Semite cannot accept in himself. Several writers follow Freud in this—e.g., Maurice Samuel in *The Great Hatred* (1940; rpt. New York, 1941), pp. 127-28, Jacques Maritain in *Redeeming the Time* (1943; rpt. London, 1946), p. 126, and Edward H. Flannery in *The Anguish of the Jews* (1965; rpt. New York and London, 1971), pp. 271-72. Clinical investigation of the problem, though less dogmatic about the ways anti-Semitism can be expressed, has in several instances reached similar conclusions about the psychodynamics involved. See, for example, Nathan W. Ackerman and Marie Jahoda, *Antisemitism and Emotional Disorder* (New York, 1950), *passim.* For the role of projection in anti-Semitism, see also T. W. Adorno *et al., The Authoritarian Personality* (New York, 1950), pp. 474-75, 485, *et passim,* and Bruno Bettelheim and Morris Janowitz, *Social Change and Prejudice, Including Dynamics of Prejudice* (London, 1964), pp. 146-47, 260-63, *et passim.*

Gertrude J. Selznick and Stephen Steinberg in *The Tenacity of Prejudice* (New York, Evanston, and London, 1969), pp. 189ff, support the idea that anti-Semitism results chiefly from ignorant acceptance of traditional superstition about Jews, and only indirectly (if at all) from individual psychopathology. Several scholars argue that this was the case in the medieval period. Ackerman and Jahoda, Adorno *et al.*, Bettelheim and Janowitz, and Flannery say, however, that there must be a predisposition that causes susceptibility to anti-Semitism.

I do not endorse the psychoanalytical view as the only explanation of anti-Semitism, though I find it to be a very useful starting point for understanding the treatment of the Jew in the mystery plays.

5 Ackerman and Jahoda observe that this differs from religious animal sacrifice in that the anti-Semite does not perceive the relationship between his treatment of the Jew and his internal conflict (pp. 56-57).

6 In the language of Ackerman and Jahoda, the Jew is a living Rorschach inkblot. "His alleged and sometimes actual qualities are so manifold and so inconsistent, so ambiguous and indeterminate, that the anti-Semite sees whatever he needs to see in the Jew" (p. 58). See also Adorno *et al.*, p. 2, and Bettelheim and Janowitz, p. 146 *et passim*.

7 The word is very rarely used in any other context. In Old Testament plays, figures such as Pharaoh may use it in order to describe the Jews as a people different from their own.

8 In the York plays the soldiers are explicitly Jews in 29/260ff, 33/389, 34/23. See also Towneley 20/152, 724, 21/66, 92, 115, 22/122-24, and elsewhere. Citations from these cycles are taken from *York Plays*, ed. Lucy Toulmin Smith (1885; rpt. New York, 1963) and *The Towneley Plays*, ed. George England and Alfred W. Pollard, EETS, e.s. 71 (1897; rpt. 1966).

9 In York 37/170, Belsabub delivers a similar line.

10 The oaths that evil figures swear by "Mahownd" associate them with Saracens. For example, in N-town 34, Ameraunt, a guard with the name of a Saracen giant, calls on Mahownde's help; see Dorothee Metlitzki's fascinating *The Matter of Araby in Medieval England* (New Haven and London, 1977), p. 197, for a discussion of Ameraunt in English romance.

11 The most important exceptions occur in the Chester Cycle, in which Expositor and Doctor offer narrative commentaries in several plays.

12 Folio 37r. Citations from the N-town Cycle are taken from the edition that I am preparing for the Early English Text Society.

13 For a history of artistic renditions of the Jews' supposed blindness, see Wolfgang Seiferth, *Synagogue and Church in the Middle Ages* (New York, 1970), *passim*.

14 All citations from the Chester plays are taken from *The Chester Mystery Cycle*, ed. R. M. Lumiansky and David Mills, EETS, s.s. 3 (1974); the present quotation comprises lines 205-09 in Play XIII.

15 Adorno *et al.* (p. 71) define anti-Semitism in broadly similar terms. The anti-Semitic "ideology," they say, consists "of stereotyped negative opinions describing the Jews as threatening, immoral, and categorically different from non-Jews. . . ."

16 In *The Jew in Early English Literature* (1926; rpt. New York, 1972), p. 56, H. Michelson notes the influence of *Romans* but nevertheless makes the unsupportable observation that "there cannot be the least doubt that, whenever a Jew was represented in a Mystery or Miracle play, they imitated one from real life rather than from an other source that would not have appealed to the public so much." Michelson's contention is repeated by Modder (p. 15).

The New Testament treatment of the Jews was of course mediated by a body of commentary and literature too large to survey here. One of the most influential commentaries on this theme was the Pseudo-Augustinian *Sermo Contra Judeos, Paganos, et Arianos,* which denounces Jews as shameful children of falsehood. The *Sermo* cites Jewish and pagan prophecies of Christ, providing the model for the prophets plays. Early dramatic portraits of the Jew are quite as hostile as those in the fifteenth-century plays, denouncing the Jew as blind, deaf, drunk, proud, and insane. The

Fleury *Visitatio Sepulchri,* for example, represents Jews as mad and damnable, and the Benediktbeuern Christmas Play has Archsynagogus justify his blindness through appeals to *ratio* and *natura,* just as the Jews do implicitly in the later cycles. These early plays stress the "otherness" of the Jew, giving no hint of the correlation between the Jew's vices and the Christian's own undesirable qualities.

17 For a persuasive discussion of medieval personifications as literal types, see Robert Frank's "The Art of Reading Medieval Personification-Allegory," *ELH,* 20 (1953), 237-50.

Note, incidentally, that the anti-Semite's perception of the Jew is also impersonal, involving a form of personification.

18 Spitzer, *Traditio,* 2 (1944), 455.

19 I wish to express my appreciation to Homer Goldberg, Richard Levin, and David Bevington, who read this paper and made very useful suggestions and corrections.

The Robin Hood Folk Plays
of South-Central England

Michael J. Preston

The British folk plays have been given considerable attention since their "discovery" in the late eighteenth century.[1] Comment on the plays has concentrated heavily upon their origins; according to the current theory, the plays are vestiges of an archetypal "life-cycle play."[2] Because of this emphasis on origins, as well as the co-ordinate assumption that the texts are either hopelessly corrupt or purely a matter of latter-day accretion, there has been a tendency to avoid detailed study of the many texts which have been recorded;[3] it is the action of the play which is considered important.[4] Accordingly, the *Revesby Sword Play,*[5] or some other atypical text,[6] has been examined in great detail because it manifests some trait which supports the current assumption made about the origins of the tradition. Although Roger Abrahams has argued that "the interdependence of life and death was [not] the dominant theme" of seasonal festivities and that "there does not seem to be any evidence for the existence of any 'original folk drama' involving this total life-cycle perspective,"[7] the theory is still maintained by a significant group of British and Irish folklorists[8] and should not too readily be discounted. In all probability the British folk play *tradition* is a set of *traditions* which differ among themselves, not merely because of oral change, but because in different areas there have been different influences, and to sort out which influence influenced the original origin produces arguments of more heat than light. Besides, although one may be interested in the origins of a tradition, it must be remembered that even certain knowledge of an origin might shed very little light on the tradition as it exists centuries or millennia later. The

British folk plays, as performed today, are certainly far removed from any ritual origin they might have.

Generally studies of the British folk plays are based on very few texts and ignore the hundreds of others which, in one way or another, tend to contradict or at least not support the ideas under consideration.[9] One example of this selection is the detailed treatment given the 1779 *Revesby Sword Play*,[10] while ignoring the traditional 1780 St. George play from Islip, Oxfordshire.[11] Rather than using the odd text to support a theory, I propose to study a number of texts from one small area—parts of Gloucestershire, Oxfordshire, Somerset, and Wiltshire—and explain what has happened within this tradition.

I

One aspect of the British folk play texts which lends support to the notion that the entirety of all texts is a matter of accretion is the apparent tendency of the texts to absorb snips and snatches from almost any conceivable source. Performances may be lengthened by adding speeches and songs, as well as by multiplying the number of combats. On occasion, a second entire play may be added to the end of a traditional text, as seems to have happened to the Ducklington "Men's Mummering."[12] Many changes seem to come about through the substitution of one speech or set of speeches for another.

Perhaps the most interesting examples of substitution involve major portions of the ballad of "Robin Hood and the Tanner" (Child 126) and two stanzas from "Robin Hood and the Shepherd" (Child 135).[13] Although the plays from Icomb[14] and Sapperton,[15] Gloucestershire, and Keynsham, Somerset[16] contain only small fragments of the ballads, large portions of the play texts are comprised of the ballad substitutions at Kempsford[17] and South Cerney,[18] Gloucestershire, Ducklington and Shipton-under-Wychwood,[19] Oxfordshire, and Inglesham,[20] Wiltshire—towns located within a few miles of each other. The texts from these five towns begin with their regionally distinct texts and change to the more broadly traditional wording only after the battle when the doctor, who is needed to raise the slain hero, enters. Perhaps because there is no organic identification of the speaker of each ballad stanza, as there often is for folk play speeches, the speaker differs somewhat from one text to the next.[21] Little John, for example, is substituted for Robin Hood in the 1958 South Cerney text.

What is of particular interest in these so-called Robin Hood plays is not what G. E. and W. H. Hadow maintained—that the separation of the May games from the Christmas festivities is not yet complete[22]—but that there is such a marked correspondence among the various versions of the inserted ballad. It appears that the ballad was inserted into the play in one town, and the whole play, together with its inserted material, spread from there. However, the presence of two fragmentary stanzas from "Robin Hood and the Shepherd" necessitates further explanation. We know that Robin Hood ballads circulated orally in this general area; "Robin Hood and Little John" (Child 125), for example, was recorded in Quenington.[23] The two ballads which were incorporated into these folk plays may also have been known locally. What seems probable is that someone "wrote in" parts of "Robin Hood and the Tanner," and that, because the eighteenth stanza of "Robin Hood and the Shepherd" corresponds quite closely with stanza twenty-nine of "Robin Hood and the Tanner," the one was simply replaced by the other—a common occurrence with ballads.[24]

From studying the ballad portions remaining in the plays, it is possible to see with some degree of probability just how the adapter worked the ballad into the structure of the play. The first four stanzas of the ballad are narrated, and these were assigned to the Tanner so that he could introduce the play in a manner not unlike that of the usual Father Christmas. Then the following stanzas (5-11) and parts of 13-15 were retained. These contain the verbal conflict and the battle between Robin Hood and the Tanner. The narrated stanza 12 was omitted, as are the narrated stanzas 16-20. Aside from the introductory passage, only those stanzas which are easily ascribable to a particular character are retained for the play text, and from these the narrated tags which identify the supposed speaker in the ballad—such as "said jolly Robin"—have all been carefully pared away.

After the battle comes the cure by the traditional doctor in which he is "aided" by his regionally characteristic helper, Jack Finney. Following the cure, more ballad stanzas are added which represent the aborted second battle of the ballad, a feature not uncommon among the folk plays. Then the play closes with traditional lines. It seems much more probable that someone rewrote this play than that it happened by a series of accidents.

Thus we see something of how external material can be grafted onto a traditional performance and survive: simply one or more traditional parts of the text are replaced by near equivalents in action. The way substitutions are rejected, as appears to have happened at Icomb, Keynsham, and Sapperton, is that the more broadly traditional version replaces the inserted material, thus repeating the process of simple substitution and demonstrating the dominance of a widespread form of a custom over a geographically restricted variant. It is significant, however, that the time-factor seems not to have played a major part in the apparently gradual process of rejecting the ballad "transplant." The text recorded longest ago, that from Keynsham in 1822, has nearly rejected the ballad, while some of the later texts, such as the 1958 South Cerney text, are no less close to the ballad original than the 1884 Ducklington Men's text.

II

The text from Bampton, Oxfordshire, is troublesome in that, although Robin Hood and Little John are present, it is quite unlike any of the eight texts discussed earlier. The version printed by P. H. Ditchfield shortly before the end of the nineteenth century[25] and that recorded by Donald C. Baker in 1966 are quite similar; both manifest the same problem of extended texts differing substantially from the ballad text. Although one unacquainted with many folk play texts might assume that this considerable difference is due to the chaotic state of these oral texts, the source of this "odd" Robin Hood tradition is to be found in John Allen Giles's *History of Bampton*.[26] In this book Giles claimed to have seen folk plays which contained Robin Hood and Little John performed in Somerset in his youth, and so he determined to introduce the Somerset characters to Bampton where he lived. But because Giles remembered only a line or two from each of the traditional speeches—these he printed within quotation marks—he was forced to compose the remainder himself. Giles's version was first performed on Christmas Eve of 1847 by the local mummers.

Although Giles's text itself does not fit in with the eight

texts based on the ballads, it does give us some valuable information indirectly about those plays. We know that Giles[27] spent the first sixteen years of his life in the parish of Mark, Somerset, which is twenty or so miles away from Keynsham where a folk play containing Robin Hood fragments was recorded in 1822. Giles was born in 1808, and so the play he witnessed may be assigned to a date approximate to that of the Keynsham version, but because of the distance between Keynsham and Mark, it is doubtful that he saw the Keynsham troupe perform. From Giles's reconstruction, faulty as it undoubtedly is except perhaps in general outline, we learn that the play performed in the vicinity of Mark must have contained speeches by Robin Hood and Little John of some size; however, since the play itself centers around the confrontation between St. George and the Turkish Knight, rather than Robin Hood and the Tanner, it can be safely maintained that the positions of Robin Hood and Little John in the play had been minimized. Thus the version Giles saw in Somerset must have represented something "halfway" between the fragmentary Robin Hood at Keynsham and the full version at South Cerney.

The texts recorded in Bampton in 1896 and in 1966 suggest a comparison, not merely because they were recorded in the same town, but because of their obvious textual relationship. Although the 1966 text follows closely the order of the original text as printed by Giles—it differs mainly in a few omitted lines and two added introductory tags—the 1896 text begins with Giles's version of Father Christmas' speech and ends with the speeches of Robin Hood and Little John. But despite the difference in the ordering of the speech units, a close comparison of the speeches themselves reveals that almost every speech present in either text also occurs in the other; it is mainly in the order of the speeches in which the difference occurs, and that order differs in a markedly constant fashion.

If one divides the two halves of the two-part 1966 text immediately preceding the entrance of the doctor—he enters after the battle in each part—the play may be divided into four units of action: the introductory speech of Father Christmas and the speeches of and battle between St. George and the Turkish Knight; the doctor's speech, the cure, and the speeches of Robin Hood and Little John; the introductory speech of Father Christmas and the speeches of and battle between Royal Aprussian King and Soldier Bold; and the second doctor episode, the appearance and speeches of Jack Finney, and the monologue of Tom the Tinker. In the 1896 version, these four parts are almost identical in internal structure, but they come in a different order. The second and fourth parts are switched so that the second cure comes after the first battle, and the first cure comes after the second battle. How this came about is easily explained: the doctor can cure either fallen man whichever text he follows because there is no internal requisite that either be applied to any particular man, and so the cures were substituted for each other.

This switching about of episodes explains another kind of change which has been generally ignored. Although whether particular speeches are deleted depends in great part upon a number of external circumstances—whether the play was performed in long or short form, for example—nonetheless, within any episode the speeches have to follow each other in a certain order to make sense. Although this structural order must be followed, the order of certain repetitious episodes which occur in the same play may be readily switched. Thus, if there were two traditional versions of the play in the same area, as at Ducklington, one set of combatants might well be substituted for the other; or, if the play were to be lengthened, one set might follow the other as at Burghclere,[28] Hampshire, differing from the practice of adding a second play onto the end as in the Ducklington "Men's Mummering." It is the substitution that accounts for the acceptance of the Robin Hood ballad into the place of the traditional battle, and it is a second substitution which appears to have removed Robin Hood from the plays at Keynsham, Sapperton, and Icomb, leaving only a tiny fragment of the ballad text as evidence that the ballad-based episode had once been present.

III

In addition to evidence concerning substitution of one pair of combatants for another, the plays which contain Robin Hood fragments give us evidence about the final portion of the play which Chambers called the *Quête*.[29] After reading a large number of plays selected at random, one might conclude that this portion of the play is rather arbitrary and may be shortened to a single speech to indicate a collection, or may be lengthened with as many local speech units as the occasion will bear. But the local speeches, like the ubiquitous Beelzebub and Big Head speeches, must come from some place, and one may well wonder why they are so commonly associated with the folk plays.

In the South Cerney play, Jack Vinney speaks a long penultimate speech in which he claims to be "old Tom the Tinker," "Old Cut and Slashum," "old Belsebub," and even "old Father Christmas." His speech also contains the lines usually spoken by "Happy Jack." Thus there are five different characters' speeches taken up by a sixth character. One explanation for this is that it was undoubtedly necessary to "double" a number of parts because of the need for three of the traditional performers to take on the new roles of the Tanner, Robin Hood, and Little John. This kind of doubling did occur in the Ducklington men's play and is common enough, but if one looks at the usual function of some of the characters whose speeches Jack Vinney has taken at South Cerney, something else may be discerned. Old Father Christmas usually introduces the play, but his place has been taken by the Tanner. "Cut and Slashum" is usually a phrase used to describe one of the traditional combatants, both of which have been displaced by Robin Hood and the Tanner. The speeches of these characters were traditional, and these speeches were retained in the play although incongruously added to the part of another character. If one looks at the Keynsham text, he sees that Father Christmas has taken back his traditional role, but he still speaks a few lines formerly assigned to the Tanner. Thus it seems that a character who has been pushed out of his traditional place in the play will often remain a very minor character in the background, sometimes represented by a couplet or two in the text. Giles's reconstruction presents evidence quite in accord with this observation. In Giles's text Robin Hood and Little John have been shoved out of their place as combatants by the more broadly traditional St. George and Turkish Knight, and as a result they speak their limited parts after the Doctor has performed his cure; it is significant that they appear in the portion of the play usually filled by the "functionless" characters. Thus we are presented with a definite possibility, if not a probability, that if the main battle of the folk plays is the product of chapbook influence or any other later influence, then the apparently functionless characters become most important in any attempt to reconstruct what the play tradition may have been like in the sixteenth and fifteenth centuries and before, if the custom existed then as is commonly believed.30

The plays which contain fragments of Robin Hood ballads seem to have had a relatively simple history. Someone, presumably in the eighteenth century, inserted major portions of "Robin Hood and the Tanner" into a traditional text. This probably took place in the general area of Oxfordshire or Gloucestershire. This new version was performed by a local troupe and spread to the neighboring towns. After a period of years, the more broadly traditional form of the play dominated the regional oddity, essentially replacing it except where it seems to have had its champions—Giles and Hadow, for example, who presumably were interested in Robin Hood for antiquarian reasons. The traditional characters who had been "written out" of the Robin Hood version were simply substituted back into the performances by the same process by which they had been removed without modifying the plot or action of the play in any substantial way, only occasionally leaving behind a tell-tale line or two in the text. In how many places the Robin Hood version disappeared without a trace we will probably never know.

NOTES

1 This article has benefited substantially from a Grant-in-Aid from the American Council of Learned Societies and a Younger Humanist Fellowship from the National Endowment for the Humanities. An earlier version of this paper appeared as Chapter III of *The Saint George Play Traditions: Solutions to Some Textual Problems* (M.A. Thesis, University of Colorado, 1972), pp. 75-112.

2 Margaret Dean-Smith, "The Life-Cycle or Folk Play," *Folk-lore,* 69 (1958), 237-53.

3 E. C. Cawte, Alex Helm, and N. Peacock, *English Ritual Drama,* Publications of the Folklore Soc. (London, 1967), contains an extensive bibliography on pp. 94-132. A valuable "Table of Locations" is given on pp. 37-73.

4 Cf. Dean-Smith, *op. cit.,* and the extensive publications of Alex Helm on the Guizer Press. Although concerned with collecting many texts, neither attempts to study any number in detail. The only "in depth" study of the plays of any region is M. W. Barley's essay, "Plough Plays in the East Midlands," *Journal of the English Folk Dance and Song Society,* 7, No. 2 (1953), 68-95. Barley's essay has been generally ignored since its publication.

5 Cf. E. K. Chambers, *The English Folk-Play* (Oxford, 1933), pp. 104-23.

6 Cf. Alan Brody, *The English Mummers and their Plays* (Philadelphia: Univ. of Pennsylvania Press, 1970), pp. 46 ff. and 131-36.

7 Roger D. Abrahams, "British West Indian Folk Drama and the 'Life Cycle' Problem," *Folklore*, 81 (1970), 241.

8 Cf. E. C. Cawte, "More on the 'Mummers' Play'," *Journal of American Folklore*, 85 (1972), 375-76.

9 Brody states (p. 29) that "the large number of verbal variants . . . must inevitably lead us to the conclusion that it was not the meaning of the action as expressed in the words that was originally the important feature." Also (p. 3), "Every new version . . . forces us back to the core of the play." And (p. 11) this "core" is what "the Cambridge scholars suggested . . . might be the fragmented remains of a pre-Christian ceremony." Brody should know that variants in no way indicate that a text is considered unimportant. The ballad texts, for example, show the same degree of textual variation.

On pp. 16ff Brody points out that the Marshfield Paper Boys do not collect money but dispense luck; this supports his contention that the collection is not really important in a consideration of the tradition. On p. 59 he uses the doctor-episode from Bellerby, Yorkshire, to connect the entire tradition to fertility matters. Both plays are atypical, but no more so than the Earsdon play which Brody says (p. 81) "is an example of the movement from verbal corruption to corruption of sense which finally leads to a thorough distortion of the action itself." How Brody determines which atypical play is significant and which is merely "corrupt" is a mystery to me, unless he is selecting plays which fit his theory rather than developing a theory to explain the plays.

10 See my article, "The Revesby Sword Play," *Journal of American Folklore*, 85 (1972), 51-57.

11 See my article, "The Oldest British Folk Play," *Folklore Forum*, 6 (1973), 168-74.

12 Cawte *et al.*, p. 56, note no surviving Ducklington text. However, Bodleian MS. Eng. Poet, c.17 contains "The Boys Mummering" (ff. 40r-40v) and "The Mens Mummering" (ff. 41r-43r). These two texts are headed by a "title page" containing the following information: "Christmas Mummering at Ducklington, Oxon. written down by Jesse Fisher, son of the Parish Clerk, at 13." It is dated "Jan. 1884."

13 Locating ballad fragments embedded in the folk plays was greatly facilitated by the availability of a KWIC concordance. This was produced through the facilities of the Center for Computer Research in the Humanities at the University of Colorado. Microfilm copies of this concordance are stored in Norlin Library at the University of Colorado, in the Archives of Popular Tradition at Sheffield University, and with the Folklore Society in London.

14 R. J. E. Tiddy, *The Mummers' Play* (Oxford, 1923), pp. 174-79.

15 Tiddy, pp. 170-73.

16 BL Add. MS. 24,542 is printed by C. R. Baskerville in "Mummers' Wooing Plays in England," *Modern Philology*, 21 (1924), 268-72. This is a transcript by an unknown person of the play Joseph Hunter witnessed on December 27, 1822. A substantially similar text is contained in BL Add. MS. 24,546 which was written out by James Cantle, one of the performers, and sent to Hunter. This has been printed by Ivor Gatty in "Two Variations of the Folk Play and a Further Account of the Old Hoss," *Journal of the English Folk Dance and Song Society*, 5 (1947), 82-85.

17 Tiddy, pp. 248-53.

18 Cf. G. E. and W. H. Hadow, *The Oxford Treasury of English Literature*

(Oxford, 1908), II, 287-94. I refer to this as the "1908 South Cerney text" out of convenience. The text was undoubtedly written down prior to 1908, perhaps many years earlier, because the Hadows' father was long the Vicar of South Cerney. The 1958 South Cerney text was sent by Mrs. J. E. Fenton to Donald C. Baker who passed it on to me. Of the play at South Cerney, Mrs. Fenton wrote in 1967: "The S. Cerney Mumming Play was performed yearly at Christmas up to 1913, after which nothing was heard of it until 1938, when a lady in the village got some of the old Mummers to play it again. It was not until 1958 that I felt we should get the words written down. This I achieved, having managed to get 2 of the 1913 team together. Helped by plenty of beer & dozens of cigarettes, they spoke it, while I wrote it down! It has since been played 3 times, 1958, 1964 & 1965."

19 Tiddy, pp. 209-13.

20 Alfred Williams, *Round About the Upper Thames* (London, n.d.), pp. 306-12.

21 John Robert Moore, in "The Influence of Transmission on the English Ballads," *Modern Language Review*, 11 (1916), 401, wrote: "Attribution of speeches, in particular, is likely to be lost."

22 G. E. and W. H. Hadow, p. 287.

23 Alfred Williams, *Folk-Songs of the Upper Thames* (London, 1923), p. 296.

24 Cf. Moore, pp. 402-04.

25 P. H. Ditchfield, *Old English Customs* (London, 1901), pp. 320-26.

26 J. A. Giles, *History of the Parish and Town of Bampton* (1848), pp. 176-78.

27 *Dictionary of National Biography*, s.v. "John Allen Giles."

28 Tiddy, pp. 185-88.

29 Chambers, pp. 63-71.

30 S. D. Malin, *Character Origins in the English Folk Play* (1970) (Ph.D. dissertation in Speech), attempts to relate the "functionless" characters of the folk play tradition to medieval witchcraft. This seems to be the first study to deal seriously with these characters.

Work and Play: Some Aspects of
Folk Drama in Russia

Elizabeth A. Warner

The date 1672 is generally regarded as an important one in the history of the Russian theatre, for it was on the seventeenth of October of that year that the first performance of the play *Esfir* or *Artakserksovo deistvo* was given in the specially built theatre at the village of Preobraʒhenskoe near Moscow before the Tsar Aleksei Mikhailovich and his court. *Esfir* has often been referred to as "the first play of the Russian theatre."

It was commissioned to celebrate the birth of Aleksei Mikhailovich's son, the future Peter the Great, and it appears to have been a tremendous success. It is said the Tsar watched engrossed for ten solid hours. Certainly we know from contemporary bills that no expense had been spared, either on the construction of the theatre or the preparation of the costumes. Many expensive materials were used for the latter—brightly coloured Persian silks, Turkish satin and fine cloth from Germany—and they were lavishly decorated with silver and gold braid, lace and embroideries. Real ermine was used for Artaxerxes' robes. It was probably the lavish spectacle and the sheer novelty of the occasion which impressed the court rather than the skill of the actors, for the cast was composed of untrained clerks, artisans, and shop-keepers from the German quarter of Moscow. They knew little Russian and were gathered together for rehearsal approximately one month before the performance by the German pastor Gregory whom Alexsei Mikhailovich had approached with his proposal for the play.

The Tsar's enjoyment of the first play he had ever seen had a certain importance for the development of theatre in Russia. Its popularity at court was ensured for many years to come, although performances took place only sporadically during the four years between its inauguration and the death of its founder in 1676. The tradition was, however, carried on by Peter's sister Natalya and Praskov'ya Fedorovna (widow of John V, Peter's half-brother) and her daughter at the royal palace at Izmailova. Later, of course, Peter the Great himself recognised the importance of the theatre both as a weapon of political propaganda and as an instrument of education and helped to introduce it to a wider audience with the building of the public theatre on Red Square in 1702.

That Aleksei Mikhailovich should thus have been instrumental in acquainting the Russian aristocracy with the pleasures of the theatrical art is ironic, for the same man failed to recognize and accept the desire to play and be entertained among his ordinary subjects. In the early years of his reign the Tsar had endorsed and indeed encouraged ecclesiastical condemnation and persecution of most forms of popular entertainment—dancing, singing, the playing of musical instruments, fisticuffs, masking at Christmastide, and taking part in the many ritual games so popular in the Russian countryside. Long before Aleksei Mikhailovich "founded" the Russian theatre, the ordinary Russian people had developed their own liking and talent for play acting in a variety of different ways.

Old Russian secular and ecclesiastical documents are full of references dating from the twelfth century onwards to the antics of the *skomorokhi,* Russia's wandering players, to mumming at Christmastide, to spring ritual games and amusements at weddings and funerals. An epistle from bishop Pamfil in 1505, for example, describes the celebrations on St. John's Eve in which almost the whole town of Pskov took part. Women and girls danced with much hand-clapping and stamping of feet to the accompaniment of tambourines, reed pipes, and various stringed instruments.[1] In Tsar Aleksei Mikhailovich's order of 1648 forbidding folk entertainments, the custom of putting on masks and costumes such as the *skomorokhi* wore, of dressing up and leading about the "devilish mare" (i.e., the hobby-horse) were among the condemned activities.[2]

The need to dramatise and "play" is clearly a deep-seated human instinct, common to all peoples including the most primitive. One of the most important impulses towards the creation of drama is almost certainly a combination of man's ability to

observe accurately the world around him and his desire to reproduce in play what he sees and hears. Man is in fact a highly
imitative animal. In this respect it is interesting to note the high
incidence of imitation in children's games. Modern British children will play at "Hospitals," "Schools," or "Mothers and Fathers"—games in which they imitate to the best of their ability
the behavior of the grown-ups involved. Russian peasant children in the past, living in small, isolated rural communities, must
have relied heavily in their imitative play upon the observance
of simple domestic scenes and familiar daily events. Indeed a
large number of such games were recorded in the last century
by ethnographers such as P. V. Shein, A. Tereshchenko, E. A.
Pokrovskii, and V. F. Kudryavtsev. Many of these are quite
predictable in content and differ only in detail from games we
have enjoyed ourselves. There was, for example, *Gostit'sya*
("Paying visits") in which little girls would "bake pies" out of
clay and build huts in which they pretended to entertain their
friends. In another game *Gorshki* ("Pots," a reference to the
earthenware pots used for the cooking and serving of food, milk,
etc.) boys and girls played at "families," building a house which
they decorated with bunches of flowers, making food from sand
and water, eating at table, going off to work, pasturing the
horses, cutting corn, and so on.3 Of greater interest are games
which describe more specific activities such as *Polotno*
("Cloth") in which the simple act of buying and selling material was reproduced with symbolic gestures. The children held
hands and stood in a long line. This was the "cloth." One child
played the part of the merchant and another that of the customer. Several yards of cloth were measured off, the merchant
using his outstretched arms as a tape measure, and a number
of children were correspondingly removed from the line. The
remainder twisted themselves up in a huddle showing that the
material had been rolled up again. This process was repeated
several times until one customer, realizing he had been cheated,
returned to complain. The game ended in confusion with the
dishonest merchant himself being rolled up in the "bale of
cloth."4 Even the seamier side of life in pre-Revolutionary
Russia found an echo in children's play. Take *Kandaly* ("Fetters").5 In this game the children stood in two facing rows. One
child shouts: "Fetters." "They're on," comes the reply. "Unlock
them." "Whose shall I unlock?" "Your friend's." "Which

friend?" "Serega." At this the child whose name has been called makes a dash for freedom to the opposite row followed by the kicks and cuffs of his former mates. Although essentially no more than a chasing game, *Kandaly* seems to recall the days of the chain-gangs, a not too unfamiliar sight in pre-Revolutionary days. New recruits, dragged unwillingly from their families for long years of service in the Russian army, were frequently chained together to prevent them escaping; prisoners were chained together for heavy work such as the building of roads, and on the main route to Siberia, the "Vladimirka," the sad columns of chained exiles, were a familiar sight. Similarly, hunts for deserters, runaway peasants, or escaped prisoners are clearly remembered in the game *Beglye* ("The Runaways"), recorded by Efimenko in the Archangel government. The players divide into two groups, the runaways and the police searchers. When they are caught the runaways are dragged back, lassoed together. A series of stylized "punishments" are inflicted upon them. Bundles of birch rods were prepared before the game began, but there is no indication that they were actually used.6

The reproduction in play of adult behavior appears to be instinctive among children of all races even in the most primitive societies and extends beyond the merely domestic to the ritual acts and observances which most closely affected both the individuals and the larger social group of which the children formed a part. Ralph Beals and Harry Hoijer write of children in *An Introduction to Anthropology:*

> But children are not continually preached at nor harassed by fears, actually they spend much of their time in games. Both sexes make and play with dolls and miniature household equipment. Boys play at hunting and war, and may even imitate in play the dancers and singers they see and hear in ceremonials.7

Russian village children also used the material of ritual as a basis for play. One of the most colorful and spectacular events of rural life until the beginning of this century was the peasant marriage ritual; therefore it is perhaps not surprising that it was a frequent subject in the dramatic games of both children and adults alike, although in the latter an element of parody was often apparent. An interesting eye-witness account of one such wedding game played with dolls by seven small girls from the village of Kholm in 1928 is given by I. M. Levina in an anthology of ethnographical material from Northern Russia.8 One is immediately struck by the intense seriousness of the players and their strict attention to the minutest details. Not only did they accurately reproduce all the important characters, speeches, songs, and formal scenes of this highly complex ritual from the arrival of the match-makers to the wedding-day feast and the post-nuptial trials undergone by the young bride in her new mother-in-law's household, but they had clearly absorbed from the attitudes of their elders something of the ritual significance of the performance. Their allocation of roles to the dolls, for example, showed a correct understanding of the focal position of the bride and her entourage as opposed to the more passive role of the groom's faction. On the male side we find that only the groom, his parents, and the best man *(tysyatskii)* were represented, whereas on the female side we find the bride and her parents, her godmother, three sisters, and a brother as well as numerous girl friends. A deep-seated regard for "correctness" is also felt in the discussion over which doll should play the part of the bride's godmother *(bozhatochka)*. It was usual for a married woman to perform this function, so the girls chose "Natal'ya Nikolaevna," a doll which had already been "married" herself in a previous game. Her long hair had been carefully wound into the two braids denoting married status, and the head was covered with the specially arranged head scarf of the married woman *(povoinik)*. There was some argument over the suitability of the doll chosen to play the bride's mother. Her pink dress *(sarafan)* was considered incorrect for a woman of that age. Similar attention to detail was noted in the preparation of the interiors. During the decoration of the bride's home prior to the first scene of the game—the match-making—someone placed a make-believe samovar on the table. It was, however, promptly removed, for the samovar was traditionally brought out only after the serious business had been concluded and refreshments were offered in token of friendship and harmony.

That children should incorporate parts of the marriage ritual into their play is not really so surprising, for apart from its more serious aspects—economic, social, and religious—it was a beautiful, moving, and memorable festive event. Stranger, however, for the modern European, was their interest in funerals. A death and burial element was quite common in children's games, as for example at the end of *Kostroma,* the Russian equivalent of the English game "Jenny Jones" or "Georgina" which died out towards the end of the last century. One girl played the part of Kostroma, another the role of her nurse. A question and answer game followed. Kostroma's friends call to see if she will come out to play, but each time they are turned away by the nurse. At first Kostroma is too busy (chopping wood, spinning flax, going to Mass, etc.), then she is sick, dying, and finally dead. A mock funeral takes place, and Kostroma is buried by her friends. The funeral, however, often degenerated into an unceremonious scuffle as the children seized the defunct Kostroma by the arms and legs and deposited her noisily some distance from the game. Miraculously brought back to life, Kostroma then pounced on her friends and the girl she caught became the new Kostroma. More realistic representations of the funeral rites were also common. Levina, who recorded the game at weddings described above, also writes of funerals where a doll was buried in a specially made coffin to the accompaniment of traditional keening.[9]

In the past the activities of children and adults were not kept apart to the extent they usually are today, and imitative games were often of considerable importance as a form of preparation, both psychological and actual, for the life of adult society. Some games involving conventionalized imitation of specific work processes can be traced to highly practical origins, for in most non-literate societies the transmission of various skills was necessarily carried out on a "watch-and-do" basis. Many heavily stylized work games with symbolic gestures and movements evolved from the basic teacher-apprentice situation and were incorporated into the rituals of initiation and other ceremonies. In time, the evolving mimetic figures of the players often became so divorced from reality that the original functional intention was lost and only the ritual purpose of the actions remained. Such games were comprehensible only to the initiated who then had to reinterpret them for the apprentice-initiates.

A classic example of the ritual transmission of work processes may be found in the initiation rites of the Poro Bush Society among the Mano people of Liberia. "Once the boys have been duly impressed by these rites, the process of instruction begins, and they learn the details of agriculture, trades, herb medicine and the like. In the Bush model gardens are planted, and forges and other paraphernalia set up."[10] Inade-

quate documentary evidence makes it difficult to draw any
definite conclusions about the presence of initiation ceremonies
among the early East Slavs. However, there are clear indications that small girls were initiated into the skills of spinning
and weaving which were the main occupations of the Russian
peasant woman at least until the Revolution. Indeed the domestic loom was retained in some villages until the last war.
Fon Kramer's description of superstitions and customs in the
village of Verkhotishanka (Voronezh government) around the
middle of the nineteenth century indicates vestigial symbolic
remains of initiation rites in the time honored tradition by which
young women in the first year of marriage were obliged to spin,
weave, and sew all the sacks and rough hempen material
(veret'e) used by the family to store and protect produce.[11]
Certainly, spinning was an occupation which was surrounded
by a great deal of superstition, ritual, and taboo. It was considered wrong, for example, to spin on Friday, the day dedicated
to Paraskeva-Friday, patron saint of spinners. Any woman foolish enough to disregard this would herself be punished by blindness. In some regions of Russia the women also did not spin
during shrove week; if they disobeyed, according to legend, mice
would gnaw at the thread and the cloth would rot.[12] It was
generally accepted that after spinning had been finished for the
day, the work had to be left tidy and a prayer spoken over it.

Among the most popular spring and summer entertainments
of the girls and younger women of the Russian village was the
performing of *khorovods* or round dances in which certain actions described in songs were mimetically reproduced to a choral
accompaniment. One of these, *Len* ("Flax"), reproduces in
some considerable detail one of the age-old traditional occupations of the Russian peasant woman; a young girl asks her
mother to show her how to grow the flax plant and how to
prepare it for weaving into fine linen. *Len* is performed by a
choir with two soloists playing the parts of mother and daughter.
It begins with an invocation to the newly sown seed; as the
dancer sways and bends this way and that, so hopefully will the
flax grow thick and abundant:

> Pod dubravoyu len, len,
> Pod zelenoyu, len, len.
> Uzh ya seyala, seyala lenok,
> Uzh ya seya, prigovarivala,

Chebotami prikolachivala,
Na vse boka povorachivala:
"Ty udaisya, udaisya,moi len,
Ty udaisya, moi belen'kii,
"Polyubisya, druzhok milen'kii!"

(At the forest's edge, flax, flax grows
By the green forest.
I have sown it, sown the little seeds of flax,
And as I sowed, stamping it down with my
Boots and swaying from side to side,
I said to it:
"Now grow up fine and strong, my flax,
Fine and strong, my white flax,
To please me, dear little friend.")

The soloist then turns to her mother and asks in successive couplets "teach me, mother, how to weed the white flax, how to pluck it, spread it out, dry it, brake it, skutch it, card it, spin it." The mother replies and shows through stylized body movements how each task is to be accomplished:

Eshche tak da vot tak, chi dochi,
Vot tak da chi dochi moi,
Vot tak da golubushki,
Vot tak da golubushki.

(Do it like this and like this daughters,
This is the way to do it little daughters,
This way my darlings,
This way my darlings.) 13

Songs of this kind were also sung during specially organized communal work activities in which the whole village would band together to help a local farmer or simply a neighbor with some extensive task requiring many hands such as the sowing of seed, haymaking, harvesting, or even the building of a new house or mill. The host on such occasions did not pay his workers but entertained them to a generous meal in the evening.

Similar in content were work scenes in some variants of the dramatic spring game *Kostroma* which enjoyed a widespread popularity in Russia up to the end of the last century. *Kostroma* belonged to the spring cycle of agricultural rituals and was performed by the young women and girls of the village some time between Whitsun and the beginning of the St. Peter Fast (on June 29). The nucleus of the game consisted of the following: A straw figure was made, dressed in female clothing and laid in a coffin. A funeral procession was formed, the women moaning and wailing as for a dead relative or friend. When the cortege reached the river the "corpse" was stripped and flung into the water. The basic elements of the ritual can be seen in the following description based on observations of the ethnographer P. V. Shein.14 In the vicinity of Murom (some 160 miles east of Moscow) and other villages along the banks of the Oka river, the "burial of Kostroma," or "farewell to spring," as it was sometimes called, took place on the last Sunday before the St. Peter Fast. The typical setting in which *Kostroma* was performed is evocatively painted by Shein: a warm summer evening, the sun just setting, a slight breeze blowing in from the river, rustling the groves of birch trees around the village, in the distance the bleating of sheep. With the day's work done, the villagers gradually emerge out of doors—the older people to enjoy the last rays of the sun and to gossip, the young to sing and play games. At some point in the evening one of the young women suggests "it is time to bury Kostroma." There is some opposition from the more God-fearing members of the community, since taking part in such ceremonies of patently pagan origin was much frowned on by the Church, even in the nineteenth century. As one woman puts it: "My man told me it's a sin . . . and when I'm dead and in the other place they'll pull my tongue out for it and make me lick a red-hot frying pan." She is overruled, and a laughing, noisy crowd of women, girls, and lads runs off to "bury Kostroma." A straw figure is made and dressed in a shirt and *sarafan,* on her feet shoes and on her head a scarf and garland of flowers. The figure is then placed in a wooden feeding-trough *(koryto)* which serves as a coffin. While this is being done, the girls sing about Kostroma, about how she was a merchant's daughter from Kostroma (a town about 140 miles north of Murom), about how she was given drugged wine at a party and subsequently died:

> Vdrug Kostroma povalilas':
> Kostromushka umerla.
> Kostromushka, Kostroma!
> K Kostrome stali skhodit'sya,
> Kostromushku ubirat'
> I vo grob polagat',
> Kak rodnye—to stali tuzhit':
> Po Kostromushke vyplakivati
> "Byla Kostroma vesela,

Byla Kostroma khorosha!"
Kostromushka, Kostroma,
Nasha belaya lebedushka!

(Suddenly Kostromka collapsed.
Kostromushka died.
Kostromushka, Kostroma!
Then people came to Kostroma
To lay her out and place her in the coffin,
And her family began to mourn
And weep for Kostromushka.
"Kostroma was gay
And Kostroma was pretty!"
Kostromushka, Kostroma,
Our little white swan.)

The funeral procession is acted out with that peculiar mixture of grotesque and yet "serious" parody typical of those ceremonies known throughout Europe in which rituals connected with marriage or death are imitated. The women wear white head scarves to show they are in mourning, and the inclinations of the village lads to play the fool are sternly quelled. The young men who carry the coffin wear rough garments of sackcloth, another sign of mourning. The procession is headed by a mock priest, swinging a bast shoe in grotesque imitation of the ecclesiastical censer. A group of girls depicting the professional keeners sing:

Kostroma, Kostroma,
Ty naryadnaya byla,
Razveselaya byla,
Ty gul'livaya byla!
A teper', Kostroma,
Ty vo grob legla!

(Kostroma, Kostroma,
Once so smart,
Once so jolly,
So fond of making merry,
Now you have lain down in your coffin.)

The ceremony ends on the banks of the nearest river or lake where Kostroma is undressed and flung into the water.

This basic framework for the game was often expanded by the addition of other dramatic scenes. Most striking in this respect are variants of *Kostroma* recorded in 1940 by L. Kulakovskii in the villages of Dorozhevo and Domashevo in the Bryansk region roughly half-way between Moscow and Kiev. One of the central themes of the play here was the mimetic reproduction of the actions of spinning a hank of tow into thread and then weaving it into cloth. In the Dorozhevo[15] variant, which was in the form of a round dance *(khorovod)*, Kostroma sits on a rug in the middle of the ring. The chorus addresses her:

> Kostryma, Kostryma,
> My lady Kostryma!
> Kostromushka has kisel'[16] made with milk,
> Kostromushka has pancakes with curds [*tvorog*].
> Good day, Kostroma! Good day to you!
> What are you doing?

A series of answers follows, describing the spinning and weaving process from preparation of the flax, retting, braking, skutching, and carding, through the spinning of the yarn, the setting up of the warp on the loom, the weaving of the cloth, to the cutting of the finished material off the loom and the final beating and laying out of the prepared material.

The original functional/ritual purpose of this game in the village of Dorozhevo became enriched over the years with the addition of purely entertaining episodes of a comic and frequently ribald nature. Thus, where in other variants of the game, including those from the neighboring village of Domashevo, Kostroma simply dies and is buried with or without a mock funeral, in the Dorozhevo variant we find a whole sociodomestic comedy. When the hard work is over, Kostroma and her husband have a hearty meal and a half-liter of wine or vodka (the food was real and actually eaten, although the wine was only water), after which Kostroma falls ill with a stomach-ache. A wise-man *(znakhar')* is summoned from the neighboring village of Komyagino, some 40 kilometers from Dorozhevo. (According to Kulakovskii, in the past there was indeed a popular wise man living there. This was not an unusual feature of Russian village life, certainly before the end of the nineteenth century. Indeed, until the spread of local medical services in the 1870's the wise man or woman performed an essential function. Such persons had certain medical skills in bone-setting and herbal remedies as well as more sinister powers displayed in the making of love potions, in the finding of lost or stolen property, or in warding off the evil eye.) However, the wise man proves to be away from home, so the local medical auxiliary *(fel'dsher)* is sent for instead. He enters dressed in an apron or with a white tablecloth round his middle and carrying a stick to represent his stethoscope. One can well imagine that the comic and bawdy potential of the scene in which he questioned Kostroma about the nature of her illness and the way in which he sounded and examined her was exploited to the full. The local men tried to forbid their wives taking part, and more decent versions were presented to visiting ethnographers as well as, indeed, to the astonished and delighted Moscow audiences before whom *Kostroma* was performed for the first time in 1940. The doctor eventually gave Kostroma a powder to take and departed. He was succeeded by the village priest *(pop)* who carried out a parody version of the Orthodox rite of *soborovanie,* "anointing of the sick" (or *podzaborovanie,* "under-the-fence-ing," as it is punningly referred to here, playing on the closeness of the words *sobor*—cathedral and *zabor*—fence in Russian). The priest was dressed in an old padded coat fitted at the waist and an old hat turned inside out. He had a cross made from bits of wood and an incongruous and highly original censer—a stuffed duck or grouse used by hunters as a decoy and swung by the neck. The language of the improvised parts of the play was fairly spicy, particularly in the scenes with the doctor and in Kostroma's confessions to the priest who absolves her "In the name of the oats and the hay and the holy chaff" ('Vo imya ovsa i sena i svyatogo Khobot'ya).17

The connection between the straw figure of Kostroma and the spinning interludes of the Bryansk region is not immediately apparent. But Kostroma is clearly one of those anthropomorphic spirits of vegetation and growth which occur so frequently in Russian agricultural ritual. The word *Kostroma* itself is probably derived from *koster* (or *kostra)* the stalk or boon of the flax plant. Vegetation figures were often made of materials other than straw, and it is probable that the original Kostroma dolls were made from this tough, strawlike residue of the flax or hemp from which the fiber had already been extracted to be spun eventually into linen.

In the above excerpt the players were clearly trying to convey a reasonably realistic representation of the work processes involved in the game. The degree to which the actions of the players appeared "true to life," however, varied considerably from one type of game to another. In some the pantomime was reduced to an almost abstract pattern of formal gestures and

movements. Such, for example was the series of *khorovod*-type
games depicting the weaving of cloth recorded in the latter half
of the nineteenth century by Shein. These took place in Trinity
week during a spring festival which included such elements as
the ritual ornamenting of a young birch tree with ribbons and
the weaving of garlands for the purpose of divination. The
dances began with the initial winding of the yarn onto the bean
roll and the formation of the warp, and continued until the final
process of weaving the material. The most striking feature was
the design or pattern formed by the players. For example, the
winding of the thread onto the bean roll was shown as follows:
a chain was formed and the girls to begin with walked round in
a circle, then the chain was broken at one point. The girl at one
end stood still while the remainder wound their way round her,
thus forming a spiral with the girl at its center. The weaving
itself was done in a most ingenious way. The girls, standing in
pairs facing each other, represented the weaving frame. Each
pair crossed hands to form the warp. One girl standing at either
end of the row was the weaver. To get the cloth woven a little
boy was seated on the crossed hands of the first couple and
from there tossed down the line to be caught by the weaver at
the other end. He was the shuttle carrying the thread of the
weft.[18] Mimetic dances of this type in which some activity or
object is represented purely by the body movements of the
dancers unaided by the use of costume, makeup, etc., may be
regarded as one of the most primitive forms of dramatic expression. It can be applied not merely to concrete subjects such as
the art of weaving as in the above example, but also, more surprisingly, to relatively abstract concepts such as the dance imitating the surf of the ocean to be found among the Fiji islanders
or the song of the Indians of the Pueblo of Laguna in New
Mexico about the rising sun, accompanied by gestures to indicate
the coming of dawn and the subsequent fertilization of the
crops.[19] Similarly, the Onas of South America, who believed
in the transmigration of souls into the heavens, the clouds, thunder, mountains, stones, dark abysses, etc., strove to represent
these natural phenomena in their masked dances.[20]

Primitive man's experiments into the realm of drama, as
indeed into other art forms, were largely limited and conditioned
by the pattern of his own existence and of the society in which
he lived. In many primitive communities before the division of

labor into specific trades and other economic developments, people had little leisure time to devote to esoteric pursuits such as art and literature, since they were almost wholly occupied with obtaining food. Such conditions can still be found among economically backward, although not necessarily primitive peoples. Where art existed (or exists) in such communities, the impulse towards its creation was almost certainly of a predominantly utilitarian nature. Many of the art forms which are characteristic of particular tribes or communities originally had a utilitarian purpose. Such, for example, is the magnificent basketry work of the Californian Indians or the pottery of the ancient Peruvians, old Russian house-carvings and highly decorated distaffs, or the intricate stylized embroidery with distinctive regional variations found on the festive garments and linen of the Slavonic peoples. However, while utilitarian (including religious/ritual) considerations were probably foremost in the mind of the primitive artist, it would be wrong to deny the existence of the aesthetic instinct which is also necessary to the production and enjoyment of true works of art. Ruth Bunzel suggests: "Most definitions of art presuppose the existence in man of an aesthetic emotion which can be evoked by the qualities inherent in objects or activities."[21] However, she also states: "But it is nevertheless true that the greater part of the art of primitive man is applied to useful objects."[22]

The content of most early "dramas" among the Russians was also, as one might expect, derived from the world of their immediate material experience—a world largely concerned with the changing seasons, the growth and wellbeing of the crops (grain and vegetable), and animal husbandry. On a more personal level, marriage and death (particularly the former) were either accompanied by or gave rise to a considerable amount of dramatic activity.[23] Hunting scenes are strangely conspicuous by their absence, although long after the Russians had settled as primitive farmers and herdsmen and ceased to rely on the hunt for food, fur-bearing animals such as the bear were still highly sought after for their pelts, a considerable source of revenue and commerce. But that the early Slav communities on what was later to become the territory of Russia did practice some sort of totemic cult involving the bear is almost certain, for it crops up again and again in superstitious beliefs and observances recorded as late as the nineteenth century in situations related to marriage, sex, fertility of crops, the health of farm-animals, happiness, and good-luck. For example, a young couple leaving the church after their wedding were often made to sit on a bearskin rug so that they would have "as many children as there were hairs on the rug." The tame dancing bear frequently seen in the pre-Revolutionary village was led around the peasants' barns and outhouses to bring good luck; sometimes a piece of its fur was burnt and the smoke used to cense the house and farm buildings. A bear's skull was sometimes hung up in the stable, again to ensure the safety and well-being of the animals.

In accordance with Frazer's principle of contagious magic, the properties of the bear itself could be passed through the wearing of its pelt (and later, by analogy, through other materials, such as sheepskin, straw, or dried pea stalks) to a human actor portraying the animal. Masked bears of this type were a common feature of village mumming during the Christmas and New Year period in Russia from the earliest times and were believed to possess the same powers as the living animal; hence the village girls would try to dance with the masked bear in the hope of catching a husband. As the old rhyme says:

> Medved' pykhtun
> Po reke plyvet.
> Komu pykhnet na dvor,
> Tomu zyat' vo terem.
>
> (Bear, the puffer,
> Swims down the river.
> Each house he puffs at
> Will gain a son-in-law.)[24]

The bear also appears in a mysterious role in several Russian folk tales which are clearly of ancient origin. There is the knight Ivan Medvedko (from *medved'*—i.e., bear) who is half human, half bear, and there are tales of encounters between bears and girls which hint at a half-forgotten belief in the possibility of mixed mating. Although ritual games specifically concerned with the hunting of the bear have not survived in Russia itself, ample evidence exists of their presence among neighboring peoples, particularly the various nomadic tribes of Siberia where the cult of the bear was highly developed and shows distinct similarities to the vestigial remains of these practices in Russia. When a bear was caught and skinned, for example, its head was boiled up and the skull hung on a nearby tree in the belief that the bear's spirit would bring good luck to the participants in his funeral celebrations. Tribes such as the Man'zy and Ostyaks held protracted festivals in honor of the bear which included many specifically ritual ceremonies as well as feasting, dancing, singing, and the acting of scenes based on the bear-hunt itself, as well as on the life of the hunters in general and on other purely social or domestic themes.25 These scenes were acted out in the presence of the bear itself, or rather the skin, complete with head and claws, of the recently captured animal. This was ceremonially laid out in a place of honor. Rings were placed on its claws, silver coins over its eyes, and a muzzle of birch bark over its nose. This was done to prevent the women from either looking directly into the bear's eyes or kissing his mouth, an honor allowed only to the men. Hunting was a purely male preserve and only male actors took part in the games. In Russia too the divisions between male and female occupations were observed in the work-derived games, with men or boys playing the part of bear, goat, bull, or horse while the women, as has been seen, acted out their traditional role as spinners and weavers. The Siberian players wore grotesque masks of birch bark with eyebrows, whiskers, and beard blacked in with soot. They wore ordinary clothing but with garments turned inside out and a humpback added. Interestingly, this last detail was also a recurring feature in the appearance of the Russian masked bear. Among the scenes performed was one depicting the arrival of strangers at the feast in honor of the dead bear. They are surprised at the great crowd which has gathered and then, when they see the cause of it—the bearskin—they are terrified and try to escape. One, bolder than the others, eventually plucks up courage to kiss the bear's muzzle, and then everyone begins to enjoy himself. Another scene tells of three brothers, the youngest of whom is an idiot, who go out to hunt for bears. They eventually find a bear's den, but unfortunately their attempts to trap it are unsuccessful and it mauls the middle brother to death. The youngest escapes up a tree, which his elder brother proceeds to chop down, bringing tree and brother crashing to the ground.

There follows a variant of a scene frequently found also in Russian ritual drama and the folk theatre—the resurrection of the corpses by literally blowing the breath of life into them through some bodily opening, usually the mouth or an ear, but in this case through the anus. More closely connected with the origins of the bear cult itself was the acting out of a Siberian legend which told how the art and custom of hunting the bear originated. Two hunters came across a bear's den in the forest and, puzzled as to the nature of the animal and how to trap it, they were forced to seek the advice of a local wise woman. She explained in great detail exactly what had to be done. The hunters followed her instructions implicitly, laying the foundations of what was to become a time honored ritual, and caught their bear (a log of wood wrapped up in a deerskin jacket). Finally they "skinned" it, leaving only the head and paws, and carried it home rejoicing.

In general, imitation of the appearance, characteristics, and function in the life of the village of various animals both wild and domestic played a significant part in the development of drama in primitive societies. Animals were necessary for food and clothing to all except perhaps the most primitive food gatherers. Moreover, animals by their very nature were an obvious target for imitation. Their bright colors or distinctive markings, their powers of swift movement or great strength and all the often grotesque similarities and disparities between the world of animals and that of men were striking and relatively easy to portray. In their games, the Russians portrayed mainly farm animals—the horse, bull, and goat—who were not only useful to them for the obvious reasons, but also closely connected with ancient pagan beliefs and ceremonies associated with fertility, the dying and rebirth of nature. Many references to such maskings are to be found in Old Russian documents, mainly in ecclesiastical literature condemning the remnants of pagan practices among the Russians. In a codicil to the Russian law codes of 1636 we find an injunction against taking part in hobby horse games at Christmastide.[26] Similarly, in Tsar' Aleksei Mikhailovich's order of 1648 the people are forbidden to wear masks or make hobby horses.[27] The continued popularity of the hobby horse and the joyful atmosphere of celebration and unharnessed enjoyment which surrounded it are attested by many descriptions through the centuries. E. Avdeeva, in her memories of a Siberian childhood at the end of the eighteenth century, recollects the coming of the Christmas hobby horse: "There was a rider on the horse dressed as a knight and with them were a lady and her cavalier. In the evenings they went from house to house and wherever they entered there was singing and dancing."28 A. N. Minkh, in his collection of Russian folk customs and superstitions, offers a description dating to 1863 of the hobby horse during the spring festival of Rusal'skoe Voskresen'e (mermaid Sunday) which took place in the Saratov government around the beginning of June on the Sunday before the start of St. Peter's Fast. The festival began with singing and dancing as the young people of the village gathered in the streets. The hobby horse, which made its first appearance in the evening, was made of straw and carried on the bent backs of two lads who "played" the legs in the traditional manner of the pantomime horse. The animal was hung all over with bells and brightly colored scraps of cloth. Perched on top a boy of about fifteen made everyone laugh with his jokes. A large crowd, consisting mainly of women and children, followed, waving rattles and banging on basins and metal dampers from the stove. The procession made its way, wending an irregular course through the village and bumping into or chasing unwary bystanders, down to the river where the horse was cast into the water.29

In a sense the first performance of the play *Artakserksovo deistvo* represented a beginning in the development of the Russian theatre, but in another sense it was not a true beginning. Behind the lavish excitement provided by the exclusive court theatre with its imported producer and actors and plays from biblical or foreign literature was another theatrical tradition, though unrecognized as such by the men who condemned it—a theatre which was an integral part of the life of the people, which sprang from their immediate needs and daily activities. This moreover was a theatre which represented a continuity of tradition (in the sense that it reflected a style of life and concept of nature which remained essentially unchanged for centuries) in a way that the court theatre, dependent upon fashions in art and politics, could not.

NOTES

1 A. S. Famintsyn, *Skomorokhi na Rusi* (St. Petersburg, 1889), pp. 80-81.

2 Ibid., p. 87.

3 V. N. Vsevolodskii-Gerngross, *Igry narodov SSSR* (Moscow and Leningrad, 1933), p. 296.

4 Ibid., p. 160.

5 Ibid., p. 156.

6 Ibid., p. 149.

7 R. L. Beals and H. Hoijer, *An Introduction to Anthropology* (New York, 1953), p. 594.

8 I. M. Levina, "Kukol'nye igry v svad'bu i metishche," *Krest'yanskoe iskusstvo SSSR: Iskusstvo severa*, II (Leningrad, 1928), 201-34.

9 Ibid., p. 224.

10 E. D. Chapple and C. S. Coon, *Principles of Anthropology* (London, 1947), p. 503.

11 F. Buslaev, "Yazycheskie predaniya sela Verkhotishanki," *Istoricheskie ocherki russkoi narodnoi slovesnosti i iskusstva*, Vol. I: *Russkaya narodnaya poeziya* (1861; rpt. The Hague, 1969), p. 249.

12 A. Afanas'ev, *Poeticheskie vozzreniya slavyan na prirodu*, I (1865; rpt. The Hague, 1970), 234.

13 P. V. Shein, *Velikoruss v svoikh pesnyakh, obryadakh, obychayakh. . . .* Part 1, No. 1 (1898), 81-82.

14 Ibid., pp. 367-70.

15 L. Kulakovskii, *Iskusstvo sela Dorozheva* (Moscow, 1965), pp. 16-28.

16 A sort of jelly made with fruit juice and potato flour.

17 A further pun based on the similar sounding benediction "Vo imya otsa i syna i svyatogo dukha" (In the name of the Father, Son, and Holy Ghost).

18 Shein, pp. 348-49.

19 Franz Boas, "Literature, music and dance," *General Anthropology*, by Franz Boas *et al.* (1938), pp. 605-06.

20 Karsten, *The Civilisation of South American Indians* (New York, 1926), p. 218.

21 Ruth Bunzel, "Art," *General Anthropology*, p. 536.

22 Ibid., p. 538.

23 For further information on this aspect of Russian drama, see E. A. Warner, *The Russian Folk Theatre* (The Hague, 1977), p. 39-78.

24 Famintsyn, p. 95.

25 N. L. Gondatti, *Sledy yazychestva u inorodtsev severo-zapodnoi Sibiri* (Moscow, 1888), pp. 61-91.

26 Famintsyn, p. 86.

27 Ibid., p. 87.

28 E. A. Avdeeva, *Zapiski i zamechaniya o Sibiri* (Moscow, 1837), p. 58.

29 A. N. Minkh, *Norodnye obychai, obryady, sueveriya i predrazsudki krest'yan saratovskoi gubernii* (St. Petersburg, 1890), p. 105.

Index

371